MW01616458

The Great Fiction

The Great Fiction

Property, Economy, Society, and the Politics of Decline

HANS-HERMANN HOPPE

aissez Faire Books

An Essential Resource for Enlightened Minds Since 1972

Copyright © 2012 — Laissez Faire Books
All rights reserved.
Printed in the United States of America.
ISBN: 978-162129-030-8 (print)
ISBN: 978-162129-031-5 (ebook)

18 17 16 15 14 13 12   1 2 3 4 5 6 7

Published by Laissez Faire Books, 808 St. Paul Street, Baltimore, Maryland.
www.LaissezFaireBooks.com
www.LFB.org

Published under the Creative Commons Attribution License 3.0.
http://creativecommons.org/licenses/by/3.0/

Contents

Editorial Preface
by Jeffrey Tucker

If you are unfamiliar with the working of Hans-Hermann Hoppe, prepare for *The Great Fiction* to cause a fundamental shift in the way you view the world. No living writer today is more effective at stripping away the illusions almost everyone has about economics and public life. More fundamentally, Professor Hoppe causes the scales to fall from one's eyes on the most critical issue facing humanity today: the choice between liberty and statism.

The title comes from a quotation by Frédéric Bastiat, the 19th century economist and pamphleteer: "The state is the great fiction by which everyone seeks to live at the expense of everyone else." He does not say that this is one feature of the state, one possible aspect of public policy gone wrong, or one sign of a state gone bad in a shift from its nightwatchman role to become confiscatory. Bastiat is characterizing the core nature of the state itself.

The whole of Hoppe's writings on politics can be seen as an elucidation on this point. He sees the state as a gang of thieves that uses propaganda as a means of disguising its true nature. In fleshing this out, Hoppe has made tremendous contributions to the literature, showing how the state originates and how the intellectual class helps perpetuate this cover up, whether in the name of science, or religion, or the provision of some service like health, security, education, or whatever. The excuses are forever changing; the functioning and goal of the state are always the same.

It is true, then, that Hoppe stands with a long line of anarchist thinkers who see the state as playing a purely destructive role in society. But unlike the main line of thinkers in this tradition, Hoppe's thinking is not encumbered by utopian illusions about society without the state. He follows Ludwig von Mises and Murray N. Rothbard in placing private property as a central element in social organization. In justifying this point of view, Hoppe goes far beyond traditional Lockean phrases. He sees private property as an inescapable institution in a world of scarcity, and draws on the work of contemporary European philosophy to make his claims more robust than any of his intellectual predecessors did.

The reader will be surprised at the approach Hoppe takes because it is far more systematic and logical than people expect of writers on these topics. I suspect that this is because he came to views after a long intellectual struggle, having moved systematically from being a conventional left-socialist to become the founder of his own anarcho-capitalist school of thought. The dramatic change happened to him in graduate school, as he reveals in the biographical sections of this book. He takes nothing for granted in the course of his argumentation. He leads the reader carefully through each step in his chain of reasoning. This approach requires extraordinary discipline and a level of brilliance that is out of the reach of most writers and thinkers.

This particular work goes beyond politics, however, to show the full range of Hoppe's thought on issues of economics, history, scientific methodology, and the history of thought. In each field, he brings that same level of rigor, that drive for uncompromising adherence to logic, the fearlessness in the fact of radical conclusions. In light of all of this, it seems too limiting to describe Hoppe as a mere member of the Austrian or libertarian tradition, for he really has forged new paths—in more ways than he makes overt in his writings. We are really dealing here with a universal genius, which is precisely why Hoppe's name comes up so often in any discussion of today's great living intellectuals.

It so happens that Hoppe is also an extremely controversial figure. I don't think he would have it any other way. Regardless, this is always the case for truly creative minds that do not shrink from the conclusions of their own premises. The perspective from which he writes stems from a passionate yet scientific attachment to radical freedom, and his work comes about in times when the state is on the march. Everything he writes cuts across the grain. It is paradigm breaking. Just when you think you have figured out his mode of thinking, he takes it in a direction that you didn't expect, which is why in writing this editorial preface I'm being careful not to give away too many of the ideas herein. It is not only his conclusions that are significant but the masterful way that he arrives at them.

It is my great honor as executive editor of Laissez Faire Books to be the publisher of a work of this significance. This is more than a collection in the libertarian tradition; it is a testimony to the fact that progress in ideas is still possible in our time. So long as that remains true, so long as the tradition Hoppe represents is living and improving, we have reason to believe that human liberty has not and will not finally succumb to the great fiction.

Preface

While the need for and value of inter-disciplinary and trans-disciplinary research is often emphasized as a welcome antidote to hyper-specialization, such commitment is typically little more than lip service. In general, in today's *academia* inter- and trans-disciplinary work is frowned on and discouraged. It hampers your professional career or even dooms it. Once you venture outside an increasingly narrowly-defined field of academic specialization, your colleagues will dismiss and disparage you for no longer being a "real" economist, philosopher, or whatever; and likewise, the certified members and gate-keepers of those fields into which you venture will either ignore or dismiss you as an intellectual outsider and trespasser and not really "one of them."

Indeed, even within a given academic field such as philosophy or economics, for instance, you are no longer expected to cover your discipline in its entirety. Instead, you are supposed to confine your work to one of your discipline's numerous branches or sub-disciplines and publish exclusively in its "officially approved 'refereed' scholarly journals." You are not supposed to be a philosopher or economist, *period*. Rather, you are supposed to be a philosopher of science, or of mathematics, or logic, language, religion, art and aesthetics, etc.; and you are supposed to be a micro-economist, a macro-economist, a game theorist, a labor or development economist, an econometrician, a mathematical economist, etc. Only as a historian of your discipline are you still somewhat exempt from these strictures and supposed to cover your entire field. However, the history of philosophy and even more so the history of economics and economic thought, for example, are increasingly eliminated from the academic *curricula*, because they are considered merely interpretative—philological or hermeneutical— endeavors, rather than real "science."

Throughout my entire academic career I ignored these strictures. First, because I did not know any better, and then, when I knew, because I consciously rejected and resisted them—and learned to live with the consequences. I earned my living as an economist, but I did not confine my work to economics. I frequently ventured out into philosophy, my first intellectual love, and from there, into law, sociology, history, and politics— wherever my intellectual curiosity led me.

The present volume bears witness to this fact. It contains articles, speeches, and interviews written and presented over almost a quarter century. Most of them have previously appeared in disparate places: in various academic journals, magazines of opinion, or popular media outlets. Yet there are also some longer, previously unpublished pieces appearing here for the very first time.

While this book freely and frequently cuts across disciplinary lines, there is one dominant and unifying theme throughout the following: property, or more precisely *private* property, defined as the exclusive control of scarce resources, its origin, and its ethical and economic rationale and justification as the ultimate source of peace and prosperity. On the other hand: the State, defined as a territorial monopolist of ultimate decision making and conflict arbitration including all cases of conflict involving the State and its agents itself, its origin, and its role as the greatest danger to private property, as a permanent source of social conflict and the greatest enemy to peace and prosperity. And finally: the constitution of a private law society, defined as a society without a state or any monopoly or monopolist whatsoever (whether legal or otherwise) and its unique function as the only conceivable guarantor of eternal peace and prosperity.

But there is much more to be found in the following: there are reflections on social evolution and the causes of the so-called Neolithic and Industrial Revolution, on monarchy and on the decivilizing effect of democracy, on war, centralization and secession, on egalitarianism, inequality and natural aristocracy, on the inevitability and virtue of discrimination, and on migration and the perils of multiculturalism—much of which is extremely "politically incorrect" and has made me a *persona non grata* not only among mainstream intellectuals but in particular also among many so-called left-, big-government, or bleeding-heart libertarians.

There are some pieces assembled here dealing with purely theoretical (value-free)—philosophical or economic—problems, others dealing with normative issues, and still others concerned with matters of politics and political strategy. Some pieces are long and intellectually "demanding" and others short and "easy." In any case, however, I hope the reader will find them always lucid, rigorously argued and, above all, intellectually stimulating.

While no one except me can be held personally responsible for any of the following, I owe a profound gratitude to Lew Rockwell and to the "gang" of radical—in politically correct lingo: "extremist"—thinkers he managed to assemble around the Ludwig von Mises Institute in Auburn, Alabama: to Walter Block, Thomas DiLorenzo, David Gordon, Jeffrey Herbener, Guido Hülsmann, Stephan Kinsella, Peter Klein, Ralph Raico, Joseph Salerno, and Mark Thornton. Special thanks go also to Jeffrey Tucker, formerly editorial vice president of the Ludwig von Mises Institute and now publisher and executive editor of Laissez Faire Books.

My deepest gratitude is to my two principal intellectual masters, however. To Ludwig von Mises (1881–1973), whom I unfortunately never met, but whose monumental work has been a constant source of inspiration to me, and to Mises's greatest student, Murray Rothbard (1926–1995), who further radicalized, expanded and completed the Misesian edifice, and with whom I was fortunate enough to spend the last ten years of his life in intimate cooperation, first in New York City and then as colleagues, office neighbors and intellectual co-combatants at the University of Nevada, Las Vegas.

Hans-Hermann Hoppe
Istanbul, June 2012

Part One

Politics and Property

1

The Role of Intellectuals and Anti-Intellectual Intellectuals

"The state is the great fictitious entity by which everyone seeks to live at the expense of everyone else." —Frédéric Bastiat

Let me begin with the definition of a state. What must an agent be able to do to qualify as a state? This agent must be able to insist that all conflicts among the inhabitants of a given territory be brought to him for ultimate decision-making or be subject to his final review. In particular, this agent must be able to insist that all conflicts involving *him* be adjudicated by him or his agent. And implied in the power to exclude all others from acting as ultimate judge, as the second defining characteristic of a state, is the agent's power to tax: to unilaterally determine the price that justice seekers must pay for his services.

Based on this definition of a state, it is easy to understand why a desire to control a state might exist. For whoever is a monopolist of final arbitration within a given territory can *make* laws. And he who can *legislate* can also *tax*. Surely, this is an enviable position.

More difficult to understand is how anyone can get away with controlling a state. Why would others put up with such an institution?

I want to approach the answer to this question indirectly. Suppose you and your friends happen to be in control of such an extraordinary institution. What would you do to maintain your position (provided you didn't have any moral scruples)? You would certainly use some of your tax income to hire some thugs. First: to make peace among your subjects so that they stay productive and there is something to tax in the future. But more importantly, because you might need these thugs for your *own* protection should the people wake up from their dogmatic slumber and challenge you.

• Originally published by *Libertarian Alliance* in 2008.

This will not do, however, in particular if you and your friends are a small minority in comparison to the number of subjects. For a minority cannot lastingly rule a majority solely by brute force. It must rule by "opinion." The majority of the population must be brought to *voluntarily* accept your rule. This is not to say that the majority must agree with every one of your measures. Indeed, it may well believe that many of your policies are mistaken. However, it must believe in the legitimacy of the institution of the state *as such*, and hence, that even if a particular policy may be wrong, such mistake is an "accident" that one must tolerate in view of some greater good provided by the state.

Yet how can one persuade the majority of the population to believe this? The answer is: only with the help of intellectuals.

How do you get the intellectuals to work for you? To this the answer is easy. The market demand for intellectual services is not exactly high and stable. Intellectuals would be at the mercy of the fleeting values of the masses, and the masses are uninterested in intellectual-philosophical concerns. The state, on the other hand, can accommodate the intellectuals' typically over-inflated egos and offer them a warm, secure, and permanent berth in its apparatus.

However, it is not sufficient that you employ just *some* intellectuals. You must essentially employ them *all*—even the ones who work in areas far removed from those that you are primarily concerned with: that is philosophy, the social sciences and the humanities. For even intellectuals working in mathematics or the natural sciences, for instance, can obviously think for themselves and so become potentially dangerous. It is thus important that you secure also their loyalty to the state. Put differently: you must become a *monopolist*. And this is best achieved if all "educational" institutions, from kindergarten to universities, are brought under state control and all teaching and researching personnel is "state-certified."

But what if the people do not *want* to become "educated"? For this, "education" must be made compulsory; and in order to subject the people to state controlled education for as long as possible, everyone must be declared equally "educable." The intellectuals know such egalitarianism to be false, of course. Yet to proclaim nonsense such as "everyone is a potential Einstein if only given sufficient educational attention" pleases the masses and, in turn, provides for an almost limitless demand for intellectual services.

None of all this guarantees "correct" statist thinking, of course. It certainly helps, however, in reaching the "correct" conclusion, if one realizes that without the state one might be out of work and may have to try one's hands at the mechanics of gas pump operation instead of concerning oneself with such pressing problems as alienation, equity, exploitation, the deconstruction of gender and sex roles, or the culture of the Eskimos, the Hopis and the Zulus.

In any case, even if the intellectuals feel underappreciated by you—that is: by one *particular* state administration—they know that help can only come from *another* state administration but not from an intellectual assault on the institution of the state as such. Hence, it is hardly surprising that, as a matter of fact, the overwhelming majority of contemporary intellectuals, including most conservative or so-called free market intellectuals, are fundamentally and philosophically statists.

Has the work of the intellectuals paid off for the state? I would think so. If asked whether the institution of a state is necessary, I do not think it is exaggerated to say that 99 percent of all people would unhesitatingly say yes. And yet, this success rests on rather shaky grounds, and the entire statist edifice can be brought down—if only the work of the intellectuals is countered by the work of intellectual *anti-intellectuals*, as I like to call them.

The overwhelming majority of state supporters are not *philosophical* statists, i.e., because they have *thought* about the matter. Most people do not think much about anything "philosophical." They go about their daily lives, and that is it. So most support stems from the mere fact that a state *exists*, and has always existed as far as one can remember (and that is typically not farther away than one's own lifetime). That is, the greatest achievement of the statist intellectuals is the fact that they have cultivated the masses' natural intellectual laziness (or incapacity) and never allowed for "the subject" to come up for serious discussion. The state is considered as an unquestionable part of the social fabric.

The first and foremost task of the intellectual anti-intellectuals, then, is to counter this dogmatic slumber of the masses by offering a precise definition of the state, as I have done at the outset, and then to ask if there is not something truly remarkable, odd, strange, awkward, ridiculous, indeed ludicrous about an institution such as this. I am confident that such simple, definitional work will produce some very first, but serious, doubt regarding an institution that one previously had been taken for granted—*a good start.*

Further, proceeding from less sophisticated (yet, not coincidentally, more popular) pro-state arguments to more sophisticated ones: To the extent that intellectuals have deemed it necessary to *argue* in favor of the state at all, their most popular argument, encountered already at kindergarten age, runs like this: Some activities of the state are pointed out: the state builds roads, kindergartens, schools; it delivers the mail and puts the policeman on the street. Imagine, there would be no state. Then we would not have these goods. Thus, the state is necessary.

At the university level, a slightly more sophisticated version of the same argument is presented. It goes like this: True, markets are best at providing many or even most things; but there are other goods markets cannot provide or cannot provide in sufficient quantity or quality. These other, so-called "public goods" are goods that bestow benefits onto people beyond those actually having produced or paid for them. Foremost among such goods ranks typically "education and research." "Education and research," for instance, it is argued, are extremely valuable goods. They would be under-produced, however, because of "free riders," i.e., of "cheats," who benefit—via so-called neighborhood effects—from "education and research" without paying for it. Thus, the state is necessary to provide otherwise un-produced or under-produced (public) goods such as education and research.

These statist arguments can be refuted by a combination of three fundamental insights: First, as for the kindergarten argument, it does not follow from the fact that the state provides roads and schools that *only* the state can provide such goods. People have little difficulty recognizing that this is a fallacy. From the fact that monkeys can ride bikes it does not follow that *only* monkeys can ride bikes. And second, immediately following, it must be recalled that the state is an institution that can legislate and tax; and hence, that state agents have little incentive to produce efficiently. State roads and schools will only be more costly and their quality lower. For there is always a tendency for state agents to use up as many resources as possible doing whatever they do but actually work as little as possible doing it.

Third, as for the more sophisticated statist argument, it involves the same fallacy encountered already at the kindergarten level. For even if one were to grant the rest of the argument, it is still a fallacy to conclude from the fact that states provide public goods that *only* states can do so.

More importantly, however, it must be pointed out that the entire argument demonstrates a total ignorance of the most fundamental fact of human life, namely, scarcity. True, markets will not provide for all desirable things. There are always unsatisfied wants as long as we do not inhabit the Garden of Eden. But to bring such unproduced goods into existence scarce resources must be expended, which consequently can no longer be used to produce other, likewise desirable things. Whether public goods exist next to private ones does not matter in this regard—the fact of scarcity remains unchanged: more "public" goods can come only at the expense of less "private" goods. Yet what needs to be demonstrated is that one good is more important and valuable than another one. This is what is meant by "economizing."

Yet can the state help economize scarce resources? *This* is the question that must be answered. In fact, however, conclusive proof exists that the state does *not* and cannot economize: For in order to produce anything, the state must resort to taxation (or legislation)—which demonstrates irrefutably that its subjects do *not* want what the state produces but prefer instead *something else* as *more* important. Rather than economize, the state can only redistribute: it can produce more of what *it* wants and less of what the people want—and, to recall, whatever the state then produces will be produced inefficiently.

Finally, the most sophisticated argument in favor of the state must be briefly examined. From Hobbes on down this argument has been repeated endlessly. It runs like this: In the state of nature—before the establishment of a state—permanent conflict reigns. Everyone claims a right to everything, and this will result in interminable war. There is no way out of this predicament by means of agreements; for who would *enforce* these agreements? Whenever the situation appeared advantageous, one or both parties would break the agreement. Hence, people recognize that there is but one solution to the *desideratum* of peace: the establishment, per agreement, of a state, i.e., a third, independent party as ultimate judge and enforcer. Yet if this thesis is correct and agreements require an outside enforcer to make them binding, then a state-by-agreement can never come into existence. For in order to enforce the very agreement that is to result in the formation of a state (to make *this* agreement binding), another outside enforcer, a prior state, would already have to exist. And in order for *this* state to have come into existence, yet another still earlier state must be postulated, and so on, in infinite regress.

On the other hand, if we accept that states exist (and of course they do), then this very fact contradicts the Hobbesian story. The state itself has come into existence *without* any outside enforcer. Presumably, at the time of the alleged agreement, no prior state existed. Moreover, once a state-by-agreement is in existence, the resulting social order still remains a self-enforcing one. To be sure, if A and B now agree on something, their agreements are made binding by an external party. However, the *state* itself is not so bound by any outside enforcer. There exists no external third party insofar as conflicts between state-agents and state-subjects are concerned; and likewise no external third party exists for conflicts between different state agents or agencies. Insofar as agreements entered into by the state *vis-à-vis* its citizens or of one state agency *vis-à-vis* another are concerned, that is, such agreements *can be only self-binding on the State*. The state is bound by nothing except its own self-accepted and enforced rules, i.e., the constraints that it imposes on itself. *Vis-à-vis* itself, so to speak, the state is still in a natural state of anarchy characterized by self-rule and enforcement, because there is no higher state, which could bind it.

Further: If we accept the Hobbesian idea that the enforcement of mutually agreed upon rules *does* require some independent third party, this would actually rule out the establishment of a state. In fact, it would constitute a conclusive argument *against* the institution of a state, i.e., of a *monopolist* of ultimate decision-making and arbitration. For then, there must also exist an independent third party to decide in every case of conflict between me (private citizen) and some state agent, and likewise an independent third party must exist for every case of intra-state conflicts (and there must be another independent third party for the case of conflicts between various third parties)—yet this means, of course, that such a "state" (or any independent third party) would be no state as I have defined it at the outset but simply one of many freely competing third-party conflict arbitrators.

Let me conclude then: the intellectual case against the state seems to be easy and straightforward. But that does not mean that it is practically easy. Indeed, almost everyone is convinced that the state is a necessary institution, for the reasons that I have indicated. So it is very doubtful if the battle against statism can be won, as easy as it might seem on the purely theoretical, intellectual level. However, even if that should turn out to be impossible—at least let's have some fun at the expense of our statist opponents.

And for that I suggest that you always and persistently confront them with the following riddle. Assume a group of people, aware of the possibility of conflicts between them. Someone then proposes, as a solution to this human problem, that he (or someone) be made the ultimate arbiter in any such case of conflict, including those conflicts in which he is involved. Is this is a deal that you would accept? I am confident that he will be considered either a joker or mentally unstable. Yet this is precisely what all statists propose.

2

The Ethics and Economics of Private Property

I. THE PROBLEM OF SOCIAL ORDER

Alone on his island, Robinson Crusoe can do whatever he pleases. For him, the question concerning rules of orderly human conduct—social cooperation—simply does not arise. Naturally, this question can only arise once a second person, Friday, arrives on the island. Yet even then, the question remains largely irrelevant so long as no *scarcity* exists. Suppose the island is the Garden of Eden; all external goods are available in superabundance. They are "free goods," just as the air that we breathe is normally a "free" good. Whatever Crusoe does with these goods, his actions have repercussions *neither* with respect to his own future supply of such goods *nor* regarding the present or future supply of the same goods for Friday (and *vice versa*). Hence, it is impossible that there could ever be a conflict between Crusoe and Friday concerning the use of such goods. A conflict is only possible if goods are scarce. Only then will there arise the need to formulate rules that make orderly—conflict-free—social cooperation possible.

In the Garden of Eden only two scarce goods exist: the physical body of a person and its standing room. Crusoe and Friday each have only one body and can stand only at one place at a time. Hence, even in the Garden of Eden conflicts between Crusoe and Friday can arise: Crusoe and Friday cannot occupy the same standing room simultaneously without coming thereby into physical conflict with each other. Accordingly, even in the Garden of Eden rules of orderly social conduct must exist—rules regarding the proper location and movement of human bodies. And outside the Garden of Eden,

---

• Originally published in the *Elgar Companion to the Economics of Private Property*, edited by Enrico Colombatto (London: Edward Elgar, 2004).

in the realm of scarcity, there must be rules that regulate not only the use of personal bodies but also of *everything* scarce so that *all* possible conflicts can be ruled out. This is the problem of social order.

II. THE SOLUTION:
PRIVATE PROPERTY AND ORIGINAL APPROPRIATION

In the history of social and political thought, various proposals have been advanced as a solution to the problem of social order, and this variety of mutually inconsistent proposals has contributed to the fact that today's search for a single "correct" solution is frequently deemed illusory. Yet as I will try to demonstrate, a correct solution exists; hence, there is no reason to succumb to moral relativism. The solution has been known for hundreds of years, if not for much longer.[1] In modern times this old and simple solution was formulated most clearly and convincingly by Murray N. Rothbard.[2]

Let me begin by formulating the solution—first for the special case represented by the Garden of Eden and subsequently for the general case represented by the "real" world of all-around scarcity—and then proceed to the explanation of why this solution, and no other, is correct.

In the Garden of Eden, the solution is provided by the simple rule stipulating that everyone may place or move his own body wherever he pleases, *provided only that no one else is already standing there and occupying the same space.* And outside of the Garden of Eden, in the realm of all-around scarcity the solution is provided by this rule:

Everyone is the proper owner of his own physical body as well as of all places and nature-given goods that he occupies and puts to use by means of his body, *provided that no one else has already occupied or used the same places and goods before him.* This ownership of "originally appropriated" places and goods by a person implies his right to use and transform these places and goods in any way he sees fit, *provided that he does not thereby forcibly change the physical integrity of places and goods originally appropriated by another*

---

1. See section V below.

2. See Murray N. Rothbard, *Man, Economy, and State* (Auburn, Ala.: Ludwig von Mises Institute, 1993 [1962]); idem, *Power and Market* (Kansas City: Sheed Andrews and McMeel, 1977 [1970]); idem, *The Ethics of Liberty* (New York: New York University Press, 1998 [1982]); idem, *Egalitarianism as a Revolt against Nature and Other Essays* (Auburn, Ala.: Ludwig von Mises Institute, 2000 [1974]); idem, *The Logic of Action*, 2 vols. (Cheltenham, Eng.: Edward Elgar, 1997).

person. In particular, once a place or good has been first appropriated, in John Locke's words, by "mixing one's labor" with it, ownership in such places and goods can be acquired only by means of a voluntary—contractual—transfer of its property title from a previous to a later owner.

In light of widespread moral relativism, it is worth pointing out that this idea of original appropriation and private property as a solution to the problem of social order is in complete accordance with our moral "intuition." Is it not simply absurd to claim that a person should *not* be the proper owner of his body and the places and goods that he originally, i.e., *prior* to anyone else, appropriates, uses and/or produces by means of his body? For who else, if not he, should be their owner? And is it not also obvious that the overwhelming majority of people—including children and primitives—in fact act according to these rules, and do so as a matter of course?

Moral intuition, as important as it is, is not proof. However, there also exists proof of the veracity of our moral intuition.

The proof is two-fold. On the one hand, the consequences that follow if one were to deny the validity of the institution of original appropriation and private property are spelled out: If person A were *not* the owner of his own body and the places and goods originally appropriated and/or produced with this body as well as of the goods voluntarily (contractually) acquired from another previous owner, then only two alternatives would exist. Either *another* person, B, must be recognized as the owner of A's body as well as the places and goods appropriated, produced or acquired by A, or *both* persons, A *and* B, must be considered equal co-owners of all bodies, places and goods.

In the first case, A would be reduced to the rank of B's slave and object of exploitation. B would be the owner of A's body and all places and goods appropriated, produced and acquired by A, but A in turn would not be the owner of B's body and the places and goods appropriated, produced and acquired by B. Hence, under this ruling two categorically distinct classes of persons would be constituted—*Untermenschen* such as A and *Übermenschen* such as B—to whom different "laws" apply. Accordingly, such ruling must be discarded as a human ethic equally applicable to everyone *qua* human being (rational animal). From the very outset, any such ruling is recognized as not universally acceptable and thus cannot claim to represent law. For a rule to aspire to the rank of a law—a *just* rule—it is necessary that such a rule apply equally and universally to everyone.

Alternatively, in the second case of universal and equal co-ownership, the requirement of equal law for everyone would be fulfilled. However, this alternative would suffer from an even more severe deficiency, because if it were applied, all of mankind would instantly perish. (Since every human ethic must permit the survival of mankind, this alternative must also be rejected.) Every action of a person requires the use of some scarce means (at least of the person's body and its standing room), but if all goods were co-owned by everyone, then no one, at no time and no place, would be allowed to do anything unless he had previously secured every other co-owner's consent to do so. Yet how could anyone grant such consent were he not the exclusive owner of his own body (including his vocal chords) by which means his consent must be expressed? Indeed, he would first need another's consent in order to be allowed to express his own, but these others could not give their consent without having first his, and so it would go on.

This insight into the praxeological impossibility of "universal communism," as Rothbard referred to this proposal, brings me immediately to an alternative way of demonstrating the idea of original appropriation and private property as the only correct solution to the problem of social order.[3] Whether or not persons have any rights and, if so, which ones, can only be decided in the course of argumentation (propositional exchange). Justification—proof, conjecture, refutation—is *argumentative* justification. Anyone who denied this proposition would become involved in a performative contradiction because his denial would itself constitute an argument. Even an ethical relativist would have to accept this first proposition, which is referred to accordingly as the *apriori of argumentation*.

From the undeniable acceptance—the axiomatic status—of this apriori of argumentation, two equally necessary conclusions follow. First, it follows from the apriori of argumentation when there is *no* rational solution to the problem of conflict arising from the existence of scarcity. Suppose in my earlier scenario of Crusoe and Friday that Friday were not the name of a man but of a gorilla. Obviously, just as Crusoe could face conflict regarding his body and its standing room with Friday the man, so might he with Friday the gorilla. The gorilla might want to occupy the same space that Crusoe already occupied. In this case, at least if the gorilla were the sort of entity

3. See also Hans-Hermann Hoppe, *A Theory of Socialism and Capitalism* (Boston: Kluwer Academic Publishers, 1989); idem, *The Economics and Ethics of Private Property* (Boston: Kluwer Academic Publishers, 1993).

that we know gorillas to be, there would be no rational solution to their conflict. Either the gorilla would push aside, crush, or devour Crusoe—that would be the gorilla's solution to the problem—or Crusoe would tame, chase, beat, or kill the gorilla—that would be Crusoe's solution. In this situation, one might indeed speak of moral relativism. However, it would be more appropriate to refer to this situation as one in which the question of justice and rationality simply would not arise; that is, it would be considered an extra-moral situation. The existence of Friday the gorilla would pose a technical, not a moral, problem for Crusoe. He would have no other choice than to learn how to successfully manage and control the movements of the gorilla just as he would have to learn to manage and control other inanimate objects of his environment.

By implication, only if both parties in a conflict are capable of engaging in argumentation with one another, can one speak of a moral problem and is the question of whether or not there exists a solution to it a meaningful question. Only if Friday, regardless of his physical appearance, is capable of argumentation (even if he has shown himself to be capable only once), can he be deemed rational and does the question whether or not a correct solution to the problem of social order exists make sense. No one can be expected to give *any* answer to someone who has never raised a question or, more to the point, who has never stated his own relativistic viewpoint in the form of an argument. In that case, this "other" cannot but be regarded and treated as an animal or plant, i.e., as an extra-moral entity. Only if this other entity can pause in his activity, whatever it might be, step back, and say yes or no to something one has said, do we owe this entity an answer and, accordingly, can we possibly claim that our answer is the correct one for both parties involved in a conflict.

Moreover, it follows from the apriori of argumentation that everything that must be presupposed in the course of an argumentation as the logical and praxeological precondition of argumentation cannot in turn be argumentatively disputed as regards its validity without becoming thereby entangled in an internal (performative) contradiction.

Now, propositional exchanges are not made up of free-floating propositions, but rather constitute a specific human activity. Argumentation between Crusoe and Friday requires that both have, and mutually recognize each other as having, exclusive control over their respective bodies (their brains, vocal cords, etc.) as well as the standing room occupied by their bodies. No one could propose anything and expect the other party to convince himself of the validity of this proposition or deny it and propose something else unless his and his opponent's right to exclusive control over their respective bodies and standing rooms were presupposed. In fact, it is precisely this mutual recognition of the proponent's as well as the opponent's property in his own body and standing room which constitutes the *characteristicum specificum* of all propositional disputes: that while one may not agree regarding the validity of a specific proposition, one can agree nonetheless on the fact that one disagrees. Moreover, this right to property in one's own body and its standing room must be considered *apriori* (or indisputably) justified by proponent and opponent alike. Anyone who claimed any proposition as valid *vis-à-vis* an opponent would already presuppose his and his opponent's exclusive control over their respective body and standing room simply in order to say "I claim such and such to be true, and I challenge you to prove me wrong."

Furthermore, it would be equally impossible to engage in argumentation and rely on the propositional force of one's arguments if one were not allowed to own (exclusively control) other scarce means (besides one's body and its standing room). If one did not have such a right, then we would all immediately perish and the problem of justifying rules—as well as any other human problem—would simply not exist. Hence, by virtue of the fact of being alive, property rights to other things must be presupposed as valid, too. No one who is alive can possibly argue otherwise.

Furthermore, if a person were not permitted to acquire property in these goods and spaces by means of an act of original appropriation, i.e., by establishing an objective (intersubjectively ascertainable) link between himself and a particular good and/or space prior to anyone else, and if instead property in such goods or spaces were granted to latecomers, then no one would ever be permitted to begin using any good unless he had previously secured such a latecomer's consent. Yet how can a latecomer consent to the actions of an early comer? Moreover, every latecomer would in turn need the consent of other and later later-comers, and so on. That is, neither we, our forefathers, nor our progeny would have been or would be able to survive if one followed this rule. However, in order for any person—past, present or future—to argue anything, survival must be possible; and in order to do just this, property rights cannot be conceived of as being timeless and unspecific with respect to the number of persons concerned. Rather, property rights must necessarily be conceived of as originating by means of action at definite points in time and space by definite individuals. Otherwise, it would be impossible for anyone to ever say anything at a definite point in time and space and for someone else to be able to reply. Simply saying, then, that the first-user-first-owner rule of the ethics of private property can be ignored or is unjustified implies a performative contradiction, as one's being able to say so must presuppose one's existence as an independent decision-making unit at a given point in time and space.[4]

III. Misconceptions and Clarifications

According to this understanding of private property, property ownership means the exclusive control of a particular person over specific *physical* objects and spaces. Conversely, property rights invasion means the uninvited *physical* damage or diminution of things and territories owned by other persons. In contrast, a widely held view holds that the damage or diminution of the *value* (or price) of someone's property also constitutes a punishable offense.

As far as the (in)compatibility of both positions is concerned, it is easy to recognize that nearly every action of an individual can alter the *value* (price) of someone else's property. For example, when person A enters the labor or the marriage market, this may change the value of B in these markets. And when A changes his relative valuations of beer and bread, or if A himself decides to become a brewer or baker, this changes the value of the property of other brewers and bakers. According to the view that *value* damage constitutes a rights violation A would be committing a punishable offense *vis-à-vis* brewers or bakers. If A is *guilty*, then B and the brewers and bakers must have the right to *defend* themselves against A's actions, and their defensive actions can only consist of physical invasions of A and his property. B must be permitted to physically prohibit A from entering the labor or

---

4. Note the "natural law" character of the proposed solution to the problem of social order—that private property and its acquisition through acts of original appropriation are not mere conventions but necessary institutions (in accordance with man's nature as a rational animal). A convention serves a *purpose*, and an *alternative* to a convention exists. For instance, the Latin alphabet serves the purpose of written communication. It has an alternative, the Cyrillic alphabet. Hence, we call it a convention. What is the purpose of norms? The avoidance of conflict regarding the use of scarce physical things. Conflict-generating norms contradict the very purpose of norms. Yet with regard to the purpose of conflict avoidance, no alternative to private property and original appropriation exists. In the absence of prestabilized harmony among actors, conflict can only be prevented if all goods are always in the private ownership of specific individuals and it is always clear who owns what and who does not. Also, conflicts can only be avoided from the very beginning of mankind if private property is acquired by acts of original appropriation (instead of by mere declarations or words of latecomers).

marriage market; the brewers and bakers must be permitted to physically prevent A from spending his money as he sees fit. However, in this case the physical damage or diminution of the property of others cannot be viewed as a punishable offense. Since physical invasion and diminution are defensive actions, they are legitimate. Conversely, if physical damage and diminution constitute a rights violation, then B or the brewers and bakers do not have the right to defend themselves against A's actions, for his actions—his entering of the labor and marriage market, his altered evaluation of beer and bread, or his opening of a brewery or bakery—do not affect B's bodily integrity or the physical integrity of the property of brewers or bakers. If they physically defend themselves nonetheless, then the right to defense would lie with A. In that case, however, it cannot be regarded as a punishable offense if one alters the value of other people's property. A third possibility does not exist.

Both ideas of property rights are not only incompatible, however. The alternative view—that one could be the owner of the value or price of scarce goods—is indefensible. While a person has control over whether or not his actions will change the *physical* properties of another's property, he has no control over whether or not his actions affect the *value* (or price) of another's property. This is determined by *other* individuals and their evaluations. Consequently, it would be impossible to know in advance whether or not one's planned actions were legitimate. The entire population would have to be interrogated to assure that one's actions would not damage the value of someone else's property, and one could not begin to act until a universal consensus had been reached. Mankind would die out long before this assumption could ever be fulfilled.

Moreover, the assertion that one has a property right in the value of things involves a contradiction, for in order to claim this proposition to be valid—universally agreeable—it would have to be assumed that it is permissible to act *before* agreement is reached. Otherwise, it would be impossible to ever propose anything. However, if one is permitted to assert a proposition—and no one could deny this without running into contradictions—then this is only possible because *physical* property borders exist, i.e., borders which everyone can recognize and ascertain independently and in complete ignorance of others' subjective valuations.[5]

---

5. While *no one* could act if *everyone* owned the value of his property, it *is* practically possible that *one* person or group, A, owns the value of his property and can determine what *another* person or group, B, may or may not do with the things under their

Another, equally common misunderstanding of the idea of private property concerns the classification of actions as permissible or impermissible based *exclusively* on their physical effects, i.e., without taking into account that every property right has a *history* (temporal genesis).

If A currently physically damages the property of B (for example by air pollution or noise), the situation must be judged differently depending on whose property right was established *earlier*. If A's property was founded first, and if he had performed the questionable activities before the neighboring property of B was founded, then A may continue with his activities. A has established an easement. From the outset, B had acquired dirty or loud property, and if B wants to have his property clean and quiet he must pay A for this advantage. Conversely, if B's property was founded first, then A must stop his activities; and if he does not want to do this, he must pay B for this advantage. Any other ruling is impossible and indefensible, because as long as a person is alive and awake he cannot *not* act. An early comer cannot, even if he wished otherwise, wait for a latecomer and his agreement before he begins acting. He must be permitted to act immediately. And if no other property besides one's own exists (because a latecomer has not yet arrived), then one's range of action can be deemed limited only by laws of nature. A latecomer can only challenge the legitimacy of an early comer if *he* is the owner of the goods affected by the early comer's actions. However, this implies that one can be the owner of un-appropriated things; i.e., that one can be the owner of things one has not yet discovered or appropriated through physical action. This means that no one is permitted to become the first user of a previously undiscovered and un-appropriated physical entity.

IV. THE ECONOMICS OF PRIVATE PROPERTY

The idea of private property not only agrees with our moral intuitions and is the sole just solution to the problem of social order; the institution of private property is also the basis of economic prosperity and of "social welfare." As long as people act in accordance with the rules underlying the institution of private property, social welfare is optimized.

---

control. This, however, means that B "owns" *neither* the value *nor* the physical integrity of the things under his control; that is, B and his property are actually owned by A. This rule can be implemented, but it does not qualify as a human ethic. Instead, it is a two-class system of exploiting Übermensch and exploited Untermensch.

Every act of original appropriation improves the welfare of the appropriator (at least *ex ante*); otherwise, it would not be performed. At the same time, no one is made worse off by this act. Any other individual could have appropriated the same goods and territories if only he had recognized them as scarce and, hence, valuable. However, since no other individual made such an appropriation, no one else can have suffered a welfare loss on account of the original appropriation. Hence, the so-called Pareto criterion (that it is scientifically legitimate to speak of an improvement of "social welfare" only if a particular change increases the individual welfare of at least one person and leaves no one else worse off) is fulfilled. An act of original appropriation meets this requirement. It enhances the welfare of one person, the appropriator, without diminishing anyone else's physical wealth (property). Everyone else has the same quantity of property as before and the appropriator has gained new, previously non-existent property. Thus, an act of original appropriation always increases social welfare.

Any further action with originally appropriated goods and territories enhances social welfare, for no matter what a person does with his property, it is done to increase his welfare. This is the case when he consumes his property as well as when he produces new property out of "nature." Every act of production is motivated by the producer's desire to transform a less valuable entity into a more valuable one. As long as acts of consumption and production do not lead to the physical damage or diminution of property owned by others, they are regarded as enhancing social welfare.

Finally, every voluntary exchange (transfer) of appropriated or produced property from one owner to another increases social welfare. An exchange of property is only possible if both owners prefer what they acquire over what they surrender and thus expect to benefit from the exchange. Two persons gain in welfare from every exchange of property, and the property under the control of everyone else is unchanged.

In distinct contrast, any deviation from the institution of private property must lead to social welfare losses.

In the case of universal and equal co-ownership—universal communism instead of private property—the price to be paid would be mankind's instant death because universal co-ownership would mean that no one would be allowed to do anything or move anywhere. Each actual deviation from a private property order would represent a system of unequal domination and hegemony. That is, it would be an order in which *one* person or group— the rulers, exploiters, or Übermenschen—would be permitted to acquire property *other than* by original appropriation, production or exchange, while another person or group—the ruled, exploited or Untermenschen—would be prohibited from doing likewise. While hegemony is possible, it would involve social welfare losses and would lead to relative impoverishment.

If A is permitted to acquire a good or territory which B has appropriated as indicated by visible signs, the welfare of A is increased at the expense of a corresponding welfare loss on the part of B. The Pareto criterion is not fulfilled, and social welfare is sub-optimal. The same is true with other forms of hegemonic rule. If A prohibits B from originally appropriating a hitherto un-owned piece of nature; if A may acquire goods produced by B without B's consent; if A may proscribe what B is permitted to do with his appropriated or produced goods (apart from the requirement that one is not permitted to physically damage or diminish others' property)—in each case there is a "winner," A, and a "loser," B. In every case, A increases his supply of property at the expense of B's corresponding loss of property. In no case is the Pareto criterion fulfilled, and a sub-optimal level of social welfare always results.

Moreover, hegemony and exploitation lead to a reduced level of future production. Every ruling which grants non-appropriators, non-producers and non-traders control, either partial or full, over appropriated, produced or traded goods, leads necessarily to a reduction of future acts of original appropriation, production and mutually beneficial trade. For the person performing them, each of these activities is associated with certain costs, and the costs of performing them increases under a hegemonic system and those of not performing them decreases. Present consumption and leisure become more attractive as compared to production (future consumption), and the level of production will fall below what it otherwise would have been. As for the rulers, the fact that they can increase their wealth by expropriating property appropriated, produced or contractually acquired by others will lead to a wasteful usage of the property at its disposal. Because they are permitted to supplement their future wealth by means of expropriation (taxes), present-orientation and consumption (high time preference) is encouraged, and insofar as they use their goods "productively" at all, the likelihood of misallocations, miscalculation, and economic loss is systematically increased.

V. THE CLASSIC PEDIGREE

As noted at the outset, the ethics and economics of private property presented above does not claim originality. Rather, it is a modern expression of a "classic" tradition, going back to beginnings in Aristotle, Roman law, Aquinas, the late Spanish Scholastics, Grotius and Locke.[6]

In contrast to the communist utopia of Plato's *Republic*, Aristotle provides a comprehensive list of the comparative advantages of private property in *Politics*. First, private property is more productive.

What is common to the greatest number gets the least amount of care. Men pay most attention to what is their own; they care less for what is common; or at any rate they care for it only to the extent to which each is individually concerned. Even when there is no other cause for inattention, men are more prone to neglect their duty when they think that another is attending to it.[7]

Secondly, private property prevents conflict and promotes peace. When people have their own separate domains of interest, "there will not be the same grounds for quarrels, and the amount of interest will increase, because each man will feel that he is applying himself to what is his."[8] "Indeed, it is a fact of observation that those who own common property, and share in its management, are far more often at variance with one another than those who have property in severalty."[9] Further, private property has existed always and everywhere, whereas nowhere have communist utopias sprung up spontaneously. Finally, private property promotes the virtues of benevolence and generosity. It allows one to be so with friends in need.

Roman law, from the *Twelve Tables* to the *Theodosian Code* and the *Justinian Corpus*, recognized the right of private property as near absolute. Property stemmed from unchallenged possession, prior usage established easements, a property owner could do with his property as he saw fit, and freedom of contract was acknowledged. As well, Roman law distinguished importantly between "national" (Roman) law—*ius civile*—and "international" law—*ius gentium*.

The Christian contribution to this classic tradition—embodied in St. Thomas Aquinas and the late Spanish Scholastics, as well as Protestants Hugo Grotius and John Locke—is twofold. Both Greece and Rome were

---

6. For details see Murray N. Rothbard, *Economic Thought Before Adam Smith: An Austrian Perspective on the History of Economic Thought*, vol. I (Aldershot, Eng.: Edward Elgar, 1995); also Tom Bethell, *The Noblest Triumph: Property and Prosperity Through the Ages* (New York: St. Martin's Press, 1998).

7. Aristotle, *Politics* (Oxford: Clarendon Press, 1946), p. 1261b.

8. *Id.*, p. 1263a.

9. *Id.*, p. 1263b.

slave-holding civilizations. Aristotle characteristically considered slavery a natural institution. In contrast, Western—Christian—civilization, notwithstanding some exceptions, has been essentially a society of free men. Correspondingly, for Aquinas as for Locke, every person had a proprietary right over himself (self-ownership). Moreover, Aristotle, and classic civilization generally, were disdainful of labor, trade, and money-making. In contrast, in accordance with the Old Testament, the Church extolled the virtues of labor and work. Correspondingly, for Aquinas as for Locke, it was by work, use, and cultivation of previously unused land that property first came into existence.

This classic theory of private property, based on self-ownership, original appropriation (homesteading), and contract (title transfer), continued to find prominent proponents, such as J. B. Say. However, from the height of its influence in the eighteenth century until quite recently, with the advance of the Rothbardian movement, the classic theory had slipped into oblivion.

For two centuries, economics and ethics (political philosophy) had diverged from their common origin in natural law doctrine into seemingly unrelated intellectual endeavors. Economics was a value-free "positive" science. It asked, "what means are appropriate to bring about a given (assumed) end?" Ethics was a "normative" science (if it was a science at all). It asked, "what ends (and what use of means) is one justified to choose?" As a result of this separation, the concept of property increasingly disappeared from both disciplines. For economists, property sounded too normative; for political philosophers property smacked of mundane economics.

In contrast, Rothbard noted, such elementary economic terms as direct and indirect exchange, markets and market prices, as well as aggression, crime, tort, and fraud, cannot be defined or understood without a theory of property. Nor is it possible to establish the familiar economic theorems relating to these phenomena without the implied notion of property and property rights. A definition and theory of property must precede the definition and establishment of all other economic terms and theorems.

Rothbard's unique contribution, from the early 1960s until his death in 1995, was the rediscovery of property and property rights as the common foundation of both economics and political philosophy, and the systematic reconstruction and conceptual integration of modern, marginalist economics and natural-law political philosophy into a unified moral science: libertarianism.

VI. CHICAGO DIVERSIONS

At the time when Rothbard was restoring the concept of private property to its central position in economics and reintegrating economics with ethics, other economists and legal theorists associated with the University of Chicago, such as Ronald Coase, Harold Demsetz, and Richard Posner, were also beginning to redirect professional attention to the subject of property and property rights.[10]

However, whereas for Rothbard private property and ethics logically precede economics, for the latter private property and ethics are subordinate to economics and economic considerations. According to Posner, whatever increases social wealth is just.[11]

The difference between the two approaches can be illustrated considering one of Coase's problem cases: A railroad runs beside a farm. The engine emits sparks, damaging the farmer's crop. What is to be done?

From the classic viewpoint, what needs to be established is who was there first, the farmer or the railroad? If the farmer was there first, he could force the railroad to cease and desist or demand compensation. If the railroad was there first, then it might continue emitting sparks and the farmer would have to pay the railroad to be spark free.

From the Coasean point of view, the answer is twofold. First and "positively," Coase claims that it does not matter *how* property rights and liability are allocated as long as they *are* allocated, and provided (unrealistically) that transaction costs are zero.

Coase claims it is wrong to think of the farmer and the railroad as either "right" or "wrong" (liable), as "aggressor" or "victim."

The question is commonly thought of as one in which A inflicts harm on B and what has to be decided is, How should we restrain A? But this is wrong. We are dealing with a problem of a reciprocal nature. To avoid the harm to B would be to inflict harm on A. The real question that has to be decided is, Should A be allowed to harm B or should B be allowed to harm A? The problem is to avoid the more serious harm.[12]

---

10. See Ronald Coase, *The Firm, The Market, and the Law* (Chicago: University of Chicago Press, 1988); Harold Demsetz, *Ownership, Control, and the Firm* (Oxford: Basil Blackwell, 1988); Richard Posner, *The Economics of Justice* (Cambridge: Harvard University Press, 1981).

11. Posner, *The Economics of Justice*, p. 74: "an act of injustice (is defined) as an act that reduces the wealth of society."

12. Ronald Coase, "The Problem of Social Cost," in idem, *The Firm, the Market,*

Further, given the "equal" moral standing of A and B, for the allocation of economic resources it allegedly does not matter to whom property rights are initially assigned. Suppose the crop loss to the farmer, A, is $1,000, and the cost of a spark apprehension device (SAD) to the railroad, B, is $750. If B is found liable for the crop damage, B will install an SAD or cease operations. If B is found not liable, then A will pay a sum between $750 and $1,000 for B to install an SAD. Both possibilities result in the installation of an SAD. Now assume the numbers are reversed: the crop loss is $750, and the cost of an SAD is $1,000. If B is found liable, he will pay A $750, but he will not install an SAD. And if B is found not liable, A is unable to pay B enough to install an SAD. Again, both scenarios end with the same result: there will be *no* SAD. Therefore, regardless of how property rights are initially assigned, according to Coase, Demsetz and Posner the allocation of production factors will be the same.

Second and "normatively"—and for the only *realistic* case of *positive* transaction costs—Coase, Demsetz and Posner demand that courts assign property rights to contesting parties in such a way that "wealth" or the "value of production" is maximized. For the case just considered this means that if the cost of the SAD is less than the crop loss, then the court should side with the farmer and hold the railroad liable. Otherwise, if the cost of the SAD is higher than the loss in crops, then the court should side with the railroad and hold the farmer liable. Posner offers another example. A factory emits smoke and thereby lowers residential property values. If property values are lowered by $3 million and the plant relocation cost is $2 million, the plant should be held liable and forced to relocate. Yet if the numbers are reversed—property values fall by $2 million and relocation costs are $3 million—the factory may stay and continue to emit smoke.

Both the positive and the normative claim of Chicago law and economics must be rejected.[13] As for the claim that it does not matter to whom property

---

and the Law, p. 96.

The moral perversity of this claim is best illustrated by applying it to the case of A raping B. According to Coase, A is not supposed to be restrained. Rather, "we are dealing with a problem of a reciprocal nature." In preventing A from raping B, harm is inflicted on A because he can no longer rape freely. The real question is: Should A be allowed to rape B, or should B be allowed to prohibit A from raping him/her? "The problem is to avoid the more serious harm."

13. See also Walter Block, "Coase and Demsetz on Private Property Rights," *Journal of Libertarian Studies* 1, no. 2 (1977); idem, "Ethics, Efficiency, Coasian Property Rights, and Psychic Income: A Reply to Harold Demsetz," *Review of Austrian Economics* 8, no. 2 (1995);

rights are initially assigned, three responses are in order. First, as Coase
cannot help but admit, it certainly matters to the farmer and the railroad,
to whom which rights are assigned. It matters not just how resources are
allocated but also who owns them.

Second and more importantly, for the value of social production it
matters fundamentally how property rights are assigned. The resources
allocated to productive ventures are not simply given. They themselves are
the outcome of previous acts of original appropriation and production, and
how much original appropriation and production there is depends on the
incentive for appropriators and producers. If appropriators and producers
are the absolute owners of what they have appropriated or produced,
i.e., if no liability *vis-à-vis* second- or third-comers arises out of acts of
appropriation and production, then the level of wealth will be maximized.
On the other hand, if original appropriators and producers can be found
liable *vis-à-vis* latecomers, as is implied in Coase's "reciprocity of harm"
doctrine, then the value of production will be lower than otherwise. That
is, the "it doesn't matter" doctrine is counterproductive to the stated goal of
wealth maximization.

Third, Coase's claim that the use of resources will be unaffected by the
initial allocation of property rights is not generally true. Indeed, it is easy to
produce counterexamples. Suppose the farmer does not lose $1,000 in crops
because of the railroad's sparks, but he loses a flower garden worth $1,000 to
him but worthless to anyone else. If the court assigns liability to the railroad,
the $750 SAD will be installed. If the court does not assign liability to the
railroad, the SAD will *not* be installed because the farmer simply does not
possess the funds to bribe the railroad to install an SAD. The allocation of
resources is *different* depending on the initial assignment of property rights.

Similarly, contra the normative claim of Chicago law and economics
that courts should assign property rights so as to maximize social wealth,
three responses are in order. First, any interpersonal comparison of utility
is scientifically impossible, yet courts must engage in such comparisons
willy-nilly whenever they engage in cost–benefit analyses. Such cost–benefit

idem, "Private Property Rights, Erroneous Interpretations, Morality and Economics,"
Quarterly Journal of Austrian Economics 3, no. 1 (2000); Gary North, *The Coase Theorem:
A Study in Epistemology* (Tyler, Texas: Institute for Christian Economics, 1992); idem,
"Undermining Property Rights: Coase and Becker," *Journal of Libertarian Studies* 16,
no. 4 (2002).

analyses are as arbitrary as the assumptions on which they rest. For example, they assume that psychic costs can be ignored and that the marginal utility of money is constant and the same for everyone.

Second, as the numerical examples given above show, courts assign property rights differently depending on changing market data. If the SAD is less expensive than the crop damage, the farmer is found in the right, while if the SAD is more expensive than the damage, the railroad is found in the right. That is, different circumstances will lead to a redistribution of property titles. No one can ever be sure of his property.[14] Legal uncertainty is made permanent. This seems neither just nor economical; moreover, who in his right mind would ever turn to a court that announced that it may reallocate existing property titles in the course of time depending on changing market conditions?

Finally, an ethic must not only have permanency and stability with changing circumstances; an ethic must allow one to make a decision about "just or unjust" *prior* to one's actions, and it must concern something under an actor's control. Such is the case for the classic private property ethic with its first-use–first-own principle. According to this ethic, to act justly means that a person employs only justly acquired means—means originally appropriated, produced, or contractually acquired from a previous owner—and that he employs them so that no physical damage to others' property results. Every person can determine *ex ante* whether or not this condition is met, and he has control over whether or not his actions physically damage the property of others. In distinct contrast, the wealth maximization ethic fails in both regards. No one can determine *ex ante* whether or not his actions will lead to social wealth maximization. If this can be determined at all, it can only be determined *ex post*. Nor does anyone have control over whether or not his actions maximize social wealth. Whether or not they do depends on *others'* actions and evaluations. Again, who in his right mind would subject himself to the judgment of a court that did not let him know in advance how to act justly and how to avoid acting unjustly, but that would judge *ex post*, after the facts?

---

14. Posner, *The Economics of Justice*, pp. 70–71, admits this with captivating frankness: "Absolute rights play an important role in the economic theory of the law.... But when transaction costs are prohibitive, the recognition of absolute rights is inefficient. ... [P]roperty rights, although absolute, (are) contingent on transaction costs and subservient or instrumental to the goal of wealth maximization."

3

The Origin of Private Property and the Family

I. THE SETTING: HISTORY

It is reasonable to begin human history 5 million years ago, when the human line of evolutionary descent separated from that of our closest non-human relative, the chimpanzee. It is also reasonable to begin it 2.5 million years ago, with the first appearance of *Homo habilis*; or 200,000 years ago, when the first representative of "anatomically modern man" made its appearance; or 100,000 years ago, when the anatomically modern man had become the standard human form. Instead, I want to begin only 50,000 years ago, when "anatomically modern man" had evolved into "behaviorally modern man." This is an eminently reasonable starting point, too.[1]

"Behaviorally modern human" refers to the existence of hunter-gatherers, of which even today some small pockets have remained. Based on archeological evidence, humans living 100,000 years ago were apparently still largely inept at hunting. They were certainly unable to take down large and dangerous animals, and it appears that they did not know how to fish. Their tools were almost exclusively made of stone and wood and made of materials of local origin, indicating the absence of any distance travel or trading. In distinct contrast, about 50,000 years later the human tool kit took on a new, greatly advanced appearance. Other materials were used besides stone and wood: bone, antler, ivory, teeth, shells, and the materials often came from distant places. The tools, including knifes, needles, barbed points, pins, borers and blades were more complex and skillfully crafted. The missile technology

---

• Previously unpublished.

1. See on the following Nicholas Wade, *Before the Dawn* (New York: Penguin Press, 2006).

27

was much improved and indicated highly developed hunting skills (although bows were invented only about 20,000 years ago). As well, man knew how to fish and was apparently able to build boats. Moreover, next to plain, functional tools, seemingly purely artistic implements—ornaments, figurines and musical instruments, such as bird-bone flutes—appeared on the scene at this time.

It has been hypothesized that what made this momentous development possible was a genetic change leading to the emergence of language, which involved a radical improvement in man's ability to learn and innovate. The archaic humans—*Homo ergaster, Homo neanderthalensis, Homo erectus*—did not have command of a language. To be sure, it can be safely assumed that they employed, as do many of the higher animals, the two so-called lower functions of language: the expressive or symptomatic function and the trigger or signal function.[2] However, they were apparently incapable of performing the two higher, cognitive functions of language: the descriptive and, especially, the argumentative function. These unique human abilities—so uniquely human, indeed, that one cannot think them "away" from our existence without falling into internal contradictions—of forming simple descriptive statements (propositions) such as "this (subject) is 'a' (predicate)," which claim to be *true*, and especially of presenting arguments (chains of propositions) such as "this is *a*; every *a* is *b*; hence, this is *b*," which claim to be *valid*, emerged apparently only about 50,000 years ago.[3]

Without language, human coordination had to occur via instincts, of which humans possess very few, or by means of physical direction or manipulation; and learning had to be either through imitation or by means of internal (implicit) inferences. In distinct contrast, with language—that is with words: sounds associated with and logically tied to certain objects and concepts (characteristics)—coordination could be achieved by mere symbols; and learning thus became independent of sense impressions

---

2. On the "lower" and "higher" functions of language see Karl Buehler, *Sprachtheorie. Die Darstellungsfunktion der Sprache* (Stuttgart: UTB, 1982 [1934]); and, in particular, also Karl R. Popper, *Conjectures and Refutations* (London: Routledge, 1963), pp. 134 ff., and idem, *Objective Knowledge* (Oxford: Oxford University Press, 1972), chap. 3, pp. 119–22, and chap. 6, sections 14–17.

3. Luigi Luca Cavalli-Sforza, *Genes, Peoples, and Languages* (Berkeley: University of California Press, 2000), p. 93, dates the origin of language at around 100,000 years ago; but given the archeological evidence cited above, the later, more recent date of only 50,000 years ago appears more likely.

(observations) and inferences could be made externally (explicitly) and hence became inter-subjectively reproducible and controllable. That is, by means of language knowledge could be transmitted to distant places and times (it was no longer tied to perception); one could communicate about matters (knowledge acquired and accumulated) far away in time and place. And because our reasoning process, our train of thought leading us to certain inferences and conclusions became "objectified" in external, inter-subjectively ascertainable arguments it could not only be easily transferred through time and space but at the same time be publicly criticized, improved, and corrected. It is no wonder, then, that hand in hand with the emergence of language revolutionary changes in technology would come about.

About 100,000 years ago, the population size of "modern humans," our immediate predecessors, is estimated to have been around 50,000, spread across the African continent and northward into the Middle East, the region of today's Israel.[4] From about 80,000 to 70,000 years ago, the earth experienced a significant cooling period. As a consequence, the Neanderthals, who lived in Europe and in the course of many millennia had adjusted to cold climates moved southward, where they clashed with and apparently destroyed their African relatives in large numbers. In addition, an extended dry period beginning about 60,000 years ago robbed "modern man" of much of his subsistence basis, such that 50,000 years ago the number of "modern humans" may not have exceeded 5,000, confined to northeast Africa.[5]

However, from then on the rise of modern humans has been uninterrupted, spreading all across the globe and eventually displacing all of their archaic relatives. The last Neanderthals, holed up in some caves near Gibraltar, are believed to have become extinct about 25,000 years ago. The last remnants of *Homo erectus*, found on the Indonesian island of Flores, date back about 13,000 years.

The "modern humans" led a nomadic hunter-gatherer lifestyle. Societies were composed of small bands of people (10–30), which occasionally met and formed a common genetic pool of about 150 and maybe up to 500 people (a size which geneticists have found to be necessary in order to avoid dysgenic effects).[6] The division of labor was limited, with the main partition being that

---

4. Cavalli-Sforza, *Genes, Peoples, and Languages*, p. 92.

5. Wade, *Before the Dawn*, pp. 8, 58; Cavalli-Sforza's estimate is significantly higher: 50,000. (*Genes, Peoples, and Languages*, p. 50)

6. Cavalli-Sforza, *Genes, Peoples, and Languages*, p. 30.

between women—acting mostly as gatherers—and men—acting mostly
as hunters. While private property of tools and implements was known and
recognized, the nomadic lifestyle only allowed for little possessions and hence
made hunter-gatherer societies comparatively egalitarian.[7] Nonetheless, life
initially appears to have been good for our forebears.[8] Only a few hours
of regular work allowed for a comfortable life, with good (high protein)
nourishment and plenty of leisure time. Indeed, fossil findings (skeletons
and teeth) seem to indicate that our hunter-gatherer forebears enjoyed a life
expectancy of well above 30 years, which was only reached again in the course
of the 19th century.[9] Contra Hobbes, their life was anything but nasty,
brutish, and short.[10]

   However, the life of hunters and gatherers faced a fundamental and
ultimately unanswerable challenge. Hunter-gatherer societies led essentially
parasitic lives. That is, they did not add anything to the nature-given supply
of goods. They only depleted the supply of goods. They did not produce
(apart from a few tools) but only consumed. They did not grow and breed
but had to wait for nature to regenerate and replenish. At best, what they
accomplished was that they did not over-hunt or over-gather so that the
natural regeneration process was not disturbed or even brought to an entire
standstill. In any case, what this form of parasitism obviously involved,
then, was the inescapable problem of population growth. In order to permit

---

7. The egalitarianism of hunter-gatherer societies should not be overemphasized or
idealized, however. These societies were also characterized by pronounced hierarchical
features. Not unlike what is known from the animal kingdom, men ranked above and
dominated women. Often women were "taken" and treated by men like goods of the "outer"
world are taken and treated: appropriated, stolen, used, abused, and traded. Children
ranked below adults. Moreover, hierarchies existed among both male and the female
members of society, down from the reigning alpha-male and female to the lowliest member
of society. Status fights occurred, and whoever did not accept the established rank-order
faced severe punishment. The losers in the fights for higher status were threatened with
injury, even death and, at the very best, expulsion from the tribe. In a word: even if tribal
life provided for a comfortable standard of living in terms of abundant food and leisure it
was anything but comfortable in terms of today's much cherished "individual autonomy."
To the contrary, life in the tribal household meant discipline, order and submission.

   8. See Richard Lee and I. De Vore, eds., *Man the Hunter* (Chicago: Aldine, 1968);
Marvin Harris, *Cannibals and Kings: The Origins of Cultures* (New York: Vintage Books,
1977), esp. chap. 2.

   9. Harris, *Cannibals and Kings*, p. 19 f.

   10. This statement refers only to the hunter-gatherer life during periods of peace,
however. On the high incidence of warfare and unnatural causes of death, see below.

the comfortable life just described, the population density had to remain extremely low. It has been estimated that one square mile of territory was needed to comfortably sustain one to two persons, and in less fertile regions even larger territories were necessary.[11] So what was one to do when the population size exceeded these more or less narrow limits?

People could of course try to prevent such population pressure from emerging, and indeed hunter-gatherer societies tried their best in this regard. They induced abortions, they engaged in infanticide, especially female infanticide, and they reduced the number of pregnancies by engaging in long periods of breast-feeding (which, in combination with the low body-fat characteristic of constantly mobile and moving women, reduces female fertility). Yet while this alleviated the problem it did not solve it. The population kept increasing.

Given that the population size could not be maintained at a stationary level, only three alternatives existed for the steadily emerging "excess" population. One could *fight* over the limited food supplies, one could *migrate*, or one could *invent* and adopt a new, technologically advanced societal organization mode that allowed for a larger population size to survive on the same, given territory.

As for the first option, i.e., fighting, a few remarks shall suffice. In the literature, primitive man has been frequently described as peaceful and living in harmony with nature. Most popular in this regard is Rousseau's portrayal of the "noble savage." Aggression and war, it has been frequently held, were the result of civilization built upon the institution of private property. In fact, matters are almost exactly the reverse.[12] True, the savagery of modern wars has produced unparalleled carnage. Both World War I and World War II, for instance, resulted in tens of millions of deaths and left entire countries in ruins. And yet, as anthropological evidence has in the meantime made abundantly clear, primitive man has been considerably more warlike than contemporary man. It has been estimated that on the average some 30 percent of all males in primitive, hunter-gatherer societies died from unnatural—violent—causes, far exceeding anything experienced in this regard in modern

---

11. Thus, for instance, writes Harris: "In all of France during the late stone age there were probably no more than 20,000 and possibly as few as 1,600 human beings." (*Cannibals and Kings*, p. 18)

12. See Wade, *Before the Dawn*, chap. 8, and pp. 150–54; also Lawrence H. Keeley, *War Before Civilization* (New York: Oxford University Press, 1996).

societies.[13] According to Keeley's estimates, a tribal society on the average lost about 0.5 percent of its population in combat each year.[14] Applied to the population of the twentieth century this would amount to a casualty rate of some 2 billion people instead of the actual number of "merely" a few hundred million. Of course, primitive warfare was very different from modern warfare. It was not conducted by regular troops on battlefields, but by raids, ambushes and surprise attacks. However, every attack was characterized by utmost brutality, carried out without mercy and always with deadly results; and while the number of people killed in each attack might have been small, the incessant nature of these aggressive encounters made violent death an ever-present danger for every man (and abduction and rape for every woman).[15] Moreover, increasing evidence for the widespread practice of cannibalism has been accumulated in recent times. Indeed, it appears that cannibalism was once upon a time an almost universal practice.[16]

More importantly, these findings regarding primitive man's war-likeness are not just anthropological curiosities, i.e., features that one might consider incidental to the true nature of hunter-gatherer societies. To the contrary, there exist fundamental theoretical reasons why such societies were characterized by incessant warfare and peaceful relations were almost impossible to attain, in particular, if the possibility of evading one another was foreclosed because all surrounding land was occupied. Because then it became unavoidable that the members of different hunter-gatherer tribes encountered each other more or less regularly on their various expeditions in search of plants and animals. Indeed, as the population size increased such encounters became

---

13. Napoleon Chagnon, "Life Histories, Blood Revenge, and Warfare in a Tribal Population," *Science* 239 (1988): pp. 985–92.

14. Keeley, *War Before Civilization*, p. 33; Wade, *Before the Dawn*, p. 151 f.

15. See also Steven LeBlanc, *Constant Battles* (New York: St. Martin's Press, 2003).

16. See Wade, *Before the Dawn*, pp. 154–58.
Contrasting the ferocity of primitive vs. modern men, Wade, following Keeley, notes (*Before the Dawn*, p. 152): When primitive warriors "met the troops of civilized societies in open battle, they regularly defeated them despite the vast disparity in weaponry. In the Indian wars, the U.S. Army 'usually suffered severe defeats' when caught in the open, such as by the Seminoles in 1834, and at the battle of Little Bighorn. In 1879 the British army in South Africa, equipped with artillery and Gatling guns was convincingly defeated by Zulus armed mostly with spears and ox-hide shields at the battles of Isandlwana, Myer's Drift and Hlobane. The French were sent off by the Tuareg of the Sahara in the 1890s. The state armies prevailed in the end only through larger manpower and attritional campaigns, not by superior fighting skill."

ever more frequent. And because hunters and gatherers did not add anything to the nature-given supply of goods but only consumed what was provided by nature, their competition for food was necessarily of an antagonistic nature: either I pick the berries or hunt a given animal or you do it. No or little trade and exchange between the members of different tribes existed, because the members of one tribe engaged in essentially the same activities as those of any other tribe and neither one accumulated any surplus of goods that could be exchanged for others' surplus goods. There existed only ineradicable conflict and the more conflict the more the population number in each tribe exceeded its optimum size. In this situation, where everything appropriated by one person (or tribe) was immediately consumed and the total supply of goods was strictly limited by natural forces, only deadly antagonism could exist between men. In the words of Ludwig von Mises, men became

> deadly foes of one another, irreconcilable rivals in their endeavors to secure a portion of the scarce supply of means of sustenance provided by nature. Each man would have been forced to view all other men as his enemies; his craving for the satisfaction of his own appetites would have brought him into an implacable conflict with all his neighbors. No sympathy could possibly develop under such a state of affairs.[17]

Only the death of one's rivals provided a solution to one's own desire to survive. Indeed, to spare another man's life would have left him equipped to create even more offspring and hence reduced one's own future chance of survival still further.[18]

---

17. Ludwig von Mises, *Human Action: A Treatise on Economics* (Chicago: Regnery, 1966), p. 144.

18. Indirectly, this insight into the irreconcilable antagonism between the members of different tribes within the framework of hunter-gatherer societies also provides a first clue as to the requirements for peaceful cooperation among men. In order for members of different tribes to view each other not as enemies but as potential collaborators, there must be genuine *production* of consumer goods (above and beyond the mere appropriation of nature-given consumer goods). At least, as a very minimum requirement, there must be production of consumer goods in the sense of the storage of surplus goods (of saving for future consumption). For only if man thus *adds* something to nature which otherwise, without his deliberate effort, would not exist at all, can there be a reason for one man to spare another man's life for his own good (for his own selfish motives and to his own advantage). To be sure, as proponents of the thesis that it is civilization, which breeds war, are fond to point out, the very fact that one man has added something to the supply of

The second available option to deal with the steadily reemerging problem of excess population was migration. While by no means costless—after all one had to leave familiar for unfamiliar territories—migration (as compared to fighting) must have appeared frequently as the less costly option, especially as long as some open frontier existed. Hence, setting out from their homeland in East-Africa, successively the entire globe was conquered by bands of people breaking away from their relatives to form new societies in areas hitherto unoccupied by humans.

It appears that this process began also about 50,000 years ago, shortly after the emergence of behaviorally modern man and the acquisition of the ability to build boats. From about this time on until around 12,000 to 11,000 years ago global temperatures gradually fell (since then we are in an interglacial warming period) and the sea levels accordingly fell.[19] People crossed over the Red Sea at the Gate of Grief, which was then merely a narrow gap of water dotted with islands, to land at the southern tip of the Arabian peninsula (which enjoyed a comparatively wet period at that time). From there onward, preferring to stay in tropical climate zones to which one had been adjusted, the migration—of possibly not more than

---

nature-given goods might also provide a reason for another man to engage in aggression: to rob him of his product. But there is certainly less reason to kill such a man than to kill a man who has added nothing but merely takes and consumes what is given (and hence inevitably reduces what remains available for another). Moreover, insofar as a man adds something to the total supply of available goods there exists also a reason for another man to *not* interfere with his activity but let him continue, and to benefit from him and his activity by engaging in mutually beneficial trade with him and hence, as a consequence, ultimately develop sympathetic feelings toward his fellow man. Thus, while civilization does not eliminate man's aggressive impulses it can and did diminish and attenuate them.

19. Actually, the last great warming period, also called interglacial period, had already ended about 120,000 years ago. During this period, i.e., more than 120,000 years ago, hippopotamuses had lived in the Rhine and the Thames and northern Europe had something of an "African appearance." From then on, glaciers moved steadily further southward and the sea level eventually fell by more than 100 meters. The Thames and the Elbe became tributaries of the Rhine, before it streamed first into the Northern Sea and from there into the Atlantic. See Josef H. Reichholf, *Eine kurze Naturgeschichte des letzten Jahrtausends* (Frankfurt/M.: Fischer, 2007), p. 15 f. When this period ended, quite suddenly, about 12,000 years ago, the glaciers rapidly retreated and the sea level rose, not by millimeters per year but very quickly in an almost flood-like fashion. Within a very brief period England and Ireland, which had previously been connected to the European continent, became islands. The Baltic Sea and much of the contemporary North Sea came thus into existence. Likewise, most of today's Persian Gulf dates from about this time. *Id.*, p. 49 f.

150 people—continued eastward. Travel was mostly by boat, because until about 6,000 years ago when man learned how to tame horses, this form of transportation was much faster and more convenient than travel by foot. Hence, migration took place along the coastline—and proceeded from there into the interior through river valleys—first all the way to India. From there, as the genetic evidence seems to indicate, the population movement split into two directions. On the one hand it proceeded around the Indian peninsula to southeast Asia and Indonesia (which was then connected to the Asian mainland) and finally to the now foundered former continent of Sahul (of Australia, New Guinea and Tasmania, which were joined until about 8,000 years ago), which was then only separated from the Asian mainland by a 60 mile wide channel of water dotted with islands permitting short-distance island hopping, as well as northward up the coast to China and eventually Japan. On the other hand, the migration process went from India in a northwesterly direction, through Afghanistan, Iran, and Turkey and ultimately Europe. As well, splitting off of this stream of migration, people pressed in northeasterly direction into southern Siberia. Later migrations, most likely in three waves, with the first about 14,000–12,000 years ago, went from Siberia across the Bering Strait—then (until about 11,000 years ago) a land bridge—and onto the American continent, apparently reaching Patagonia only about 1,000 years later (archeological findings of human remains in southern Chile have been dated as 12,500 years old). The last migration route set out from Taiwan, which was occupied about 5,000 years ago, sailing across the Pacific to reach the Polynesian islands and finally, only about 800 years ago, New Zealand.[20]

The process was essentially always the same: a group invaded some territory, population pressure mounted, some people stayed put, a subgroup moved further on, generation after generation, along the coastline, following rivers and game and avoiding deserts and high mountains. The migration from Africa all the way to Australia may have taken about 4,000 to 5,000 years, and migration to Europe 7,000 years (the oldest artifacts there ascribed to modern humans, found in Bulgaria, date about 43,000 years back) and another 7,000 years to reach western Spain.[21] Once broken up, practically no contact existed between the various hunter-gatherer societies. Consequently,

---

20. For further details see Wade, *Before the Dawn*, chap. 5; also Jared Diamond, *Guns, Germs, and Steel: The Fates of Human Societies* (New York: Norton, 1997), chap. 1.

21. See Cavalli-Sforza, *Genes, Peoples, and Languages*, p. 94.

although initially closely related to one another through direct kinship relations, these societies formed separated genetic pools and, confronted with different natural environments and as the result of mutations and genetic drift interacting with natural selection, in the course of time they took on distinctly different appearances. By and large, the genetic difference between various societies increased in correlation with the spatial distance between societies and the duration of their separation time.[22] Different ethnicities emerged and, further on, also distinctly different human races. These emerging, genetically based differences concerned matters such as skin color, physical build and strength, resistance to cold temperatures and to various diseases, and tolerance *vis-à-vis* certain substances. They also concerned cognitive matters, however. Thus, genetic evidence exists for two significant further developments regarding the size and cognitive powers of the human brain. One such development occurred about 37,000 years ago and affected most of the population in Europe as well as in East Asia (but left very few traces in Africa), and another occurred about 6,000 years ago and affected mostly people in the Middle East and Europe (but had less impact in East Asia and almost none in sub-Saharan Africa).[23]

Moreover, hand in hand with the geographical and correlated genetic differentiation of humans went a linguistic differentiation. Very much in agreement with and supported by genetic (biological) evidence, some linguists, in particular Merritt Ruhlen,[24] following in the footsteps of the pioneering work of Joseph Greenberg, have made the plausible case for a single human proto-language, from which all human languages can be derived as more or less distant relatives. Obviously, the original emigrants from the African homeland, some 50,000 years ago, would have spoken the same language, and so it seems hardly surprising that the above-sketched population movement, and the splitting of groups of people into different genetic pools, more or less separated in time and space from one another, should be closely mirrored by a differentiation of languages, the grouping of different languages into language families, and the grouping of these into still larger super-families.[25] Likewise, the process of the proliferation

---

22. *Id.*, pp. 20–25.

23. See Wade, *Before the Dawn*, pp. 96–99.

24. *The Origin of Language: Tracing the Evolution of the Mother Tongue* (New York: Wiley, 1994).

25. See Cavalli-Sforza, *Genes, Peoples, and Languages*, chap. 5, esp. p. 144, for a table showing the correlation between genetic and linguistic families and trees of descent. See

of languages appears to have followed a predictable pattern. First, with the spread of humans around the world as hunters and gatherers and the concomitant proliferation of distinct, separated genetic pools, a successively increasing number of different languages emerged. Thus, for instance, of the 6,000 different languages still spoken today, some 1,200 languages are spoken in New Guinea, one of the most "primitive" remaining world regions, half of which have no more than the "magic" number of 500 speakers and none more than 100,000. Then, however, with the beginning of human settlement some 11,000 years ago and the following transition to agriculture and the attendant expansion and intensification of the division of labor (more on which later on), a countervailing and even contrary tendency appears to have come into existence: just as the genetic pools appear to have widened, so the number of different languages spoken has successively diminished.

II. The Problem: Theory

About 35,000 years ago, i.e., 15,000 years after the initial exodus from Africa, practically all of Europe, Asia, Australia and, of course, Africa itself had been occupied by our ancestors, the modern humans, and archaic humans, *Homo neanderthalensis* and *Homo erectus*, were on the verge of extinction. About 12,000 years ago, humans had also spread all across the Americas. Apart from the Polynesian islands, then, all land and all of the naturally given supply of earthly (economic) goods, of plants and animals, had been taken into human possession; and, given the parasitic lifestyle of hunter-gatherers, humans did not *add* anything to this land and the nature-given supply of goods but merely reacted to natural *changes*.

These changes were at times quite drastic. Changes in global climate, for instance, could and did significantly affect how much inhabitable land was available and the natural vegetation and animal population. In the time period under consideration, in the 20,000 plus years between 35,000 and 11,000 years ago, drastic changes in such natural conditions occurred. 20,000 years ago, for instance, during the period know as the *Last Glacial Maximum*, temperatures fell sharply and most of Northern Europe and Siberia became uninhabitable. Britain and all of Scandinavia were covered by glaciers, most of Siberia turned into polar desert and steppe-tundra extended as far south

---

also Luigi Luca Cavalli-Sforza and Francesco Cavalli-Sforza, *The Great Human Diasporas: The History of Diversity and Evolution* (Cambridge: Perseus Books, 1995), chap. 7; Wade, *Before the Dawn,* chap. 10, pp. 102 ff.

as the Mediterranean, the Black Sea and the Caspian Sea. After 5,000 years, about 15,000 years ago, the glaciers began to retreat, allowing people, animals and plants to re-occupy previously deserted regions. Two and a half thousand years later, however, within merely a decade, temperatures again plummeted back to almost the previous frigid conditions; and only another 1,000 years later, about 11,500 years ago, and again quite suddenly, did temperatures then experience a long-sustained increase and the earth entered the so-called *Holocene*, the latest and still lasting interglacial warming period.[26] (The Sahara began to turn into the present, extremely hot desert only less than 3,000 years ago. In pre-Roman times, the Sahara—and similarly the central-Asian deserts—was still a green savanna with an abundant supply of wildlife. The power and the attraction of Carthage, for instance, was based largely on the fertility of its hinterland as a center of wheat production; this fact was an important reason for Rome's desire to destroy Carthage and gain control of its North-African territories.[27])

In any case and regardless of all complicating details and all changes that future empirical researchers will no doubt bring about concerning the foregoing historical narrative, at some point in time the landmass available to help satisfy human needs could no longer be enlarged. In economic jargon, the supply of the production factor "land" became fixed, and every increase in the size of the human population had to be sustained by the same, unchanged quantity of land. Of the formerly three available options in response to an increasing population pressure: to move, to fight or to invent, only the latter two remained open. What to do when faced with this challenge?

To bring the problem faced into even sharper relief it is useful to first take another, more detailed look at the admittedly rather limited extent of the division of labor within a hunter-gatherer society.

---

26. During the present *Holocene* period temperatures continued to show significant variations, however. About 10,000 years ago, after a warming period of thousands of years, temperatures reached the present level. Several times thereafter, temperatures rose significantly above this level (by up to 2 degrees Celsius): 8,000 to 6,800 years ago, 6,000 to 5,500 years ago, 5,000 to 4,000 years ago, 2,500 to 2,000 years ago, and again from the 10th to the 14th century, during the so-called medieval warming period. As well, several periods with significantly lower than present temperatures existed: 9,000 to 8,000 years ago, 6,800 to 6,000 years ago, 4,000 to 2,500 years ago, from the 2nd to the 8th century and again from the 14th until the mid-19th century, the so-called Little Ice Age. See Reichholf, *Eine kurze Naturgeschichte des letzten Jahrtausends*, p. 27.

27. *Id.*, p. 23 f.

So far the antagonism between the members of *different* bands or clans has been explained while it has been taken for granted that *within* a given band or clan collaboration — peaceful cooperation — exists. But why should this be so? Intra-group cooperation is almost universally assumed as a matter of course. Nonetheless, it too requires an explanation, because a world without even this limited degree of cooperation is certainly *conceivable*. To be sure, there exists a biological basis for *some* forms of human cooperation. "The mutual sexual attraction of male and female," writes Mises, "is inherent in man's animal nature and independent of any thinking and theorizing. It is permissible to call it original, vegetative, instinctive, or mysterious."[28] The same can be said about the relationship between mother and child: if mothers did not take care of their offspring for an extended period of time, their children would instantly die and mankind would be doomed. However, this necessary, biologically determined degree of cooperation is a far cry from that actually observed in hunter-gatherer societies. Thus, Mises continues,

> neither cohabitation, nor what precedes it or follows, generates social cooperation and societal modes of life. The animals too join together in mating, but they have not developed social relations. Family life is not merely a product of sexual intercourse. It is by no means natural and necessary that parents and children live together in the way they do in the family. The mating relation need not result in a family organization. The human family is an outcome of thinking, planning, and acting. It is this fact which distinguishes it radically from those animal groups which we call *per analogiam* animal families.[29]

Why, for instance, did not each man and each woman, after they had left infancy, hunt or gather alone only to meet for occasional sex? Why did it *not* occur what has been described as having occurred for *groups* of humans *already on the level of individuals*: one person, faced with a strictly limited supply of nature-given goods, breaking away from another in order to avoid conflict until all land was taken into possession and then a war of everyone against everyone else (rather than merely a war of the members of one group against the members of all other groups) breaking out? The answer to this is: because of the recognition that cooperation was more productive than

---

28. Mises, *Human Action*, p. 167.
29. *Id.*

isolated, self-sufficient action. Division of labor and cooperation based on such division of labor increased the productivity of human labor.

There are three reasons for this: First, there exist tasks which exceed the powers of any single man and require instead the combined efforts of several men in order to be successfully executed. Certain animals, for instance, might be too large or too dangerous to be hunted by single individuals but require the cooperative engagement of many. Or there exist tasks which could, in principle, be executed by a single individual but that would take up so much time for an isolated actor that the final result does not appear worth the effort. Only concerted action can accomplish these tasks in a time span sufficiently short to deem the task worthwhile. Searching for edible plants or animals, for instance, is fraught with uncertainties. On one day one might stumble across suitable plants or animals quickly, but at another time one might search for them in vain seemingly without end. But if one pools this risk, i.e., if a large number of gatherers or hunters begin their search separately only to call upon each other once anyone of them has turned out to be lucky in his search, then gathering and hunting might be turned into routinely successful endeavors for each participant.

Second: Even though the natural environment faced by each person might be more or less the same, each individual (even identical twins) is different from any other. Men, for instance, are significantly different in their abilities than women. By their very nature, men are typically better hunters and women better gatherers. Adults are significantly different in their abilities than kids. Some people are physically strong and others show great dexterity. Some are tall and others are quick. Some have great vision and others a good sense of smell. Given such differences it is obviously advantageous to partition the various tasks necessary to perform in order to secure a comfortable life in such a way that each person specializes in those activities in which he has an advantage over others. Women gather and men hunt. Tall individuals pick fruits of trees and short ones specialize in hunting mushrooms. Quick runners relay messages. Individuals with good eyesight will spot distant events. Kids are used for the exploration of small and narrow holes. People with great dexterity produce tools. The strong will specialize in going in for the kill, etc.

Third: Moreover, even if the members of one tribe are so distinguished from one another that one person is more efficient in every conceivable task than another, division of labor is still all-around more productive than isolated labor. An adult might be better at any task than a kid, for instance. Given the inescapable fact of the scarcity of time, however, even in this conceivably worst-case scenario it makes economic sense—that is, it leads to a greater physical output of goods produced per unit of labor—if the adult specializes in those tasks in which his greater efficiency (as compared to that of the kid) is particularly pronounced and leaves those tasks for the kid to perform in which the latter's all-around lower efficiency is comparatively smaller. Even though the adult might be more efficient than the child in collecting small firewood, for instance, the adult's far greater superiority in hunting large game would make it a waste of his time to gather wood. Instead, he would want the child to collect firewood and use all of his own precious time to perform that task in which his greater efficiency is especially marked, namely large game hunting.

Nonetheless: While these advantages offered by the division of labor can explain intra-tribal cooperation (rather than fight) and, based on such, initially, maybe purely "selfishly-motivated" collaboration, the gradual development of feelings of sympathy (good will) toward one's fellowmen, which go above and beyond whatever *biological* basis there may exist for the special, more-than-normally-friendly relationship between close kin, this explanation still only goes so far. Given the peculiar, parasitic nature of hunter-gatherer societies and assuming land to be fixed, invariably the moment must arise when the number of people exceeds the optimal group size and average living standards will fall, threatening whatever degree of intra-group solidarity previously might have existed.[30]

This situation is captured and explained by the economic *law of returns*.

The law of returns, popularly but somewhat misleadingly also called the *law of diminishing returns*, states that for any combination of two or more production factors an optimum combination exists (such that any deviation

---

30. Empirically, it appears that the "magic number," i.e., the optimum population size for a hunter-gatherer society, was somewhere between 50 to 100 people for a territory of about 50 to 100 square miles (one person per square mile). At around this combination point, all advantages offered by the division of labor were exhausted. If the population size increased beyond this "magic" number, average living standards became increasingly endangered and this threat grew still more if neighboring tribes, due to their own internal population growth, increased their territorial incursions thus further diminishing the nature-given supply of goods available to the members of the first tribe. Internal as well as external population pressure then called for a solution to an increasingly urgent problem: namely sheer survival.

from it involves material waste, or "efficiency losses").[31] Applied to the two original factors of production, labor and land (nature-given goods), the law implies that if one were to increase the quantity of labor (population) while the quantity of land and the available technology (hunting and gathering) remained fixed, eventually a point will be reached where the physical output per labor-unit input is maximized. This point marks the optimal population size. If there is no additional land available and technology remains fixed at a "given" level, any population increase beyond the optimal size will lead to a progressive decline in per capita income. Living standards, on the average, will fall. A point of (absolute) overpopulation has been reached. This is, as Mises has termed it, the *Malthusian law of population.*

Because of the fundamental importance of this *Malthusian law of population* and in order to avoid any possible misunderstanding, it is advisable to make also explicit what the law does *not* state. The law does not assert where exactly this optimal combination point is located—at so-and-so many people per square mile, for instance—but only *that* such a point exists. Otherwise, if every quantity of output could be produced by increasing only one factor (labor) while leaving the other (land) unchanged, the latter (land) would cease to be scarce—and hence an economic good—at all; one could increase without limit the return of any piece of land by simply increasing the input of labor applied to this piece without ever having to consider expanding the size of one's land. The law also does not state that *every* increase of one factor (labor) applied to a fixed quantity of another (land) must lead to a less than proportional increase of the output produced. In fact, as one approaches the optimum combination point an increase of labor applied to a given piece of land might lead to a more than proportional increase of output (increasing returns). One additional man, for instance, might make it possible that an animal species can be hunted that cannot be hunted at all without this one extra hunter. The law of returns merely states that this cannot occur without definite limits. Nor does the law assert that the optimum combination point cannot be shifted up- and outward. In fact, as will be explained in the following, owing to technological advances the optimum combination point can be so moved, allowing a larger population to enjoy a higher average living

---

31. See Mises, *Human Action*, pp. 127–31; idem, *Socialism: An Economic and Sociological Analysis* (Indianapolis, Ind.: Liberty Classics, 1981), pp. 174–75; also Hans-Hermann Hoppe, *Kritik der sozialwissenschaftlichen Sozialforschung. Untersuchungen zur Grundlegung von Soziologie und Ökonomie* (Opladen: Westdeutscher Verlag, 1985), pp. 59–64.

standard on the same quantity of land. What the law of returns does say is only that *given* a state of technological development (mode of production) and a corresponding degree of specialization, an optimum combination point exists beyond which an increase in the supply of labor must necessarily lead to a less then proportional increase of the output produced or no increase at all.

Indeed, for hunter-gatherer societies the difficulties of escaping the Malthusian trap of absolute overpopulation are even more severe than these qualifications regarding the law of returns might indicate. For while these qualifications might leave the impression that it is "only" a technological innovation that is needed to escape the trap, this is not the full truth. Not just any technological innovation will do. Because hunter-gatherer societies are, as explained, "parasitic" societies, which do not add anything to the supply of goods but merely appropriate and consume what nature provides, any productivity increase *within* the framework of this mode of production does not (or only insignificantly so) result in a greater output of goods produced (of plants gathered or animals hunted) but rather merely (or mostly) in a reduction of the time necessary to produce an essentially unchanged quantity of output. The invention of bow and arrow that appears to have been made some 20,000 years ago, for instance, will not so much lead to a greater quantity of available animal meat to consume, thus allowing a larger number of people to reach or exceed a given level of consumption, but rather only to the same number of people enjoying more leisure with an unchanged standard of living in terms of meat-consumption (or else, if the population increases, the gain of more leisure time will have to be paid for by a reduction in meat consumption per capita). In fact, for hunter-gatherers the productivity gains achieved by technological advances such as the invention of bow and arrow may well turn out to be no blessing at all or only a very short-term blessing. Because the greater ease of hunting that is thus brought about, for instance, may lead to over-hunting, increasing the supply of meat per capita in the short-run, but diminishing or possibly eliminating the meat supply in the long-run by reducing the natural rate of animal reproduction or hunting animals to extinction and thus magnifying the Malthusian problem, even without any increase in population size.[32]

---

32. In fact, over-hunting and animal extinction played a fateful role especially in the Americas, which were only occupied after the invention of bow and arrow. While the Americas originally exhibited pretty much the same fauna as the Eurasian continent—after all, for thousands of years animals could move from one continent to another across the

III. The Solution: Theory and History

The technological invention, then, that solved (at least temporarily[33]) the problem of a steadily emerging and re-emerging "excess" of population and the attendant fall of average living standards was a revolutionary change in the entire mode of production. It involved the change from a parasitic lifestyle to a genuinely productive life. Instead of merely appropriating and consuming what nature had provided, consumer goods were now actively produced and nature was augmented and improved upon.

This revolutionary change in the human mode of production is generally referred to as the "Neolithic Revolution": the transition from food production by hunting and gathering to food production by the raising of plants and animals.[34] It began about 11,000 years ago in the Middle East, in the region typically referred to as the "Fertile Crescent." The same invention was made again, seemingly independently, less than 2,000 years later in central China, and again a few thousand years later (about 5,000 years ago) also in the Western hemisphere: in Mesoamerica, in South America, and in the eastern part of today's United States. From these centers of innovation the new technology then spread to conquer practically the entire earth.

The new technology represented a fundamental cognitive achievement and was reflected and expressed in two interrelated institutional innovations, which from then on until today have become the dominant feature of human life: the appropriation and employment of ground land as private property, and the establishment of the family and the family household.

Beringian land bridge—by the time of the European rediscovery of America some 500 years ago all large domesticable mammals (except for the llama in South America) had been hunted to extinction. Likewise, it appears now that the entire mega-fauna that once inhabited Australia was hunted to extinction (except for the red kangaroo). It seems that this event occurred around 40,000 years ago, only a few thousand years after man had first arrived in Australia, and even without the help of bow and arrow, only with very primitive weapons and the help of fires used for the trapping of animals. See on this Diamond, *Guns, Germs, and Steel*, pp. 42 ff.

33. While the changes brought about by the "Neolithic Revolution" allowed for a significantly higher sustainable population size, the Malthusian problem was bound to eventually arise again, and the seemingly ultimate solution to the problem was only reached with the so-called "Industrial Revolution" that began in Europe at the end of the 17th century.

34. See also Michael H. Hart, *Understanding Human History* (Augusta, Ga.: Washington Summit Publishers, 2007), pp. 139 ff.

To understand these institutional innovations and the cognitive achievement underlying them one must first take a look at the treatment of the production factor "land" by hunter-gatherer societies.

It can be safely assumed that private property existed within the framework of a tribal household. Private property certainly existed with regard to things such as personal clothing, tools, implements and ornaments. To the extent that such items were produced by particular, identifiable individuals or acquired by others from their original makers through either gift or exchange they were considered individual property. On the other hand, to the extent that goods were the results of some concerted or joint effort they were considered collective household goods. This applied most definitely to the means of sustenance: to the berries gathered and the game hunted as the result of some intra-tribal division of labor. Without doubt, then, collective property played a highly prominent role in hunter-gatherer societies, and it is because of this that the term "primitive communism" has been often employed to describe primitive, tribal economies: each individual contributed to the household income "according to his abilities," and each received from the collective income "according to his needs" (as determined by the existing hierarchies within the group)—not quite unlike the "communism" in "modern" households.

Yet what about the ground land on which all group activities took place? One may safely rule out that ground land was considered private property in hunter-gatherer societies. But was it collective property? This has been typically assumed to be the case, almost as a matter of course. However, the question is in fact more complicated, because a third alternative exists: that ground land was neither private nor collective property but instead constituted part of the *environment* or more specifically the *general conditions* of action or what has also been called "common property" or, in short, "the commons."[35]

In order to decide this question, standard anthropological research is of little or no help. Instead, some elementary as well as fundamental economic theory, including a few precise definitions, is required. The external world in which man's actions take place can be divided into two categorically distinct parts. On the one hand, there are those things that are considered *means*—

---

35. See on this distinction Murray N. Rothbard, *Man, Economy, and State* (Los Angeles: Nash, 1970), chap. 1.

or *economic goods*; and on the other hand, there are those things that are considered *environment*—or also referred to sometimes, if somewhat misleadingly, as *free goods*. The requirements for an element of the external world to be classified as a means or an economic good have been first identified with all due precision by Carl Menger.[36] They are threefold. First, in order for something to become an economic good (henceforth simply: a *good*), there must be a human need (an unachieved end or an unfulfilled human desire or want). Second, there must be the human perception of a thing believed to be equipped or endowed with properties or characteristics causally connected (standing in a causal connection) with, and hence capable of bringing about, the satisfaction of this need. Third, and most important in the present context, an element of the external world so perceived must be under human *control* such that it can be employed (actively, deliberately used) to satisfy the given need (reach the end sought). Writes Mises: "A thing becomes a means when human reason plans to employ it for the attainment of some end and human action really employs it for this purpose."[37] Only if a thing is thus brought into a causal connection with a human need *and* this thing is under human control can one say that this entity is appropriated— has become a good—and hence, is someone's (private or collective) property. If, on the other hand, an element of the external world stands in a causal connection to a human need but no one can (or believes that he can) control and interfere with this element (but must leave it unchanged instead, left to its own natural devices and effects) then such an element must be considered part of the un-appropriated environment and hence is no one's property. Thus, for instance, sunshine or rainfall, atmospheric pressure or gravitational forces may have a causal effect on certain wanted or unwanted ends, but insofar as man thinks himself incapable of interfering with such elements they are mere *conditions* of acting, not the part of any action. E.g., rainwater may be causally connected to the sprouting of some edible mushrooms and this causal connection may well be known. However, if nothing is done about the rainwater, then this water is also not owned by anyone; it might be a factor contributing to production, but it is not strictly speaking a production factor. Only if there is an actual interference with the natural rainfall, if the rainwater is collected in a bucket or in a cistern, for instance, can it be considered someone's property and does it become a factor of production.

---

36. Carl Menger, *Principles of Economics* (Grove City: Libertarian Press, 1994 [1871]), p. 52.
37. Ludwig von Mises, *Human Action*, p. 92.

Before the backdrop of these considerations one can now proceed to address the question regarding the status of ground land in a hunter-gatherer society.[38] Certainly, the berries picked off a bush were property; but what about the bush, which was causally associated with the picked berries? The bush was only lifted from its original status as an environmental condition of action and a mere contributing factor to the satisfaction of human needs to the status of property and a genuine production factor once it had been appropriated: that is, once man had purposefully interfered with the natural causal process connecting bush and berries by, for instance, watering the bush or trimming its branches in order to produce a certain outcome (an increase of the berry harvest above the level otherwise, naturally attained). Further, once the bush had thus become property by grooming it or tending to it also *future* berry harvests became property, whereas previously only the berries actually harvested were someone's property; moreover, once the bush had been lifted out of its natural, un-owned state by watering it so as to increase the future berry harvest, for instance, also the ground land supporting the bush had become property.

Similarly, there is also no question that a hunted animal was property; but what about the herd, the pack or the flock of which this animal was a part? Based on our previous considerations, the herd must be regarded as unowned nature as long as man had done *nothing* that could be interpreted (and that was in his own mind) causally connected with the satisfaction of a perceived need. The herd became property only once the requirement of *interfering* with the natural chain of events in order to produce some desired result had been fulfilled. This would have been the case, for instance, as soon as man engaged in the *herding* of animals, i.e., as soon as he actively tried to control the movements of the herd. The herder then did not only own the herd, he thus became also the owner of all future offspring naturally generated by the herd.

What, however, about the ground land on which the controlled movement of the herd took place? According to our definitions, the herdsmen could not be considered the owner of the ground land, at least not automatically so, without the fulfillment of a further requirement. Because herders as conventionally defined merely followed the natural movements of the herd and their interference with nature was restricted to keeping the flock together so as

---

38. See also Hans-Hermann Hoppe, *Eigentum, Anarchie und Staat. Studien zur Theorie des Kapitalismus* (Leipzig: Manuscriptum, 2005 [1987]), chap. 4, esp. pp. 106 ff.

to gain easier access to any one of its members should the need for the supply of animal meat arise. Herdsmen did not interfere with the land itself, however. They did not interfere with the land in order to control the movements of the herd; they only interfered with the movements of the members of the herd. Land only became property once herders gave up herding and turned to animal husbandry instead, i.e., once they treated land as a (scarce) means in order to control the movement of animals by controlling land. This only occurred when land was somehow enclosed, by fencing it in or constructing some other obstacles (such as trenches), which restricted the free, natural flow of animals. Rather than being merely a contributing factor in the production of animal herds, land thus became a genuine production factor.

What these considerations demonstrate is that it is erroneous to think of land as the collectively owned property of hunter-gatherer societies. Hunters were not herdsmen and still less were they engaged in animal husbandry; and gatherers were not gardeners or agriculturalists. They did not exercise control over the nature-given fauna and flora by tending to it or grooming it. They merely picked pieces from nature for the taking. Land to them was no more than a condition of their activities, not their property.

At best, very small sections of land had been appropriated (and were thus turned into collective property) by hunters and gatherers, to be used as permanent *storage* places for surplus goods for use at future points in time and as shelters, all the while the surrounding territories continued to be treated and used as unowned conditions of their existence.

What can be said, then, to have been the decisive step toward a (temporary) solution of the Malthusian trap faced by growing hunter-gatherer societies was the establishment of property in land going above and beyond the establishment of mere storage places and sheltering facilities. Pressured by falling standards of living as a result of absolute overpopulation, members of the tribe (separately or collectively) successively appropriated more and more of the previously un-owned surrounding nature (land). And underlying and motivating this appropriation of surrounding ground land—and turning former places of storage and shelter into residential centers of agriculture and animal husbandry—was an eminent intellectual achievement. As Michael Hart has noted, "the idea of planting crops, protecting them, and eventually harvesting them is not obvious or trivial, and it requires a considerable degree of intelligence to conceive of that notion. No apes ever conceived of that idea, nor did *Australopithecus*, *Homo habilis*, *Homo erectus*, nor even archaic *Homo sapiens.*"[39] Nor did any of them conceive of the even more difficult idea of the tending, taming, and breeding of animals.

Formerly, all consumer goods had been appropriated in the most direct and quickest way possible: through foraging, i.e., by "picking" such goods wherever they happened to be or go. In contrast, with agriculture and animal husbandry consumer goods were attained in an indirect and roundabout way: by producing them through the deliberate control of ground land. This was based on the discovery that consumer goods (plants and animals) were not simply "given" to be picked, but that there were natural causes affecting their supply *and* that these natural causes could be manipulated by taking control of ground land. The new mode of production required more time in order to reach the ultimate goal of food consumption (and insofar involved a loss of leisure), but by interposing ground land as a genuine factor of production it was more productive and led to a greater total output of consumer goods (food), thus allowing for a larger population size to be sustained on the same quantity of land.[40]

More specifically with respect to plants: Seeds and fruits suitable for nutritional purposes were no longer just picked (and possibly stored), but the wild plants bearing them were actively cultivated. Besides for their taste, seeds and fruits were selected for size, durability (storability), the ease of harvesting and of seed-germination, and they were not consumed but used as inputs for the *future* output of consumer goods, leading in the relatively short time span of maybe twenty to thirty years to new, domesticated plant varieties with significantly improved yields per unit land. Among the first plants thus domesticated in the Near and Middle East were the einkorn wheat, emmer wheat, barley, rye, peas and olives. In China it was rice and millet; much later, in Mesoamerica it was corn, beans and squash; in South America potatoes and manioc; in Northeast America sunflowers and goosefoot; and in Africa sorghum, rice, yams and oil palm.[41]

The process of animal domestication proceeded along similar lines, and in this regard it was possible to draw on the experience gained by the first

---

39. Hart, *Understanding Human History*, p. 162.

40. It has been estimated that with the appropriation of land and the corresponding change from a hunter-gatherer existence to that of agriculturists-gardeners and animal husbandry, a population size ten to one hundred times larger than before could be sustained on the same amount of land.

41. Diamond, *Guns, Germs, and Steel*, pp. 100, 167.

domestication and breeding of dogs, which had taken place some 16,000 years ago, i.e., still under hunter-gatherer conditions, somewhere in Siberia.[42]

Dogs are the descendants of wolves. Wolves are excellent hunters. However, they are also scavengers, and it has been plausibly argued that as such wolves regularly hung around human campsites for scraps. As scavengers, those wolves who were least afraid of humans and who displayed the friendliest behavior toward them obviously enjoyed an evolutionary advantage. It was likely from these semi-tame, camp-following wolves that cubs were adopted into tribal households as pets and where it was then discovered that these could be trained for various purposes. They could be used in the hunt of other animals, they could be used to pull, they made for good bed-warmers during cold nights, and they even provided a source of meat in cases of emergency. Most importantly, however, it was discovered that some of the dogs could bark (wolves rarely bark) and be selected and bred for their ability to bark and as such perform the invaluable task of warning and guarding their owners of strangers and intruders. It was this service above all, that appears to be the reason why, once the dog had been "invented," this invention spread like wildfire from Siberia all across the world. Everyone everywhere wanted to possess some offspring of this new, remarkable kind of animal, because in an era of constant inter-tribal warfare, the ownership of dogs proved to be a great advantage.[43]

Once the dog had arrived in the region of the Near East, which was to become the first center of human civilization, it must have added considerable momentum to the human "experiment" of productive living and its success. For while a dog used for sentry duty was an asset for mobile hunter-gatherers, it was an even greater asset for stationary settlers. The reason for this is straightforward: because in sedentary societies there were simply *more* things to be protected. In hunter-gatherer societies one had to fear for one's life, be it from external or internal aggression. However, because no member of society owned much of anything, there was little or no reason to steal. Matters were different, though, in a society of settlers. From its very inception, sedentary

---

42. Wade, *Before the Dawn*, pp. 109–13.

43. Incidentally, genetic analyses have revealed that all present dogs, including those in the Americas, stem most likely from a single litter to be located somewhere in East Asia. That is, it appears that the domestication of the dog did not occur independently at various places but at a single place from where it spread outward to ultimately encompass the entire globe.

life was marked by the emergence of significant differences in the property and wealth owned by different members of society; hence, insofar as envy existed in any way, shape or form (as can be safely assumed)[44] each member (each separate household) also faced the threat of theft or destruction of his property by others, including especially also members of his own tribe. Dogs provided invaluable help in dealing with this problem, especially because dogs, as a matter of biological fact, attach themselves to *individual* "masters," rather than to people in general or, like cats, for instance, to particular places.[45] As such, they themselves represented a prime example of something owned *privately*, rather than collectively. That is, they offered a "natural refutation" of whatever taboo might have existed in a primitive society against the private ownership of property. Moreover and more importantly, because dogs were unquestionably the property of particular individuals they proved also uniquely serviceable in guarding the private property of their natural owners from every kind of "foreign" invader.[46]

Animals, even more so than plants, were valuable for humans for a variety of reasons: as sources of meat, milk, skin, fur and wool and also as potential means of transportation, pull and traction, for instance. However, as a matter of biological fact, most animals turn out to be un-domesticable.[47] The first and foremost selection criterion, then, in the "production" of animals as livestock or pets was an animal species' perceived degree of tamability or controllability. To test one's hypothesis, in a first step it was checked whether or not an animal was suitable to herding. If so, it was then tried if a herd of wild animals could also be penned. If so, one would subsequently select the tamer animals as parents of the next generation—but not all animals breed in captivity!—and so on and on. Finally, one would select among the tamed animal variety for other desirable properties such as size, strength, etc., thus breeding eventually a new, domesticated animal species. Among the first large mammalian animals thus domesticated in the Near and Middle East (around 10,000 years ago) were sheep, goats and pigs (from wild boars), then cattle (from wild aurochs). Cattle were also domesticated, apparently

---

44. See Helmut Schoeck, *Envy: A Theory of Social Behavior* (New York: Harcourt, Brace and World, 1970).

45. See Konrad Lorenz, *Man Meets Dog* (New York: Routledge, 2002 [1954]).

46. Remarkably, even today, with the availability of highly sophisticated electronic alarm systems, it remains barking dogs, which offer the most effective protection against burglary.

47. See Diamond, *Guns, Germs, and Steel*, chap. 9, esp. pp. 168–75.

independently, in India at about the same time (about 8,000 years ago). Roughly at about the same time as in the Near and Middle East, sheep, goats and pigs were domesticated independently also in China, and China was also to contribute the domesticated water buffalo (about 6,000 years ago). Central Asia and Arabia contributed the domesticated Bactrian and Arabian camel respectively (around 4,500 years ago). And the Americas, or more precisely the Andes region of South America, were to contribute the guinea pig (about 7,000 years ago), the llama and alpaca (about 5,500 years ago). Finally, an "invention" of particularly momentous consequences was the domestication of the horse, which occurred about 6,000 years ago in the region of today's Russia and Ukraine. This achievement initiated a genuine revolution in land transportation. Up until then, on land man had to walk from place to place, and the fastest way to cover distances was by boat. This changed dramatically with the arrival of the domesticated horse, which from then on until the 19th century with the invention of the locomotive and the motorcar, was to provide the fastest means of over-land transportation. Accordingly, not quite unlike the "invention" of the dog some 16,000 years ago, the "invention" of the horse was to spread like wildfire. However, coming some 10,000 years later, the latter invention could no longer diffuse as widely as the former. While the dog had reached practically all corners of the world, the climactic changes—the global warming—that had taken place in the meantime made it impossible for the same success to be repeated in the case of the horse. In the meantime, the Eurasian land mass was separated from the Americas and from Indonesia, New Guinea and Australia by bodies of water too wide to be bridged. Thus, it was only thousands of years later, after the European rediscovery of the Americas, for instance, that the horse was finally introduced there. (Wild horses had apparently existed on the American continent, but they had been hunted to extinction there so as to make any independent domestication impossible.)

The appropriation of land as property and basis of agriculture and animal husbandry was only half of the solution to the problem posed by an increasing population pressure, however. Through the appropriation of land a more effective use was made of land, allowing for a larger population size to be sustained. But the institution of land ownership in and of itself did not affect the other side of the problem: the continued proliferation of new and more offspring. This aspect of the problem required some solution as well. A social institution had to be invented that brought this proliferation under control. The institution designed to accomplish this task is the institution of the family, which developed not coincidentally hand in hand with that of land ownership. Indeed, as Thomas Malthus pointed out, in order to solve the problem of overpopulation, along with the institution of private property "the commerce between the sexes" had to undergo some fundamental change as well.[48]

What was the commerce between the sexes before and what was the institutional innovation brought about in this regard by the family? A precise answer to the first question is notoriously difficult, but it is possible to identify the principal structural change. In terms of economic theory, the change can be described as one from a situation where both the benefits of creating offspring—by creating an additional potential *producer*—and especially the costs of creating offspring—by creating an additional *consumer* (eater)—were socialized, i.e., reaped and paid for by society at large rather than the "producers" of this offspring, to a situation where both benefits as well as costs involved in procreation were internalized by and economically imputed back to those individuals causally responsible for producing them.

Whatever the details may have been, it appears that the institution of a stable monogamous and also of a polygamous relationship between men and women that is nowadays associated with the term family is fairly new in the history of mankind and was preceded for a long time by an institution that may be broadly defined as "unrestricted" or "unregulated" sexual intercourse or as "group marriage."[49] The commerce between the sexes during this stage of human history did not rule out the existence of temporary pair relationships between one man and one woman. However, in principle every woman was considered a potential sexual partner of every man, and vice versa. "Männer (lebten) in Vielweiberei und ihre Weiber gleichzeitig in Vielmännerei," noted Friedrich Engels, following in the footsteps of Lewis H. Morgan's researches in *Ancient Society* (1871), "und die gemeinsamen Kinder (galten) daher auch als ihnen allen gemeinsam (gehörig) ... jede Frau (gehörte) jedem Mann und jeder Mann jeder Frau gleichmässig."[50]

---

48. *Essay on the Principle of Population*, chap. 10.

49. See on this Friedrich Engels, *Der Ursprung der Familie, des Privateigentums und des Staates*, in Karl Marx and Friedrich Engels, *Werke*, Vol. 21 (Berlin: Dietz Verlag, 1972 [1884]).

50. *Id.*, p. 38 f. "Men lived in polygamy and their women simultaneously in polyandry,

What Engels and countless later socialists failed to notice in their glori-fying description of the past—and supposedly again future—institution of "free love," however, is the plain fact that this institution has a direct and clear effect on the production of offspring. As Ludwig von Mises has commented: "it is certain that even if a socialist community may bring 'free love,' it can in no way bring free birth."[51] What Mises implied with this remark, and what socialists such as Engels and Bebel apparently ignored, is that, certainly in the age before the availability of effective means of contraception, free love has consequences, namely pregnancies and births, and that births involve benefits as well as costs. This does not matter as long as the benefits exceed the costs, i.e., as long as an additional member of society adds more to it as a producer of goods than it takes from it as a consumer—and this may well be the case for some time. But it follows from the law of returns that this situation cannot last forever, without limits. Inevitably, the point must arrive when the costs of additional offspring will exceed its benefits. Then, any further procreation must be stopped—moral restraint must be exercised—unless one wants to experience a progressive fall in average living standards. However, if children are considered everyone's or no one's children, because everyone entertains sexual relations with everyone else, then the incentive

---

and their children were considered as belonging to all of them.... Each woman belonged to every man and each man to every woman."

Incidentally, socialist authors such as Friedrich Engels did not merely describe but glorified this institution, very much like they glorified the already mentioned institution of "primitive communism." Indeed, socialists typically recognized, quite correctly, the joint emergence of private property and the institution of the family, and they thought (and hoped) that both institutions—private property in the means of production, including land, and the (monogamous) family—would ultimately disappear again with the establishment of a future socialist society characterized by plenty (plentitude) of wealth and free love. Thus, after an arduous if necessary historical detour characterized by misery, exploitation and male sexual domination, mankind would at long last return—on a higher level—to the very institutions characteristic of its own prehistoric "golden age." Under socialism, monogamous marriage was to disappear along with private property. Choice in love would become free again. Men and women would unite and separate as they pleased. And in all of this, as socialist August Bebel wrote in his, at the time (in the 1880s and 1890s), enormously popular book *Die Frau und der Sozialismus*, socialism would not create anything really new, but only "recreate on a higher level of culture and under new social forms what was universally valid on a more primitive cultural level and before private ownership dominated society." Bebel, *Die Frau und der Sozialismus* (Stuttgart, 1879), p. 343; see also Mises, *Socialism*, p. 87.

51. Mises, *Socialism*, p. 175.

to refrain from procreation disappears or is at least significantly diminished. Instinctively, by virtue of man's biological nature, each woman and each man is driven to spread and proliferate her or his genes into the next generation of the species. The more offspring one creates the better, because the more of one's genes will survive. No doubt, this natural human instinct can be controlled by rational deliberation. But if no or little economic sacrifice must be made for simply following one's animal instincts, because all children are maintained by society at large, then no or little incentive exists to employ reason in sexual matters, i.e., to exercise any moral restraint.

From a purely economic point of view, then, the solution to the problem of overpopulation should be immediately apparent. The ownership of children or more correctly the trusteeship over children must be privatized. Rather than considering children as collectively owned by or entrusted to "society" or viewing childbirths as some uncontrolled and uncontrollable natural event and accordingly considering children as owned by or entrusted to no one (as mere favorable or unfavorable "environmental changes"), children must instead be regarded as entities which are privately produced and entrusted into private care. As Thomas Malthus first perceptively noted, this, essentially, is what is accomplished with the institution of a family:

> the most natural and obvious check (on population) seemed to be to make every man provide for his own children; that this would operate in some respect as a measure and guide in the increase of population, as it might be expected that no man would bring beings into the world, for whom he could not find the means of support; that where this notwithstanding was the case, it seemed necessary, for the example of others, that the disgrace and inconvenience attending such a conduct should fall upon the individual, who had thus inconsiderately plunged himself and innocent children in misery and want.—The institution of marriage, or at least, of some express or implied obligation on every man to support his own children, seems to be the natural result of these reasonings in a community under the difficulties that we have supposed.[52]

Moreover and finally: with the formation of monogamous or polygamous families came another decisive innovation. Earlier on, the members of a tribe formed a single, unified household, and the intra-tribal division of labor was essentially an intra-household division of labor. With the formation of

---

52. *Essay on the Principle of Population*, chap. 10.

families came the breakup of a unified household into several, independent households and with that also the formation of "several"—or private—ownership of land. That is, the previously described appropriation of land was not simply a transition from a situation where something that was earlier on un-owned became now owned, but more precisely something previously un-owned was turned into something owned by separate households (thus allowing also for the emergence of inter-household division of labor).

Consequently, then, the higher social income made possible by the ownership of land was no longer distributed, as was formerly the case, to each member of society "according to his need." Rather, each separate household's share in the total social income came to depend on the product economically imputed to it, that is, to its labor and its property invested in production. In other words: the formerly pervasive "communism" might have still continued *within* each household, but communism vanished from the relation between the members of different households. The incomes of different households differed, depending on the quantity and quality of invested labor and property, and no one had a claim on the income produced by the members of a household other than one's own. Thus, "free riding" on others' efforts became largely if not entirely impossible. He who did not work could no longer expect to still eat.[53]

---

53. Rationally motivated as the institution of the family was, the transition from a regime of "free love" to one of family life did not come without costs, and the associated benefits and costs were different for men and women.

Surely, from the male's point of view it was advantageous to have every woman accessible for sexual gratification. In addition, this greatly improved his chances of reproductive success. By having children with as many women as possible the likelihood of his genes being passed on into future generations was increased. And this was accomplished seemingly without any cost to him if the responsibility of raising children to maturity could be externalized onto society at large. In contrast, if sexual access was restricted to just one woman (in the case of monogamy) or a few women (in the case of polygamy) his chances of sexual gratification and of reproductive success were diminished. Moreover, men now had to weigh and compare the pros (benefits) and cons (costs) of sex and procreation—something they previously did not have to do. On the other hand, also primitive men could not fail to notice, at least eventually, that even under a regime of free love the chances of sexual gratification and reproductive success were by no means equal. Some males—the stronger and more attractive alpha males—had much better chances than others. In fact, as every animal breeder knows, just one male is sufficient to keep all females constantly impregnated. Thus, free love effectively meant that very few males "had" most of the women, and especially most of the attractive and reproductively most appealing women, and fathered most of the offspring, while most of the males had the dubious obligation of helping to bring up other men's children. Surely, even the dimmest recognition of this fact must have posed a permanent threat to any intra-tribal solidarity and especially to any inter-male solidarity that was called for, for instance, in the defense against rival tribes; and this threat must have grown ever more intense the farther the population exceeded its optimum size. In contrast, the institution of a monogamous family and to a somewhat lesser degree also of a polygamous family offered to each male a somewhat equal chance of reproductive success and thus created a much greater incentive for every male to engage and invest in cooperative behavior.

Matters are significantly different from the female point of view. After all, it is women who must bear the risk of pregnancy associated with sexual intercourse. It is they who are particularly vulnerable during pregnancy and following childbirth. Moreover, it is women who have a unique natural tie to children; for while there can be always some doubt as to paternity no doubt is possible as far as maternity is concerned. Every woman knows who *her* children are and who the children of *other* women are. In light of these natural facts the principal advantage of a regime of free love from a female point of view becomes apparent. Because of the greater risk and investment associated with sex for women, women tend to be more selective as far as their mating partner is concerned. Thus, in order to increase the likelihood of their own reproductive success, they exhibit a strong preference for mating partners who appear healthy, vigorous, attractive, bright, etc., i.e., in a word, for alpha males. And because males are less choosy in their selection of sex objects, under a system of free love even the least attractive females can realistically expect to be able to mate occasionally with some of the most attractive males and hence possibly pass their "superior" genes on to one's own offspring.

Obviously, this advantage disappears as soon as the institution of the family replaces a regime of free love. Each woman is now supposed to try her reproductive luck with just one or maybe a few sets of male genes, and in the great majority of cases these genes do not rank among the very best. What did women get out of marriage, then? Very little, it would seem, as long as the population was at or around its optimum size and the life of the hunter-gatherer tribe was characterized by comfort and plenty. This had to change, however, as soon as the population grew beyond this point. The more the population exceeded its optimum size the more intense grew the competition for the limited food supplies. Whatever inter-female solidarity existed before increasingly weakened now. Naturally, each woman was interested in assuring her own reproductive success and helping her own children reach maturity and thus came into conflict with every other woman and her children. Even killing another woman's child in order to further the prospect of survival for one's own children was increasingly considered an option in this situation. (Incidentally, the same sort of inter-female competition for reproductive success still prevails to some extent within the framework of polygamous relationships and explains some of the peculiar instabilities and tensions inherent in such relationships.) In this situation, each woman (and her kids) is in increasing need for personal protection. But who would be willing to provide such protection? Most children have the same father—from among the few alpha males endowed with more-than-equal chances of procreation—but they have different mothers. Accordingly, the protection of one woman and her children from another cannot be expected to come from the children's father, because the father is very often the same

Thus, in response to mounting population pressure a new mode of societal organization had come into existence, displacing the hunter-gatherer lifestyle that had been characteristic of most of human history. As Ludwig von Mises summarized the matter:

> Private ownership in the means of production is the regulating principle which, within society, balances the limited means of subsistence at society's disposal with the less limited ability of consumers to increase.

---

one. Nor can it be expected to come from another male; for why should a male offer personal support and protection to a woman who entertained sexual relations with other men and whose children were fathered by other men, especially if this offspring threatened his own standard of living? A woman could only secure personal protection from a man if she forewent all of the advantages of free love and promised instead to grant her sexual favors exclusively to him and thus managed to assure him also that her children were always his as well.

Distinctly male and female perspectives exist not only as far as the very establishment of the institution of the family is concerned but also regarding the importance of marital fidelity in maintaining its stability. The difference between male and female calculations in this regard has its reason in the natural fact that, at least until the very recent development of reliable genetic paternity tests, a child's mother was always known in a way—with a degree of certainty—that was unavailable and unattainable for the child's father. As folk-wisdom has it: mother's baby, father's maybe. This fact, again quite "naturally," had to lead to significantly different—asymmetric—expectations regarding appropriate (and inappropriate) male and female marital conduct. Of course, in order to assure the stability of the institution of the family any form of marital infidelity had to be socially disapproved; but disapproval had to be far more pronounced and the possible sanctions far more severe in the case of female infidelity than in the case of male infidelity. While this may appear "unfair," it was in fact quite rational and in accordance with the "nature of things," because female infidelity involved a far greater risk for betrayed husbands than male infidelity involved for betrayed wives. A wife's infidelity can be the first step leading to a divorce from her husband just as a husband's infidelity can be the first step leading to a divorce from his wife. In this regard, the situation is the same (symmetric) in both cases and the "sin" committed is equally grave. However, if and insofar as marital infidelity does *not* lead to divorce, the "sin" committed by a woman must be considered far graver than that committed by a man. Because extramarital sexual affairs may lead to pregnancies, and if a so-impregnated woman then stays with her husband, the real danger arises that she might be tempted to present her illegitimate offspring to her husband as his own, thus deceiving him to support another man's child. No such danger exists in the opposite case: no man can submit his illegitimate offspring to his wife without her knowing the truth of the matter. Hence, the far greater social stigma attached to female as compared to male infidelity. (Incidentally—and also quite rationally—in the case of male infidelity a similar distinction is made: the offence is considered more severe if a man has an affair with a married woman than with an unmarried one; for in the former case he becomes a potential accomplice to a further female act of deception whereas in the latter case he does not. Accordingly, in recognition of this distinction and so as to accommodate the rather indiscriminate male sex-drive, prostitution has become a near-universal social institution.)

By making the share in the social product which falls to each member of society depend on the product economically imputed to him, that is, to his labour and his property, the elimination of surplus human beings by the struggle for existence, as it rages in the vegetable and animal kingdom, is replaced by a reduction in the birth-rate as a result of social forces. 'Moral restraint,' the limitations of offspring imposed by social positions, replaces the struggle for existence.[54]

Having first established some permanent storage and sheltering places, then, step by step, having appropriated more and more surrounding land as the basis for agricultural production and the raising of livestock and transforming erstwhile centers of storage and shelter into extended settlements composed of houses and villages occupied by separate family households, the new lifestyle of the people of the Near and Middle East as well as the other regions of original human settlement began to spread outward, slowly but inescapably.[55] In principle, two modes are conceivable by which this diffusion could have taken place. Either the original settlers gradually displaced the neighboring nomadic tribes in search of new to-be-cultivated land (demic diffusion), or else the latter imitated and adopted the new lifestyle on their own initiative (cultural diffusion). Until recently, it had been generally believed that the first mode of diffusion was the predominant one.[56] However, based on newly discovered genetic evidence this view now appears to be questionable, at least insofar as the spread of the new, sedentary lifestyle from the Near East to Europe is concerned. If present Europeans were the descendants of Near Eastern people at the time of the Neolithic revolution, genetic traces for this should exist. In fact, however, very few such traces can be found among present-day Europeans. Thus, it appears more likely that the spread of the new sedentary lifestyle occurred largely, if not exclusively, via the latter, second-mentioned route, while the role in this process played by the original Near Eastern settlers was only a minor one. Perhaps a few such settlers pushed in northern and western direction, where they were then absorbed by neighboring people adopting their new and successful lifestyle, with the effect that their own genetic imprint became more and more diluted with increasing distance from their Near Eastern point of origin.

---

54. Mises, *Socialism*, p. 282.

55. Based on archeological records, the speed of this diffusion process has been estimated at about one kilometer per year on land (and somewhat higher along coastlines and river valleys). See Cavalli-Sforza, *Genes, Peoples, and Languages*, p. 102.

56. See for instance Cavalli-Sforza, *Genes, Peoples, and Languages*, pp. 101–13; Cavalli-Sforza and Cavalli-Sforza, *The Great Human Diasporas*, chap. 6, esp. pp. 144 ff.

In any case, with the Neolithic Revolution the formerly universal hunter-gatherer lifestyle essentially died out or was relegated to the outer fringes of human habitation. Without doubt, the newly developing farming communities were attractive targets for nomadic raiders, and owing to their greater mobility neighboring nomadic tribes for a long time posed a serious threat to agricultural settlers. But ultimately, nomads were no match for them, because of their greater numbers. More specifically, it was the organization of larger numbers of people in communities of households— the location of separate households in close physical proximity to each other—that made for military superiority. Community life did not merely lower the transaction costs as far as intra-tribal exchange was concerned. Community life also offered the advantage of easily and quickly coordinated joint defense in the case of external aggression. Moreover, besides the strength of greater numbers, settled agricultural communities allowed also for an intensified and expanded division of labor and for greater savings and thus facilitated the development of a weaponry superior to anything available to bands of nomads.[57]

Fifty thousand years ago the human population size has been estimated to have been as low as 5,000 or possibly 50,000 people. At the beginning of the Neolithic revolution, some 11,000 years ago, when essentially the entire globe had been conquered by tribes of hunters and gatherers having spread out in the course of thousands of years from their original homeland somewhere in East Africa, the world population size has been estimated to have reached about 4 million.[58] Since then, slowly but steadily, the new mode of production: of agriculture and animal husbandry based on private (or collective) ownership of land and organized around separate family households, successively displaced the original hunter-gatherer order.

---

57. More than 10,000 years ago already some early-neolithic settlements, such as Catal Höyük in present-day Turkey, for instance, reached an estimated size of 4,000–5,000 inhabitants. Findings made at such sites include sanctuaries à la Stonehenge (alas, more than 6,000 years older!), spacious houses built of stone and with elaborate wall paintings, megalith columns with animal reliefs, sculptures, carvings with writing-like symbols, ornaments, stone-vessels with elaborate decorations, stone-daggers, mirrors made from obsidian (a volcanic stone), bone needles, arrow heads, mill-stones, jugs and vases made of stone and clay, rings and chains made from colorful stones, even the beginning of metal works.

58. See Colin McEvedy and Richard Jones, *Atlas of World Population History* (Harmondsworth: Penguin Books, 1978).

Consequently, at the beginning of the Christian era, the world population had increased to 170 million, and in 1800, which marks the onset of the so-called Industrial Revolution (the topic of the following chapter) and the close of the agrarian age or as it has also been termed the "old biological order," it had reached 720 million. (Today's world population exceeds 7 billion!) During this agrarian age, the size of cities occasionally reached or even surpassed one million inhabitants, but until the very end less than 2 percent of the population lived in big cities and even in the economically most advanced countries 80–90 percent of the population was occupied in agricultural production (while this number has fallen to less than 5 percent today).

4

From the Malthusian Trap to the Industrial Revolution: An Explanation of Social Evolution

I. Economic Theory

For economic theory the question of how to increase wealth and get rich has a straightforward answer.

It has three components: you get richer (a) through capital accumulation, i.e., the construction of intermediate "producer" or "capital" goods that can produce more consumer goods per unit of time than can be produced without them or goods that cannot be produced at all with just land and labor (and capital accumulation in turn has something to do with (low) time preference); (b) through participation and integration in the division of labor; and (c) through population control, i.e., by maintaining the optimal population size.

Robinson Crusoe, alone on his island, has originally only his own "labor" and "land" (nature) at his disposal. He is as rich (or poor) as nature happens to make him. Some of his most urgently felt needs he may be able to satisfy directly, equipped only with his bare hands. At the very least, he can always satisfy his desire of leisure in this way: immediately. However, the satisfaction of most of his wants requires more than bare nature and hands, i.e., some indirect or roundabout—and time-consuming—production method. Most, indeed almost all goods and associated sorts of satisfaction require the help of some only indirectly useful tools: of producer or capital goods. With the help of producer goods it becomes possible to produce more per unit of time of the very goods that can be produced also with bare hands (such as leisure) or to produce goods that cannot be produced at all with just land and labor. In order to catch more fish than with his bare hands Crusoe builds

---

• Previously unpublished.

63

a net; or in order to build a shelter that he cannot build with his bare hands at all, he must construct an axe.

However, to build a net or an axe requires a sacrifice (saving). To be sure, production with the help of producer goods is expected to be more productive than without it; Crusoe would not spend any time building a net if he did not expect that he could catch more fish per unit time with the net than without it. Nonetheless, the production of a producer good involves a sacrifice; for it takes time to build a producer good and the same time cannot be used for the enjoyment or consumption of leisure or other immediately available consumer goods. In deciding whether or not to build the productivity enhancing net, Crusoe must compare and rank two expected states of satisfaction: the satisfaction which he can attain now, without any further waiting, and the satisfaction that he can attain only later, after a longer waiting time. In deciding to build the net, Crusoe has determined that he ranks the sacrifice: the value forgone of greater consumption now, in the present, below the reward: the value of greater consumption later, in the future. Otherwise, if he had ranked these magnitudes differently, he would have abstained from building the net.

This weighing and the possible exchange of present against future goods and associated satisfactions are governed by time preference. Present goods are invariably more valuable than future ones, and we exchange the former against the latter only at a premium. The degree, however, to which present goods are preferred to future ones, or the willingness to forego some possible present consumption for a greater future consumption, i.e., the willingness to save, is different from person to person and one point in time to another. Depending on the height of his personal time preference Crusoe will save and invest more or less and his standard of living will be higher or lower. The lower his time preference, i.e., the easier it is for Crusoe to delay current gratification in exchange for some anticipated greater satisfaction in the future, the more capital goods Crusoe will accumulate and the higher will be his standard of living.

Second, people can increase their wealth through participation in the division of labor. We assume that Crusoe is joined by Friday. Because of their natural, physical or mental differences or the differences of the "land" (nature) they face, almost automatically absolute and comparative advantages in the production of various goods emerge. Crusoe is better equipped to produce one good and Friday another. If they specialize in what each is particularly good at producing, the total output of goods will be larger than if they had not specialized and remained in a position of an isolated and self-sufficient producer. Alternatively, if either Crusoe or Friday is the superior producer of every good, the all-around superior producer is to specialize in those activities in which his advantage is especially great and the all-around inferior producer must specialize in those activities in which his disadvantage is comparatively smaller. Thereby, too, the overall output of goods produced will be greater than if each had remained in self-sufficient isolation.

Third, the wealth in society depends on the population size, i.e., on whether or not the population is kept at its optimum size. That wealth depends on the population size follows from the "law of returns" and the "Malthusian law of population," which Ludwig von Mises has hailed as

> one of the great achievements of thought. Together with the principle of the division of labor it provided the foundations of modern biology and for the theory of evolution; the importance of these two fundamental theorems for the sciences of human action is second only to the discovery of the regularity in the intertwinement and sequence of market phenomena and their inevitable determination by the market data. The objections raised against the Malthusian law as well as against the law of returns are vain and trivial. Both laws are indisputable.[1]

In its most general and abstract form, the law of returns states that for any combination of two or more production factors there exists an optimum combination (such that any deviation from it involves material waste, or "efficiency losses"). Applied to the two original factors of production, labor and land (nature-given goods), the law implies that if one were to continuously increase the quantity of labor (population) while the quantity of land (and the available technology) remained fixed and unchanged, eventually a point will be reached where the physical output per labor-unit input is maximized. This point marks the optimal population size. If the population were to grow beyond this size, income per head would fall; and likewise, income per head would be less if the population were to fall below this point (as the division of labor would shrink, with an accompanying efficiency loss). To maintain the optimal level of income per person, then, the population

---

1. Ludwig von Mises, *Human Action: A Treatise on Economics* (Chicago: Regnery, 1966), p. 667.

must no longer grow but remain stationary. Only one way exists for such a stationary society to further increase real income per head or to grow in size without a loss in per capita income: through technological innovation, i.e., by the employment of better, more efficient tools made possible through savings brought about by the abstention from leisure or other immediate consumption. If there is no technological innovation (technology is fixed), the only possible way for the population to grow in size without a concomitant fall in per capita income is through taking more (and possibly better) land into use. If there is no additional land available and technology is fixed at a "given" level, however, then any population increase beyond the optimal size must lead to a progressive decline in per capita income.

This latter situation has been referred to also as the "Malthusian trap." Ludwig von Mises has characterized it thus:

> The purposive adjustment of the birthrate to the supply of the material potentialities of well-being is an indispensable condition of human life and action, of civilization, and of any improvement in wealth and welfare.... Where the average standard of living is impaired by the excessive increase in population figures, irreconcilable conflicts of interest arise. Each individual is again a rival of all other individuals in the struggle for survival. The annihilation of rivals is the only means to increase one's well-being.... As natural conditions are, man has only the choice between the pitiless war of each against each or social cooperation. But social cooperation is impossible if people give rein to the natural impulses of proliferation.[2]

It has been already described and explained (in the previous chapter) how all this worked out in hunter-gatherer societies. It is conceivable that mankind had never left the seemingly comfortable hunter-gatherer lifestyle. This would have been possible, if only mankind had been able to restrict all population growth beyond the optimal size of a hunter-gatherer band (of a few dozen members). In that case, we might still live today very much like all of our direct forebears had lived for tens of thousands of years, until some 11,000 or 12,000 years ago. As a matter of fact, however, mankind did not manage to do so. The population did grow, and accordingly increasingly larger territories had to be taken into possession until one ran out of additional land. Moreover, technological advances made within the framework of hunter-gatherer societies (such as the invention of bow and

---

2. Mises, *Human Action*, p. 672.

arrow some 20,000 years ago, for instance) increased (rather than decreased) the speed of this expansionism. Because hunters and gatherers (like all nonhuman animals) only depleted (consumed) the supply of nature-given goods, but did not produce and thus add to this supply, better tools in their hands fastened (rather then delayed) the process of territorial expansion.

The Neolithic Revolution, which began about 11,000 years ago, brought some temporary relief. The invention of agriculture and animal husbandry allowed for a larger number of people to survive on the same, unchanged quantity of land, and the institution of the family, in privatizing (internalizing) the benefits as well as the costs of the production of offspring, provided a new, hitherto unknown check on the growth of population. But neither innovation brought a permanent solution to the problem of excess population. Men still could not keep their pants up, and the greater productivity brought about by the new, non-parasitic mode of production represented by agriculture and animal husbandry was quickly exhausted again by a growing population size. A significantly larger number of people could be sustained on the globe than before, but mankind did not yet escape from the Malthusian trap—until some 200 years ago with the beginning of the so-called Industrial Revolution.

II. Economic History: The Problem

The problem to be explained in the following has been captured by two charts depicting world population growth on the one hand and the development of per capita income (average living standards) on the other.

Figure 1, adapted from Colin McEvedy and Richard Jones,[3] shows human population growth from 400 BC until the present (AD 2012). The population size was about 4 million at the beginning of the Neolithic Revolution. But up until about 7,000 years ago (5000 BC) the area under crops (first merely in the region of the Fertile Crescent and then also in northern China) was too small to have much of an effect on the global population size. By then the population had grown to about 5 million. But since then, population growth increased rapidly: 2,000 years later (3000 BC) it had almost tripled to 14 million, 3,000 years ago (1000 BC) it had reached 50 million,[4] and only some 500 years later, when the chart sets in, the world

---

3. Colin McEvedy and Richard Jones, *Atlas of World Population History* (Harmondsworth: Penguin Books, 1978), p. 342.

4. *Id.*, p. 344.

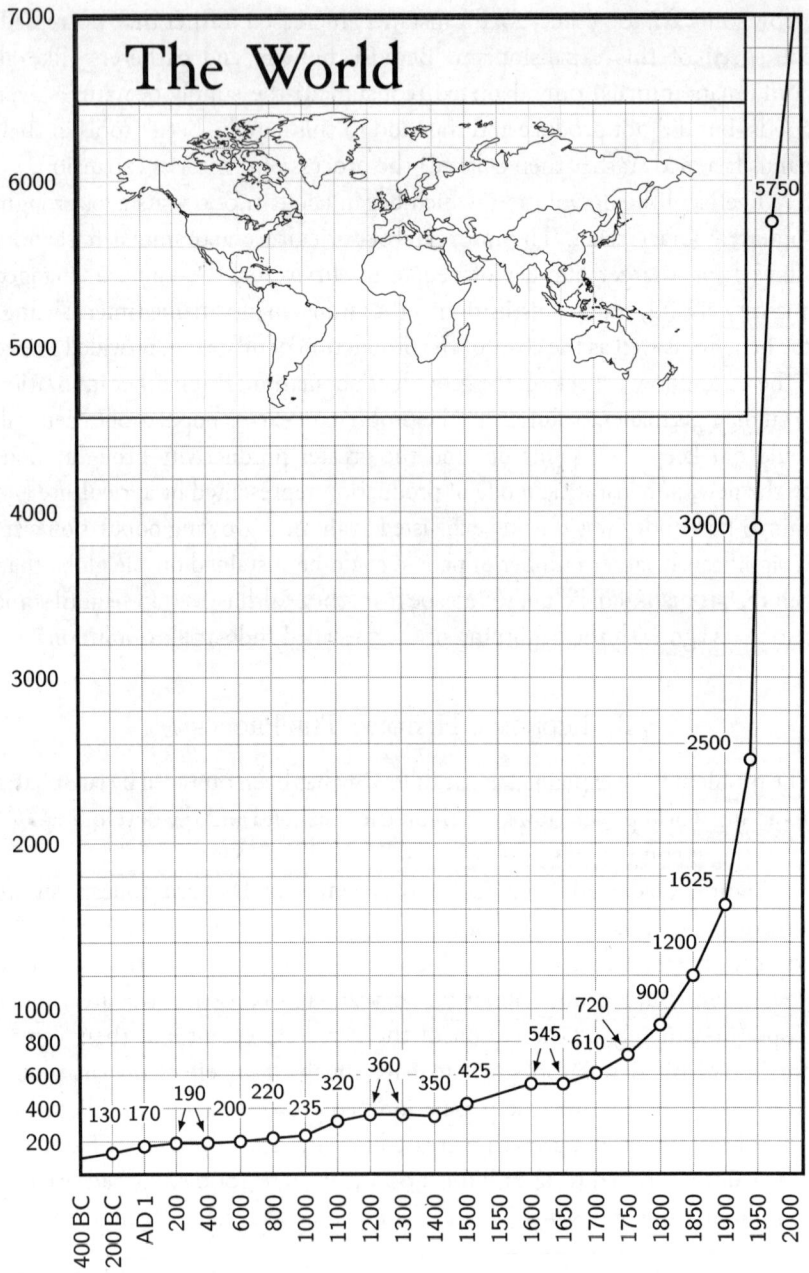

Figure 1: Total world population (millions)

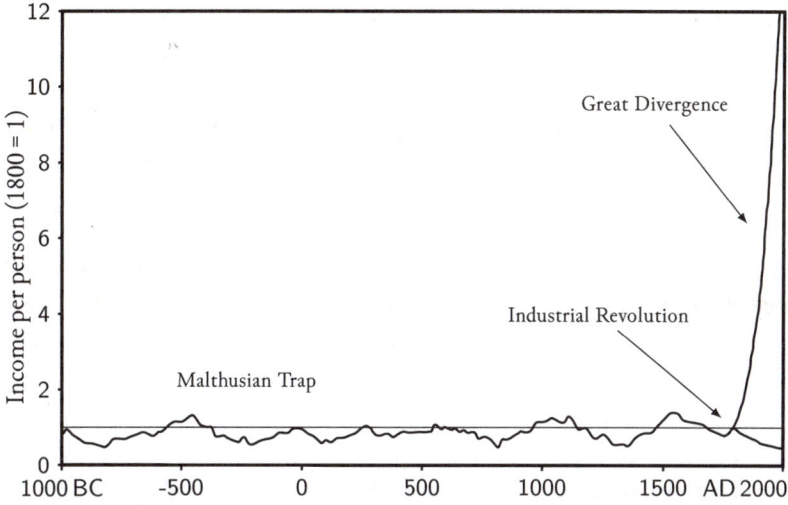

Figure 2: World economic history in one picture. Incomes rose sharply in many countries after 1800 but declined in others.

population size stood at about 100 million. Since then, as the chart indicates, the population size has continued to increase slowly but more or less steadily up until about 1800 (to about 720 million), when a significant break occurred and the population growth sharply increased to presently, only some two hundred years later reach 7 billion.

Figure 2, taken from Gregory Clark,[5] shows the development of per capita income from the beginning of recorded human history to the present. It, too, shows a significant break occurring at around 1800. Until that time, i.e., for most of recorded human history, real income per capita (in terms of food, housing, clothing, heating and lighting) did not rise. That is, average living standards in 18th century England were not significantly higher than those in ancient Babylon, where the oldest records of wage rates and various consumer goods prices could be found. Naturally, with sedentary life and private landownership distinct differences in wealth and income came into existence. There existed large landowners (lords) who lived in enormous luxury, even by today's standards, almost from the beginnings of settled life. Nor were average living standards always and everywhere equally

---

5. Gregory Clark, *Farewell to Alms: A Brief Economic History of the World* (Princeton, N.J.: Princeton University Press, 2007), p. 2.

low. There existed pronounced regional differences between, for instance, English, Indian, and West African real incomes in 1800. And of course, as far as cross-time comparisons are concerned, many technologies existed in 1800 England, which were unknown in ancient Rome, Greece, China, or Babylon. Yet in any case, everywhere and at all times the overwhelming majority of the population, the mass of small landowners and most laborers, lived near or only a little bit above subsistence level. There were ups and downs in real incomes, due to various external events, but nowhere was there a continuous upward trend in real income per person discernable until about 1800.

In combination, both charts capture the world-historic significance of the so-called Industrial Revolution, which occurred some 200 years ago, as well as the significance—and in particular the length—of the previous, Malthusian, stage of human development. Until sometime around 1800, little difference in the economies of humans and nonhuman animals existed. For animals (and plants) it is always and invariably true that an increase in their number will encroach upon the available means of subsistence and eventually lead to overpopulation, to "supernumerary specimens," as Mises has called them, which must be "weeded out" due to a lack of sustenance. Today, we know that as far as humans are concerned, this *must* not be so: no supernumerary specimens who are thus weeded out exist in modern, western societies. But for most of human life this was indeed the case.

To be sure, the population size could grow, mostly because more land was taken into possession for agricultural use, and partly because of better technology incorporated in producer goods and an extended and intensified division of labor. But all such economic "gains" were always eaten up quickly by a growing population that again encroached upon the available means of subsistence and led to overpopulation and the emergence of "supernumerary specimens" for whom there was no space in the division of labor and who consequently had to die out silently or become a menace (an economic "bad") in the form of beggars, vagrants, plunderers, bandits or warriors. Throughout most of human history, then, the iron law of wages held sway. Income and wages were held down near subsistence level owing to the existence of a substantial class of supernumerary specimens.

III. History Explained

Why did it take so long to get out of the Malthusian trap; and what happened that we finally succeeded? Why did it take so long until we gave up a hunter-gatherer existence in favor of an existence as agricultural settlers? And why, even after the invention of agriculture and animal husbandry, did it take more than another 10,000 years until mankind's seemingly final escape from the Malthusian trap? Economic theory, or what I have said about it, does not and can not answer these questions.

The standard answer among economists, in particular also among libertarian economists, is: there must have been institutional impediments, in particular an insufficient protection of private property rights, that prevented a quicker development and these impediments were removed only recently (about 1800). This, essentially, is also Ludwig von Mises's explanation.[6] Likewise, Murray N. Rothbard has advanced similar ideas.[7] I want to argue that this explanation is mistaken or at least insufficient and present the outline of an alternative (hypothetical) explanation.

For one, hunters and gatherers, from all we know, had plenty of free time on their hands to invent agriculture and animal husbandry. Again and again and at countless places, they suffered from excess population and consequently falling incomes; and yet, although the opportunity cost of foregone leisure must have been low, no one anywhere, for tens of thousands of years, thought of agriculture and animal husbandry as an (at least temporary) escape from Malthusian conditions. Instead, until about 11,000 years ago hunter-gatherer tribes answered the recurring challenge of overpopulation always either by migration, i.e., by taking additional land into use (until they finally ran out of land) or by fighting each other to the death until the population size was sufficiently reduced to prevent real incomes from falling.

Also, property rights in settled societies were well protected at many places and times. The idea of private property and the successful protection thereof are not inventions and institutions of the recent past, but have been known for a long time and practiced almost from the beginnings of settled life. From all we know, for instance, property rights in 1200 England and in much of feudal Europe were better protected than they are in contemporary England and Europe. That is, every institutional incentive favorable to capital accumulation and division of labor was in place—and yet nowhere, until about 1800, did mankind succeed in extricating itself from the Malthusian trap of excess population and stagnating per capita incomes. Thus the institution of property-protection can and should be regarded only as a necessary, but not a sufficient, condition of economic growth (rising per capita incomes).

---

6. Mises, *Human Action*, pp. 617–23.

7. Rothbard, "Left and Right," in idem, *Egalitarianism as a Revolt Against Nature and Other Essays*, (Auburn, Ala.: Ludwig von Mises Institute, 2000).

There must be something else—some other factor, not appearing in economic theory—which will have to explain all this.

Part of the answer is obvious: mankind did not get out of the Malthusian trap because, as noted before, men could not keep their pants up. If they had done so, there would have been no excess population. This can be only part of the answer, however. Because population control can prevent that real incomes will fall, but it cannot make incomes rise.[8] Some other, "empirical" factor not figuring in pure (aprioristic) economic theory must explain the length of the Malthusian age and how we finally got out of it. This missing factor is the historical *variable* of human intelligence, and the simple answer to the above questions, then, (to be elaborated in the following) is: because for most of history mankind was simply not intelligent enough—and it takes time to breed intelligence.[9]

Until some 11,000 or so years ago, mankind was not intelligent enough, such that not even its brightest members were capable of conceiving the idea of indirect or roundabout consumer goods' production that underlies agriculture and animal husbandry. The idea of first planting crops, then tending and protecting and finally harvesting them is not obvious or trivial. Nor is the idea of taming, husbanding and breeding animals obvious or trivial. It requires a considerable degree of intelligence to conceive of such notions. It took tens of thousands of years of natural selection under hunter-gatherer conditions to finally breed enough intelligence to make such cognitive achievements possible.

Similarly, it took several thousand years more of natural selection under agricultural conditions, then, to reach a threshold in the development of human intelligence (or more precisely: of low time preference correlated with

---

8. When Tahiti was rediscovered by Europeans in 1767, some 1,000 or possibly 2,000 years after it had been first settled by Austronesian farmers, its population was estimated at 50,000 (today: 180,000). According to all accounts, the Tahitians lived paradisiacal lives. Real income per capita was high, not least because of highly favorable climatic conditions in the Polynesian islands. Tahitian men could not keep their pants up either, but in order to maintain their high standard of living, the Tahitians practiced a most rigorous and ruthless form of population control, involving infanticide and deadly warfare. The place was paradise, but a paradise only for the living. Yet all the while Tahitians were still living in the stone-age. Their tool kit had remained essentially unchanged since their first arrival on the island(s). There had been no further capital accumulation, and real income per capita, even if high due to favorable external circumstances, had remained stagnant.

9. See Michael H. Hart, *Understanding Human History: An Analysis Including the Effects of Geography and Differential Evolution* (Augusta, Ga.: Washington Summit Publishers, 2007).

high intelligence) such that productivity growth could continuously outstrip any population growth. From the beginning of the Neolithic revolution until about 1800 enough inventions (technological improvements) were made by bright people (and imitated by others of lesser intelligence) to account (in addition to more agriculturally used land) for a significant increase in world population: from about 4 million to 720 million (now: 7 billion). But during the entire era, the rate of technological progress was never sufficient to allow for population growth *combined* with increasing per capita incomes.

Today, we take it for granted that it is solely the unwillingness to consume less and to save more that imposes limits on economic growth. We have a seemingly endless supply of natural resources and recipes of how to produce more, better and different goods, and it is only our limited savings that prevent us from employing these resources and implement such recipes. Yet this phenomenon is actually quite new. For most of human history savings were held back by a lack of ideas of how to productively invest them, i.e., of how to convert plain savings (storing) into productive savings (producer goods' production). For Crusoe, for instance, it was not sufficient to have a low time preference and to save. Rather, Crusoe also had to conceive the idea of a net and must have known how to build it from scratch. Most people are not intelligent enough to invent and implement anything new but can at best only imitate, more or less perfectly, what other, brighter people have invented before them. Yet if no one is capable to do this or to imitate what others have invented before, then even the safest of property rights will make no difference. Every incentive needs a receptor to work, and if a receptor is lacking or insufficiently sensitive, different incentive structures do not matter. Hence, the institution of property-protection must be regarded as only a necessary (but not sufficient) condition of economic growth (rising per capita incomes). Likewise, it requires intelligence to recognize the higher physical productivity of the division of labor, and it requires intelligence to recognize the laws of human reproduction and thus allow for any form of deliberate population control, let alone an efficient—low-cost—control.

The mechanism through which higher human intelligence (combined with low time preference) was bred over time is straightforward. Given that man is physically weak and ill equipped to deal with brute nature, it was advantageous for him to develop his intelligence.[10] Higher intelligence translated into economic success, and economic success in turn translated into

---

10. See also Arnold Gehlen, *Man* (New York: Columbia University Press, 1988).

reproductive success (producing a larger number of surviving descendants). For the existence of both relationships massive amounts of empirical evidence are available.[11]

There can be no doubt that a hunter-gatherer existence requires intelligence: the ability to classify various external objects as good or bad, the ability to recognize a multiplicity of causes and effects, to estimate distances, time, and speed, to survey and recognize landscapes, to locate various (good or bad) things and to remember their position in relation to each other, etc.; most importantly, the ability to communicate with others by means of language and thus facilitate coordination. Not every member of a band was equally capable of such skills. Some were more intelligent than others. These differences in intellectual talents would lead to some visible status differentiation within the tribe—of "excellent" hunters, gatherers and communicators and "lousy" ones—and this status differentiation would in turn result in differences in the reproductive success of various tribe members, especially given the "loose" sexual mores prevailing among hunter-gatherers. That is, by and large "excellent" tribe members would produce a larger number of surviving offspring and thus transmit their genes more successfully into the next generation than "lousy" ones. Consequently, if and insofar as human intelligence has some genetic basis (which seems undeniable in light of the evolution of the entire species), hunter-gatherer conditions would over time produce (select for) a population of increasing average intelligence and at the same time an increasingly higher level of "exceptional" intelligence.

The competition within and between tribes, and the selection for and breeding of higher intelligence via differential rates of reproductive success, did not come to a halt once the hunter-gatherer life had been given up in favor of agriculture and animal husbandry. However, the intellectual requirements of economic success became somewhat different under sedentary conditions.

The invention of agriculture and animal husbandry was in and of itself an outstanding cognitive achievement. It required a lengthened planning horizon. It required longer provisions and deeper and farther-reaching insights into the chains of natural causes and effects. And it required more work, patience and endurance than under hunter-gatherer conditions. In addition, it was instrumental for success as a farmer that one possessed some

11. See also Hart, *Understanding Human History*; Clark, *Farewell to Alms*, chap. 6; and Richard Lynn, *Dysgenics: Genetic Deterioration in Modern Populations* (London: Ulster Institute for Social Research, 2011), chap. 2.

degree of numeracy so as to count, measure and proportion. It required intelligence to recognize the advantages of inter-household division of labor and to abandon self-sufficiency. It required some literacy to design contracts and establish contractual relations. And it required some skill of monetary calculation and of accountancy to economically succeed. Not every farmer was equally apt in these skills and had an equally low degree of time preference. To the contrary, under agricultural conditions, where each household was responsible for its own production of consumer goods and offspring and there was no longer any "free riding" as under hunter-gatherer conditions, the natural inequality of man, and the corresponding social differentiation of and between more or less successful members of a tribe became increasingly and strikingly visible (in particular through the size of one's land holdings). Consequently, the translation of economic (productive) success and status into reproductive success, i.e., the breeding of a comparatively larger number of surviving offspring by the economically successful, became even more direct and pronounced.

Further, this tendency of selecting for higher intelligence would be particularly pronounced under "harsh" external conditions. If the human environment is unchangingly constant and "mild"—as in the seasonless tropics, where one day is like another year in and out—high or exceptional intelligence offers a lesser advantage than in an inhospitable environment with widely fluctuating seasonal variations. The more challenging the environment, the higher the premium placed on intelligence as a requirement of economic, and consequently reproductive success. Hence, the growth of human intelligence would be most pronounced in harsher (historically, generally northern) regions of human habitation.

Humans live off—consume—animals and plants, and animals live off other animals or plants. Plants, thus, stand at the beginning of the human food chain. The growth of plants in turn depends on the presence (or absence) of four factors: carbon dioxide (which is evenly distributed across the globe and hence of no interest here), sun energy, water, and, very importantly, minerals (such as potassium, phosphates, etc.).[12]

At the equator, where (nearby) the first modern humans lived, two of the three conditions of biological growth were met perfectly. There existed

---

12. See on the following Josef H. Reichholf, *Stabile Ungleichgewichte. Die Ökologie der Zukunft* (Frankfurt: Suhrkamp, 2008); also Carroll Quigley, *The Evolution of Civilizations: An Introduction to Historical Analysis* (Indianapolis, Ind.: Liberty Classics, 1979), chap. 6.

an abundance of sunlight and of rain. Rain fell predictably almost daily. Days and nights were equally long and temperatures year-round comfortably warm, with little to no difference between day vs. night and summer vs. winter temperatures. In the tropical rainforest, temperatures rarely exceed 30 degrees Celsius and rarely fall below 20 degrees Celsius. Winds were generally calm, interrupted only by sudden brief storms. The conditions for human habitation, then, would appear quite appealing; and yet, the population density in tropical regions is and has always been extremely low as compared to that in regions further north (and south), sometimes, as in the rainforests of the Amazon, nearly as low as the population density typical of deserts or arctic regions. The reason for this is the extreme shortage of soil minerals in the tropics.

The soil of the tropics is, geologically speaking, old (as compared in particular to those regions affected by the earth-historical sequence of glacial and interglacial periods) and almost completely drained of minerals (except for equatorial regions with volcanic—mineral producing—activity as on some Indonesian islands such as Java, for instance, where the human population density has in fact always been significantly higher). As a result, the enormous biomass characteristic of the tropics produces no new, surplus or excess growth. Growth is year-round, but it is slow, and it does not lead to an increase in the total biomass. Once grown up, the rainforest only recycles itself. Moreover, the overwhelming proportion of this biomass is in the form of slow growing hard-wood trees, i.e., of dead matter; and the leaves of most tropical plants, due to their peculiar need for protection (cooling) against the intense equator sun, are not only hard and tough but often poisonous or at least distasteful to humans and other plant-eaters such as cattle and deer. This absence of surplus growth and the special chemistry of tropical plants explains the fact that, contrary to what is frequently imagined, the tropics support only amazingly few and smallish animals. Indeed, the only animals existing in abundance are ants and termites. A tropical biomass (mostly of wood) of more than 1,000 tons per hectare produces no more than 200 kilograms of meat (animal mass), i.e., one five thousandth of the plant mass. (In contrast, in the East-African grassland savannah a mere 50 tons of plant mass per square kilometer (100 hectare) produces some 20 tons of animal mass: of elephants, buffalos, zebras, gnus, antelopes and gazelles.) Yet where there are so few and non-sizeable animals, only few humans can be sustained. (In fact, most people who lived in the tropics lived near rivers and sustained their lives essentially from fishing rather than hunting and gathering.)

At their place of origin, then, humans very quickly arrived at the point where they had to leave the paradisiacal, warm, stable and predictable environment of the tropics and enter other regions in search of food. The regions northward (and southward) of the equator were seasonal regions, however. That is, they had less, and less constant rainfall than the tropics, and the temperatures increasingly fell and varied more widely as one moved northward (or southward). In northern regions of human habitation, temperatures could easily vary by more than 40 degrees Celsius per day and seasonal temperatures by more than 80 degrees. The total biomass produced under such conditions was significantly less than in the tropics. However, further away from the equator the soil had (often) sufficient or even ample minerals to compensate for these climatic disadvantages and offered optimal conditions for the growth of vegetation suited for animal and human consumption: of plants that grew fast and, in spurts, produced large seasonal surpluses of fresh biomass — in particular of grasses (including grains) — that could support a large number of sizable animals.

During the last ice age, which ended some 10,000 years ago, the regions which offered thus less than paradisiacal climatic conditions but a superior food supply included (concentrating here on the northern hemisphere, where most of the considered development took place) all of supra-equatorial Africa — including the Sahara — and most of the Eurasian land mass (except for still-arctic northern Europe and Siberia). Since then, and essentially continuing until today, a northern belt of deserts, which widens toward the east, has come to separate the entire zone of seasonal regions into a southern one of subequatorial regions and a northern one that includes now also most of northern Europe and Siberia. From the hunter-gatherer stage of human development essentially until today, then, the highest population density could be found in these "moderate" seasonal regions (a picture further modified only by altitudes).

It is important to realize in this context, however, that what we have come to regard as "moderate" regions of human habitation were actually quite harsh living conditions, and in far northern latitudes even extremely harsh conditions as compared to those in the constantly warm tropics, to which humans first had been adapted. In contrast to the stable and unchanging environment of the tropics, moderate regions presented increased change and fluctuation and thus posed (increasingly) difficult intellectual challenges to hunters and gatherers. Not only did they have to learn how to deal with large animals, which did not exist in the tropics (except for the volcanic parts of Indonesia), and their movements. More importantly, outside equatorial regions seasonal changes and fluctuations in the human environment played an increasingly greater role, and it became increasingly important to predict such changes and fluctuations and to anticipate their effects on the future food supply (of plants and animals). Those, who could do so successfully and make appropriate preparations and adjustments, had a better chance of survival and proliferation than those who could not.

Outside the equatorial rainforest, to the north (and south), pronounced rainy seasons existed and had to be taken into account. It rained during the summer and was dry in the winter. As well, the growth and distribution of plants and animals was affected by northeasterly (or, in the southern hemisphere, southeasterly) trade winds. In regions still further to the north (or south), increasingly separated since the end of the last ice-age from the subequatorial regions by a belt of (northern and southern) deserts, the rain seasons shifted, with rain in the winter and drought in the summer. The winds affecting the distribution of rain were prevailingly westerlies. Summers were hot and dry, while winter temperatures, even in low altitudes, could easily reach "deadly" freezing levels, even if only for short periods. Growing seasons were accordingly limited. Lastly, in the northernmost regions of human habitation, i.e., north of Mediterranean latitudes, rain fell irregularly throughout the year and, with prevailing westerly winds, more in the west (northern Europe) than in the east (northern Asia). Otherwise, however, seasonal changes and fluctuations in this zone of human habitation were extreme. The lengths of days (light) and nights (dark) varied remarkably throughout the year. In extreme northern regions, a light summer day and a dark winter night both could last for more than a month. More importantly, the entire region (and especially pronounced as one moved in a northeasterly direction) experienced extended periods of often extremely freezing conditions during the winter. During these periods, lasting from many months to most of the year, all plant growth came essentially to a standstill. Plants died or went dormant. Nature stopped supplying food, and humans (and animals) were threatened with starvation and the danger of freezing to death. The growing seasons, during which a surplus of food and shelter could possibly be built up for this contingency, were accordingly short. Moreover, the extreme differences between long, harsh and freezing winters and the short, mild to warm growing seasons affected the migration of animals. Unless they had fully adapted to arctic conditions and could go into some form of hibernation during "dead" seasons, animals had to migrate from season to season, often over long distances to and from far apart locations. And since animals constituted a major part of the human food supply, hunter-gatherers, too, had to migrate regularly over large distances.

Before the background of this rough picture of human ecology and geography, further modified and complicated of course by the existence of mountain ranges, rivers and bodies of water, it becomes apparent why the natural selection in favor of higher intelligence among hunter-gatherers would be more pronounced as one moved in northern (or southern) direction toward the coldest regions of human habitation. No doubt, significant intelligence was required of humans to live successfully in the tropics. However, the equilibrium-like constancy of the tropics acted as a natural constraint on the further development of human intelligence. Because one day was much like any other day in the tropics, little or no need existed for anyone to take anything into account in his actions except his immediate surroundings or to plan beyond anything but the immediately impending future. In distinct contrast, the increasing seasonality of regions outside the tropics made for an intellectually increasingly challenging environment.

The existence of seasonal changes and fluctuations—of rain and drought, summer and winter, scorching heat and freezing cold, winds and calms— required that more, and more remote factors including the sun, the moon and the stars, and longer stretches of time had to be taken into account if one wanted to act successfully and survive and procreate. More and longer chains of causes and effects had to be recognized and more and longer chains of argument thought through. The planning horizon had to be extended in time. One had to act now, in order to be successful much later. Both the period of production—the time lapse between the onset of a productive effort and its completion—and the period of provision—the time span into the future for which present provisions (savings) had to be made—needed to be lengthened. In the northernmost regions, with long and deadly winters, provisions of food, clothing, shelter and heating had to be made that would last through most of a year or beyond. Planning had to be in terms of years, instead of days or months. As well, in pursuit of seasonally widely migrating animals, extensive territories had to be traversed, requiring exceptional skills of orientation and navigation. Only groups intelligent enough on average to generate exceptional leaders who possessed such superior intellectual skills and abilities were rewarded with success—survival and procreation. Those groups and leaders, on the other hand, who were not capable of these achievements, were punished with failure, i.e., extinction.

The greatest progress on the way toward the invention of agriculture and animal husbandry some 11,000 years ago, then, should have occurred in the northernmost regions of human habitation. Here, the competition within and between hunter-gatherer groups should have produced over time the most intelligent—provisionary and farsighted—population. And indeed, during the tens of thousands of years until about 11,000 years ago, every significant technological advance originated in northern regions: mostly in Europe or, in the case of ceramics, in Japan. In contrast, during the same period the tool kit used in the tropics remained almost unchanged.

But the explanatory power of the above sketch of social evolution goes much further. The admittedly hypothetical theory presented here can explain why it took so long to get out of the Malthusian trap, and how such a feat was possible at all and we did not remain under Malthusian conditions forever: Mankind was simply not intelligent enough to achieve productivity increases that could continuously outstrip population growth. A certain threshold of average and exceptional intelligence had to be reached first for this to become possible, and it took time (until about 1800) to "breed" such level of intelligence. The theory can explain the well-established and corroborated (and yet for "political correctness" reasons persistently ignored) fact of intelligence research: that the average IQ of nations gradually declines as one moves from north to south (from about 100 or more points in northern countries to about 70 in sub-Saharan Africa).[13] More specifically, the theory can thus explain why the Industrial Revolution originated and then took hold immediately in some—generally northern—regions but not in others, why there had always existed persistent regional income differences, and why these differences could have increased (rather than decreased) since the time of the Industrial Revolution.

As well, the theory can explain what may at first appear as an anomaly: that it was not in the northernmost regions of human habitation where the Neolithic revolution began some 11,000 years ago and whence it gradually and successively conquered the rest of the world, but in regions significantly further south—yet still far north of the tropics: in the Middle East, in central

---

13. See Richard Lynn and Tatu Vanhanen, *IQ and Global Inequality* (Augusta, Ga.: Washington Summit Publishers, 2006); Richard Lynn, *The Global Bell Curve: Race, IQ and Inequality Worldwide* (Augusta, Ga.: Washington Summit Publishers, 2008); idem, *Race Differences in Intelligence: An Evolutionary Analysis* (Augusta, Ga.: Washington Summit Publishers, 2008).

China (the Yangtze Valley), and in Mesoamerica. The reason for this seeming anomaly is easy to detect, however. In order to invent agriculture and animal husbandry two factors were necessary: sufficient intelligence and favorable natural circumstances to apply such intelligence. It was the second factor that was lacking in extreme northern regions and thus prevented its inhabitants from making the revolutionary invention. The extreme freezing conditions and the extreme brevity of the growing season there made agriculture and animal husbandry practically impossible, even if the idea might have been conceived. What was necessary to actually implement the idea were natural circumstances favorable to sedentary life: of a long and warm growing season (besides suitable crops, and domesticable animals). (The greater scarcity of such crops and animals on the American continent is the likely reason for the somewhat belated third independent invention of agriculture and animal husbandry in Mesoamerica.) Such climatic conditions existed in the mentioned "temperate" regions. Here, the competitive development of human intelligence among hunter-gatherers had made sufficient progress (even if it lagged behind that in the north) so that, combined with favorable natural circumstances, the idea of agriculture and animal husbandry could be implemented. Since the end of the last ice age about 10,000 years ago, then, the zone of temperate climates expanded northward into higher latitudes, rendering agriculture and animal husbandry increasingly feasible there as well. Meeting there an even more intelligent people, the new revolutionary production techniques were not merely quickly imitated and adopted, but most subsequent improvements in these techniques had its origins here. South of the centers of the original invention, too, the new technique would be gradually adopted (with the exception of the tropics)—after all, it is easier to imitate something than to invent it. Meeting a less intelligent people there, however, little or no contribution to the further development of more efficient practices of agriculture or animal husbandry would come from there. All further efficiency gains in these regions would stem from the imitation of techniques invented elsewhere, in regions further north.

IV. Implications and Outlook

Several implications and suggestions follow from this. First, the theory of social evolution sketched here entails a fundamental criticism of the egalitarianism rampant within the social sciences generally but also among many libertarians. True, economists allow for human "differences" in the form of different labor productivities. But these differences are generally interpreted as the result of different external conditions, i.e., of different endowments or training. Only rarely are internal, biologically anchored characteristics admitted as possible sources of human differences. Yet even when economists admit the obvious: that human differences have internal, biological sources as well, as Mises and Rothbard certainly do, they still typically ignore that these differences are themselves in turn the outcome of a lengthy process of natural selection in favor of human characteristics and dispositions (physical and mental) determinant of economic success and, more or less highly positively correlated with economic success, of reproductive success. That is, it is still largely overlooked that we, modern man, are a very different breed from our predecessors hundreds or even thousands of years ago.

Second, once it is realized that the Industrial Revolution was first and foremost the outcome of the evolutionary growth of human intelligence (rather than the mere removal of institutional barriers to growth), the role of the State can be recognized as fundamentally different under Malthusian vs. post-Malthusian conditions. Under Malthusian conditions the State doesn't matter much, at least as far as macro-effects are concerned. A more exploitative State will simply lead to a lower population number (much like a pest would), but it does not affect per capita income. In fact, in lowering the population density, income per capita may even rise, as it did after the great pestilence in the mid-fourteenth century. And in reverse: a "good," less-exploitative State will allow for a growing number of people, but per capita incomes will not rise or may even fall, because land per capita is reduced. All this changes with the Industrial Revolution. For if productivity gains continuously outstrip population increases and allow for a steady increase in per capita incomes, then an exploitative institution such as the State can continuously grow without lowering per capita income and reducing the population number. The State then becomes a permanent drag on the economy and per capita incomes.

Third, whereas under Malthusian conditions positive eugenic effects reign: the economically successful produce more surviving offspring and the population stock is thus gradually bettered (cognitively improved), under post-Malthusian conditions the existence and the growth of the State produces a two-fold dysgenic effect, especially under democratic welfare-state conditions.[14] For one, the "economically challenged," as the principal "clients" of the welfare State, produce more surviving offspring, and the economically successful less. Secondly, the steady growth of a parasitic State, made possible by a growing underlying economy, systematically affects the requirements of economic success. Economic success becomes increasingly dependent on politics and political talent, i.e., the talent of using the State to enrich oneself at others' expense. In any case, the population stock becomes increasingly worse (as far as the cognitive requirements of prosperity and economic growth are concerned), rather than better.

Finally, it is important to note in conclusion, then, that just as the Industrial Revolution and the attendant escape from the Malthusian trap was by no means a necessary development in human history so its success and achievements are also not irrevocable.

---

14. Lynn, *Dysgenics.*

5

Of Common, Public, and Private Property and the Rationale for Total Privatization

I have three goals. First, I want to clarify the nature and function of private property. Second, I want to clarify the distinction between "common" goods and property and "public" goods and property, and explain the construction error inherent in the institution of public goods and property. Third, I want to explain the rationale and principle of privatization.

I. Theoretical Preliminaries

I will begin with some abstract but fundamental theoretical considerations concerning the sources of conflicts and the purpose of social norms. If there were no interpersonal conflicts, there would be no need for norms. It is the purpose of norms to help avoid otherwise unavoidable conflicts. A norm that generates conflict, rather than helps avoid it, is contrary to the purpose of norms, i.e., it is a dysfunctional norm or a perversion.

It is sometimes thought that conflicts result from the mere fact of different people having different interests or ideas. But this is false, or at least very incomplete. From the diversity of individual interests and ideas alone it does not follow that conflicts must arise. I want it to rain, and my neighbor wants the sun to shine. Our interests are contrary. However, because neither I, nor my neighbor controls the sun or the clouds, our conflicting interests have no practical consequences. There is nothing that we can do about the weather. Likewise, I may believe that A causes B, and you believe that B is caused by C; or I believe in and pray to God, and you don't. But if this is all the difference there is between us nothing of any practical consequence follows. Different interests and beliefs can lead to conflict only when they are put

---

• Originally published in *Libertarian Papers* 3, no. 2 (2011).

into action—when our interests and ideas are attached to or implemented in physically controlled objects, i.e., in *economic goods* or *means of action*.

Yet even if our interests and ideas are attached to and implemented in economic goods, no conflict results so long as our interests and ideas are concerned exclusively with different—physically separate—goods. Conflict only results if our different interests and beliefs are attached to and invested in one and the same good. In the *Schlaraffenland*,[1] with a superabundance of goods, no conflict can arise (except for conflicts regarding the use of our physical bodies that embody our very own interests and ideas). There is enough around of everything to satisfy everyone's desires. In order for different interests and ideas to result in conflict, goods must be *scarce*. Only scarcity makes it possible that different interests and ideas can be attached to and invested in one and the same stock of goods. Conflicts, then, are physical clashes regarding the control of one and the same given stock of goods. People clash because they want to use the same goods in different, incompatible ways.

Even under conditions of scarcity, when conflicts are possible, however, they are not necessary or unavoidable. All conflicts regarding the use of any good can be avoided if only every good is privately owned, i.e., exclusively controlled by some specified individual(s) and it is always clear which thing is owned, and by whom, and which is not. The interests and ideas of different individuals may then be as different as can be, and yet no conflict arises so long as their interests and ideas are concerned always and exclusively with their own, separate property.

What is needed to avoid all conflict, then, is only a norm regarding the privatization of scarce things (goods). More specifically, in order to avoid all conflict *from the very beginning of mankind on*, the required norm must concern the *original privatization* of goods (the first transformation of nature-given "things" into "economic goods" and private property). Further, the original privatization of goods *cannot* occur by verbal declaration, i.e., by the mere utterance of words, because this could work and not lead to permanent and irresolvable conflict only if, contrary to our initial assumption of different interests and ideas, a prestabilized harmony of the interests and ideas of all people existed. (Yet in that case no norms were needed in the first place!)

---

1. See the Wikipedia entry for "Cockaigne," http://en.wikipedia.org/wiki/Cockaigne.

Rather, to avoid all otherwise unavoidable conflict, the original privatization of goods must occur through actions: through acts of original appropriation of what were previously "things." Only through actions, taking place in time and space, can an objective—inter-subjectively ascertainable—link be established between a particular person and a particular good. And only the *first* appropriator of a previously un-appropriated thing can acquire this thing without conflict. For, by definition, as the *first* appropriator he *cannot* have run into any conflict with anyone in appropriating the good in question, as everyone else appeared on the scene only *later.* All property must go back, then, directly or indirectly, through a chain of mutually beneficial and hence likewise conflict-free property-title transfers, to original appropriators and acts of original appropriation.

As a matter of fact, this answer is apodictically, i.e., non-hypothetically, true. In the absence of a prestabilized harmony of all individual interests, only private property can help avoid otherwise—under conditions of scarcity—unavoidable conflict. And only the principle of property acquisition by means of original appropriation or mutually beneficial transfer from an earlier to a later proprietor makes it possible that conflict can be avoided throughout—from the very beginning of mankind until the end. No other solution exists. Every other ruling is contrary to the nature of man as a rational actor.

In conclusion, even under conditions of all-around scarcity it is possible that people with divergent interests and ideas can peacefully—without conflict—coexist, provided they recognize the institution of private (i.e., exclusive) property and its ultimate foundation in and through acts of original appropriation.

II. Private Property, Common Goods and Public Property

Let me now move from theory to practice and application. Let us assume a small village with privately owned houses, gardens, and fields. In principle, all conflicts regarding the use of these goods can be avoided, because it is clear who owns and has exclusive control of what house, garden, and field, and who doesn't.

But then there runs a "public" street in front of the private houses, and a "public" path leads through the woods at the edge of the village to some lake. What is the status of this street and this path? They are not private property. Indeed, we assume that no one claims that he is the street's or the path's private owner. Rather, street and path are part of the natural *environment* in which everyone acts. Everyone uses the street, but no one owns it or exercises exclusive control regarding its utilization.

It is conceivable that this state of affairs with ownerless public streets can go on forever without leading to any conflict. It is not very realistic, however, because this requires the assumption of a stationary economy. Yet with economic change and growth, and in particular with a growing population, conflicts concerning the use of the public street are bound to increase. While "street conflicts" initially might have been so infrequent and so easy to avoid as not to cause anyone to worry, now they are ubiquitous and intolerable. The street is constantly congested and in permanent disrepair. A solution is required. The street must be taken out of the realm of the environment—of external "things" or *common property*—and brought into the realm of "economic goods." This, the increasing economization of things previously considered and treated as "free goods," is the way of civilization and progress.

Two solutions to the problem of managing increasingly intolerable conflicts concerning the use of "common property" have been proposed and tried. The first—and correct—solution is to privatize the street. The second—incorrect—solution is to turn streets into what is nowadays called "public property" (which is very different from the former, unowned "common" goods and property). Why the second solution is incorrect or dysfunctional can best be grasped in contradistinction to the alternative privatization option.

How is it possible that formerly unowned common streets can be privatized without thereby generating conflict with others? The short answer is that this can be done provided only that the appropriation of the street does not infringe on the previously established rights—the easements—of private-property owners to use such streets "for free." Everyone must remain free to walk the street from house to house, through the woods, and onto the lake, just as before. Everyone retains a right-of-way, and hence no one can claim to be made worse off by the privatization of the street. Positively, in order to objectify—and validate—his claim that the formerly common street is now a private one and that he (and no one else) is its owner, the appropriator (whoever it may be) must perform some visible maintenance and repair work on and along the street. Then, as its owner, he—and no one else—can further develop and improve the streets as he sees fit. He sets the rules and regulations concerning the use of his street so as to avoid all street conflicts. He can build a hot dog or a bratwurst stand on his road, for instance, and exclude others from doing the same; or he can prohibit loitering on his street and collect a fee for the removal of garbage. *Vis-à-vis* foreigners or strangers, the street owner can determine the rules of entry regarding uninvited strangers. Last but not least, as its private owner he can sell the street to someone else (with all previously established rights-of-way remaining intact).

In all of this, it is more important *that* a privatization takes place than what specific *form* it assumes. On one end of the spectrum of possible privatizations we can imagine a single owner. A wealthy villager, for example, takes it upon himself to maintain and repair the street and thus becomes its owner. On the other end of the spectrum, we can imagine that the initial maintenance or repair of the street is the result of a genuine community effort. In that case, there is not just one owner of the street, but every community member is (initially) its equal co-owner. In the absence of a prestabilized harmony of all interest and ideas, such co-ownership requires a decision-making mechanism regarding the further development of the street. Let us assume that, as in a joint-stock company, it is the majority of the street owners that determines what to do or not to do with it. This, i.e., majority rule, smacks of conflict, but it isn't so in this case. Every owner who is dissatisfied with the decisions made by the majority of owners, who believes that the burdens imposed on him by the majority are greater than the benefits he can derive from his (partial) street ownership, can always and at all times drop out or "exit." He can sell his ownership share to someone else, thus opening the possibility for the concentration of ownership titles, conceivably in a single hand, all the while retaining his original right-of-way.

In contrast, a very different sort of street property is created if the exit option does *not* exist, i.e., if a person is not permitted to sell his share of street property or he is stripped of his former right-of-passage. This is, however, precisely what defines and characterizes the second "public"-property option. The public street in this modern sense of the word "public" is not unowned as it once was. There *is* a street owner—whether it is a particular individual, the king of the road, or a democratically elected street government—who has an exclusive say in setting the traffic rules and determining the future development of the street. But the street government does not permit its electors, i.e., the people, who supposedly are the street's equal co-owners, to sell their ownership share (and so renders them compulsory owners of something of which they might rather want to divest themselves). And neither government nor king allow the village-residents unrestricted access and passage on the formerly free street but make its further use conditional on the payment of some user fee or contribution (thus rendering the village residents compulsory street owners again if only they want to continue using it as before).

The results of this arrangement are predictable. In denying the "exit" option, the owner of the "public" street has gained a stranglehold on the village population. Accordingly, the fees and other conditions imposed on the village residents for the continued use of the formerly "free" street will tend to become increasingly more burdensome. Conflicts will not be avoided; quite to the contrary, conflicts are institutionalized. Because the exit option is closed, i.e., because the public-street users must now pay for what they formerly had for free, and no resident can sell and divest himself of his supposed street ownership but remains continuously bound by the decisions made by the street government or king, not only are conflicts regarding the further use, maintenance and development of the street itself rendered permanent and ubiquitous. More importantly, with "public" streets conflict is also introduced into areas where it formerly did *not* exist. For if the private owners of the houses, gardens, and fields along the street must pay contributions to the street owner in order to continue doing what they had done before, i.e., if they must pay taxes to the street owner, then, by the same token, the street owner has thereby gained control over their private properties. A private owner's control concerning the use of his own house is then no longer an exclusive one. Rather, the owner of the adjacent street can interfere with a house owner's decisions regarding his own house. He can tell the house owner what to do or not to do with his house if he wants to leave or enter it as before. That is, the public-street owner is in a position where he can limit, and ultimately even eliminate, i.e., expropriate, all private property and property rights and thus render conflict unavoidable and all-around.

III. The Rationale for Privatization

It should be clear now why the institution of public property is dysfunctional. Institutions and the norms underlying them are supposed to help avoid conflict. But the institution of "public" property—of "public" streets—creates and increases conflict. For the purpose of conflict avoidance (of peaceful human cooperation), then, public property must go. All public property must become private property.

But how to privatize in the "real world," which has developed far beyond the simple village model that I have so far considered? In this "real world" we have not just public streets, but also public parks, land, rivers, lakes, coastlines, housing, schools, universities, hospitals, barracks, airports, harbors, libraries, museums, monuments, and on and on. Further, on top of local governments we have a hierarchy of "superior" provincial and ultimately "supreme" national or central governments as the owners of such goods. Predictably, moreover, parallel to the territorial extension and expansion of the domain of public goods, in which private-property owners have become implicated without any "way out," the range of choices left to people regarding their private property has been increasingly limited and narrowed. Only a small and increasingly smaller realm is left wherein private-property owners can still make free decisions, i.e., free from possible intrusion or interference by some public authority. Not even within the four walls of one's own house is one left free and can one exercise exclusive control over one's property. Today, in the name of the public and as the owner of all "public goods," governments can invade your house, confiscate any and all of your belongings, and even kidnap your children.

Obviously, in the "real world," the question of how to privatize is more difficult than in the simple village model. But the village model and elementary social theory can help us recognize the *principle* (if not all the complicating details) involved and to be applied in this task. The privatization of "public" goods must occur in such a way that does not infringe on the preestablished rights of private-property owners (in the same way as the first appropriator of a formerly unowned *common* street did not infringe on anyone's rights if and insofar as he recognized every resident's unrestricted right-of-way).

Because "public" *streets* were the springboards from which all other "public goods" sprang, the privatization process should begin with streets. With the transformation of formerly *common* streets into "public" streets the expansion of the domain of public goods and the powers of government started, and here one should begin with the solution.

The privatization of "public" streets has a twofold result. On the one hand, no resident is henceforth forced to pay any tax for the upkeep or development of any local, provincial, or federal street. The future funding of all streets is solely the responsibility of their new private owners (whomever they may be). On the other hand, insofar as a resident's rights-of-way are concerned, the privatization must leave no one worse off than he was originally (while it also cannot make anyone better off). Originally, every village resident could travel freely on the local street along his property, and he could proceed equally freely from there as long as things around him were unowned. However, if in his travels he came across something that was visibly owned, whether a house, a field, or a street, his entrance was conditional on the owner's permission or invitation. Likewise, if a nonresident stranger came across a local street, entrance to this street was subject to its (domestic) owner's permission. The stranger had to be invited by some resident onto his property. That is, people could move around, but no one had an entirely unrestricted right of passage. No one was free to move just anywhere without ever requiring anyone's permission or invitation. The privatization of streets cannot change this fact and remove such original, natural restrictions on the "freedom of movement."

Applied to the world of local, provincial, and federal streets, this means that as the result of the privatization of streets every resident must be permitted to travel freely on every local, provincial, and federal street or highway as before. Entrance onto the streets of *different* states or provinces, and especially of *different localities*, however, is not equally free, but conditional on the permission or invitation of the owners of such streets. Local streets always—praxeologically—precede any inter- or trans-local streets, and hence entry into different localities was never free but always and everywhere conditional on some local permission or invitation. This original *datum* is reinstated and reinforced with privatized streets.

Today, on "public" streets, where everyone is essentially permitted to go everywhere and anywhere, without any "discriminatory" access restriction whatsoever, conflict in the form of "forced integration," i.e., of having to accept uninvited strangers into one's midst and onto one's property, has become ubiquitous. In distinct contrast, with every street and in particular every local street privatized, neighborhoods and communities regain their original right of exclusion, which is a defining element of private property (just as much as the right of inclusion, i.e., the right to invite someone else onto one's property). The owners of neighborhood and community streets, while not infringing on any resident's right-of-way or right to invite, can determine the entrance requirement for uninvited strangers (undocumented aliens) onto their streets and thus prevent the phenomenon of forced integration.

Yet who *are* the streets' owners? Who can claim, and validate his claim, that he owns the local, provincial, or federal streets? These streets are not the result of some sort of community effort, nor are they the result of the work of some clearly identifiable person or group of persons. True, literally speaking, the street workers built the streets. But that does not make them the streets' owners because these workers had to be paid to do their work. Without funding, there would be no street. Yet the funds paid to the workers are the result of tax payments by various taxpayers. Accordingly, streets should be regarded as these taxpayers' property. The former taxpayers, in accordance with their amount of local, state, and federal taxes paid, should be awarded tradable property titles in local, state, and federal streets. They then can either keep these titles as an investment, or they can divest themselves of their street property and sell it, all the while retaining their unrestricted right-of-way.

The same essentially applies to the privatization of all other public goods, such as schools, hospitals, etc. As a result, all tax payments for the upkeep and operation of such goods stop. The funding and development of schools and hospitals, etc., is henceforth solely up to their new, private owners. Likewise, the new owners of such formerly "public" goods are those residents who actually financed them. They, in accordance with their amount of taxes paid, should be awarded saleable property shares in the schools, hospitals, etc. Other than in the case of streets, however, the new owners of schools and hospitals are unrestricted by any easements or rights-of-way in the future uses of their property. Schools and hospitals, unlike streets, were *not* first *common goods* before being turned into "public" goods. Schools and hospitals simply did not exist at all as goods before, i.e., until they had been first produced; and hence no one (except the producers) can have acquired a prior easement or right-of-way concerning their use. Accordingly, the new private owners of schools, hospitals, etc., are at liberty to set the entrance requirements for their properties and determine if they want to continue operating these properties as schools and hospitals or prefer to employ them for a different purpose.

IV. ADDENDUM
PRIVATIZATION: PRINCIPLE AND APPLICATIONS

The only effective solution to the problem of conflict, i.e., the only rule or norm that can assure conflict avoidance from the beginning of mankind onward and produce "eternal peace" is the institution of private property, ultimately grounded in acts of original appropriation of previously unowned or "common" resources. In contrast, the institution of public property begins with conflict, i.e., with an act of original expropriation of some formerly private property (rather than the appropriation of previously unowned goods); and public property does not end conflict and expropriation but institutionalizes them and makes them permanent. Hence arises the imperative of privatization—and hence the principle of restitution, i.e., the notion that public property be returned *qua* private property to those from whom it had been forcibly taken. That is, public goods should become the private property of those who financed or otherwise funded these goods and who can establish an objective—inter-subjectively ascertainable—claim to this effect.

Applying this principle to the existing world is often complicated and requires considerable legal effort. I shall only consider three realistic privatization cases in order to address some central questions and decisions.

The first case, most closely approximated by the former Soviet Union, is that of a society where each and every property is public property, administered by a state government. Everyone is a state employee and works in public offices, enterprises, factories, and shops; and everyone moves and lives on public land and in public housing. There is no private property except in immediate consumer goods, in one's underwear, toothbrush, etc. Moreover, all records concerning the legal past are lost or destroyed such that no one, based on such records, can substantiate a claim to any identifiable part of public property.

In this case, the principle that every claim to public property must be based on objective, inter-subjectively ascertainable "data" would lead one to award private ownership (and saleable property titles) based on present or past occupancy: the bureaus go to the bureaucrats who occupy them, the factories to the workers, the fields to the farmers, and the houses to the residents. Retired workers are awarded property titles in their former workplaces in accordance with the duration of their employment. As present or past occupants of the property in question, only they have an objective tie to this property. They are the ones who have maintained the property as it is while others were working elsewhere at other public workplaces.

Everything else, i.e., all public property that is *not* currently occupied and maintained by anyone (e.g., the "wilderness") becomes "common" property and is opened up to all members of the society for privatization by way of original appropriation.

This solution only leaves out one important question. All legal documents are presumably lost. But people have not lost their memories. They still remember past crimes. There are victims and witnesses to acts of murder, battery, torture, and imprisonment. What to do with those who committed these crimes, who ordered or commissioned them, or who cooperated in their execution? Should the torturers of the secret police and the Communist *nomenklatura*,[2] for instance, be included in this privatization scheme and become the private owners of the police stations and government palaces where they administered and planned their crimes? Justice requires instead that every alleged criminal offender be brought to trial by his supposed victims and, if sentenced and convicted, not only be excluded from obtaining any public property whatsoever, but also possibly be handed much harsher punishment (such as having his throat cut).

The second case differs from the first one in only one respect: the legal past has not been wiped out. Documents and records exist to prove past expropriations, and based on such documents specific people can lay objective claim to specific pieces of public property. This was essentially the case in the Soviet Union's former vassal states, such as East Germany, Czechoslovakia, Poland, etc., where the Communist takeover had taken place only some 40 years or about one generation before (rather than more than 70 years, as in the Soviet Union).

In this case, the original, expropriated owners or their legal heirs should be restored as private owners to the public property in question. But what about capital improvements? More specifically, what about newly erected structures (of houses and factories)—that would come to be privately owned by their current or past occupants—that were built on land restored to a different, original landowner? How many property shares should the landowner receive and how many the owners of the structure? Structures and land cannot be physically separated. In terms of economic theory, they are absolutely specific, complementary production factors whose relative contribution to their joint-value product cannot be disentangled. In this case no alternative exists for the contending parties but to bargain.

The third case is that of the so-called mixed economies. In these societies a public sector exists side by side with a nominally private sector. There are

---

2. See the Wikipedia entry for "Nomenklatura," http://en.wikipedia.org/wiki/Nomenklatura.

public goods and public employees next to nominally private property and the owners and employees of private business. Typically, the public employees who administer public property do not produce goods or services that are sold on the market. (For the atypical case of value-productive public enterprises, see below.) Their sales revenue and their market income are zero. Their salaries and all other costs involved in the operation of public goods are instead paid for by *others*. These others are the owners and employees of *private* business. Private business and employees, in contrast to their public counterparts, produce goods and services that are sold in the market and thus earn an income. Out of this income, private business does not merely pay the salaries of its own employees and provide for the maintenance of its own property; it also pays—in the form of income and property taxes—the (net) salaries of all public employees and the operating costs of all public property.

In this case, the principle that public property should be restored *qua* private property to those who actually funded it would lead one to assign ownership titles exclusively to *private* owners, producers, and employees in accordance with their past property and income tax payments, while *public* managers and employees would be excluded. All government offices and palaces, for instance, would have to be vacated by their current occupants. Public-sector salaries were paid only—and public property exists only—because of the funding provided by private-business owners and their employees. Hence, while public employees may keep their private property, they have no claim to the public property that they used and administered.

(This is different only in the atypical case where a public enterprise, such as a government-owned car factory, produced marketable goods and services and thus earned a market income. In that case, the public employees may have a legitimate claim to ownership, depending on the circumstances. They have a claim to full ownership of the factory, if no previously expropriated owner exists who can lay claim to the factory *and* if the factory never received any tax subsidies. If a previous owner exists, the factory employees can claim at best partial ownership and must bargain with the owner concerning their relative share of ownership titles. And if and to the extent that the factory had been tax subsidized, the factory workers would have to further divide their proportion of ownership titles with private-sector employees *qua* taxpayers.)

Simultaneously with the privatization of all public property, all *nominally* private property would be restored to its original state as *real* private property. That is, all nominally private property would be freed of all property or income taxes and of all legislative restrictions on its use (while previously concluded agreements concerning the use of property between private parties remain in effect). Without taxes, then, there are no government expenditures, and without government expenditures all public employees will be unsalaried and must look for productive work to earn a living. Likewise, every recipient of government grants, subsidies, or purchase orders will see his income reduce or disappear entirely and must look for alternatives.

This solution leaves still one important question unresolved. Once all net tax*payers* have been allotted their appropriate number of public-property shares, how do they take hold of this property and exercise their rights as private-property owners? Even if an inventory of all public property exists, most people do not have the faintest idea of what it is that they now (partially) own. Most people have a fairly good idea of *local* public property, but about the public property at other, distant locations, they know next to nothing, except regarding a few "national monuments." It is practically impossible for anyone to reach a realistic appraisal of the "correct" price for all of public property, and hence also of the "correct" price of an individual share in this property. Consequently, the prices asked and paid for such shares would be highly indeterminate and widely fluctuating and divergent, at least initially; and it would be rather unwieldy and highly time-consuming until some investor or group of investors had bought up the majority of all shares in order to then begin operating or selling off parts of this property to earn a return on its investment.

This difficulty can be overcome by bringing the idea of original appropriation back into play. The titles in the hands of net taxpayers are not only saleable tickets. More importantly, they entitle their owners to repossess formerly public and now-vacated property. Public property is opened to original appropriation, and the tickets are claims to vacated, momentarily unowned public property. Everyone can take his titles to specific pieces of public property and register as their owner. Since the first one to register with a particular piece of property would be its initial owner, it is assured that all pieces of public property would be almost instantly repossessed. More specifically, most public property would thus, at least initially, come to be owned by *local* residents, i.e., by people living in close proximity to a given piece of property and most knowledgeable concerning its potential value productivity. Moreover, because the value per property share increasingly falls as additional ticket-holders register with one and the same piece of property, any over-subscription or under-subscription of specific properties would be avoided or weeded out quickly. Very quickly, each piece of property would be appraised realistically according to its value productivity.

6

Natural Order, the State, and the Immigration Problem

I.

Human cooperation is the result of three factors: the differences among men and/or the geographical distribution of nature-given factors of production; the higher productivity achieved under the division of labor based on the mutual recognition of private property (the exclusive control of every man over his own body and his physical appropriations and possessions) as compared to either self-sufficient isolation or aggression, plunder and domination; and the human ability to recognize this latter fact. Were it not for the higher productivity of labor performed under division of labor and the human ability to recognize this fact, explains Ludwig von Mises, men would have forever remained deadly foes of one another, irreconcilable rivals in their endeavors to secure a portion of the scarce supply of means of sustenance provided by nature. Each man would have been forced to view all other men as his enemies; his craving for the satisfaction of his own appetites would have brought him into an implacable conflict with all his neighbors. No sympathy could possibly develop under such a state of affairs.[1]

• Originally published in *Journal of Libertarian Studies* 16, no. 1 (2002).

1. Ludwig von Mises, *Human Action: A Treatise on Economics* (Auburn, Ala.: Ludwig von Mises Institute, 1998), p. 144. "Within the frame of social co-operation," Mises explains,

> there can emerge between members of society feelings of sympathy and friendship and a sense of belonging together. These feelings are the source of man's most delightful and most sublime experiences. However, they are not, as some have asserted, the agents that have brought about social relationships. They are fruits of social cooperation, they thrive only within its frame; they did not precede the establishment of social relations and are not the seed from which they spring.

The higher productivity achieved under the division of labor and man's ability to recognize this fact explain the origin of the most elementary and fundamental of human institutions: the family and the family household.[2] Second, it explains the fact of neighborhood (community) among homogeneous people (families, clans, tribes): of neighborhood in the form of adjacent properties owned by separate and "equal" owners and in the "unequal" form of the relationship characteristic of a father and his son, a landlord and his tenant, or a community founder and his follower-residents.[3] Third and most important for our purposes, it explains the possibility of the peaceful coexistence of heterogeneous and alien communities. Even if the members of different communities find each other physically and/or behaviorally strange, irritating, or annoying, and do not want to associate as neighbors, they may still engage in mutually beneficial trade if they reside spatially separated from each other.[4]

Let us broaden this picture and assume the existence of different races, ethnicities, languages, religions, and cultures (henceforth summarily: ethno-

---

2. As regards the family, Mises explains,

> the mutual sexual attraction between male and female is inherent in man's animal nature and independent of any thinking and theorizing. It is permissible to call it original, vegetative, instinctive, or mysterious. ...However, neither cohabitation, nor what precedes it and follows, generates social cooperation and societal modes of life. The animals too join together in mating, but they have not developed social relations.
>
> Family life is not merely a product of sexual intercourse. It is by no means natural and necessary that parents and children live together in the way they do in the family. The mating relation need not result in a family organization. The human family is an outcome of thinking, planning, and acting. (*Human Action*, p. 167)

3. See on this also Spencer H. MacCallum, *The Art of Community* (Menlo Park, Calif.: Institute for Humane Studies, 1970).

4. Mises notes in this regard that

> even if such a thing as a natural and inborn hatred between various races existed, it would not render social cooperation futile.... Social cooperation has nothing to do with personal love or with a general commandment to love one another. They cooperate because this best serves their own interests. Neither love nor charity nor any other sympathetic sentiments but rightly understood selfishness is what originally impelled man to adjust himself to the requirements of society, to respect the rights and freedoms of his fellow men and to substitute peaceful cooperation for enmity and conflict. (*Human Action*, p. 168)

cultures). Based on the insight that "likes" associate with other likes and live spatially separated from "unlikes," the following picture emerges: People of one ethno-culture tend to live in close proximity to one another and spatially separated and distant from people of another ethno-culture. Whites live among Whites and separate from Asians and Blacks. Italian speakers live among other Italians and separate from English speakers. Christians live among other Christians and separate from Muslims. Catholics live among Catholics and separate from Protestants, etc. Naturally, some "overlap" and "mixing" of different ethno-cultures in various "border-territories" exists. Moreover, as centers of interregional trade, cities naturally display a higher degree of ethno-cultural heterogeneity. This notwithstanding, however, neighborhoods and communities are internally homogeneous (uni-cultural). In fact, even in border territories and cities the same spatial association and separation of likes and unlikes is found. Nothing like a society where members of different ethno-cultures live as neighbors or in close physical proximity to each other (as propagated by some American multiculturalists) emerges. Rather, the emerging multiculturalism is one in which many distinctly different ethno-cultures coexist in physical-spatial separation and distance from one another, and trade with each other from afar.[5]

Let us take one more step and assume that all property is owned privately and the entire globe is settled. Every piece of land, every house and building, every road, river, and lake, every forest and mountain, and all of the coastline is owned by private owners or firms. No such thing as "public" property or "open frontier" exists. Let us take a look at the problem of migration under this scenario of a "natural order."

First and foremost, in a natural order, there is no such thing as "freedom of migration." People cannot move about as they please. Wherever a person moves, he moves on private property; and private ownership implies the owner's right to include as well as to exclude others from his

---

5. See also Hans-Hermann Hoppe, *Democracy: The God That Failed—The Economics and Politics of Monarchy, Democracy, and Natural Order* (New Brunswick, N.J.: Transaction Publishers, 2001), esp. chap. 9.

On the significance of race and ethnicity, and especially on "genetic similarity and dissimilarity" as a source of attraction and repulsion see J. Phillippe Rushton, *Race, Evolution, and Behavior* (New Brunswick, N.J.: Transaction Publishers, 1995); idem, "Gene-Culture, Co-Evolution, and Genetic Similarity Theory: Implications for Ideology, Ethnic Nepotism, and Geopolitics," *Politics and the Life Sciences* 4 (1986); and Michael Levin, *Why Race Matters* (Westport, Conn.: Praeger, 1997).

property. Essentially, a person can move only if he is invited by a recipient property owner, and this recipient-owner can revoke his invitation and expel his invitees whenever he deems their continued presence on his property undesirable (in violation of his visitation code).

There will be plenty of movement under this scenario because there are powerful reasons to open access to one's property, but there are also reasons to restrict or close access. Those who are the most inclusive are the owners of roads, railway stations, harbors, and airports, for example. Interregional movement is their business. Accordingly, their admission standards can be expected to be low, typically requiring no more than the payment of a user fee. However, even they would not follow a completely non-discriminatory admission policy. For instance, they would exclude intoxicated or unruly people and eject all trespassers, beggars, and bums from their property, and they might videotape or otherwise monitor or screen their customers while on their property.

The situation for the owners of retail establishments, hotels, and restaurants is similar. They are in the business of selling and renting and thus offer easy access to their property. They have every economic incentive *not* to discriminate unfairly against "strangers" or "foreigners," because this would lead to reduced profits or losses. However, they must be significantly more circumspect and restrictive in their admission policy than the owners of roads or airports. They must take into account the local-domestic repercussions that the presence of strangers may have. If local-domestic sales suffer due to a retailer's or hotel's open admission policy *vis-à-vis* foreigners, then discrimination is economically justified. In order to overcome this possible problem, commercial establishments can be expected to require of their "foreign" visitors at a minimum adherence to local standards of conduct and appearance.[6]

The situation is similar for local employers. They prefer lower to higher wage rates; hence, they are not predisposed against foreigners. However, they must be sensitive to the repercussions on the local labor force that may result from the employment of foreigners; that is, they must be fearful of the possibility that an ethno-culturally heterogeneous work force might lead to lower productivity. Moreover, employment requires housing, and it is in

---

6. On the law and economics of "affirmative action" and discrimination, see Richard A. Epstein, *Forbidden Grounds* (Chicago: University of Chicago Press, 1992); Walter Block and Michael Walker, eds., *Discrimination, Affirmative Action, and Equal Opportunity* (Vancouver, B.C.: Fraser Institute, 1982).

the residential housing and real estate market where discrimination against and exclusion of ethnocultural strangers will tend to be most pronounced. For it is in the area of *residential* as contrasted to commercial property where the human desire to be private, secluded, protected, and undisturbed from external events and intrusions is most pronounced. The value of residential property to its owner depends essentially on its almost total exclusivity. Only family members and occasionally friends are included. And if residential property is located in a neighborhood, this desire for undisturbed possession — peace and privacy — is best accomplished by a high degree of ethno-cultural homogeneity (as this lowers transaction costs while simultaneously increasing protection from external disturbances and intrusions). By renting or selling residential property to strangers (and especially to strangers from ethno-culturally distant quarters), heterogeneity is introduced into the neighborhood. Transaction costs tend to increase, and the peculiar peace-and-privacy security — the freedom from external, foreign intrusions — sought and expected of residential property tends to fall, resulting in lower residential property values.[7]

---

7. Empirically, man's demand for ethno-cultural homogeneity in residential areas finds expression in two important institutional developments. On one hand, demand is accommodated by the development of proprietary communities — "gated" or "restrictive" communities or covenants — owned by a founder-developer and leased to follower-tenants. Here, from the outset, the owner imposes his own standards of community admission and membership conduct. The follower-tenants, in associating with the owner, agree to abide by this code. Of course, any such code restricts a person's range of permissible choices (as compared to the range available outside a proprietary community). By the same token, though, the code protects each community member from various forms of external disturbances. Presumably, in residing where they do community members demonstrate that they prefer the added "protection" offered by the code over its added "restrictiveness."

On the other hand, in communities of multiple independent proprietors, the demand for ethno-cultural homogeneity finds expression in the institution of insurance (mutual or capital-based). The essence of insurance is the grouping of individual risks into a pool (or class) of risks. However, in order to be so grouped, each individual risk must be "homogeneous" as regards the risk under consideration to every other individual risk within the same class. "Heterogeneous" risks either cannot be insured or must be insured separately (in different pools, jointly with other homogeneous risks, and at different prices). Ethno-cultural homogeneity of neighborhoods, then, is simply a device for making insurance against external threats and interferences possible and thus lowering the cost of residential property protection. Homogeneity facilitates mutual property insurance. Capital-based insurers will charge lower premiums for clusters of homogeneous territories (while at the same time revealing the different ranks in cultural development of various ethno-cultures, as reflected in the price-spread of the premium charged at different locations).

Under the scenario of a natural order, then, it can be expected that there will be plenty of interregional trade and travel. However, owing to the natural discrimination against ethno-cultural strangers in the area of residential housing and real estate, there will be little actual migration, i.e., permanent resettlement. And whatever little migration there is, it will be by individuals who are more or less completely assimilated to their newly adopted community and its ethno-culture.[8]

II.

Let us now introduce the institution of a State. The definition of a State assumed here is rather uncontroversial: A State is an agency which possesses the exclusive monopoly of ultimate decision-making and conflict arbitration within a given territory. In particular, a State can insist that all conflicts involving itself be adjudicated by itself or its agents. Implied in the power to exclude all others from acting as ultimate judge, as the second defining element of a State, is its power to tax: to unilaterally determine the price justice seekers must pay to the State for its services as the monopolistic provider of law and order.[9]

Certainly, based on this definition it is easy to understand why there might be a desire to establish a State. It is not, as we are told in kindergarten, in order to attain the "common good" or because there would be no order without a State, but for a reason far more selfish and base. For he who is a monopolist of final arbitration within a given territory can *make* and *create* laws in his own favor rather than recognize and apply existing law; and he who can legislate can also tax and thus enrich himself at the expense of others.

Here it is impossible to cover the fascinating question of how such an extraordinary institution as a State with the power to legislate and tax can possibly arise, except to note that ideologies and intellectuals play a decisive

---

8. Mass migration, in contrast to small-scale individual migration of skilled laborers in pursuit of a more productive environment, is entirely a state-made phenomenon (see also section IV below). Most typically, mass migration is the outcome of inter-state warfare, state resettlement programs, group expulsion, or general economic destructionism.

9. See Murray N. Rothbard, *For A New Liberty* (New York: Macmillan, 1978), esp. chap. 3; Murray N. Rothbard, *The Ethics of Liberty* (New York: New York University Press, 1998), esp. part III; Hans-Hermann Hoppe, *A Theory of Socialism and Capitalism* (Boston: Kluwer Academic Publishers, 1989); also Franz Oppenheimer, *The State* (New York: Vanguard Press, 1914).

role.[10] Rather, States are assumed "given," and the changes as regards migration that result from their existence will be considered.

First, with the establishment of a state and territorially defined state borders, "immigration" takes on an entirely new meaning. In a natural order, immigration is a person's migration from one neighborhood-community into a different one (micro-migration). In contrast, under statist conditions immigration is immigration by "foreigners" from across state borders, and the decision whom to exclude or include, and under what conditions, rests not with a multitude of independent private property owners or neighborhoods of owners but with a single central (and centralizing) state-government as the ultimate sovereign of all domestic residents and their properties (macro-migration). If a domestic resident-owner invites a person and arranges for his access onto the resident-owner's property but the government excludes this person from the state territory, it is a case of *forced exclusion* (a phenomenon that does not exist in a natural order). On the other hand, if the government admits a person while there is no domestic resident-owner who has invited this person onto his property, it is a case of *forced integration* (also non-existent in a natural order, where all movement is invited).

III.

In order to comprehend the significance of this change from decentralized admission by a multitude of property owners and owner-associations (micro-migration) to centralized admission by a state (macro-migration), and in particular to grasp the potentialities of forced integration under statist conditions, it is necessary first to briefly consider a state's policy of *domestic migration*. Based on the state's definition as a territorial monopolist of legislation and taxation and the assumption of "self-interest," the basic features of its policy can be predicted.

Most fundamentally, it can be predicted that the state's agents will be interested in increasing (maximizing) tax revenues and/or expanding the range of legislative interference with established private property rights, but they will have little or no interest in actually doing what a state is supposed

---

10. See Hoppe, *Democracy: The God That Failed*; idem, "Natural Elites, Intellectuals, and the State," pamphlet (Auburn, Ala.: Ludwig von Mises Institute, 1995); Murray N. Rothbard, *For A New Liberty*, esp. chap. 7; idem, *Education: Free and Compulsory* (Auburn, Ala.: Ludwig von Mises Institute, 1999).

to do: protecting private property owners and their property from domestic and foreign invasion.

More specifically, because taxes and legislative interference with private property rights are not paid voluntarily but are met with resistance, a state, to assure its own power to tax and legislate, must have an existential interest in providing its agents access to everyone and all property within the state's territory. In order to accomplish this, a state must take control of (expropriate) all existing private roads and then use its tax revenue to construct more and additional "public" roads, places, parks and lands, until everyone's private property borders onto or is encircled by public lands and roads.

Many economists have argued that the existence of public roads indicates an imperfection of the natural—free market—order. According to them, the free market "under-produces" the so-called "public" good of roads; and tax-funded public roads rectify this deficiency and enhance overall economic efficiency (by facilitating interregional movement and trade and lowering transaction costs). Obviously, this is a starry-eyed view of the situation.[11]

Free markets *do* produce roads, although they may well produce fewer and different roads than under statist conditions. And viewed from the perspective of a natural order, the increased production of roads under statist conditions represents not an improvement but an "overproduction," or better yet "malproduction," of roads. Public roads are not simply harmless facilitators of interregional exchange. First and foremost, they are facilitators of state taxation and control, for on public roads the government's taxmen, police, and military can proceed directly to everyone's doorstep.[12]

In addition, public roads and lands lead to a distortion and artificial breakup of the spatial association and separation characteristic of a natural order. As explained, there are reasons to be close and inclusive, but there are also reasons to be physically distant and separated from others. The over-production of roads occurring under statist conditions means on the one hand that different communities are brought into greater proximity to one another than they would have preferred (on grounds of demonstrated

---

11. On the fallacies of the theory of public goods see Murray N. Rothbard, *Man, Economy, and State* (Auburn, Ala.: Ludwig von Mises Institute, 1993), pp. 883–90; Hoppe, *A Theory of Socialism and Capitalism*, chap. 10; on roads in particular see Walter Block, "Public Goods and Externalities: The Case of Roads," *Journal of Libertarian Studies* 7, no. 1 (1983).

12. Even the famed roadways of ancient Rome were typically regarded as a *plague* (rather than an advantage) because they were essentially military rather than trade routes. See Max Weber, *Soziologie, Weltgeschichtliche Analysen, Politik* (Stuttgart: Kroener, 1964), p. 4.

preference). On the other hand, it means that one coherent community is broken up and divided by public roads.[13]

Moreover, under the particular assumption of a *democratic* state even more specific predictions can be made. Almost by definition, a state's territory extends over several ethno-culturally heterogeneous communities, and dependent on recurring popular elections, a state-government will predictably engage in redistributive policies.[14] In an ethno-culturally mixed territory this means playing one race, tribe, linguistic or religious group against another; one class within any one of these groups against another (the rich versus the poor, the capitalists versus the workers, etc.); and finally, mothers against fathers and children against parents. The resulting income and wealth redistribution is complex and varied. There are simple transfer payments from one group to another, for instance. However, redistribution also has a spatial aspect. In the realm of spatial relations it finds expression in an ever more pervasive network of non-discriminatory "affirmative action" policies imposed on private property owners.

An owner's right to exclude others from his property is the means by which he can avoid "bads" from happening: events that will lower the value of his property. By means of an unceasing flood of redistributive legislation, the democratic state has worked relentlessly not only to strip its citizens of all arms (weapons) but also to strip domestic property owners of their right of exclusion, thereby robbing them of much of their personal and physical protection. Commercial property owners such as stores, hotels, and restaurants are no longer free to exclude or restrict access as they see fit. Employers can no longer hire or fire who they wish. In the housing market, landlords are no longer free to exclude unwanted tenants. Furthermore, restrictive covenants are compelled to accept members and actions in violation of their very own rules and regulations. In short, forced integration is ubiquitous, making all aspects of life increasingly uncivilized and unpleasant.[15]

---

13. See also Edward Banfield, *The Unheavenly City Revisited* (Boston: Little, Brown, 1974).

14. On the practical impossibility of democracy (majority rule) in multi-ethnic states, see Ludwig von Mises, *Nation, State, and Economy* (New York: New York University Press, 1983).

15. See also Murray N. Rothbard, "Marshall, Civil Rights and the Courts," in Llewellyn H. Rockwell, Jr., ed., *The Irrepressible Rothbard* (Burlingame, Calif.: Center for Libertarian Studies, 2000), pp. 370–77; Michael Levin, "The President as Social Engineer," in John V. Denson, ed., *Reassessing the Presidency* (Auburn, Ala.: Ludwig von Mises Institute, 2001), pp. 651–66.

IV.

With this backdrop of domestic state policies we can return to the problem
of immigration under statist conditions. It is now clear what state admission
implies. It does not merely imply centralized admission. By admitting
someone onto its territory, the state also permits this person to proceed
on public roads and lands to every domestic resident's doorsteps, to make
use of all public facilities and services (such as hospitals and schools),
and to access every commercial establishment, employment, and residential
housing, protected by a multitude of non-discrimination laws.[16]

Only one more element is missing in this reconstruction. Why would
immigration ever be a problem for a state? Who would want to migrate
from a natural order into a statist area? A statist area would tend to lose its
residents, especially its most productive subjects. It would be an attraction
only for potential state-welfare recipients (whose admission would only
further strengthen the emigration tendency). If anything, *emigration* is
a problem for a state. In fact, the institution of a State is a *cause* of emigration;
indeed, it is the most important or even the sole cause of modern *mass*
migrations (more powerful and devastating in its effects than any hurricane,
earthquake or flood and comparable only to the effects on migration of the
various ice ages).

What has been missing in this reconstruction is the assumption of
a multitude of states partitioning the entire globe (the absence of natural
orders anywhere). Then, as one state causes mass emigration, another state

---

16. "If every piece of land in a country were owned by some person, group or
corporation," elaborates Murray N. Rothbard,

> this would mean that no immigrant could enter unless invited to enter and
> allowed to rent or purchase property. A totally privatized country would
> be as closed as the particular inhabitants and property owners desire. It
> seems clear, then, that the regime of open borders that exists *de facto* in
> the U.S. really amounts to a compulsory opening by the central state, the
> state in charge of all streets and public land areas, and does not genuinely
> reflect the wishes of the proprietors. ("Nations by Consent: Decomposing
> the Nation-State," *Journal of Libertarian Studies* 11, no. 2 (1994): p. 7)

On U.S. immigration, see Peter Brimelow, *Alien Nation: Common Sense About America's
Immigration Disaster* (New York: Random House, 1995); George J. Borjas, *Friends or
Strangers: The Impact of Immigrants on the U.S. Economy* (New York: Basic Books, 1990);
idem, *Heaven's Door: Immigration Policy and the American Economy* (Princeton, N.J.:
Princeton University Press, 1999).

will be confronted with the problem of mass immigration; and the general direction of mass migration movements will be from territories where states exploit (legislatively expropriate and tax) their subjects more (and wealth accordingly tends to be lower) to territories where states exploit less (and wealth is higher).

We have finally arrived in the present, when the Western world—Western Europe, North America, and Australia—is faced with the specter of State-caused mass immigration from all over the rest of the world. What can be and is being done about this situation?

Out of sheer self-interest States will not adopt an "open border" policy. If they did, the influx of immigrants would quickly assume such proportions that the domestic state-welfare system would collapse. On the other hand, the Western welfare states do not prevent tens or even hundreds of thousands (and in the case of the United States well in excess of a million) of uninvited foreigners per year from entering and settling their territories. Moreover, as far as legal (rather than tolerated illegal) immigration is concerned, the Western welfare states have adopted a non-discriminatory "affirmative action" admission policy. That is, they set a maximum immigration target and then allot quotas to various emigration countries or regions, irrespective of how ethno-culturally similar or dissimilar such places and regions of origin are, thus further aggravating the problem of forced integration. As well, they typically allow an "open" (unspecified) number of "political asylum" seekers to enter—of government approved "victim" groups (to the exclusion of other, "politically incorrect" victims).[17]

---

17. Typically, it is easier for a certified "political" mass murderer, such as a socialist dictator, for instance, who has been overthrown by another, to gain entrance into Western countries than it is for the (his) "true" victims.

While he who qualifies as a victim changes with the political winds, a relative constant in Western asylum policy is the preference for Jewish immigration (at the exclusion of non-Jews). In the U.S., for instance, it has been a long-standing tradition that Jews from the former Soviet Union qualify as "victims," while regular Russians or Ukrainians do not. Not to be outdone, Germany currently accepts every Russian Jew who desires entrance, but excludes as non-victims all other Russians. Consequently, the demand for German asylum among Russian "Jews," two thirds of whom are supported entirely through "public" welfare, has risen to such a level that the Central Committee of Jews in Germany demanded of the German government (successfully) that applicants be "tested" for Jewishness. Essentially, the test is the same as that employed by the National Socialists in the infamous Nuremberg Race Laws of 1934 (while it is used to the opposite effect), which in turn was based on the official (self-acknowledged) religious strictures of orthodox

In light of the unpopularity of this policy, one might wonder about the motive for engaging in it. However, given the nature of the state it is not difficult to discover a rationale. States, as will be recalled, are also promoters of forced domestic integration. Forced integration is a means of breaking up all intermediate social institutions and hierarchies (in between the state and the individual) such as family, clan, tribe, community, and church and their internal layers and ranks of authority. Through forced integration individuals are isolated (atomized) and their power of resistance *vis-à-vis* the State is weakened.[18]

In the "logic" of the state, a hefty dose of foreign invasion, especially if it comes from strange and far-away places, is reckoned to further strengthen this tendency. And the present situation offers a particularly opportune time to do so, for in accordance with the inherently centralizing tendency of States and statism generally and promoted here and now in particular by the U.S. as the world's only remaining superpower, the Western world—or more precisely the neoconservative-social-democratic elites controlling the state governments in the U.S. and Western Europe—is committed to the establishment of supra-national states (such as the European Union) and ultimately one world state. National, regional or communal attachments are the main stumbling blocks on the way to this goal. A good measure of uninvited foreigners and government imposed multiculturalism is calculated to further weaken and ultimately destroy national, regional, and communal identities and thus promote the goal of a One World Order, led by the U.S., and a new "universal man."[19]

Judaism. Incidentally, Israel, which defines itself as "a Jewish State," practically prohibits all immigration by non-Jews (while allowing any Jew from anywhere, under the Law of Return, to enter Israel with full citizenship rights). Ninety-two percent of Israel's land is state-owned and regulated by the Jewish National Fund. According to its regulations, the right to reside, to open a business, and frequently also to work on this land is prohibited to anyone except Jews. While Jews may rent from non-Jews, non-Jews are prohibited from renting from Jews. See Israel Shahak, *Jewish History, Jewish Religion* (London: Pluto Press, 1994), esp. chap. 1.

18. See also Robert A. Nisbet, *Community and Power* (New York: Oxford University Press, 1962); idem, *Conservatism* (Minneapolis: University of Minnesota Press, 1986).

19. For a summary presentation of the neoconservative worldview, see Francis Fukuyama, *The End of History and the Last Man* (New York: Avon Books, 1993); for a critical assessment of the neoconservatives and their agenda, see Paul Gottfried, *The Conservative Movement* (New York: Twayne Publishers, 1993); idem, *After Liberalism* (Princeton, N.J.: Princeton University Press, 1999). For a brilliant literary treatment of the subject of mass immigration and the Western welfare state, see Jean Raspail, *The Camp of the Saints* (New York: Charles Scribner's Sons, 1975).

V.

What, if anything, can be done to spoil these statist designs and regain security and protection from invasion, whether domestic or foreign? Let us begin with a proposal made by the editors of the *Wall Street Journal*, the Cato Institute, the Foundation for Economic Education, and various left-libertarian writers of an open- or no-border policy—not because this proposal has any merit, but because it helps to elucidate what the problem is and what needs to be done to solve it.

It is not difficult to predict the consequences of an open border policy in the present world. If Switzerland, Austria, Germany or Italy, for instance, freely admitted everyone who made it to their borders and demanded entry, these countries would quickly be overrun by millions of third-world immigrants from Albania, Bangladesh, India, and Nigeria, for example. As the more perceptive open-border advocates realize, the domestic state-welfare programs and provisions would collapse as a consequence.[20] This would not be a reason for concern, for surely, in order to regain effective protection of person and property the welfare state must be abolished. But then there is the great leap—or the gaping hole—in the open border argument: out of the ruins of the democratic welfare states, we are led to believe, a new natural order will somehow emerge.

The first error in this line of reasoning can be readily identified. Once the welfare states have collapsed under their own weight, the masses of immigrants who have brought this about are still there. They have not been miraculously transformed into Swiss, Austrians, Bavarians or Lombards, but remain what they are: Zulus, Hindus, Ibos, Albanians, or Bangladeshis. Assimilation can work when the number of immigrants is small. It is entirely impossible, however, if immigration occurs on a mass scale. In that case, immigrants will simply transport their own ethno-culture onto the new territory. Accordingly, when the welfare state has imploded there will be a multitude of "little" (or not so little) Calcuttas, Daccas, Lagoses, and Tiranas strewn all over Switzerland, Austria, and Italy. It betrays a breathtaking sociological naiveté to believe that a natural order will emerge out of this admixture. Based on all historical experience with such forms of multiculturalism, it can safely be predicted that in fact the result will be civil war. There will be widespread plundering and squatterism leading to massive capital consumption, and civilization as we know it will disappear from

---

20. See, for instance, Walter Block, "A Libertarian Case for Free Immigration," *Journal of Libertarian Studies* 13, no. 2 (1998).

Switzerland, Austria and Italy. Furthermore, the host population will quickly be outbred and, ultimately, physically displaced by their "guests." There will still be Alps in Switzerland and Austria, but no Swiss or Austrians.[21]

However, the error in the open border proposal goes further than its dire consequences. The fundamental error of the proposal is moral or ethical in nature and lies in its underlying assumption that foreigners are "entitled," or have a "right," to immigrate. In fact, they have no such right whatsoever.

Foreigners would have a right to enter Switzerland, Austria or Italy only if these places were uninhabited (unowned) territories. However, they *are* owned, and no one has a right to enter territories that others own unless invited by the owner. Nor is it permissible to argue, as some open border proponents have done, that while foreigners may not enter *private* property without the owner's permission they may do so with *public*

---

21. Peter Brimelow, *Alien Nation*, pp. 124–27, has provided some recent evidence for the thesis that no multicultural state, and especially no democratic one, has ever worked peacefully for very long. Working back from the present, here is the evidence: *Eritrea*, ruled by Ethiopia since 1952, splits off in 1993; *Czechoslovakia*, founded in 1918, splits into Czech and Slovak ethnic components in 1993; the *Soviet Union* of 1917 splits into multiple ethnic components in 1991, and many of these components are threatened with further ethnic fragmentation; *Yugoslavia*, founded in 1918, splits into several ethnic components in 1991, and further breakup is still under way; *Lebanon*, founded in 1920, has effectively partitioned Christians and Muslims (under Syrian domination) since 1975; *Cyprus*, independent since 1960, effectively partitions Greek and Turkish territories in 1974; *Pakistan*, independent since 1947, ethnically distinct Bangladesh splits off in 1971; *Malaysia*, independent since 1963, Chinese-dominated Singapore is expelled in 1965. The list goes on with still unresolved cases: *India* and the Sikhs and Kashmiris; *Sri Lanka* and the Tamils; *Turkey*, *Iraq* and *Iran* and the Kurds; *Sudan* and *Chad* and the Arabs versus Blacks; *Nigeria* and the Ibos; *Ulster* and the Protestants versus the Catholics; *Belgium* and the Flemish versus the Walloons; *Italy* and the German-speaking South Tyrolians; *Canada* and the French versus the English; *Zimbabwe* and *South Africa* and Blacks versus Whites.

Yet, is not Switzerland, with an assemblage of Germans, French, Italians, and Romansh an exception? Hardly. All essential powers in Switzerland, in particular those determining educational and cultural matters (schools), are concentrated in the hands of the cantons rather than in those of the central government. And almost all of the twenty-six cantons and half-cantons are ethno-culturally homogeneous. Seventeen cantons are almost exclusively German; four cantons are almost exclusively French; and one canton is predominantly Italian. Only three cantons are bilingual, the Swiss ethno-cultural balance has been essentially stable, and there is only a limited amount of inter-cultural cantonal migration. Even given these favorable circumstances, Switzerland did experience an unsuccessful, violently suppressed war of secession, the Sonderbundskrieg of 1847. Furthermore, the creation of the new, breakaway French-speaking canton of Jura from the predominantly German canton of Berne in 1979 was preceded by years of terrorist activity.

property. In their eyes, public property is akin to unowned property and thus "open" to everyone, domestic citizen and foreigners alike.[22] However, this analogy between public property and unowned resources is wrong. There is a categorical difference between unowned resources (open frontier) and public property. Public property is the result of state-government confiscations—of legislative expropriations and/or taxation—of originally privately owned property. While the state does not *recognize* anyone as its private owner, all of government controlled public property has in fact been brought about by the tax-paying members of the domestic public. Austrians, Swiss, and Italians, in accordance with the amount of taxes paid by each citizen, have funded the Austrian, Swiss, and Italian public property. Hence, *they* must be considered its legitimate owners. Foreigners have not been subject to domestic taxation and expropriation; hence, they cannot claim any rights regarding Austrian, Swiss or Italian public property.

The recognition of the moral status of public property as expropriated private property is not just sufficient grounds for rejecting the open border proposal as a moral outrage. It is equally sufficient for combating the present semi-open "affirmative action" immigration policies of the Western welfare States.

Up to now, in the debate on immigration policy too much emphasis has been placed on consequentialist (utilitarian) arguments. Apologists of the *status quo* have argued that most immigrants work and become productive, so immigration contributes to a rising domestic standard of living. Critics have argued that the existing State-welfare institutions and provisions increasingly invite welfare-immigration, and they have warned that the only advantage of the current policies over the open border alternative is that the former will take decades until it ultimately leads to similarly dire effects, while the latter will produce such effects within years. As important as the resolution of these issues is, it is not decisive. The opposition against current immigration policies is ultimately independent of whether immigration will make per capita GDP (or similar statistical measures) rise or fall. It is a matter of justice: of right and wrong.

Understandably, the democratic welfare States try to conceal the *source* of public property (i.e., acts of expropriation). However, they do acknowledge that public property is "somehow" the property of their citizens and that

---

22. See, for instance, Block, "A Libertarian Case for Free Immigration."

they are the citizens' trustees in regard to public property. Indeed, the modern state's *legitimacy* is derived from its claim to protect its citizens and their property from domestic and foreign invaders, intruders, and trespassers. Regarding foreigners, this would require that the state act like the gatekeepers in private gated communities. The State would have to check every newcomer for an invitation and monitor his movement while en route to his final destination. Once it is made clear that the government actually tolerates or even promotes the intrusion and invasion of masses of aliens who by no stretch of the imagination can be deemed welcome or invited by domestic residents, this is or may become a threat to a government's legitimacy and exert enough pressure on it to adopt a more restrictive and discriminatory admission policy.[23]

---

23. Against many left-libertarian open border enthusiasts, it is incorrect to infer from the fact that an immigrant has found someone willing to employ him that his presence on a given territory must henceforth be considered "invited." Strictly speaking, this conclusion is true only if the employer also assumes the full costs associated with the importation of his immigrant-employee. This is the case under the much-maligned arrangement of a "factory town" owned and operated by a proprietor. Here, the full cost of employment, the cost of housing, healthcare, and all other amenities associated with the immigrant's presence, is paid for by the proprietor. No one else's property is involved in the immigrant-worker settlement. Less perfectly (and increasingly less so), this full-cost-principle of immigration is realized in Swiss immigration policy. In Switzerland immigration matters are decided on the local rather than federal government level, by the local owner-resident community in which the immigrant wants to reside. These owners are interested that the immigrant's presence in their community increase rather than decrease their property values. In places as attractive as Switzerland, this typically means that the immigrant (or his employer) is expected to buy his way into a community, which often requires multimillion-dollar donations.

Unfortunately, welfare states are not operated like factory towns or even Swiss communities. Under welfare-state conditions the immigrant employer must pay only a small fraction of the full costs associated with the immigrant's presence. He is permitted to socialize (externalize) a substantial part of such costs onto other property owners. Equipped with a work permit, the immigrant is allowed to make free use of every public facility: roads, parks, hospitals, schools, and no landlord, businessman, or private association is permitted to discriminate against him as regards housing, employment, accommodation, and association. That is, the immigrant comes invited with a substantial fringe benefits package paid for not (or only partially) by the immigrant employer (who allegedly has extended the invitation), but by other domestic proprietors as taxpayers who had no say in the invitation whatsoever. This is not an "invitation," as commonly understood. This is an imposition. It is like inviting immigrant workers to renovate one's own house while feeding them from other people's refrigerators. Consequently, because the cost of importing immigrant workers is lowered, more employer-sponsored immigrants will arrive

But this can only be the beginning; even if public opinion induced the state to adopt an immigration stance more in accordance with popular sentiments and justice, this fact would not change that the interests of private property owners and those of the State as a territorial monopolist of legislation and taxation are incompatible and in permanent conflict with each other. A State is a contradiction in terms: it is a property protector who may expropriate the property of the protected through legislation and taxation. Predictably, a State will be interested in maximizing its tax revenues and power (its range of legislative interference with private property rights) and disinterested in protecting anything except itself. What we experience in the area of immigration is only one aspect of a general problem. States are

---

than otherwise. Moreover, the character of the immigrant changes, too. While Swiss communities choose well-heeled, highly value-productive immigrants, whose presence enhances communal property values all-around, employers under democratic welfare-state conditions are permitted by state law to externalize their employment costs on others and tend to import increasingly cheap, low-skilled and low value-productive immigrants, regardless of their effect on all-around communal property values.

Theoretically bankrupt, the left-libertarian open border stance can be understood only psychologically. One source can be found in the Randian upbringing of many left-libertarians. Big businessmen-entrepreneurs are portrayed as "heroes" and, according to Ayn Rand in one of her more ridiculous statements, are viewed as the welfare state's "most severely persecuted minority." In this view (and untainted by any historical knowledge or experience), what can possibly be wrong with a businessman hiring an immigrant worker? In fact, as every historian knows, big businessmen are among the worst sinners against private property rights and the law of the market. Among other things, in an unholy alliance with the central state they have acquired the privilege of importing immigrant workers at other people's expense (just as they have acquired the privilege of exporting capital to other countries and being bailed out by taxpayers and the military when such investments turn sour).

A second motive for the open border enthusiasm among contemporary left-libertarians is their egalitarianism. They were initially drawn to libertarianism as juveniles because of its "anti-authoritarianism" (trust no authority) and seeming "tolerance," in particular toward "alternative"—non-bourgeois—lifestyles. As adults, they have been arrested in this phase of mental development. They express special "sensitivity" in every manner of discrimination and are not inhibited in using the power of the central state to impose non-discrimination or "civil rights" statutes on society. Consequently, by prohibiting other property owners from discrimination as they see fit, *they* are allowed to live at others' expense. They can indulge in their "alternative" lifestyle without having to pay the "normal" price for such conduct, i.e., discrimination and exclusion. To legitimize this course of action, they insist that one lifestyle is as good and acceptable as another. This leads first to multiculturalism, then to cultural relativism, and finally to "open borders." See further on this Hoppe, *Democracy: The God That Failed*, esp. chap. 10.

also supposed to protect their citizens from domestic intrusion and invasion, yet as we have seen, they actually disarm them, encircle them, tax them, and strip them of their right to exclusion, thus rendering them *helpless.*

Accordingly, the solution to the immigration problem is at the same time the solution to the general problem inherent in the institution of a State and of public property. It involves the return to a natural order by means of secession. To regain security from domestic and foreign intrusion and invasion, the central nation States will have to be broken up into their constituent parts. The Austrian and the Italian central States do not own Austrian and Italian public property; they are its citizens' trustees. Yet they do not protect them and their property. Hence, just as the Austrians and the Italians (and not foreigners) are the owners of Austria and Italy, so by extension of the same principle do the Carinthians and the Lombards (in accordance with individual tax payments) own Carinthia and Lombardy, and the Bergamese, Bergamo (and not the Viennese and the Roman governments).

In a decisive first step, individual provinces, regions, cities, towns and villages must declare their independence from Rome, Vienna, Berlin, Paris, and proclaim their status as "free territories." Extensive efforts by the central States to the contrary notwithstanding, strong provincial affiliations and attachments still exist in many regions, cities and villages all across Europe. It is vital to tap into these provincial and local sentiments in taking this first step. With every successive act of regional secession the power of the central State will be diminished. It will be stripped of more of its public property, its agents' range of access will increasingly be restricted, and its laws will apply in smaller and smaller territories, until it ultimately withers away.

However, it is essential to go beyond "political secession" to the *privatization* of property. After all, provincial and local political bodies (governments) have no more right to provincial property than the central government had to national property. The secession process must proceed further. Provincial or communal public property: roads, parks, government buildings, schools, courthouses, etc., must be returned to their genuine *private* owners and owner associations. Who owns what share of provincial or communal property? In principle, each owns according to his (compulsory) contribution to this property! In the case in which private property was expropriated by local government for purposes of "eminent domain," the property is simply returned to its original owner. As for the rest (and most) of public property, tradable property shares should be distributed among community members in accordance with their individual tax-payments. Every public road, park, school, etc., was funded by taxpayers; hence, local taxpayers, in accordance with their tax payments, should be awarded local public property.[24] This has a twofold implication. First, some residents have paid more taxes than others, so it is only natural and just that the former should be awarded more shares than the latter. Second and more specifically, some residents will be excluded altogether from receiving public property shares. For one, welfare recipients should be excluded. Presumably, they have paid no taxes but lived instead on taxes paid by others. Hence, they cannot claim any ownership share in public property. Likewise, all government officials and civil servants must be excluded from receiving ownership shares in public property, for their net (after tax) salary has been paid out of taxes paid by others. Just like welfare recipients, civil servants have not been tax-*payers* but tax-*consumers*. Hence, they too have no claim to communal property.[25]

With the central state withered away and the privatization of public property complete, the right to exclusion inherent in private property and essential for personal security and protection is returned into the hands of a multitude of independent private decision-making units. Immigration once again becomes a micro-phenomenon and disappears as a social "problem."

---

24. It should be emphasized that the distributed property shares must be *tradable* in order to constitute genuine *private* property. On the one hand, the tradability of shares makes it possible that people can cash-in (sell) their property. Not everyone has the patience and is willing to assume the risk associated with the ownership of capital goods. On the other hand, by the same token tradability makes it possible that the shares can be bought and put to productive use by capitalist-entrepreneurs who do have the requisite patience and are willing to assume the associated risk (of profit *and* loss).

25. To be sure, a number of complications would arise with this privatization strategy. In order to determine the ownership shares granted to various individuals in buildings and structures currently owned by federal, regional, and local governments, these individuals would have to provide documentation of their past payments of federal, regional and local taxes respectively, and in each case past welfare payments received must be deducted from taxes paid in order to arrive at a figure for the amount of net taxes paid. In a fully privatized market society, the task of finding a detailed solution to this problem would be typically assumed by private accountants, lawyers, and arbitration agencies, financed directly or indirectly, for a contingency fee, by the individual claimants.

7

The Case for Free Trade and
Restricted Immigration

It is frequently maintained that "free trade" belongs to "free immigration" as "protectionism" does to "restricted immigration." That is, the claim is made that while it is not impossible that someone might combine protectionism with free immigration, or free trade with restricted immigration, these positions are intellectually inconsistent, and thus erroneous. Hence, insofar as people seek to avoid errors, they should be the exception rather than the rule. The facts, to the extent that they have a bearing on the issue, appear to be consistent with this claim. As the 1996 Republican presidential primaries indicated, for instance, most professed free traders are advocates of relatively (even if not totally) free and nondiscriminatory immigration policies, while most protectionists are proponents of highly restrictive and selective immigration policies.

Appearances to the contrary notwithstanding, I will argue that this thesis and its implicit claim are fundamentally mistaken. In particular, I will demonstrate that free trade and restricted immigration are not only perfectly consistent but even mutually reinforcing policies. That is, it is not the advocates of free trade and restricted immigration who are wrong, but rather the proponents of free trade and free immigration. In thus taking the "intellectual guilt" out of the free-trade-and-restricted-immigration position and putting it where it actually belongs, I hope to promote a change in the present state of public opinion and facilitate substantial political realignment.

I. THE CASE FOR FREE TRADE

Since the days of Ricardo, the case for free trade has been logically unassailable. For the sake of argumentative completeness, it would be useful to briefly

---

• Originally published in *Journal of Libertarian Studies* 13, no. 2 (1998).

summarize it. The restatement will be in the form of a *reductio ad absurdum* of the protectionist thesis as proposed most recently by Pat Buchanan.

The central argument advanced in favor of protectionism is one of domestic job protection. How can American producers who pay their workers $10 per hour possibly compete with Mexican producers paying $1 or less per hour? They cannot, and American jobs will be lost unless import tariffs are imposed to insulate the American wages from Mexican competition. Free trade is possible only between countries that have equal wage rates, and thus that compete "on a level playing field." As long as this is not the case—as with the U.S. and Mexico—the playing field must be made level by means of tariffs. As for the consequences of a policy of domestic job protection, Buchanan and other protectionists claim that it will lead to domestic strength and prosperity. In support of their claim, examples are cited of free-trade countries that lost their once-preeminent international economic position, such as 19th-century England, as well as of protectionist countries which gained such preeminence, such as 19th-century America.

This or any other alleged empirical proof of the protectionist thesis must be rejected out of hand as containing a *post hoc, ergo propter hoc* fallacy. The inference drawn from historical data is no more convincing than if one were to conclude from the observation that rich people consume more than poor people that it must be consumption that makes a person rich. Indeed, protectionists such as Buchanan characteristically fail to understand what is actually involved in defending their thesis. Any argument in favor of international protectionism is simultaneously an argument in favor of interregional and inter-local protectionism. Just as different wage rates exist between the U.S. and Mexico, Haiti, or China, for instance, such differences also exist between New York and Alabama, or between Manhattan, the Bronx, and Harlem. Thus, if it were true that international protectionism could make an entire nation prosperous and strong, it must also be true that interregional and inter-local protectionism could make regions and localities prosperous and strong. In fact, one may even go further. If the protectionist argument were right, it would amount to an indictment of all trade, and a defense of the thesis that everyone would be the most prosperous and strongest if he never traded with anyone else and remained in self-sufficient isolation. Certainly, in this case, no one would ever lose his job, and unemployment due to "unfair" competition would be reduced to zero. In thus deducing the ultimate implication of the protectionist argument, its complete absurdity is revealed, for such a "full-employment society" would not be prosperous and strong; it would be composed of people who, despite working from dawn to dusk, would be condemned to destitution, or even death from starvation.

International protectionism, while obviously less destructive than a policy of interpersonal or interregional protectionism, would result in precisely the same effect and constitute a sure recipe for America's further economic decline. To be sure, some American jobs and industries would be saved, but such savings would come at a price. The standard of living and the real income of the American consumers of foreign products would be forcibly reduced. The cost to all U.S. producers who employ the protected industry's products as their own input factors would be raised, and they would be rendered internationally less competitive. Moreover, what could foreigners do with the money they earned from their U.S. imports? They could either buy American goods, or they could leave it here and invest it, and if their imports were stopped or reduced, they would buy fewer American goods or invest smaller amounts. Hence, as a result of saving a few inefficient American jobs, a far greater number of efficient American jobs would be destroyed or prevented from coming into existence.

Thus, it is nonsense to claim that England lost its former preeminence because of its free-trade policies. It lost its position *despite* its free-trade policy, and *because* of the socialist policies, which later took hold. Likewise, it is nonsense to claim that the rise of the U.S. to economic preeminence in the course of the 19th century was due to its protectionist policies. The U.S. attained this position *despite* its protectionism, and *because* of its unrivaled internal laissez-faire policies. Indeed, America's current economic decline, which Buchanan wishes to reverse, is the result not of her alleged free-trade policies, but of the circumstance that America, in the course of the 20th century, has gradually adopted the same socialist policies that earlier ruined England.

II. TRADE AND IMMIGRATION

Given the case for free trade, we will now develop the case for immigration restrictions to be combined with free-trade policies. More specifically, we will build a successively stronger case for immigration restrictions: from the initial weak claim that free trade and immigration restrictions can be combined and do not exclude each other to the final strong claim that the principle underlying free trade actually requires such restrictions.

From the outset, it must be emphasized that not even the most restrictive immigration policy or the most exclusive form of segregationism has anything to do with a rejection of free trade and the adoption of protectionism. From the fact that one does not want to associate with or live in the neighborhood composed of Mexicans, Haitians, Chinese, Koreans, Germans, Catholics, Moslems, Hindus, etc., it does not follow that one does not want to trade with them from a distance. Moreover, even if it were the case that one's real income would rise as a result of immigration, it does not follow that immigration must be considered "good," for material wealth is not the only thing that counts. Rather, what constitutes "welfare" and "wealth" is *subjective*, and one might prefer lower material living standards and a greater distance from certain other people to higher material living standards and a smaller distance. It is precisely the absolute voluntariness of human association *and* separation—the absence of any form of forced integration—which makes peaceful relationships—free trade—between racially, ethnically, linguistically, religiously, or culturally distinct people possible.

The relationship between trade and migration is one of elastic substitutability (rather than rigid exclusivity): the more (or less) you have of one the less (or more) you need of the other. Other things being equal, businesses move to low wage areas, and labor moves to high wage areas, thus effecting a tendency toward the equalization of wage rates (for the same kind of labor) as well as the optimal localization of capital. With political borders separating high- from low-wage areas, and with national (nation-wide) trade and immigration policies in effect, these normal tendencies—of immigration and capital export—are weakened with free trade and strengthened with protectionism. As long as Mexican products—the products of a low-wage area—can freely enter a high-wage area such as the U.S., the incentive for Mexican people to move to the U.S. is reduced. In contrast, if Mexican products are prevented from entering the American market, the attraction for Mexican workers to move to the U.S. is increased. Similarly, when U.S. producers are free to buy from and sell to Mexican producers and consumers, capital exports from the U.S. to Mexico will be reduced; however, when U.S. producers are prevented from doing so, the attraction of moving production from the U.S. to Mexico is increased.

Similarly, as the *foreign* trade policy of the U.S. affects immigration, so does its *domestic* trade policy. Domestic free trade is what is typically referred to as *laissez-faire* capitalism. In other words, the national government follows a policy of non-interference with the voluntary transactions between domestic parties (citizens) regarding their private property. The government's policy is one of helping to protect its citizens and their private property from domestic aggression, damage, or fraud (exactly as in the case of foreign trade and aggression). If the U.S. followed strict domestic free-trade policies, immigration from low-wage regions such as Mexico would be reduced, while when it pursues "social welfare" policies, immigration from low-wage areas becomes more attractive.

III. "OPEN BORDERS," INVASION, AND FORCED INTEGRATION

Insofar as a high-wage area such as the U.S. engaged in unrestricted free trade, internationally as well as domestically, the immigration pressure from low-wage countries would be kept low or reduced, and hence, the question as to what to do about immigration would be less urgent. On the other hand, insofar as the U.S. engaged in protectionist policies against the products of low-wage areas and in welfare policies at home, immigration pressure would be kept high or even raised, and the immigration question would assume great importance in public debate.

Obviously, the world's major high-wage regions—North America and Western Europe—are presently in this latter situation, in which immigration has become an increasingly urgent public concern. In light of steadily mounting immigration pressure from the world's low-wage regions, three general strategies of dealing with immigration have been proposed: unconditional free immigration, conditional free immigration, and restrictive immigration. While our main concern will be with the latter two alternatives, a few observations regarding the unconditional free immigration position are appropriate, if only to illustrate the extent of its intellectual bankruptcy.

According to proponents of unconditional free immigration, the U.S. *qua* high-wage area would invariably benefit from free immigration; hence, it should enact a policy of open borders, regardless of any existing conditions, i.e., even if the U.S. were ensnarled in protectionism and domestic welfare. Yet surely, such a proposal strikes a reasonable person as fantastic. Assume that the U.S., or better still Switzerland, declared that there would no longer be any border controls, that anyone who could pay the fare might enter the country, and, as a resident then be entitled to every "normal" domestic welfare provision. Can there be any doubt how disastrous such an experiment would turn out in the present world? The U.S., and Switzerland even faster, would be overrun by millions of third-world immigrants, because life on and off American and Swiss public streets is comfortable compared to life in many areas of the third world. Welfare costs would skyrocket, and the strangled economy would disintegrate and collapse, as the subsistence fund—the stock of capital accumulated in and inherited from the past—was plundered. Civilization in the U.S. and Switzerland would vanish, just as it once did from Rome and Greece.

Since unconditional free immigration must be regarded as a prescription for national suicide, the typical position among free traders is the alternative of conditional free immigration. According to this view, the U.S. and Switzerland would have to first return to unrestricted free trade and abolish all tax-funded welfare programs, and only then should they open their borders to everyone who wanted to come. In the meantime, while the welfare state is still in place, immigration would have to be made subject to the condition that immigrants are excluded from domestic welfare entitlements.

While the error involved in this view is less obvious and the consequences less dramatic than those associated with the unconditional free immigration, the view is nonetheless erroneous and harmful. To be sure, the immigration pressure on Switzerland and the U.S. would be reduced if this proposal were followed, but it would not disappear. Indeed, with free-trade policies, both foreign and domestic, wage rates within Switzerland and the U.S. may further increase relative to those at other locations (with less enlightened economic policies). Hence, the attraction of both countries might even increase. In any event, some immigration pressure would remain, so some form of immigration policy would have to exist. Do the principles underlying free trade imply that this policy must be one of conditional "free immigration"? They do not. There is no analogy between free trade and free immigration, and restricted trade and restricted immigration. The phenomena of trade and immigration are different in a fundamental respect, and the meaning of "free" and "restricted" in conjunction with both terms is categorically different. People can move and migrate; goods and services, of themselves, cannot.

Put differently, while someone can migrate from one place to another without anyone else wanting him to do so, goods and services cannot be shipped from place to place unless both sender and receiver agree. Trivial as this distinction may appear, it has momentous consequences. For *free* in conjunction with trade then means trade by invitation of private households and firms only; and *restricted* trade does not mean protection of households and firms from uninvited goods or services, but invasion and abrogation of the right of private households and firms to extend or deny invitations to their own property. In contrast, *free* in conjunction with immigration does not mean immigration by invitation of individual households and firms, but unwanted invasion or forced integration; and *restricted* immigration actually means, or at least can mean, the protection of private households and firms from unwanted invasion and forced integration. Hence, in advocating free trade and restricted immigration, one follows the same principle: requiring an invitation for people as for goods and services.

In contrast, the advocate of free trade and free markets who adopts the (conditional) free immigration position is involved in intellectual inconsistency. Free trade and markets mean that private property owners may receive or send goods from and to other owners without government interference. The government stays inactive *vis-à-vis* the process of foreign and domestic trade, because a willing (paying) recipient exists for every good or service sent, and hence all locational changes, as the outcome of agreements between sender and receiver, must be deemed mutually beneficial. The government's sole function is that of maintaining the trading process (by protecting citizen and domestic property).

However, with respect to the movement of people, the same government will have to do more in order to fulfill its protective function than merely permit events to take their own course, because people, unlike products, possess a will and can migrate. Accordingly, population movements, unlike product shipments, are not *per se* mutually beneficial events because they are not always—necessarily and invariably—the result of an agreement between a specific receiver and sender. There can be shipments (immigrants) without willing domestic recipients. In this case, immigrants are foreign invaders, and immigration represents an act of invasion. Surely, a government's basic protective function includes the prevention of foreign invasions and the expulsion of foreign invaders. Just as surely then, in order to do so and subject immigrants to the same requirement as imports (of having been invited by domestic residents), this government cannot rightfully allow the kind of free immigration advocated by most free traders. Just imagine again that the

U.S. and Switzerland opened their borders to whomever wanted to come—provided only that immigrants be excluded from all welfare entitlements, which would be reserved for U.S. and Swiss citizens. Apart from the sociological problem of thus creating two distinct classes of domestic residents and thus causing severe social tensions, there is also little doubt about the outcome of this experiment in the present world. The result would be less drastic and less immediate than under the scenario of unconditional free immigration, but it too would amount to a massive foreign invasion and ultimately lead to the destruction of American and Swiss civilization. Thus, in order to fulfill its primary function as protector of its citizens and their domestic property, a high-wage-area government cannot follow an immigration policy of laissez-passer, but must engage in restrictive measures.

IV. THE ANARCHO-CAPITALIST MODEL

From the recognition that proponents of free trade and markets cannot advocate free immigration without falling into inconsistency and contradiction, and hence, that immigration must—logically—be restricted, it is but a small step to the further recognition of *how* it must be restricted. As a matter of fact, all high-wage-area governments presently restrict immigration in one way or another. Nowhere is immigration "free," unconditionally or conditionally. Yet the restrictions imposed on immigration by the U.S. and by Switzerland, for instance, are quite different. What restrictions *should* then exist? Or, more precisely, what immigration restrictions is a free trader and free marketeer logically compelled to uphold and promote? The guiding principle of a high-wage-area country's immigration policy follows from the insight that immigration, to be free in the same sense as trade is free, must be *invited immigration.* The details follow from the further elucidation and exemplification of the concept of invitation versus invasion and forced integration.

For this purpose, it is necessary to assume first, as a conceptual benchmark, the existence of what political philosophers have described as a private property anarchy, anarcho-capitalism, or ordered anarchy: all land is privately owned, including all streets, rivers, airports, harbors, etc. With respect to some pieces of land, the property title may be unrestricted, that is, the owner is permitted to do with his property whatever he pleases as long as he does not physically damage the property of others. With respect to other territories, the property title may be more or less restricted. As is currently the case in some developments, the owner may be bound by contractual limitations on what he can do with his property (restrictive covenants, voluntary zoning), which might include residential rather than commercial use, no buildings more than four stories high, no sale or rent to unmarried couples, smokers, or Germans, for instance.

Clearly, in this kind of society, there is no such thing as freedom of immigration, or an immigrant's right of way. What does exist is the freedom of independent private property owners to admit or exclude others from their own property in accordance with their own restricted or unrestricted property titles. Admission to some territories might be easy, while to others it might be nearly impossible. Moreover, admission to one party's property does not imply the "freedom to move around," unless other property owners have agreed to such movements. There will be as much immigration or non-immigration, inclusivity or exclusivity, desegregation or segregation, non-discrimination or discrimination as individual owners or owners associations desire.

The reason for citing the model of an anarcho-capitalist society is that by definition no such thing as forced integration (uninvited migration) is possible (permitted) within its framework. Under this scenario, no difference between the physical movement of goods and the migration of people exists. As every product movement reflects an underlying agreement between sender and receiver, so all movements of immigrants into and within an anarcho-capitalist society are the result of an agreement between the immigrant and one or a series of receiving domestic property owners. Hence, even if the anarcho-capitalist model is ultimately rejected—and if for realism's sake the existence of a government and of "public" (in addition to private) goods and property is assumed—it brings into clear relief what a government's immigration policy would have to be, if and insofar as this government derived its legitimacy from the sovereignty of the "people" and was viewed as the outgrowth of an agreement or "social contract" (as is the case with all modern, post-monarchical governments, of course). A "popular" government which assumed as its primary task the protection of its citizen and their property (the production of domestic security) would surely want to preserve, rather than abolish, this no-forced-integration feature of anarcho-capitalism!

In order to realize what this involves, it is necessary to explain how an anarcho-capitalist society is altered by the introduction of a government, and how this affects the immigration problem. Since in an anarcho-capitalist society there is no government, there is no clear-cut distinction between inlanders (domestic citizens) and foreigners. This distinction appears only with the establishment of a government. The territory over which a government's power extends then becomes inland, and everyone residing outside of this territory becomes a foreigner. State borders (and passports), as distinct from private property borders (and titles to property), come into existence, and immigration takes on a new meaning. Immigration becomes immigration by foreigners across state borders, and the decision as to whether or not a person should be admitted no longer rests exclusively with private property owners or associations of such owners but with the government *qua* domestic security producer. Now, if the government excludes a person while there exists a domestic resident who wants to admit this very person onto his property, the result is forced exclusion; and if the government admits a person while there exists no domestic resident who wants to have this person on his property, the result is forced integration.

Moreover, hand in hand with the institution of a government comes the institution of public property and goods, that is, of property and goods owned collectively by all domestic residents and controlled and administered by the government. The larger or smaller the amount of public-government ownership, the greater or lesser will be the potential problem of forced integration. Consider a socialist society like the former Soviet Union or East Germany, for example. All factors of production, including all land and natural resources, are publicly owned. Accordingly, if the government admits an uninvited immigrant, it potentially admits him to any place within the country; for without private land ownership, there exist no limitations on his internal migrations other than those decreed by government. Under socialism, therefore, forced integration can be spread everywhere and thus immensely intensified. (In fact, in the Soviet Union and East Germany, the government could quarter a stranger in someone else's private house or apartment. This measure—and the resulting high-powered forced integration—was justified by the "fact" that all private houses rested on public land.)

Socialist countries will not be high-wage areas, of course, or at least will not remain so for long. Their problem is not immigration but emigration pressure. The Soviet Union and East Germany prohibited emigration and killed people for trying to leave the country. However, the problem of the extension and intensification of forced integration persists outside of socialism. To be sure, in non-socialist countries such as the U.S.,

Switzerland, and the Federal Republic of Germany, which *are* favorite immigration destinations, a government-admitted immigrant could not move just anywhere. The immigrant's freedom of movement would be severely restricted by the extent of private property, and private land ownership in particular. Yet, by proceeding on public roads, or with public means of transportation, and in staying on public land and in public parks and buildings, an immigrant can potentially cross every domestic resident's path, even move into anyone's immediate neighborhood and practically land on his very doorsteps. The smaller the quantity of public property, the less acute the problem will be. But as long as there exists *any* public property, it cannot be entirely escaped.

V. Correction and Prevention

A popular government that wants to safeguard its citizens and their domestic property from forced integration and foreign invaders has two methods of doing so, a corrective and a preventive one. The corrective method is designed to ameliorate the effects of forced integration once the event has taken place (and the invaders are there). As indicated, to achieve this goal, the government must reduce the quantity of public property as much as possible. Moreover, whatever the mix of private and public property, the government must uphold—rather than criminalize—any private property owner's right to admit *and* exclude others from his property. If virtually all property is owned privately and the government assists in enforcing private ownership rights, then uninvited immigrants, even if they succeeded in entering the country, would not likely get much farther.

The more completely this corrective measure is carried out (the higher the degree of private ownership), the less there will be a need for protective measures, such as border defense. The cost of protection against foreign invaders along the U.S.–Mexico border, for instance, is comparatively high, because for long stretches no private property on the U.S. side exists. However, even if the cost of border protection can be lowered by means of privatization, it will not disappear as long as there are substantial income and wage differentials between high- and low-wage territories. Hence, in order to fulfill its basic protective function, a high-wage-area government must also be engaged in preventive measures. At all ports of entry and along its borders, the government, as trustee of its citizens, must check all newly arriving persons for an entrance ticket—a valid invitation by a domestic property owner—and everyone not in possession of such a ticket will have to be expelled at his own expense.

Valid invitations are contracts between one or more private domestic recipients, residential or commercial, and the arriving person. *Qua* contractual admission, the inviting party can dispose only of his own private property. Hence, the admission implies negatively—similarly to the scenario of conditional free immigration—that the immigrant is excluded from all publicly funded welfare. Positively, it implies that the receiving party assumes legal responsibility for the actions of his invitee for the duration of his stay. The invitor is held liable to the full extent of his property for any crimes the invitee commits against the person or property of any third party (as parents are held accountable for the crimes of their offspring as long as they are members of the parental household). This obligation, which implies practically speaking that inviters will have to carry liability insurance for all of their guests, ends once the invitee has left the country, or once another domestic property owner has assumed liability for the person in question (by admitting him onto his property).

The invitation may be private (personal) or commercial, temporally limited or unlimited, concerning only housing (accommodation, residency) or housing and employment (but there cannot be a valid contract involving only employment and no housing). In any case, however, as a contractual relationship, every invitation may be revoked or terminated by the inviter; and upon termination, the invitee—whether tourist, visiting businessman, or resident alien—will be required to leave the country (unless another resident citizen enters an invitation-contract with him).

The invitee may lose his legal status as a non-resident or resident alien, who is at all times subject to the potential risk of immediate expulsion, only upon acquiring citizenship. In accordance with the objective of making all immigration (as trade) invited-contractual, the fundamental requirement for citizenship is the acquisition of property ownership, or more precisely the ownership of real estate and residential property.

In contrast, it would be inconsistent with the very idea of invited migration to award citizenship according to the territorial principle, as in the U.S., whereby a child born to a non-resident or resident alien in a host country automatically acquires this country's citizenship. In fact, such a child acquires, as most other high-wage-area governments recognize, the citizenship of his parents. For the host country's government to grant this child citizenship instead involves the non-fulfillment of its basic protective function, and actually amounts to an invasive act perpetrated by the government against its own citizenry. Rather, becoming a citizen means acquiring the right to stay in a country permanently, and a permanent invitation cannot be secured other than by purchasing residential property from a citizen resident. Only by selling real estate to a foreigner does a citizen indicate that he agrees to a guest's permanent stay (and only if the immigrant has purchased and paid for real estate and residential housing in the host country will he assume a permanent interest in his new country's well-being and prosperity). Moreover, finding a citizen willing to sell residential property and being prepared and able to pay for it, although a necessary requirement for the acquisition of citizenship, may not also be sufficient. If and insofar as the domestic property in question is subject to restrictive covenants, the hurdles to be taken by a prospective citizen may be significantly higher. In Switzerland, for instance, citizenship requires that the sale of residential property to foreigners be ratified by a majority or even all directly affected local property owners.

VI. CONCLUSION

Judged by the immigration policy required to protect one's own citizens from foreign invasion and forced integration—and to render all international population movements invited and contractual migrations—the Swiss government does a significantly better job than the United States. It is more difficult to enter Switzerland as an uninvited person or to stay on as an uninvited alien. In particular, it is far more difficult for a foreigner to acquire citizenship, and the legal distinction between resident citizens and resident aliens is more clearly preserved. These differences notwithstanding, the governments of both Switzerland and the U.S. pursue immigration policies that must be deemed far too permissive.

Moreover, the excessive permissiveness of their immigration policies and the resulting exposure of the Swiss and American population to forced integration with foreigners is aggravated by the fact that the extent of public property in both countries (and other high-wage areas) is quite substantial; that tax-funded welfare provisions are high and growing, and foreigners are not excluded; and that contrary to official pronouncements, even the adherence to free-trade policies is anything but perfect. Accordingly, in Switzerland, the U.S., and most other high-wage areas, popular protests against immigration policies have grown increasingly louder.

It has been the purpose of this essay not only to make the case for the privatization of public property, domestic laissez faire, and international free trade, but in particular also for the adoption of a restrictive immigration policy. By demonstrating that free trade is inconsistent with (unconditionally or conditionally) free immigration, and that free trade requires instead that migration be subject to the condition of being invited and contractual, it is our hope to contribute to more enlightened future policies in this area.

Part Two

Money and the State

8

Why the State Demands the Control of Money

Imagine you are in command of the state, defined as an institution that possesses a territorial monopoly of ultimate decision-making in every case of conflict, including conflicts involving the state and its agents itself, and, by implication, the right to tax, i.e., to unilaterally determine the price that your subjects must pay you to perform the task of ultimate decision-making.

To act under these constraints—or rather, lack of constraints—is what constitutes politics and political action, and it should be clear from the outset that politics, then, by its very nature, always means mischief. Not from your point of view, of course, but mischief from the point of view of those subject to your rule as ultimate judge. Predictably, you will use your position to enrich yourself at other people's expense.

More specifically, we can predict in particular what your attitude and policy *vis-à-vis* money and banking will be.

Assume that you rule over a territory that has developed beyond the stage of a primitive barter economy and where a common medium of exchange, i.e., a money, is in use. First off, it is easy to see why you would be particularly interested in money and monetary affairs. As state ruler, you can in principle confiscate whatever you want and provide yourself with an unearned income. But rather than confiscating various producer or consumer goods, you will naturally prefer to confiscate money. Because money, as the most easily and widely saleable and acceptable good of all, allows you the greatest freedom to spend your income as you like, on the greatest variety of goods. First and foremost, then, the taxes you impose on society will be money taxes, whether on property or income. You will want to maximize your money-tax revenues.

• Originally published on *Mises Daily*, Mises.org, October 13, 2011.

In this attempt, however, you will quickly encounter some rather intractable difficulties. Eventually, your attempts to further increase your tax income will encounter resistance in that higher tax rates will not lead to higher but to lower tax revenue. Your income—your spending money— declines, because producers, burdened with increasingly higher tax rates, simply produce less.

In this situation, you only have one other option to further increase or at least maintain your current level of spending: by borrowing such funds. And for that you must go to banks—and hence your special interest also in banks and the banking industry. If you borrow money from banks, these banks will automatically take an active interest in your future well-being. They will want you to stay in business, i.e., they want the state to go on in its exploitation business. And since banks tend to be major players in society, such support is certainly beneficial to you. On the other hand, as a negative, if you borrow money from banks you are not only expected to pay your loan back, but to pay interest on top.

The question, then, that arises for you as the ruler is, How can I free myself of these two constraints, i.e., of tax-resistance in the form of falling tax revenue and of the need to borrow from and pay interest to banks?

It is not too difficult to see what the ultimate solution to your problem is. You can reach the desired independence of taxpayers and tax payments and of banks, if only you establish yourself first as a territorial monopolist of the production of money. On your territory, only you are permitted to produce money. But that is not sufficient. Because as long as money is a regular good that must be expensively produced, there is nothing in it for you except expenses. More importantly, then, you must use your monopoly position in order to lower the production cost and the quality of money as close as possible to zero. Instead of costly quality money such as gold or silver, you must see to it that worthless pieces of paper that can be produced at practically zero cost will become money. (Normally, no one would accept worthless pieces of paper as payment for anything. Pieces of paper are acceptable as payment only insofar as they are titles to something else, i.e., property titles. In other words then, you must replace pieces of paper that were titles to money with pieces of paper that are titles to nothing.)

Under competitive conditions, i.e., if everyone were free to produce money, a money that can be produced at almost zero cost would be produced up to a quantity where marginal revenue equals marginal cost, and because marginal cost is zero the marginal revenue, i.e., the purchasing power of this money, would be zero as well. Hence, the necessity to monopolize the production of paper money, so as to restrict its supply, in order to avoid hyperinflationary conditions and the disappearance of money from the market altogether (and a flight into "real values")—and the more so the cheaper the money commodity.

In a way, you have thus accomplished what all alchemists and their sponsors wanted to achieve: you have produced something valuable (money with purchasing power) out of something practically worthless. What an achievement. It costs you practically nothing and you can turn around and buy yourself something really valuable, such as a house or a Mercedes; and you can achieve these wonders not just for yourself but also for your friends and acquaintances, of which you discover that you have all of a sudden far more than you used to have (including many economists, who explain why your monopoly is really good for everyone).

What are the effects? First and foremost, more paper money does not in the slightest affect the quantity or quality of all other, nonmonetary goods. There exist just as many other goods around as before. This immediately refutes the notion—apparently held by most if not all mainstream economists —that "more" money can somehow increase "social wealth." To believe this, as everyone proposing a so-called easy-money policy as an efficient and "socially responsible" way out of economic troubles apparently does, is to believe in magic: that stones—or rather paper—can be turned into bread.

Rather, what the additional money you printed will effect is twofold. On the one hand, money prices will be higher than they would otherwise be, and the purchasing power per unit of money will be lower. In a word, the result will be *inflation*. More importantly, however, all the while the greater amount of money does not increase (or decrease) the total amount of presently existing social wealth (the total quantity of all goods in society), it redistributes the existing wealth in favor of you and your friends and acquaintances, i.e., those who get your money first. You and your friends are relatively enriched (own a larger part of the total social wealth) at the expense of impoverishing others (who as a result own less).

The problem, for you and your friends, with this institutional setup is not that it doesn't work. It works perfectly, always to your own (and your friends') advantage and always at the expense of others. All you have to do is to avoid hyperinflation. For in that case people would avoid using money and flee into real values, thus robbing you of your magic wand. The problem with your paper-money monopoly, if there is one at all, is only that this fact will be immediately noticed also by others and recognized as the big, criminal rip-off that it indeed is.

But this problem can be overcome, too, if, in addition to monopolizing the production of money, you also set yourself up as a banker and enter the banking business with the establishment of a central bank.

Because you can create paper money out of thin air, you can also create credit out of thin air. In fact, because you can create credit out of nothing (without any savings on your part), you can offer loans at cheaper rates than anyone else, even at an interest rate as low as zero (or even at a negative rate). With this ability, not only is your former dependency on banks and the banking industry eliminated; you can, moreover, make banks dependent on you, and you can forge a permanent alliance and complicity between banks and state. You don't even have to become involved in the business of investing the credit yourself. That task, and the risk involved in it, you can safely leave to commercial banks. What you, your central bank, need to do is only this: You create credit out of thin air and then loan this money, at below-market interest rates, to commercial banks. Instead of you paying interest to banks, banks now pay interest to you. And the banks in turn loan out your newly created easy credit to their business friends at somewhat higher but still submarket interest rates (to earn from the interest differential). In addition, to make the banks especially keen on working with you, you may permit the banks to create a certain amount of their own new credit (of checkbook money) in addition and on top of the credit that you have created (fractional-reserve banking).

What are the consequences of this monetary policy? To a large extent they are the same as with an easy money policy: First, an easy credit policy is also inflationary. More money is brought into circulation and prices will be higher, and the purchasing power of money lower, than would have been the case otherwise. Second, the credit expansion too has no effect on the quantity or quality of all goods currently in existence. It neither increases nor decreases their amount. More money is just this: more paper. It does not and cannot increase social wealth by one iota. Third, easy credit also engenders a systematic redistribution of social wealth in favor of you, the central bank, and the commercial banks within your cartel. You receive an interest return on money that you have created at practically zero cost out of thin air (instead of on money costly saved out of an existing income), and so do the banks, who earn additional interest on your costless money loans. Both you and your banker friends thereby appropriate an "unearned income." You and the banks are enriched at the expense of all "real" money savers (who receive a lower interest return than they otherwise would, i.e., without the injection of your and the banks' cheap credit into the credit market).

On the other hand, there also exists a fundamental difference between an easy, print-and-spend money policy and an easy, print-and-loan credit policy.

First off, an easy credit policy changes the production structure—what is produced and by whom—in a highly significant way.

You, the chief of the central bank, can create credit out of thin air. You do not have to first save money out of your money income, i.e., cut your own expenses, and thus abstain from buying certain non-money goods (as every normal person must, if he extends credit to someone). You only have to turn on the printing press and can thus undercut any interest rate demanded of borrowers by savers elsewhere in the market. Granting credit does not involve any sacrifice on your part (which is why this institution is so "nice"). If things then go well, you will be paid a positive-interest return on your paper investment, and if they don't go well—well, as the monopoly producer of money, you can always make up losses more easily than anyone else: by covering your losses with even more printed paper.

Without costs and no genuine, personal risk of losses, then, you can grant credit essentially indiscriminately, to everyone and for any purpose, without concern for the creditworthiness of the debtor or the soundness of his business plan. Because of your "easy" credit, certain people (in particular investment bankers) who otherwise would not be deemed sufficiently credit-worthy, and certain projects (in particular of banks and their main clients) that would not be considered profitable but wasteful or too risky instead do get credit and do get funded.

Essentially, the same applies to the commercial banks within your banking cartel. Because of their special relationship to you, as the first recipients of your costless low-interest paper-money credit, the banks, too, can offer loans to prospective lenders at interest rates below market interest rates—and if things go well for them they go well; and if they don't, they can rely on you, as the monopolistic producer of money, to bail them out in the same way as you bail yourself out of any financial trouble: by more paper money. Accordingly, the banks too will be less discriminating in the selection of their clients and their business plans and more prone to funding the "wrong" people and the "wrong" projects.

And there is a second significant difference between a print-and-spend and a print-and-loan policy and this difference explains why the income and wealth redistribution in your and your banker friends' favor that is set in motion by easy credit takes the specific form of a temporal—boom–bust—cycle, i.e., of an initial phase of seeming general prosperity (of expected increases in future incomes and wealth) followed by a phase of widespread impoverishment (when the prosperity of the boom period is revealed as a widespread illusion).

This boom–bust feature is the logical—and physically necessary—consequence of credit created out of thin air, of credit un-backed by savings, of fiduciary credit (or however else you may call it) and of the fact that every investment takes time and only shows later on, at some time in the future, whether it is successful or not.

The reason for the business cycle is as elementary as it is fundamental. Robinson Crusoe can give a loan of fish (which he has not consumed) to Friday. Friday can convert these savings into a fishing net (he can eat the fish while constructing the net), and with the help of the net, then, Friday, in principle, is capable of repaying his loan to Robinson, plus interest, and still earn a profit of additional fish for himself. But this is physically impossible if Robinson's loan is only a paper note, denominated in fish, but un-backed by real fish savings, i.e., if Robinson has no fish because he has consumed them all.

Then, and necessarily so, Friday must fail in his investment endeavor. In a simple barter economy, of course, this becomes immediately apparent. Friday will not accept Robinson's paper credit in the first place (but only real, commodity credit), and because of this, the boom–bust cycle will not get started. But in a complex monetary economy, the fact that credit was created out of thin air is not noticeable: every credit note looks like any other, and because of this the notes are accepted by the takers of credit.

This does not change the fundamental fact of reality that nothing can be produced out of nothing and that investment projects undertaken without any real funding whatsoever (by savings) must fail, but it explains why a boom—an increased level of investment accompanied by the expectation of higher future income and wealth—can get started (Friday does accept the note instead of immediately refusing it). And it explains why it then takes a while until the physical reality reasserts itself and reveals such expectations as illusory.

But what's a little crisis to you? Even if your path to riches is through repeated crises, brought about by your paper-money regime and central-bank policies, from your point of view—from the viewpoint as the head of state and chief of the central bank—this form of print-and-loan wealth redistribution in your own and your banker friends' favor, while less immediate than that achieved with a simple print-and-spend policy, is still much preferable, because it is far more difficult to see through and recognize for what it is. Rather than coming across as a plain fraud and parasite, in pursuing an easy-credit policy you can even pretend that you are engaged in the selfless task of "investing in the future" (rather than spending on present frivolities) and "healing" economic crises (rather than causing them).

What a world we live in!

9

Entrepreneurship with Fiat Property and Fiat Money

Let me begin with a brief description of what a capitalist-entrepreneur does, and then explain how the job of the capitalist-entrepreneur is changed under statist conditions.

What the capitalist does is this: He saves (or borrows saved funds), hires labor, buys or rents capital goods and land, and he buys raw materials. Then he proceeds to produce his product or service, whatever it may be, and he hopes that he will make a profit.

Profits are defined simply as an excess of sales revenue over the costs of production. The costs of production, however, do not determine the revenue. If the cost of production determined price and revenue, everyone could be a capitalist. No one would ever fail. Rather, it is anticipated prices and revenues that determine what production costs the capitalist can possibly afford.

The capitalist does not know what the future prices will be or what quantity of his product will be bought at such prices. This depends on the consumers, and the capitalist has no control over them. The capitalist must speculate what the future demand for his products will be, and he can go wrong in his speculation, in which case he does not make profits but will incur losses instead.

To risk your own money in anticipation of an uncertain future demand is obviously a difficult task. Great profits may await you, but so also may total financial ruin. Few people are willing to take this risk, and even fewer are good at it and stay in business for any length of time.

In fact, there is even more to be said about the difficulty of being a capitalist.

• A speech delivered at the Edelweiss Holdings Symposium held in Zurich, Switzerland, on September 17, 2011.

Every capitalist stands in permanent competition with every other one for the invariably limited amounts of money to be spent on their goods and services by consumers. Every product competes with every other product. Whenever consumers spend more (or less) on one thing, they must spend less (or more) on another. Even if a capitalist has produced a successful product and earned a profit, there is nothing that guarantees that this will go on. Other businessmen can imitate his product, produce it more cheaply, underbid his price and out compete him. To prevent this, every capitalist must thus continuously strive to lower his production costs. Yet even trying to produce whatever you produce ever more cheaply is not enough.

The set of products offered by various capitalists is in constant flux, and so is the evaluation of these products by consumers. Continuously new or improved products are offered on the market and consumer tastes constantly change. Nothing remains constant. The uncertainty of the future facing every capitalist never disappears. There is always the lure of profits but also the threat of losses. Again, then, it is very difficult to be continuously successful as a businessman and not to sink back to the rank of an employee.

In all of this there is only one thing that the businessman can count on and take for granted, and that is his real, physical property—and even that is not safe, as we will see.

His real property comes in two forms. First, there are the physical resources, the means of production, including labor services, that the capitalist has bought or rented for some time and that he combines in order to produce whatever he produces. The value of all of these items is variable, as already explained. It depends ultimately on consumer evaluations. What is stable about them is only their physical character and capability. But without this physical stability of his productive property the capitalist could not produce what he produces.

Second, besides his productive property, the capitalist can count on his ownership of real money. Money is neither a consumer good nor a producer good. It is the common medium of exchange. As such, it is the most easily and widely sold good. And it is used as the unit of account. In order to calculate profit and loss, the capitalist needs recourse to money. The input factors and the output, his products to be produced, are incommensurable, like apples and oranges. They are made commensurable only insofar as they can all be expressed in terms of money. Without money, economic calculation is impossible, as Ludwig von Mises above all has explained. The value of money, too, is variable, like the value of everything else. But money, too, has physical characteristics. It is commodity money, such as gold or silver, and money profits are reflected in an increase in the supply of this commodity, gold or silver, at the disposal of the capitalist.

What can be said, then, about both the capitalist's means of production and his money, is this: their physical characteristics do not determine their value, but without their physical characteristics, they would have no value at all, and changes in the physical quality and quantity of his property do affect the value of his property, whatever other factors (such as changing consumer evaluations) may affect the value of his property also.

Now let me introduce the state and see how it affects the business of the capitalist.

The state is conventionally defined as an institution that possesses a territorial monopoly of ultimate decision-making in every case of conflict, including conflicts involving the state and its agents, and, by implication, the right to tax—i.e., to unilaterally determine the price that its subjects must pay to perform the task of ultimate decision-making.

To act under these constraints—or rather, lack of constraints—is what constitutes politics and political action, and it should be clear from the outset that politics, then, by its very nature, always means mischief.

More specifically, we can make two interrelated predictions as to the effect of a state on the business of business. First, and most fundamentally, under statist conditions real property will become what may be called fiat property. And secondly and more specifically, real money will be turned into fiat money.

First, with the state being the ultimate arbiter in every case of conflict including those in which it is involved itself, the state has essentially become the ultimate owner of all property. In principle, it can provoke a conflict with a businessman and then decide against him by expropriating him and making itself (or someone of its liking) the owner of the businessman's physical property. Or else, if it doesn't want to go as far, it can pass legislation or regulations that involve only a partial expropriation. It can restrict the uses that the businessman can make of his physical property. Certain things the businessman is no longer permitted to do with his property.

The state cannot increase the quality and quantity of real property. But it can redistribute it as it sees fit. It can reduce the real property at the disposal of businessmen or it can limit the range of control that they are allowed over their property; and it can thereby increase its own property (or that of its allies) and increase its own range of control over existing physical things.

The businessmen's property, then, is their property in name only. It is granted to them by the state, and it exists only as long as the state does not decide otherwise. Constantly, the sword of Damocles is hanging over the heads of businessmen. The execution of their business plans is based on their assumption of the existence, at their disposal, of certain physical resources and their physical capabilities, and all of their value speculations are based on this physical basis being given. But these assumptions about the physical basis can be rendered incorrect at any time—and their value calculations vitiated as well —if only the state decides to change its current legislation and regulations.

The existence of a state, then, heightens the uncertainty facing the businessman. It makes the future less certain than would be the case otherwise. Realizing this, many people who might otherwise become businessmen will not become businessmen at all. And many businessmen will see their business plans spoiled—not because they did not correctly anticipate future consumer demand, but because the physical basis, on which their plan was based, was altered by some unexpected and unanticipated change in state laws and regulations.

Second, rather than meddling with a businessman's productive capital through confiscation and regulation, however, the state prefers to meddle with money. Because money is the most easily and widely salable good, it allows the state operators the greatest freedom to spend their income as they like. Hence the state's preference for money taxes, i.e., for confiscating money income and money profits. Real money becomes subject to confiscation and changing rates of confiscation. This is the first sense in which money becomes fiat money under statist conditions. People own their money only insofar as the state allows them to keep it.

But there is also a second, even more perfidious, way in which money becomes fiat money under statist conditions.

States everywhere have discovered an even smoother way of enriching themselves at the expense of productive people: by monopolizing the production of money and replacing real, commodity money and commodity credit with genuine fiat money and fiat or fiduciary credit.

On its territory, per legislation, only the state is permitted to produce money. But that is not sufficient. For as long as money is a real good, i.e., a commodity that is costly to produce, there is nothing in it for the state except expenses. More importantly, then, the state must use its monopoly position in order to lower the production cost and the quality of money as close as possible to zero. Instead of costly, quality money such as gold or silver, the state must see to it that worthless pieces of paper, which can be produced at practically zero cost, will become money.

Under competitive conditions—i.e., if everyone is free to produce money—a money that can be produced at zero cost would be produced up to a quantity where marginal revenue equals marginal cost. And since marginal cost is zero, the marginal revenue, i.e., the purchasing power of this money, would be zero as well. Hence, the necessity to monopolize the production of paper money, so as to be able to restrict its supply, in order to avoid hyperinflationary conditions and the disappearance of money from the market altogether (and a flight into "real values")—and the more so the cheaper the money commodity.

Having monopolized the production of money and reduced its production cost and quality to virtually zero, the state has made a marvelous accomplishment. It costs almost nothing to print money and one can turn around and buy oneself something really valuable, such as a house or a Mercedes.

What are the effects of such fiat money, and in particular what are the effects for the business of business? First and in general, more paper money does not in the slightest affect the quantity or quality of all other, nonmonetary goods. Rather, what the additional money does is twofold. On the one hand, money prices will be higher than they would otherwise be and the purchasing power per unit of money will be lower. And secondly, with the injection of additional paper money existing wealth will be redistributed in favor of those receiving and spending the new money first and at the expense of those receiving and spending it later or last.

And specifically regarding the capitalist, then, paper money adds another dose of uncertainty to his business. If and as long as money is a commodity, such as gold or silver, it may not be exactly "easy" to predict the future supply and purchasing power of money. However, based on information about current production costs and industry profits, it is very well possible to come up with a realistic estimate. In any case, the task is not pure guesswork. And while it is conceivable that, with gold or silver as money, nominal money profits may not always equal "real" profits, it is at least impossible that a nominal profit should ever amount to nothing at all. There is always something left: quantities of gold or silver.

In distinct contrast, with paper money, the production of which is unconstrained by any kind of natural (physical) limitations (scarcity) but dependent solely on subjective whim and will, the prediction of the future money supply and purchasing power does become guesswork. What will the money printers do? And it is not just conceivable but a very real possibility that nominal money profits will turn out to represent literally nothing but bundles of worthless paper.

Moreover, hand in hand with fiat money comes fiat or fiduciary credit, and this creates still more uncertainty.

If the state can create money out of thin air it also can create money credit out of thin air. And because it can create credit out of thin air, i.e., without any previous savings on its part, it can offer cheaper loans than anyone else, at below-market rates of interest, even at rates as low as zero. The interest rate is thus distorted and falsified, and the volume of investment will become divorced from the volume of savings. Systematic mal-investment is thus generated, i.e., investment un-backed by savings. An unsustainable investment boom is set in motion, necessarily followed by a bust, revealing large-scale clusters of entrepreneurial errors.

Last but not least, under statist conditions, i.e., under a regime of fiat property and fiat money, the character of businessmen and of doing business is changed, and this change introduces another hazard into the world.

Absent a state, it is consumers that determine what will be produced, in what quality and quantity, and who among businessmen will succeed or fail. With the state, the situation facing businessmen becomes entirely different. It is now the state and its operators, not consumers, who ultimately decide who will succeed or fail. The state can keep any businessman alive by subsidizing him or bailing him out; or else it can ruin anyone by deciding to investigate him and find him in violation of state laws and regulations.

Moreover, the state is flush with taxes and fiat money and can spend more money than anyone else. It can make any businessman rich (or not). And the state and its operators have a different spending behavior than normal consumers. They do not spend their own money, but other people's money, and in most cases not for their own, personal purposes, but for those of some anonymous third parties. Accordingly, they are frivolous and wasteful in their spending. Neither the price nor the quality of what they buy is of great concern to them.

In addition, the state can go into business itself. And because it doesn't have to make profits and avoid losses, as it can always supplement its earnings through taxes or made-up money, it can always outcompete any private producer of the same or similar goods or services.

And finally, by virtue of its ability to legislate, to make laws, the state can grant exclusive privileges to some businesses, insulating or shielding them from competition, and by the same token partially expropriate and disadvantage other businesses.

In this environment, it is imperative for every businessman to pay constant and close attention to politics. In order to stay alive and possibly prosper, he must spend time and effort to concern himself with matters that have nothing to do with satisfying consumers, but with power politics. And based on his understanding of the nature of the state and of politics, then, he must make a choice: a moral choice.

He can either join in and become a part of the vast criminal enterprise that is the state. He can bribe politicians, political parties or public officials, whether with cash or in kind (including promises of future employment in the "private" sector as "board-members," "advisors," or "consultants"), in order to gain for himself economic advantages at the expense of other businesses. That is, he can pay bribes to secure state contracts or subsidies for himself and at the exclusion of others. Or he can pay bribes for the passing or maintenance of legislation that secures him and his business legal privileges and monopoly profits (and capital gains) while partially expropriating and thus screwing his competitors. Needless to say, countless businessmen have chosen this path. In particular big banking and big industry have thus become intricately involved in the state, and many a wealthy businessman has made his fortune more on account of his political skills than his abilities as a consumer-serving economic entrepreneur.

Or else, a businessman can choose the honorable but at the same time also the most difficult path. This businessman is aware of the nature of the state. He knows that the state and its operators are out to get him and bully him, to confiscate his property and money and, even worse, that they are arrogant, self-righteous, haughty, and full of themselves. Based on such understanding, this very different breed of businessman then tries his best to anticipate and adjust to the state's every evil move. But he does not join the gang. He does not pay bribes to secure contracts or privileges from the state. Instead, he tries as well as he can to defend whatever is still left of his property and property rights and make as large profits as possible in doing so.

10

The Yield from Money Held

Franz Cuhel occupies an honored place in the history of economic thought
and of the "Viennese" or "Austrian" School of economics in particular. In his
book *Zur Lehre von den Bedürfnissen* (1907), Cuhel presented for the first
time a strictly ordinal interpretation of marginal utility and thus contributed
to a systematic advance of pure economic theory. Since this lecture is named
in Cuhel's honor, I felt it appropriate that I, too, should discuss here a purely
theoretical problem of economics. My subject is not the general theory of
value, however, but, more specifically, the theory of money.

I have chosen the title of my lecture after a famous article by William H.
Hutt, "The Yield from Money Held."[1] Like Hutt, I want to attack the
following notion: that money held in cash balances and deposit accounts
is somehow "unproductive," "barren," or "sterile," offering a "yield of nil";
that only consumer goods and producer (investment) goods are productive of
human welfare; that the only productive use of money lies in its "circulation,"
i.e., in its spending on consumer or producer goods; and that the holding, i.e.,
the not-spending, of money diminishes future consumption and production.

This view is extremely popular within the economics profession and
outside. Hutt offers many examples of its proponents. I will offer only
two here. The first is John Maynard Keynes. One famous quote from his
General Theory will suffice for my purpose: "An act of individual saving," by
which Keynes means cash holding or "hoarding" instead of consumption or
investment spending,

> means—so to speak—a decision not to have dinner today. But it
> does not necessitate a decision to have dinner or buy a pair of boots

---

• The Franz Cuhel Memorial Lecture, Prague, April 24, 2009.

1. William H. Hutt, "The Yield from Money Held," in M. Sennholz, ed., *Freedom
and Free Enterprise: Essays in Honor of Ludwig von Mises* (Chicago: Van Nostrand, 1956),
pp. 196–216.

a week hence or a year hence or to consume any specified thing
at any specified date. Thus it depresses the business of preparing
today's dinner without stimulating the business of making ready for
some future act of consumption. It is not a substitution of future
consumption-demand for present consumption-demand—it is a net
diminution of such demand.[2]

Here it is: the holding of money, i.e., the not-spending of it on
either consumer or investment goods, is unproductive, indeed detrimental.
According to Keynes, the government or its central bank must create and
then spend the money that "savers," i.e., the holders of cash balances, are
unproductively holding back, so as to stimulate both consumption and
investment. (Needless to say, this is precisely what governments and central
banks are presently doing to supposedly rectify the current economic crisis.)

The second example is from closer to home, i.e., from the proponents
of "free banking" such as Lawrence White, George Selgin, and Roger
Garrison. According to them, an (unanticipated) increase in the demand for
money "pushes the economy below its potential" (Garrison), and requires
a compensating money-spending injection from the banking system.

Here it is again: an "excess demand for money" (Selgin and White)
has no positive yield or is even detrimental; hence, help is needed. For the
free bankers help is not supposed to come from the government and its
central bank, but from a system of freely competing fractional-reserve banks.
However, the idea involved is the same: the holding of (some "excess") money
is unproductive and requires a remedy.[3]

I do not want to engage in a textual critique of Keynes or the "free
bankers" here. I only mentioned them to further elucidate the idea that
I want to attack, and to indicate how widespread—and consequential—its
acceptance is within the economics profession, both inside and outside
Keynesian circles. Unlike Hutt, who proceeds "critically" in his article, i.e.,
through a textual examination of various authors, and arrives at his own
contrary view of the (positive) yield from money held in a rather indirect and

---

2. John Maynard Keynes, *The General Theory of Employment, Interest, and Money*
(New York: Harcourt, Brace, and World, 1964), p. 210.

3. Roger Garrison, "Central Banking, Free Banking, and Financial Crises," *Review of
Austrian Economics* 9, no. 2 (1996): p. 117; George Selgin and Lawrence White, "In Defense
of Fiduciary Media," *Review of Austrian Economics* 9, no. 2 (1996): pp. 100–101.

circumstantial way, I want to proceed "apodictically": by way of a positive demonstration of money's unique productivity.[4]

The first natural response to the thesis that money held in or added to cash balances is unproductive is to counter, Why, then, if money held in or added to cash balances is unproductive of human welfare, do people hold them or add to them? If cash holdings are indeed "good for nothing," no one would hold or add to them—and yet almost everyone does so all the time! And since all money is always held or hoarded by someone—when it "circulates," it only leaves one holding hand to be passed into another—money must be *continuously* "good for something" all the while it is being held (which is always).

To understand what this "good for something" of money is, it is best to ask, When, under what conditions, would there be *no* demand for cash holdings? Interestingly, wide agreement exists within the economics profession on the answer. It has been most lucidly stated by Ludwig von Mises. No money, and no demand for cash balances, would exist in "general equilibrium," or as Mises calls it, within the imaginary construction of an "evenly rotating economy." In this construction, all uncertainty is by assumption removed from human action. Everyone knows precisely the terms, times, and locations of every future action, and accordingly all exchanges can be prearranged and take the form of direct exchanges.

Writes Mises,

> In a system without change in which there is no uncertainty whatever about the future, nobody needs to hold cash. Every individual knows precisely what amount of money he will need at any future date. He is therefore in a position to lend all the funds he receives in such a way that the loans fall due on the date he will need them.[5]

---

4. For a detailed critique of Keynes see Hans-Hermann Hoppe, "Theory of Employment, Money, Interest, and the Capitalist Process: The Misesian Case Against Keynes," in idem, *The Economics and Ethics of Private Property* (Boston: Kluwer Academic Publishers, 1993); for a detailed critique of the free banking doctrine see idem, "How is Fiat Money Possible?" *Review of Austrian Economics* 7, no. 2 (1994); and idem, "Against Fiduciary Media," *Quarterly Journal of Austrian Economics* 1, no. 1 (1998). These articles are collected in Hans-Hermann Hoppe, *The Economics and Ethics of Private Property*, 2nd ed. (Auburn, Ala.: Ludwig von Mises Institute, 2006).

5. Ludwig von Mises, *Human Action: A Treatise on Economics* (Chicago: Regnery, 1966), p. 249.

Based on this fundamental insight, we can state as a first provisional conclusion concerning the positive theory of money that money and cash balances would disappear with the disappearance of uncertainty (never) and, *mutatis mutandis*, that the investment in money balances must be conceived of as an investment in certainty or an investment in the reduction of subjectively felt uneasiness about uncertainty.

In reality, outside the imaginary construction of an evenly rotating economy, uncertainty exists. The terms, times, and locations of all future actions and exchanges cannot be predicted perfectly (with certitude). Action is by nature speculative and subject to error. Presently unpredictable surprises can occur. Whenever double coincidences of wants between pairs of prospective buyers and sellers are absent, for instance, i.e., when one does not want what the other has to sell or vice versa, any direct trade (exchange) becomes impossible.

Faced with this challenge of unpredictable contingencies, man can come to value goods on account of their degree of marketability (rather than their use-value for him as consumer or producer goods) and consider trading also whenever a good to be acquired is more marketable than that to be surrendered, such that its possession would facilitate the future acquisition of other directly or indirectly serviceable goods and services. That is, a demand for *media of exchange* can arise, i.e., a demand for goods valued on account of their marketability or re-salability.

And since a more easily and widely resalable good is preferable to a less easily and widely resalable good as a medium of exchange, "there would be," as Mises writes,

> an inevitable tendency for the less marketable of a series of goods used as media of exchange to be one by one rejected until at last only a single commodity remained, which was universally employed as a medium of exchange; in a word, money.[6]

While this brief reconstruction of the origin of money is familiar, insufficient attention has been drawn to the fact that, as the most easily and widely salable good, money is at the same time the most universally *present* — *instantly* serviceable — good (which is why the interest rate, i.e., the discount rate of future goods against present goods, is expressed in terms

---

6. Ludwig von Mises, *Theory of Money and Credit* (Irvington, N.Y.: Foundation for Economic Education, 1971), pp. 32–33.

of money) and, as such, the good uniquely suited to alleviate presently felt uneasiness about uncertainty.

Because money can be employed for the *instant satisfaction of the widest range of possible needs*, it provides its owner with the best humanly possible protection against uncertainty. In holding money, its owner gains in the satisfaction of being able to meet instantly, as they unpredictably arise, the widest range of future contingencies. The investment in cash balances is an investment contra the (subjectively felt) aversion to uncertainty. A larger cash balance brings more relief from uncertainty aversion.

The term *uncertainty aversion* is meant here in its technical sense, as opposed to risk aversion. The categorical distinction between *uncertainty* on the one hand and *risk* on the other was introduced into economics by Frank H. Knight and further elaborated on by Ludwig von Mises with his distinction between *case probability* and *class probability*.[7]

Risks (instances of class probability) are contingencies against which it is possible to take out insurance, because objective long-run probability distributions concerning all possible outcomes are known and predictable. We know nothing about an individual outcome, but we know everything about the whole class of events, and we are *certain* about the future.

Insofar as man faces a risky future, then, he does not need to hold cash. To satisfy his desire to be protected against risk, he can buy or produce insurance. The sum of money that he spends on insurance is an indication of the height of his aversion to risk. Insurance premiums are money *spent*, not held, and are as such invested in the physical production structure of producer and consumer goods. The payment of insurance reflects a man's subjectively felt *certainty* concerning (predictable) future contingencies (risks).

In distinct contrast, insofar as man faces *un*certainty he is, quite literally, *not* certain concerning future contingencies, i.e., as to what he might want or need and when. In order to be protected against unpredictable contingencies at unpredictable moments, he cannot invest in producer goods (as in the case of risk insurance); for such investments would reflect his *certainty* concerning particular future needs.

---

7. Frank H. Knight, *Risk, Uncertainty and Profit* (Chicago: University of Chicago Press, 1971); Ludwig von Mises, *Human Action*, chap. VI. See also Hans-Hermann Hoppe, "The Limits of Numerical Probability," *Quarterly Journal of Austrian Economics* 10, no. 1 (2007), reprinted chapter 15 herein; and idem; "On Certainty and Uncertainty," *Review of Austrian Economics* 10, no. 1 (1997).

Only *present*, instantly serviceable goods can protect against unpredictable contingencies (uncertainty). Nor does a man want to invest in consumer goods for uncertainty protection. For an investment in consumer goods, too, is an expression of certainty concerning specific momentary or immediately impending wants. Only money, on account of its instant and unspecific wide-ranging salability, can protect him against uncertainty. Thus, just as insurance premiums are the price paid for protection against risk aversion, so cash holdings are the price paid for protection against uncertainty aversion.

To the extent that a man feels certain regarding his future needs, he will invest in consumer or producer goods. To invest in money balances is to invest neither in consumer goods nor producer goods. Unlike consumer and producer goods, which are used up in consumption or production, money is neither used up through its use as a medium of exchange nor transformed into another commodity. To invest in cash balances means, "I am uncertain about my present and future needs and believe that a balance of the most easily and widely saleable good on hand will best prepare me to meet my as-of-yet unknown needs at as-of-yet unknown times."

If a person then adds to his cash balance, he does so because he is confronted with a situation of (subjectively perceived) increased uncertainty regarding his future. The addition to his cash balance represents an investment in presently felt certainty *vis-à-vis* a future perceived as less certain. In order to add to his cash balance, a person must restrict his purchases or increase his sales of non-money goods (producer or consumer goods). In either case, the outcome is an immediate fall in certain non-money goods' prices. As the result of restricting his purchases of *x*, *y*, or *z*, the money price of *x*, *y*, or *z* will be lowered (as compared to what it would have been otherwise), and likewise, by increasing his sales of *a*, *b*, or *c*, their prices will fall.

The actor thus accomplishes exactly and immediately what he wants. He commands a larger (nominal and real) cash balance and is better prepared for an increasingly uncertain future. The marginal utility of the added cash is higher than (ranks above) the marginal utility of the non-money goods sold or un-bought. He is better off with more cash on hand and less non-money goods, otherwise he would not have reallocated his assets in this way. There is more investment in the removal of perceived uncertainty, and there is less investment in needs, present or future, considered as certain.

The situation does not change if there is a *general* increase in the demand for money, i.e., if all or most people try to increase their cash holdings, in response to heightened uncertainty. With the total quantity of money given, the average size of cash holdings cannot increase, of course. Nor is the total quantity of producer and consumer goods that make up the physical production structure affected by a general increase in the demand for money. It remains unchanged.

In generally striving to increase the size of their cash holdings, however, the money prices of non-money goods will be bid down, and the purchasing power per unit of money will correspondingly rise. Thus, the (increased) demand for and the (given) supply of money are equilibrated again, but at a higher purchasing power per unit of money and lower prices of non-money goods. That is, even if nominal cash balances cannot rise as a result of a general increase in the demand for money, the *real* value of cash balances can; and it is this increase in the value of real cash balances that brings about precisely and immediately the effect desired: being better prepared for a future deemed as less certain.

No one cares about the nominal number of money units in his possession. Rather, people want to keep cash with a definite amount of purchasing power on hand. If the purchasing power per unit of money increases as the result of an increased demand for cash holdings, each unit of money confronted with an array of generally lower non-money goods prices can do a better job in affording its owner protection against uncertainty.

This shall suffice as my attempt to provide a positive demonstration of the unique productivity of cash holdings as "yielders of certainty" in an uncertain world. Only a brief additional comment concerning the present, unprecedentedly severe economic crisis and the consequences that our theoretical considerations imply for its solution seems to be in order.

I shall say nothing here about the cause of the present crisis, except that I consider it another, spectacular vindication of the so-called Austrian — or "Mises–Hayek"—business-cycle theory. In any case, the crisis has led to heightened uncertainty. People want more certainty *vis-à-vis* a future considered far less certain than before. Accordingly, their demand for cash increases. With the quantity of money given, the higher demand for money can be satisfied only by bidding down non-money goods' prices. Consequently, as the overall "level" of prices falls, the purchasing power per unit of money correspondingly rises. Each unit of money is productive now of more certainty, and the desired level of uncertainty protection is restored. The crisis is ended.

The solution to the crisis suggested instead by most economists and pundits and officially adopted by governments everywhere is entirely different. It is motivated by the here-criticized, fundamentally flawed doctrine that money held in or added to cash balances is money unproductively withheld from production and consumption. The additions to their cash holdings that people want to bring about are thus interpreted, wrongly, as a diminution of human welfare. Accordingly, huge efforts are now undertaken to increase the amount of spending.

But this stands at cross-purpose to the general public's needs and desires: in order to be better protected against heightened perceived uncertainty, prices must fall and the purchasing power of money must rise. Yet with an influx of additional, newly created money, prices will be higher and the purchasing power per unit of money will be lower than otherwise. Thus, as the result of the current monetary policy, the restoration of the desired level of uncertainty protection will be *delayed* and the crisis *prolonged*.

11

State or Private-Law Society?

I. The Problem of Social Order

Alone on his island, Robinson Crusoe can do whatever he pleases. For him, the question concerning rules of orderly human conduct—social cooperation—simply does not arise. This question can only arise once a second person, Friday, arrives on the island. Yet even then, the question remains largely irrelevant so long as no *scarcity* exists. Suppose the island is the Garden of Eden. All external goods are available in superabundance. They are "free goods," just as the air that we breathe is normally a "free" good. Whatever Crusoe does with these goods, his actions have no repercussions— *neither* with respect to his own future supply of such goods *nor* regarding the present or future supply of the same goods for Friday (and vice versa). Hence, it is impossible that a conflict concerning the use of such goods could arise between Crusoe and Friday. A conflict is possible only if goods are scarce; and only then is there a need to formulate rules that make orderly, conflict-free social cooperation possible.

In the Garden of Eden only two scarce goods exist: a person's physical body and its standing room. Crusoe and Friday each have only one body and can stand only at one place at a time. Hence, even in the Garden of Eden conflicts between Crusoe and Friday can arise: Crusoe and Friday cannot occupy the same standing room simultaneously without coming into physical conflict with each other. Accordingly, even in the Garden of Eden rules of orderly social conduct must exist—rules regarding the proper location and movement of human bodies. Outside the Garden of Eden, in the realm of all-around scarcity, there must be rules that regulate the use not only of personal

---

• A speech given at the Ludwig von Mises Institute Brazil, 2011.

159

bodies, but of *everything* scarce, such that *all* possible conflicts can be ruled out. This is the problem of social order.

II. THE SOLUTION: THE IDEA OF PRIVATE PROPERTY

In the history of social and political thought, myriad proposals have been offered as solutions to the problem of social order, and this multitude of mutually incompatible proposals has contributed to the widespread belief that the search for a single "correct" solution is futile and illusory. Yet a correct solution does exist. There is no reason to succumb to moral relativism. Indeed, the solution to the problem of social order has been known for hundreds of years. The solution is the idea of private property.

Let me formulate the solution first for the special case represented by the Garden of Eden and subsequently for the general case represented by the *real* world of all-around scarcity.

In the Garden of Eden, the solution is provided by the simple rule stipulating that everyone may place or move his own body wherever he pleases, *provided only that no one else is already standing there and occupying the same space.*

Outside of the Garden of Eden, in the realm of all-around scarcity, the solution is provided by four logically interrelated rules:

1. Every person is the private (exclusive) owner of his own physical body. Indeed, who else, if not Crusoe, should be the owner of Crusoe's body? Friday? Or Crusoe and Friday jointly? Yet that would not help *avoid* conflict. Rather, it would *create* conflict and make it permanent.

2. Every person is the private owner of all nature-given goods that he has perceived as scarce and put to use by means of his body, *before* any other person. Again, who else, if not the first user, should be their owner? The second user? Or the first and the second user jointly? Yet such rulings again would be contrary to the very purpose of norms: of helping to avoid conflict, rather than to create it.

3. Every person who, with the help of his body and his originally appropriated goods, produces new products thereby becomes the proper owner of these products, provided only that in the process of production he does not physically damage the goods owned by another person.

4. Once a good has been first appropriated or produced, ownership in it can be acquired only by means of a voluntary, contractual transfer of its property title from a previous to a later owner.

I can spare myself here the task of providing a detailed ethical as well as economic justification of these rules. This has been done elsewhere. However, a few statements in this connection are in order.

Contrary to the frequently heard claim that the institution of private property is only a *convention*, it must be categorically stated: a convention serves a *purpose, and* it is something to which an *alternative* exists. The Latin alphabet, for instance, serves the purpose of written communication and there exists an alternative to it, the Cyrillic alphabet. That is why it is referred to as a convention.

What, however, is the purpose of action norms? If no interpersonal conflict existed—that is: if, due to a prestabilized harmony of all interests, no situation ever arose in which two or more people wanted to use one and the same good in incompatible ways—then no norms would be needed. It is the purpose of norms to help avoid otherwise unavoidable conflict. A norm that generates conflict rather than helping to avoid it is *contrary to the very purpose of norms*. It is a dysfunctional norm or a perversion.

With regard to the purpose of conflict avoidance, however, the institution of private property is definitely *not* just a convention, because no alternative to it exists. Only private (exclusive) property makes it possible that all otherwise unavoidable conflicts can be avoided. And only the principle of property acquisition through acts of original appropriation, performed by specific individuals at a specific time and location, makes it possible to avoid conflict *from the beginning of mankind* onward, because only the *first* appropriation of some previously un-appropriated good can be conflict-free—simply, because —*per definitionem*—no one else had any previous dealings with the good.

III. The Enforcement of Social Order and the Protection of Private Property: The State

As important as this insight is—that the institution of private property, ultimately grounded in acts of original appropriation, is without alternative given the desideratum of conflict avoidance (peace)—it is not sufficient to *establish* social order. For even if everyone knows how conflict can be avoided, it is still possible that people simply do not want to avoid conflict, because they expect to benefit from it at the expense of others.

In fact, as long as mankind is what it is, there will always exist murderers, robbers, thieves, thugs and con artists, i.e., people *not* acting in accordance with the above-mentioned rules. Hence, every social order, if it is to be successfully maintained, requires institutions and mechanisms designed to keep such rule breakers in check. How to accomplish this task, and by whom?

The standard reply to this question is to say that this task, i.e., the enforcement of law and order, is the first and primary duty—indeed, the *raison d'être*—of the *state*. In particular, this is the answer also given by classical liberals such as my own intellectual master, Ludwig von Mises. Whether or not this answer is correct depends on how "state" is defined.

The state, according to the standard definition, is not a regular, specialized firm. Rather, it is defined as an agency characterized by two unique, logically connected features. First, the state is an agency that exercises a territorial monopoly of ultimate decision-making. That is, the state is the ultimate arbiter in every case of conflict, including conflicts involving itself. It allows no appeal above and beyond itself. Second, the state is an agency that exercises a territorial monopoly of taxation. That is, it is an agency that unilaterally fixes the price that private citizens must pay for the state's service as ultimate judge and enforcer of law and order.

IV. The Fundamental Error of "Statism"

As widespread as the standard view regarding the necessity of the institution of a state as the provider of law and order is, it stands in clear contradiction to elementary economic and moral laws and principles.

First of all, among economists and philosophers two near-universally accepted propositions exist:

1. Every "monopoly" is "bad" from the viewpoint of consumers. Monopoly is here understood in its classic meaning as an exclusive *privilege* granted to a single producer of a commodity or service, or as the absence of "free entry" into a particular line of production. Only one agency, A, may produce a given good or service, X. Such a monopoly is "bad" for consumers, because, shielded from potential new entrants into a given area of production, the price of the product will be higher and its quality lower than otherwise, under free competition.

2. The production of law and order, i.e., of security, is the primary function of the state (as just defined). Security is here understood in the wide sense adopted in the American Declaration of Independence: as the protection of life, property, and the pursuit of happiness from domestic violence (crime) as well as external (foreign) aggression (war).

Both propositions are apparently incompatible with each other. This has rarely caused concern among philosophers and economists, however, and in so far as it has, the typical reaction has been one of taking exception to the first proposition rather than the second. Yet there exist fundamental theoretical reasons (and mountains of empirical evidence) that it is indeed the second proposition that is in error.

As a territorial monopolist of ultimate decision-making and law enforcement, the state is not just like any other monopoly, such as a milk or a car monopoly that produces milk and cars of comparatively lower quality and higher prices. In contrast to all other monopolists, the state not only produces inferior goods, but "bads" (non-goods). In fact, it must first produce bads (such as taxes) before it can produce anything that might be considered a (inferior) good.

If an agency is the ultimate judge in every case of conflict, then it is also judge in all conflicts involving itself. Consequently, instead of merely preventing and resolving conflict, a monopolist of ultimate decision-making will also *cause and provoke* conflict in order to settle it to his own advantage. That is, if one can only appeal to the state for justice, justice will be perverted in the favor of the state, constitutions and supreme courts notwithstanding.

These constitutions and courts are *state* constitutions and courts, and whatever limitations on state action they may set or find are invariably determined by agents of the very same institution under consideration. Predictably, the definition of property and protection will be continually altered and the range of jurisdiction expanded to the state's advantage. The idea of some "given" eternal and immutable law that must be *discovered* will disappear and be replaced by the idea of law as *legislation*—as arbitrary, state-*made* law.

Moreover, as ultimate judge the state is also a monopolist of taxation, i.e., it can unilaterally, without the consent of everyone affected, determine the price that its subjects must pay for the state's provision of (perverted) law. However, a tax-funded life-and-property protection agency is a contradiction in terms: an expropriating property protector. Motivated, as everyone is, by self-interest and the disutility of labor, but equipped with the unique power to tax, state agents will invariably strive to *maximize expenditures* on protection—and almost all of a nation's wealth can conceivably be consumed by the cost of protection—and at the same time to *minimize the actual production* of protection. The more money one can spend and the less one must work for it, the better off one will be.

V. THE ERROR COMPOUNDED: THE DEMOCRATIC STATE

Apart from the fundamental error of statism generally, additional errors are involved in the special case of a *democratic* state. A detailed treatment of this subject has been provided elsewhere, but a brief mention is indicated.

The traditional, pre-modern state form is that of a (absolute) monarchy. Yet monarchy was faulted, in particular also by classical liberals, for being incompatible with the basic principle of "equality before the law." Monarchy instead rested on personal *privilege*. Thus, the critics of monarchy argued, the monarchical state had to be replaced by a democratic one. In opening participation and entry into state government to everyone on equal terms, not just to a hereditary class of nobles, it was thought that the principle of the equality of all before the law had been satisfied.

However, this democratic equality before the law is something entirely different from and incompatible with the idea of *one* universal law, equally applicable to everyone, everywhere, and at all times. In fact, the former objectionable schism and inequality of a higher law of kings versus a subordinate law of ordinary subjects is fully preserved under democracy in the separation of "public" versus "private" law and the supremacy of the former over the latter.

Under democracy, everyone is equal insofar as entry into government is open to all on equal terms. Everyone can become king, so to say, not only a privileged circle of people. Thus, in a democracy no *personal* privileges or privileged persons exist. However, *functional* privileges and privileged functions exist. Public officials, as long as they act in an official capacity, are governed and protected by public law and occupy thereby a privileged position *vis-à-vis* persons acting under the mere authority of private law.

In particular, public officials are permitted to finance or subsidize their own activities through taxes. That is, they do not, as every private-law subject must, earn their income through the production and subsequent sale of goods and services to voluntarily buying or not-buying consumers. Rather, as public officials, they are permitted to engage in, and live off, what in private dealings between private-law subjects is considered "theft" and "stolen loot." Thus, privilege and legal discrimination—and the distinction between rulers and subjects—will not disappear under democracy. To the contrary. Rather than being restricted to princes and nobles, under democracy, privileges will be available to all: everyone can engage in theft and live off stolen loot if only he becomes a public official.

Predictably, then, under democratic conditions the tendency of every monopoly of ultimate decision-making to increase the price of justice and to lower its quality and substitute injustice for justice and is not diminished but aggravated. As hereditary monopolist, a king or prince regards the territory and people under his jurisdiction as his personal property and engages in the monopolistic exploitation of his "property."

Under democracy, monopoly and monopolistic exploitation do not disappear. Rather, what happens with democracy is this: instead of a prince and a nobility who regard the country as their private property, a temporary and interchangeable caretaker is put in monopolistic charge of the country. The caretaker does not own the country, but as long as he is in office he is permitted to use it to his and his protégés' advantage. He owns its current use—*usufruct*—but not its capital stock. This does not eliminate exploitation. To the contrary, it makes exploitation less calculating and carried out with little or no regard to the capital stock. Exploitation becomes shortsighted and capital consumption will be systematically promoted.

VI. THE SOLUTION: PRIVATE-LAW SOCIETY INSTEAD OF STATE

If the state, and especially the democratic state, is demonstrably incapable of creating and maintaining social order; if, instead of helping avoid conflict, the state is the source of permanent conflict; and if, rather than assuring legal security and predictability, the state itself continuously generates insecurity and unpredictability through its legislation and replaces constant law with "flexible" and arbitrary whim, then inescapably the question as to the correct—obviously, non-statist—solution to the problem of social order arises.

The solution is a *private-law society*, i.e., a society in which every individual and institution is subject to one and the same set of laws. No public law granting privileges to specific persons or functions (and no public property) exists in this society. There is only private law (and private property), equally applicable to each and everyone. No one is permitted to acquire property by any means other than through original appropriation, production, or voluntary exchange, and no one possesses a privilege to tax and expropriate. Moreover, in a private-law society no one is permitted to prohibit anyone else from using his property in order to enter any line of production he wishes and compete against whomever he pleases.

Specifically regarding the problem at hand: in a private-law society the production of security—of law and order—will be undertaken by freely financed individuals and agencies competing for a voluntarily paying (or not-paying) clientele, just as the production of all other goods and services.

It would be presumptuous to predict the precise shape and form of the security industry emerging within the framework of a private-law society. However, it is not difficult to predict a few central changes that would fundamentally—and favorably—distinguish a competitive security industry from the present, all-too-well-known statist production of (in)justice and (dis)order.

First, while in a complex society based on the division of labor *self*-defense will play only a secondary role (for reasons yet to be explained), it should be emphasized from the outset that in a private-law society everyone's right to defend oneself from aggression against one's person and property is entirely undisputed. In distinct contrast to the present, statist practice, which renders people increasingly unarmed and defenseless against aggressors, in a private-law society no restrictions on the private ownership of firearms and other weapons exist. Everyone's elementary right to engage in self-defense to protect his life and property against invaders would be sacrosanct, and as one knows from the experience of *The Not So Wild, Wild West*, as well as numerous recent empirical investigations into the relationship between the frequency of gun ownership and crime rates, more guns imply less crime.

Just as in today's complex economy we do not produce our own shoes, suits, and telephones, however, but partake in the advantages of the division of labor, so it is to be expected that we will also do so when it comes to production of security, especially the more property a person owns and the richer a society as a whole. Hence, most security services will without doubt be provided by specialized agencies competing for voluntarily paying clients: by various private police, insurance, and arbitration agencies.

If one wanted to summarize in one word the decisive difference and advantage of a competitive security industry as compared to the current statist practice, it would be this: *contract*. The state, as ultimate decision-maker and judge, operates in a contract-less legal vacuum. There exists no contract between the state and its citizens. It is not contractually fixed, what is actually owned by whom, and what, accordingly, is to be protected. It is not fixed, what service the state is to provide, what is to happen if the state fails in its duty, nor what the price is that the "customer" of such "service" must pay.

Rather, the state unilaterally fixes the rules of the game and can change them, per legislation, during the game. Obviously, such behavior is inconceivable for freely financed security providers. Just imagine a security provider, whether police, insurer, or arbitrator, whose offer consisted in something like this:

> I will not contractually guarantee you anything. I will not tell you what specific things I will regard as your to-be-protected property, nor will I tell you what I oblige myself to do if, according to your opinion, I do not fulfill my service to you—but in any case, I reserve the right to unilaterally determine the price that you must pay me for such undefined service.

Any such security provider would immediately disappear from the market due to a complete lack of customers. Each private, freely financed security producer instead must offer its prospective clients a *contract*. And these contracts must, in order to appear acceptable to voluntarily paying consumers, contain clear property descriptions as well as clearly defined mutual services and obligations. Moreover, each party to a contract, for the duration or until the fulfillment of the contract, would be bound by its terms and conditions; and every change of terms or conditions would require the unanimous consent of all parties concerned.

Specifically, in order to appear acceptable to security buyers, these contracts must contain provisions about what will be done in the case of a conflict or dispute between the protector or insurer and his own protected or insured clients as well as in the case of a conflict between different protectors or insurers and their respective clients. And in this regard only one mutually agreeable solution exists: in these cases the conflicting parties contractually agree to arbitration by a mutually trusted but independent *third party*.

And as for this third party, it too is freely financed and stands in competition with other arbitrators or arbitration agencies. Its clients, i.e., the insurers and the insured, expect of it that it come up with a verdict that is recognized as fair and just by all sides. Only arbitrators capable of forming such judgments will succeed in the arbitration market. Arbitrators incapable of this and viewed as biased or partial will disappear from the market.

From this fundamental advantage of a private-law society all other advantages follow.

First, competition among police, insurers, and arbitrators for paying clients would bring about a tendency toward a continuous fall in the price of protection (per insured value), thus rendering protection increasingly more affordable, whereas under monopolistic conditions the price of protection will steadily rise and become increasingly unaffordable.

Furthermore, as already indicated, protection and security are goods and services that compete with others. If more resources are allocated to protection, fewer can be expended on cars, vacations, food, or drink, for example. Also, resources allocated to the protection of group A (people living along the Pacific, for instance) compete with resources expended on the protection of group B (people living along the Atlantic).

The state, as a tax-funded protection monopolist, will necessarily allocate resources arbitrarily. There will be overproduction (or underproduction) of security as compared to other competing goods and services, and there will be over-protection of some individuals, groups, or regions and under-protection of others.

In distinct contrast, in a system of freely competing protection agencies all arbitrariness of allocation (all over- and underproduction) would disappear. Protection would be accorded the relative importance that it has in the eyes of voluntarily paying consumers, and no person, group, or region would receive protection at the expense of any other one. Each and every one would receive protection in accordance with his own payments.

The most important advantage of a private, contract-based production of law and order, however, is of a qualitative nature.

First, there is the fight against crime. The state is notoriously inefficient in this regard, because the state agents entrusted with this task are paid out of taxes, i.e., independent of their productivity. Why should one work if one is also paid for doing nothing at all?

In fact, it can be expected that state agents will have an interest in maintaining a moderately high crime rate, because this way they can justify ever-increased funding. Worse, for state agents the victims of crime and the indemnification and compensation of such victims play an at best negligible role. The state does not indemnify the victims of crime. To the contrary, the harmed victims are still further insulted in making them, *qua* taxpayers, pay for the incarceration and "rehabilitation" of the criminal (should he be captured).

The situation in a private-law society is entirely different. Security providers, insurers in particular, have to indemnify their clients in the case of actual damage (otherwise they would find no clients) and hence, they must operate efficiently. They must be efficient in the prevention of crime, for unless they can prevent a crime, they would have to pay up. Further, even if a criminal act could not be prevented, they must be efficient in detecting and recovering stolen loot, because otherwise they must pay to replace these goods. In particular, they must be efficient in the detection and apprehension of the criminal, for only if the criminal is apprehended is it possible for them to make *him* pay for the compensation owed to the victim and thus reduce their costs.

Moreover, a private, competitive, and contract-based security industry has a general peace-promoting effect. States are, as already explained, by nature aggressive. They can cause or provoke conflict in order to then "solve" it to their own advantage.

Or, to put it differently, as tax-funded monopolists of ultimate decision-making, states can externalize the costs associated with aggressive behavior onto others, i.e., the hapless taxpayers, and accordingly will tend to be more aggressive *vis-à-vis* their own population as well as "foreigners."

In distinct contrast, competing private insurers are by nature defensive and peaceful. On the one hand this is because every act of aggression is costly, and an insurance company engaged in aggressive conduct would require comparatively higher premiums, involving the loss of clients to cheaper nonaggressive competitors.

On the other hand, it is not possible to insure oneself against every conceivable "risk." Rather, it is only possible to insure oneself against "accidents," i.e., risks over whose outcome the insured has no control and to which he contributes nothing. Thus, it is possible to insure oneself against the risk of death and fire, for instance, but it is impossible to insure oneself against the risk of committing suicide tomorrow or setting one's own house on fire.

Similarly, it is impossible to insure oneself against the risk of business failure, of unemployment, or of disliking one's neighbors, for in each case one has some control over the event in question. Most significantly, the un-insurability of individual actions and sentiments (in contradistinction to accidents) implies that it is also impossible to insure oneself against the risk of damages resulting from one's own prior aggression or provocation.

Instead, every insurer must restrict the actions of his clients so as to exclude all aggression and provocation on their part. That is, any insurance against social disasters such as crime must be contingent on the insured submitting themselves to specified norms of civilized, nonaggressive conduct.

Further, due to the same reasons and financial concerns, insurers will tend to require that their clients abstain from all forms of vigilante justice (except perhaps under quite extraordinary circumstances), for vigilante justice, even if justified, invariably causes uncertainty and provokes possible third-party intervention. By obliging their clients instead to submit to regular publicized procedures whenever they think they have been victimized, these disturbances and associated costs can be largely avoided.

Lastly, it is worthwhile pointing out that while states as tax-funded agencies can—and do—engage in the large-scale prosecution of victimless crimes such as "illegal-drug" use, prostitution, or gambling, these "crimes" would tend to be of little or no concern within a system of freely funded protection agencies. "Protection" against such "crimes" would require higher insurance premiums, but since these "crimes"—unlike genuine crimes against persons and property—do not create victims, very few people would be willing to spend money on such "protection."

Still more: while states, as already noted, are always and everywhere eager to disarm their populations and thus rob them of an essential means of self-defense, private-law societies are characterized by an unrestricted right to self-defense and hence by widespread private gun and weapon ownership. Just imagine a security producer who demanded of its prospective clients that they would first have to completely disarm themselves before it would be willing to defend the clients' life and property. Correctly, everyone would think of this as a bad joke and refuse such an offer.

Freely financed insurance companies that demanded potential clients first hand over all of their means of self-defense as a prerequisite of protection would immediately arouse the utmost suspicion as to their true motives, and they would quickly go bankrupt. In their own best interest, insurance companies would reward armed clients, in particular those able to certify some level of training in the handling of arms, charging them lower premiums reflecting the lower risk that they represent. Just as insurers charge less if homeowners have an alarm system or a safe installed, so would a trained gun owner represent a lower insurance risk.

Last and most importantly, a system of competing protection agencies would have a twofold impact on the development of law. On the one hand, it would allow for *greater variability* of law. Rather than imposing a uniform set of standards onto everyone (as under statist conditions), protection agencies could compete against each other not just via price but also through product differentiation. There could exist side by side, for instance, Catholic protection agencies or insurers applying canon law, Jewish agencies applying Mosaic law, Muslim agencies applying Islamic law, and agencies applying secular law of one variety or another, all of them sustained by a voluntarily paying clientele. Consumers could choose the law applied to them and their property. No one would have to live under "foreign" law.

On the other hand, the very same system of private law-and-order production would promote a tendency toward the *unification and harmonization of law*. The "domestic"—Catholic, Jewish, Roman, etc.—law would apply only to the person and property of those who had chosen it. Canon law, for instance, would apply only to professed Catholics and deal solely with intra-Catholic conflict and conflict resolution.

Yet it is also possible, of course, that a Catholic might come into conflict with the subscriber of some other law code, e.g., a Muslim. If both law codes reached the same or a similar conclusion, no difficulties exist. However, if competing law codes arrived at distinctly different conclusion (as they would at least in some cases), a problem arises.

In this case, "domestic" (intragroup) law would be useless, but naturally every insured person would want protection against the contingency of intergroup conflicts as well. In this situation, it cannot be expected that one insurer and the subscribers of its law code simply subordinate their judgment to that of another insurer and its law. Rather, as I have already explained, in this situation there exists only one credible and acceptable way out of this predicament: from the outset, every insurer would have to be contractually obliged to submit itself and its clients to arbitration by an independent third party. This party would not only be independent but at the same time the unanimous choice of both parties.

It would be agreed upon because of its commonly perceived ability to find mutually agreeable (fair) solutions in cases of intergroup disagreement. If an arbitrator failed in this task and arrived at conclusions that were perceived as "unfair" or "biased" by either one of the insurers or their clients, this person or agency would not likely be chosen as an arbitrator in the future.

As a result of the constant cooperation of various insurers and arbitrators, then, a tendency toward the unification of property and contract law and the harmonization of the rules of procedure, evidence, and conflict resolution would be set in motion. Thus, in buying protection insurance, every insurer and insured becomes a participant in an integrated system of conflict avoidance and peacekeeping. Every single conflict and damage claim, regardless of where and by or against whom, would fall under the jurisdiction of one or more specific insurance agencies and would be handled either by an individual insurer's "domestic" law or by the "international" or "universal" law provisions and procedures agreed upon by everyone in advance.

Hence, instead of permanent conflict, injustice, and legal insecurity—as under the present statist conditions—in a private-law society, peace, justice, and legal security would hold sway.

12

The Private Production of Defense

Among the most popular and consequential beliefs of our age is the belief in collective security. Nothing less significant than the legitimacy of the modern state rests on this belief.

I will demonstrate that the idea of collective security is a myth that provides no justification for the modern state, and that all security is and must be private. Yet, before coming to the conclusion let me begin with the problem. First, I will present a two-step reconstruction of the myth of collective security, and at each step raise a few theoretical concerns.

The myth of collective security can also be called the Hobbesian myth. Thomas Hobbes, and countless political philosophers and economists after him, argued that in the state of nature, men would constantly be at each others' throats. *Homo homini lupus est.* Put in modern jargon, in the state of nature a permanent underproduction of security would prevail. Each individual, left to his own devices and provisions, would spend too little on his own defense, and hence, permanent interpersonal warfare would result. The solution to this presumably intolerable situation, according to Hobbes and his followers, is the institution of a state. In order to institute peaceful cooperation among themselves, two individuals, A and B, require a third independent party, S, as ultimate judge and peacemaker. However, this third party, S, is not just another individual, and the good provided by S, that of security, is not just another "private" good. Rather, S is a *sovereign* and has as such two unique powers. On the one hand, S can insist that his *subjects*, A and B, not seek protection from anyone but him; that is, S is a compulsory territorial monopolist of protection. On the other hand, S can determine unilaterally how much A and B must spend on their own security; that is, S has the power to impose taxes in order to provide security "collectively."

• Originally published in *Journal of Libertarian Studies* 14, no. 1 (Winter 1998–1999).

In commenting on this argument, there is little use in quarreling over whether man is as bad and wolf-like as Hobbes supposes, except to note that Hobbes's thesis obviously cannot mean that man is driven only and exclusively by aggressive instincts. If this were the case, mankind would have died out long ago. The fact that he did not demonstrates that man also possesses reason and is capable of constraining his natural impulses. The quarrel is only with the Hobbesian solution. Given man's nature as a rational animal, is the proposed solution to the problem of insecurity an improvement? Can the institution of a state reduce aggressive behavior and promote peaceful cooperation, and thus provide for better private security and protection? The difficulties with Hobbes's argument are obvious. For one, regardless of how bad men are, S—whether king, dictator, or elected president—is still one of them. Man's nature is not transformed upon becoming S. Yet how can there be better protection for A and B, if S must tax them in order to provide it? Is there not a contradiction within the very construction of S as an expropriating property protector? In fact, is this not exactly what is also—and more appropriately—referred to as a *protection racket*? To be sure, S will make peace between A and B but only so that he himself in turn can rob both of them more profitably. Surely S is better protected, but the more he is protected, the less A and B are protected from attacks by S. Collective security, it would seem, is not better than private security. Rather, it is the private security of the state, S, achieved through the expropriation, i.e., the economic disarmament, of its subjects. Further, statists from Thomas Hobbes to James Buchanan have argued that a protective state S would come about as the result of some sort of "constitutional" contract.[1] Yet who in his right mind would agree to a contract that allowed one's protector to determine unilaterally—and irrevocably—the sum that the protected must pay for his protection? And the fact is, no one ever has![2]

---

1. James M. Buchanan and Gordon Tullock, *The Calculus of Consent* (Ann Arbor: University of Michigan Press, 1962); James M. Buchanan, *The Limits of Liberty* (Chicago: University of Chicago Press, 1975); for a critique, see Murray N. Rothbard, "Buchanan and Tullock's *Calculus of Consent*," in idem, *The Logic of Action*, vol. 2, *Applications and Criticism from the Austrian School* (Cheltenham, Eng.: Edward Elgar, 1995); idem, "The Myth of Neutral Taxation," in *The Logic of Action*, vol. 2; Hans-Hermann Hoppe, *The Economics and Ethics of Private Property* (Boston: Kluwer Academic Publishers, 1993), chap. 1.

2. See on this particular point, Lysander Spooner, *No Treason: The Constitution of No Authority* (Larkspur, Colo.: Pine Tree Press, 1996).

Let me interrupt my discussion here, and return to the reconstruction of the Hobbesian myth. Once it is assumed that in order to institute peaceful cooperation between A and B it is necessary to have a state S, a two-fold conclusion follows. If more than one state exists, S_1, S_2, S_3, then, just as there can presumably be no peace among A and B without S, so there can be no peace between the states S_1, S_2, and S_3 as long as they remain in a state of nature (i.e., a state of anarchy) with regard to each other. Consequently, in order to achieve *universal* peace, political centralization, unification, and ultimately the establishment of a single world government are necessary.

Commenting on this argument, it is first useful to indicate what can be taken as non-controversial. To begin with, the argument is correct, as far as it goes. If the premise is correct, then the consequence spelled out follows. The empirical assumptions involved in the Hobbesian account appear at first glance to be borne out by the facts, as well. It is true that states are constantly at war with each other, and a historical tendency toward political centralization and global rule does indeed appear to be occurring. Quarrels arise only with the explanation of this fact and tendency, and the classification of a single unified world state as an improvement in the provision of private security and protection. First, there appears to be an empirical anomaly for which the Hobbesian argument cannot account. The reason for the warring among different states S_1, S_2, and S_3, according to Hobbes, is that they are in a state of anarchy *vis-à-vis* each other. However, before the arrival of a single world state not only are S_1, S_2, and S_3 in a state of anarchy relative to each other but in fact every subject of one state is in a state of anarchy *vis-à-vis* every subject of any other state. Accordingly, there should exist just as much war and aggression between the private citizens of various states as between different states. Empirically, however, this is not so. The private dealings between foreigners appear to be significantly less warlike than the dealings between different governments. Nor does this seem to be surprising. After all, a state agent S, in contrast to every one of its subjects, can rely on domestic taxation in the conduct of his foreign affairs. Given his natural human aggressiveness, however pronounced it may initially be, is it not obvious that S will be more brazen and aggressive in his conduct toward foreigners if he can externalize the cost of such behavior onto others? Surely, I am willing to take greater risks and engage in more provocation and aggression if I can make others pay for it. And surely there is a tendency of one state—one protection racket—to want to expand its territorial protection monopoly at the expense of other states and thus bring about, as the ultimate result of interstate competition, world government.[3] But how is this an improvement in the provision of private security and protection? The opposite seems to be the case. The world state is the winner of all wars and the last surviving protection racket. Doesn't this make it particularly dangerous? And will not the physical power of any single world government be overwhelming as compared to that of any one of its individual subjects?

I. THE EMPIRICAL EVIDENCE

Let me pause here in my abstract theoretical considerations to take a brief look at the empirical evidence bearing on the issue at hand. As noted at the outset, the myth of collective security is as widespread as it is consequential. I am not aware of any survey on this matter, but I would venture to predict that the Hobbesian myth is accepted more or less unquestioningly by well over 90 percent of the adult population. However, to believe something does not make it true. Rather, if what one believes is false, one's actions will lead to failure. What about the evidence? Does it support Hobbes and his followers, or does it confirm the opposite anarchist fears and contentions?

The U.S. was explicitly founded as a protective state à la Hobbes. Let me quote to this effect from Jefferson's *Declaration of Independence*:

> We hold these truths to be self-evident: that all men are created
> equal; that they are endowed by their creator with inalienable rights;
> that among these are life, liberty, and the pursuit of happiness:
> that to secure these rights, governments are instituted among men,
> deriving their just powers from the consent of the governed.

Here we have it: The U.S. government was instituted to fulfill one and only one task: the protection of life and property. Thus, it should provide the perfect example for judging the validity of the Hobbesian claim as to the status of states as protectors. After more than two centuries of protective statism, what is the status of our protection and peaceful human cooperation? Was the American experiment in protective statism a success?

According to the pronouncements of our state rulers and their intellectual bodyguards (of whom there are more than ever before), we are better protected and more secure than ever. We are supposedly protected from global warming and cooling, from the extinction of animals and plants, from the abuses of

---

3. See Hans-Hermann Hoppe, "The Trouble With Classical Liberalism," *Roth-bard–Rockwell Report* 9, no. 4 (1998).

husbands and wives, parents and employers, from poverty, disease, disaster, ignorance, prejudice, racism, sexism, homophobia, and countless other public enemies and dangers. In fact, however, matters are strikingly different. In order to provide us with all this protection, the state managers expropriate more than 40 percent of the incomes of private producers year in and year out. Government debt and liabilities have increased without interruption, thus increasing the need for future expropriations. Owing to the substitution of government paper money for gold, financial insecurity has increased sharply, and we are continually robbed through currency depreciation. Every detail of private life, property, trade, and contract is regulated by ever higher mountains of laws (legislation), thereby creating permanent legal uncertainty and moral hazard. In particular, we have been gradually stripped of the right to exclusion implied in the very concept of private property. As sellers we cannot sell to, and as buyers we cannot buy from whomever we wish. And as members of associations we are not permitted to enter into whatever restrictive covenant we believe to be mutually beneficial. As Americans, we must accept immigrants we do not want as our neighbors. As teachers, we cannot get rid of lousy or ill-behaved students. As employers, we are stuck with incompetent or destructive employees. As landlords, we are forced to cope with bad tenants. As bankers and insurers, we are not allowed to avoid bad risks. As restaurant or bar owners, we must accommodate unwelcome customers. And as members of private associations, we are compelled to accept individuals and actions in violation of our own rules and restrictions. In short, the more the state has increased its expenditures on social security and public safety, the more our private property rights have been eroded, the more our property has been expropriated, confiscated, destroyed, or depreciated, and the more we have been deprived of the very foundation of all protection: economic independence, financial strength, and personal wealth.[4] The path of every president and practically every member of Congress is littered with hundreds of thousands if not millions of nameless victims of personal economic ruin, financial bankruptcy, impoverishment, despair, hardship, and frustration.

The picture appears even bleaker when we consider foreign affairs. Never during its entire history has the continental U.S. been territorially attacked by any foreign army. (Pearl Harbor was the result of a preceding U.S. provocation.) Yet the U.S. has the distinction of having possessed

---

4. See Hans-Hermann Hoppe, "Where The Right Goes Wrong," *Rothbard–Rockwell Report* 8, no. 4 (1997).

a government that declared war against a large part of its own population and engaged in the wanton murder of hundreds of thousands of its own citizens. Moreover, while the relations between American citizens and foreigners do not appear to be unusually contentious, almost from its very beginnings the U.S. government pursued relentless aggressive expansionism. Beginning with the Spanish–American War, culminating in World War I and World War II, and continuing to the present, the U.S. government has become entangled in hundreds of foreign conflicts and risen to the rank of the world's dominant imperialist power. Thus, nearly every president since the turn of this century also has been responsible for the murder, killing, or starvation of countless innocent foreigners all over the world. In short, while we have become more helpless, impoverished, threatened, and insecure, the U.S. government has become ever more brazen and aggressive. In the name of national security, it defends us, equipped with enormous stockpiles of weapons of aggression and mass destruction, by bullying ever new "Hitlers," big or small, and all suspected Hitlerite sympathizers anywhere and everywhere outside of the territory of the U.S.[5]

The empirical evidence thus seems clear. The belief in a protective state appears to be a patent error, and the American experiment in protective statism a complete failure. The U.S. government does not protect us. To the contrary, there exists no greater danger to our life, property, and prosperity than the U.S. government, and the U.S. president in particular is the world's single most threatening and armed danger, capable of ruining everyone who opposes him and destroying the entire globe.

II. How to Think About the Statist Response

Statists react much like socialists when faced with the dismal economic performance of the Soviet Union and its satellites. They do not necessarily deny the disappointing facts, but they try to argue them away by claiming that these facts are the result of a systematic discrepancy (deviancy) between "real" and "ideal" or "true" statism, respectively socialism. To this day, socialists claim that "true" socialism has not been refuted by the empirical evidence, and everything would have turned out well and unparalleled prosperity would have resulted, if only Trotsky's, or Bucharin's, or better still their very own

---

5. See John Denson, ed., *The Costs of War* (New Brunswick, N.J.: Transaction Publishers, 1997).

brand of socialism, rather than Stalin's, had been implemented. Similarly, statists interpret all seemingly contradictory evidence as only accidental. If only some other president had come to power at this or that turn in history, or if only this or that constitutional change or amendment had been adopted, everything would have turned out beautifully, and unparalleled security and peace would have resulted. Indeed, this may still happen in the future, if their own policies are employed.

We have learned from Ludwig von Mises how to respond to the socialists' evasion (immunization) strategy.[6] As long as the defining characteristic— the essence—of socialism, i.e., the absence of the private ownership of the factors of production, remains in place, no reform will be of any help. The idea of a socialist economy is a *contradictio in adjecto*, and the claim that socialism represents a higher, more efficient mode of social production is absurd. In order to reach one's own ends efficiently and without waste within the framework of an exchange economy based on division of labor, it is necessary that one engage in monetary calculation (cost-accounting). Everywhere outside the system of a primitive self-sufficient single household economy, monetary calculation is the sole tool of rational and efficient action. Only by being able to compare inputs and outputs arithmetically in terms of a common medium of exchange (money) can a person determine whether his actions are successful or not. In distinct contrast, socialism means to have no economy, no economizing, at all, because under these conditions monetary calculation and cost-accounting is impossible by definition. If no private property in the factors of production exists, then no prices for any production factor exist; hence, it is impossible to determine whether or not they are employed economically. Accordingly, socialism is not a higher mode of production but rather economic chaos and regression to primitivism.

How to respond to the statists' evasion strategy has been explained by Murray N. Rothbard.[7] But Rothbard's lesson, while equally simple and clear and with even more momentous implications, has remained to this day far less known and appreciated. So long as the defining characteristic—the essence—of a state remains in place, he explained, no reform, whether on

---

6. Ludwig von Mises, *Socialism* (Indianapolis, Ind.: Liberty Classics, 1981); Hans-Hermann Hoppe, *A Theory of Socialism and Capitalism* (Boston: Kluwer Academic Publishers, 1989), chap. 6.

7. Murray N. Rothbard, *The Ethics of Liberty* (New York: New York University Press, 1998), esp. chaps. 22 and 23.

the level of personnel or of the constitution, will be to any avail. *Given* the principle of government—judicial monopoly and the power to tax—any notion of limiting its power and safeguarding individual life and property is illusory. Under monopolistic auspices the price of justice and protection must rise and its quality must fall. A tax-funded protection agency is a contradiction in terms and will lead to ever more taxes and less protection. Even if a government limited its activities exclusively to the protection of pre-existing property rights (as every protective state is supposed to do), the further question of *how much* security to provide would arise. Motivated (like everyone else) by self-interest and the disutility of labor, but with the unique power to tax, a government's answer will invariably be the same: to *maximize expenditures* on protection—and almost all of a nation's wealth can conceivably be consumed by the cost of protection—and at the same time to *minimize* the *production* of protection. Furthermore, a judicial monopoly must lead to a deterioration in the quality of justice and protection. If one can only appeal to government for justice and protection, justice and protection will be perverted in favor of government, constitutions, and supreme courts notwithstanding. After all, constitutions and supreme courts are *state* constitutions and courts, and whatever limitations to government action they might contain is determined by agents of the very institution under consideration. Accordingly, the definition of property and protection will continually be altered and the range of jurisdiction expanded to the government's advantage.

Hence, Rothbard pointed out, it follows that just as socialism cannot be reformed but must be abolished in order to achieve prosperity, so can the institution of a state not be reformed but must be abolished in order to achieve justice and protection. "Defense in the free society (including such defense services to person and property as police protection and judicial findings)," Rothbard concluded,

> would therefore have to be supplied by people or firms who (a) gained their revenue voluntarily rather than by coercion and (b) did not—as the State does—arrogate to themselves a compulsory monopoly of police or judicial protection ... defense firms would have to be as freely competitive and as noncoercive against noninvaders as are all other suppliers of goods and services on the free market. Defense services, like all other services, would be marketable and marketable only.[8]

---

8. Murray N. Rothbard, *Power and Market* (Kansas City: Sheed Andrews and McMeel, 1977), p. 2.

That is, every private property owner would be able to partake of the advantages of the division of labor and seek better protection of his property than that afforded through self-defense by cooperation with other owners and their property. Anyone could buy from, sell to, or otherwise contract with anyone else concerning protective and judicial services, and one could at any time unilaterally discontinue any such cooperation with others and fall back on self-reliant defense, or change one's protective affiliations.

III. The Case for Private Security

Having reconstructed the myth of collective security—the myth of the state—and criticized it on theoretical and empirical grounds, I now must take on the task of constructing the positive case for private security and protection. In order to dispel the myth of collective security, it is not just sufficient to grasp the *error* involved in the idea of a protective state. It is just as important, if not more so, to gain a clear understanding of how the non-statist security alternative would effectively work. Rothbard, building on the path-breaking analysis of the French-Belgian economist Gustave de Molinari,[9] has given us a sketch of the workings of a free-market system of protection and defense.[10] As well, we owe Morris and Linda Tannehill for their brilliant insights and analyses in this regard.[11] Following their lead, I will proceed deeper in my analysis and provide a more *comprehensive* view of the alternative-non-statist-system of security production and its ability to handle attacks, not just by individuals or gangs but in particular also by *states*.

There exists widespread agreement—among liberal-libertarians such as Molinari, Rothbard, and the Tannehills as well as most other commentators on the matter—that defense is a form of insurance, and defense expenditures represent a sort of insurance premium (price). Accordingly, as Rothbard and the Tannehills in particular would emphasize, within the framework of a complex modern economy based on a worldwide division of labor the most likely candidates for offering protection and defense services are insurance agencies. The better the protection of insured property, the lower are the damage claims and hence an insurer's costs. Thus, to provide efficient

---

9. Gustave de Molinari, *The Production of Security* (New York: Center for Libertarian Studies, 1977).

10. Murray N. Rothbard, *Power and Market*, chap. 1; idem, *For A New Liberty* (New York: Collier, 1978), chaps. 12 and 14.

11. Morris Tannehill and Linda Tannehill, *The Market for Liberty* (New York: Laissez Faire Books, 1984), esp. part 2.

protection appears to be in every insurer's own financial interest; and in fact even now, although restricted and hampered by the state, insurance agencies provide wide-ranging services of protection and indemnification (compensation) to injured private parties. Insurance companies fulfill a second essential requirement. Obviously, anyone offering protection services must appear able to deliver on his promises in order to find clients. That is, he must possess the economic means—the manpower as well as the physical resources—necessary to accomplish the task of dealing with the dangers, actual or imagined, of the real world. On this count insurance agencies appear to be perfect candidates, too. They operate on a nationwide and even international scale, and they own large property holdings dispersed over wide territories and beyond single state boundaries. Accordingly, they have a manifest self-interest in effective protection, and are big and economically powerful. Furthermore, all insurance companies are connected through a network of contractual agreements of mutual assistance and arbitration as well as a system of international reinsurance agencies, representing a combined economic power which dwarfs that of most if not all existing governments.

I want to further analyze and systematically clarify this suggestion: that protection and defense are insurance and can be provided by insurance agencies. To reach this goal, two issues must be addressed. First, it is not possible to insure oneself against every risk of life. I cannot insure myself against committing suicide, for instance, or against burning down my own house, or becoming unemployed, or not feeling like getting out of bed in the morning, or not suffering entrepreneurial losses, because in each case I have full or partial control over the likelihood of the respective outcome. Risks such as these must be assumed individually. No one except myself can possibly deal with them. Hence, the first question will have to be what makes protection and defense an insurable rather than an uninsurable risk? After all, as we have just seen, this is not self-evident. In fact, doesn't everyone have considerable control over the likelihood of an attack on and invasion of his person and property? Do I not deliberately bring about an attack by assaulting or provoking someone else, for instance, and is not protection then an uninsurable risk, like suicide or unemployment, for which each person must assume sole responsibility?

The answer is a qualified yes and no. Yes, insofar as no one can possibly offer *un*conditional protection, i.e., insurance against any invasion whatsoever. That is, unconditional protection can only be provided, if at all, by each individual on his own and for himself. But the answer is no, *insofar* as conditional protection is concerned. Only attacks and invasions that are provoked by the victim cannot be insured. However, unprovoked and thus accidental attacks can be insured against.[12] That is, protection becomes an insurable good only if and insofar as an insurance agent contractually restricts the actions of the insured so as to exclude every possible provocation on their part. Various insurance companies may differ with respect to the specific definition of provocation, but there can be no difference between insurers with regard to the principle that each must systematically exclude (prohibit) all provocative and aggressive action among its own clients.

As elementary as this first insight into the essentially defensive—non-aggressive and non-provocative—nature of protection-insurance may seem, it is of fundamental importance. For one, it implies that any known aggressor and provocateur would be unable to find an insurer, and hence, would be economically isolated, weak, and vulnerable. On the other hand, it implies that anyone wanting more protection than that afforded by self-reliant self-defense could do so only if and insofar as he submitted himself to specified norms of non-aggressive, civilized conduct. Furthermore, the greater the number of insured people—and in a modern exchange economy most people want more than just self-defense for their protection—the greater would be the economic pressure on the remaining uninsured to adopt the same or similar standards of non-aggressive social conduct. Moreover, as the result of competition between insurers for voluntarily paying clients, a tendency toward falling prices per insured property values would come about. At the same time, a tendency toward the standardization and unification of property and contract law would be set in motion. Protection contracts with standardized property and product descriptions would come into existence; and out of the steady cooperation between different insurers in mutual arbitration proceedings, a tendency toward the standardization and unification of the rules of procedure, evidence, and conflict resolution

---

12. On the "logic" of insurance, see Ludwig von Mises, *Human Action* (Chicago: Regnery, 1966), chap. 6; Murray N. Rothbard, *Man, Economy, and State* (Auburn, Ala.: Ludwig von Mises Institute, 1993), pp. 498 ff.; Hans-Hermann Hoppe, "On Certainty and Uncertainty, Or: How Rational Can Our Expectations Be?" *Review of Austrian Economics* 10, no. 1 (1997), reprinted chapter 14 herein; also Richard von Mises, *Probability, Statistics, and Truth* (New York: Dover, 1957); Frank H. Knight, *Risk, Uncertainty, and Profit* (Chicago: University of Chicago Press, 1971).

(including compensation, restitution, punishment, and retribution), and steadily increasing legal certainty would result. Everyone, by virtue of buying protection insurance, would be tied into a global competitive enterprise of striving to minimize aggression (and thus maximize defensive protection), and every single conflict and damage claim, regardless of where and by or against whom, would fall into the jurisdiction of exactly one or more enumerable and specific insurance agencies and their mutually defined arbitration procedures.

IV. More on Aggression Insurance

Now a second question must be addressed. Even if the status of defensive protection as an insurable good is granted, distinctly different forms of insurance exist. Let us consider just two characteristic examples: insurance against natural disasters, such as earthquakes, floods, and hurricanes, and insurance against industrial accidents or disasters, such as malfunctions, explosions, or defective products. The former can serve as an example of group or mutual insurance. Some territories are more prone to natural disasters than others; as a result the demand for and price of insurance will be higher in some areas than others. However, every location *within* certain territorial borders is regarded by the insurer as homogeneous with respect to the risk concerned. The insurer presumably knows the frequency and extent of the event in question for the region as a whole, but he knows nothing about the particular risk of any specific location within the territory. In this case, every insured person will pay the same premium per insured value, and the premiums collected in one time period are presumably sufficient to cover all damage claims during the same time period (otherwise the insurance industry will have losses). Thus, the particular individual risks are pooled and insured mutually.

In contrast, industrial insurance can serve as an example of individual insurance. Unlike natural disasters, the insured risk is the outcome of human action, i.e., of production efforts. Every production process is under the control of an individual producer. No producer *intends* failure or disaster, and as we have seen only accidental—non-intended—disasters are insurable. Yet even if largely controlled and generally successful, every producer and production technology is subject to occasional mishaps and accidents beyond his control—a margin of error. However, as the outcome, even if unintended, of individual production efforts and production techniques, this risk of industrial accidents is essentially different from one producer and production process to another. Accordingly, the risk of different producers and production technologies cannot be pooled, and every producer must be insured individually. In this case, the insurer presumably will have to know the frequency of the questionable event over time, but he knows nothing of the likelihood of the event at any specific moment in time, except that at all times the same producer and production technology is in operation. There is no presumption that the premiums collected during any given period will be sufficient to cover all damage claims arising during that period. Rather, the profit-making presumption is that all premiums collected over many time periods will be sufficient in order to cover all claims during the same multi-period time span. Consequently, in this case an insurer must hold capital reserves in order to fulfill its contractual obligation, and in calculating his premiums he must take the present value of these reserves into account.

The second question is, then, what kind of insurance can protect against aggression and invasion by other actors? Can it be provided as group insurance, as for natural disasters, or will it have to be offered in the form of individual insurance, as in the case of industrial accidents?

Let me note at the outset that both forms of insurance represent only the two possible extremes of a continuum, and that the position of any particular risk on this continuum is not definitively fixed. Owing to scientific and technological advances in meteorology, geology, or engineering, for instance, risks that were formerly regarded as homogeneous (allowing for mutual insurance) can become more and more de-homogenized. Noteworthy is this tendency in the field of medical and health insurance. With the advances of genetics and genetic engineering—genetic fingerprinting—medical and health risks previously regarded as homogeneous (unspecific) with respect to large numbers of people have become increasingly more specific and heterogeneous.

With this in mind, can anything specific be said about protection insurance in particular? I would think so. After all, while all insurance requires that the risk be accidental from the standpoint of the insurer and the insured, the accident of an aggressive invasion is distinctly different from that of natural or industrial disasters. Whereas natural disasters and industrial accidents are the outcome of natural forces and the operation of laws of nature, aggression is the outcome of human actions; and whereas nature is blind and does not discriminate between individuals, whether at the same point in time or over time, an aggressor can discriminate and deliberately target specific victims and choose the timing of his attack.

V. POLITICAL BORDERS AND INSURANCE

Let me first contrast defense-protection insurance with that against natural disasters. Frequently an analogy between the two is drawn, and it is instructive to examine if or to what extent it holds. The analogy is that just as every individual within certain geographical regions is threatened by the same risk of an earthquake, a flood, or a hurricane, so does every inhabitant within the territory of the U.S. or Germany, for instance, face the same risk of being victimized by a foreign attack. Some superficial similarity—to which I shall come shortly—notwithstanding, it is easy to recognize two fundamental shortcomings in the analogy. For one, the borders of earthquake, flood, or hurricane regions are established and drawn according to objective physical criteria and hence can be referred to as natural. In distinct contrast, political boundaries are artificial boundaries. The borders of the U.S. changed throughout the entire 19th century, and Germany did not exist as such until 1871, but was composed of nearly 50 separate countries. Surely, no one would want to claim that this redrawing of the U.S. or German borders was the outcome of the discovery that the security risk of every American or German within the greater U.S. or Germany was, contrary to the previously held opposite belief, homogeneous (identical).

There is a second obvious shortcoming. Nature—earthquakes, floods, hurricanes—is blind in its destruction. It does not discriminate between more and less valuable locations and objects, but attacks indiscriminately. In distinct contrast, an aggressor-invader can and does discriminate. He does not attack or invade worthless locations and things, like the Sahara Desert, but targets locations and things that are valuable. Other things being equal, the more valuable a location and an object, the more likely it will be the target of an invasion.

This raises the crucial next question. If political borders are arbitrary and attacks are in any case never indiscriminate but directed specifically toward valuable places and things, are there any non-arbitrary borders separating different security-risk (attack) zones? The answer is yes. Such non-arbitrary borders are those of private property. Private property is the result of the appropriation and/or production of particular physical objects or effects by specific individuals at specific locations. Every appropriator-producer (owner) demonstrates with his actions that he regards the appropriated and produced things as valuable (goods), otherwise he would not have appropriated or produced them. The borders of everyone's property are objective and inter-subjectively ascertainable. They are simply determined by the extension and dimension of the things appropriated and/or produced by any one particular individual. And the borders of all valuable places and things are coextensive with the borders of all property. At any given point in time, every valuable place and thing is owned by someone; only worthless places and things are owned by no one.

Surrounded by other men, every appropriator and producer can also become the object of an attack or invasion. Every property—in contrast to things (matter)—is necessarily valuable; thus, every property owner becomes a possible target of other men's aggressive desires. Consequently, every owner's choice of the location and form of his property will, among countless other considerations, also be influenced by security concerns. Other things being equal, everyone will prefer safer locations and forms of property to locations and forms that are less safe. Yet, regardless of where an owner and his property are located and whatever the property's physical form, every owner, by virtue of not abandoning his property even in view of potential aggression, demonstrates his personal willingness to protect and defend these possessions.

However, if the borders of private property are the only non-arbitrary borders standing in systematic relation to the risk of aggression, then it follows that as many different security zones as there are separately owned property holdings exist, and that these zones are no larger than the extension of these holdings. That is, even more so than in the case of industrial accidents, the insurance of property against aggression would seem to be an example of individual rather than group (mutual) protection.

Whereas the accident-risk of an individual production process is typically independent of its location—such that if the process were replicated by the same producer at different locations his margin of error would remain the same—the risk of aggression against private property—the production plant—is different from one location to another. By its very nature, as privately appropriated and produced goods, property is always separate and distinct. Every property is located at a different place and under the control of a different individual, and each location faces a unique security risk. It can make a difference for my security, for instance, if I reside in the countryside or the city, on a hill or in a valley, or near or far from a river, ocean, harbor, railroad or street. In fact, even contiguous locations do not face the same risk. It can make a difference, for instance, if I reside higher or lower on the mountain than my neighbor, upstream or downstream, closer to or more distant from the ocean, or simply north, south, west, or east of him. Moreover, every property, wherever it is located, can be shaped and transformed by its owner so as to increase its safety and reduce the likelihood of an aggression. I may acquire a gun or safe-deposit box, for instance, or I may be able to shoot down an attacking plane from my backyard or own a laser gun that can kill an aggressor thousands of miles away. Thus, no location and no property are like any other. Every owner will have to be insured individually, and to do so every aggression-insurer must hold sufficient capital reserves.

VI. The Democratic State and Total War

The analogy typically drawn between insurance against natural disasters and external aggression is fundamentally flawed. As aggression is never indiscriminate but selective and targeted, so is defense. Everyone has different locations and things to defend, and no one's security risk is the same as anyone else's. And yet the analogy also contains a kernel of truth. However, any similarity between natural disasters and external aggression is due *not* to the nature of aggression and defense but to the rather specific nature of *state* aggression and defense (interstate warfare). As explained above, a state is an agency that exercises a compulsory territorial monopoly of protection and the power to tax, and any such agency will be comparatively more aggressive because it can externalize the costs of such behavior onto its subjects. However, the existence of a state does not just increase the frequency of aggression; it changes its entire character. The existence of states, and especially of democratic states, implies that aggression and defense—war— will tend to be transformed into total, undiscriminating, war.[13]

---

13. On the relationship between state and war, and on the historical transformation from limited (monarchical) to total (democratic) war, see Ekkehard Krippendorff, *Staat und Krieg* (Frankfurt/M.: Suhrkamp, 1985); Charles Tilly, "War Making and State Making as Organized Crime," in Peter B. Evans, Dietrich Rueschemeyer, and Theda Skocpol, eds., *Bringing the State Back In* (Cambridge: Cambridge University Press, 1985); John F. C. Fuller, *The Conduct of War* (New York: Da Capo Press, 1992); Michael Howard, *War in European History* (New York: Oxford University Press, 1976); Hans-Hermann Hoppe, "Time Preference, Government, and the Process of Decivilization," in John V. Denson, ed., *The Costs of War* (New Brunswick, N.J.: Transaction Publishers, 1997); Erik von Kuehnelt-Leddihn, *Leftism Revisited* (Washington, D.C.: Regnery, 1990).

Consider for a moment a completely stateless world. Most property owners would be individually insured by large, often multinational insurance companies endowed with huge capital reserves. Most if not all aggressors, being bad risks, would be left without any insurance whatever. In this situation, every aggressor or group of aggressors would want to limit their targets, preferably to uninsured property, and avoid all "collateral damage," as they would otherwise find themselves confronted with one or many economically powerful professional defense agencies. Likewise, all defensive violence would be highly selective and targeted. All aggressors would be specific individuals or groups, located at specific places and equipped with specific resources. In response to attacks on their clients, insurance agencies would specifically target these locations and resources for retaliation, and they would want to avoid any collateral damage, as they would otherwise become entangled with and liable to other insurers.

All of this fundamentally changes in a statist world with interstate warfare. For one, if a state, the U.S., attacks another, for instance Iraq, this is not just an attack by a limited number of people, equipped with limited resources and located at a clearly identifiable place. Rather, it is an attack by all Americans and with all of their resources. Every American supposedly pays taxes to the U.S. government and is thus *de facto*, whether he wishes to be or not, implicated in every government aggression. Hence, while it is obviously false to claim that every American faces an equal risk of being attacked by Iraq, (low or nonexistent as such a risk is, it is certainly higher in New York City than in Wichita, Kansas, for instance) every American is rendered equal with respect to his own active, if not always voluntary, participation in each of his government's aggressions.

Second, just as the attacker is a state, so is the attacked, Iraq. As its U.S. counterpart, the Iraqi government has the power to tax its population or draft it into its armed forces. As taxpayer or draftee, every Iraqi is implicated in his government's defense just as every American is drawn into the U.S. government's attack. Thus, the war becomes a war of all Americans against all Iraqis, i.e., total war. The strategy of both the attacker and the defender state will be changed accordingly. While the attacker still must be selective regarding the targets of his attack, if for no other reason than that even taxing agencies (states) are ultimately constrained by scarcity, the aggressor has little or no incentive to avoid or minimize collateral damage. To the contrary, since the entire population and national wealth is involved in the defensive effort, collateral damage, whether of lives or property, is even desirable. No clear distinction between combatants and non-combatants exists. Everyone is an enemy, and all property provides support for the attacked government. Hence, everyone and everything becomes fair game. Likewise, the defender state will be little concerned about collateral damage resulting from its own retaliation against the attacker. Every citizen of the attacker state and all of their property is a foe and enemy property and thus becomes a possible target of retaliation. Moreover, every state, in accordance with this character of interstate war, will develop and employ more weapons of mass destruction, such as atomic bombs, rather than long-range precision weapons, such as my imaginary laser gun.

Thus, the similarity between war and natural catastrophes—their seemingly indiscriminate destruction and devastation—is exclusively a feature of a statist world.

VII. Insurance and Incentives

This brings on the last problem. We have seen that just as all property is private, all defense must be insured individually by capitalized insurance agencies, very much like industrial accident insurance. Yet, we have also seen that both forms of insurance differ in one fundamental respect. In the case of defense insurance, the location of the insured property matters. The premium per insured value will be different at different locations. Furthermore, aggressors can move around, their arsenal of weapons may change, and their entire character of aggression can alter with the presence of states. Thus, even given an initial property location, the price per insured value can alter with changes in the social environment or surroundings of this location. How would a system of competitive insurance agencies respond to this challenge? In particular, how would it deal with the existence of states and state aggression?

In answering these questions it is essential to recall some elementary economic insights. Other things being equal, private property owners generally, and business owners in particular, prefer locations with low protection costs (insurance premiums) and rising property values to those with high protection costs and falling property values. Consequently, there is a tendency toward the migration of people and goods from high-risk and falling property-value areas into low-risk and increasing property-value areas. Furthermore, protection costs and property values are directly related.

Other things being equal, higher protection costs (greater attack risks) imply lower or falling property values, and lower protection costs imply higher or increasing property values. These laws and tendencies shape the operation of a competitive system of insurance-protection agencies.

First, whereas a tax-funded monopolist will manifest a tendency to raise the cost and price of protection, private profit-loss insurance agencies strive to reduce the cost of protection and thus bring about falling prices. At the same time insurance agencies are more interested than anyone else in rising property values, because this implies not only that their own property holdings appreciate but in particular that there will also be more of other people's property for them to insure. In contrast, if the risk of aggression increases and property values fall, there is less value to be insured while the cost of protection and price of insurance rises, implying poor business conditions for an insurer. Consequently, insurance companies would be under permanent economic pressure to promote the former favorable and avert the latter unfavorable condition.

This incentive structure has a fundamental impact on the operation of insurers. For one, as for the seemingly easier case of the protection against common crime and criminals, a system of competitive insurers would lead to a dramatic change in current crime policy. To recognize the extent of this change, it is instructive to look first at the present and thus familiar statist crime policy. While it is in the interest of state agents to combat common private crime (if only so that there is more property left for them to tax), as tax-funded agents they have little or no interest in being particularly effective at the task of preventing it, or else, if it has occurred, at compensating its victims and apprehending and punishing the offenders. Moreover, under democratic conditions, insult will be added to injury. For if everyone — aggressors as well as non-aggressors and residents of high crime locations as well as those of low-crime locations — can vote and be elected to government office, a systematic redistribution of property rights from non-aggressors to aggressors and the residents of low-crime areas to those of high crime areas comes into effect and crime will actually be promoted. Accordingly, crime, and consequently the demand for private security services of all kinds are currently at an all-time high. Even more scandalously, instead of compensating the victims of the crimes it did not prevent (as it should have), the government forces victims to pay again as taxpayers for the cost of the apprehension, imprisonment, rehabilitation, and/or entertainment of their aggressors. And rather than requiring higher protection prices in high crime locations and lower ones in low-crime locations, as insurers would, the government does the exact opposite. It taxes more in low-crime and high property-value areas than in high-crime and low property-value ones, or it even subsidizes the residents of the latter locations—the slums—at the expense of those of the former and thus erodes the social conditions unfavorable to crime while promoting those favorable to it.[14]

The operation of competitive insurers would be in striking contrast. For one, if an insurer could not prevent a crime, it would have to indemnify the victim. Thus, above all insurers would want to be effective in crime prevention. And if they still could not prevent it, they would want to be efficient in the detection, apprehension, and punishment of criminal offenders, because in finding and arresting an offender, the insurer could force the criminal—rather than the victim and its insurer—to pay for the damages and cost of indemnification.

More specifically, just as insurance companies currently maintain and continually update a detailed local inventory of property values so they would then maintain and continually update a detailed local inventory of crimes and criminals. Other things being equal, the risk of aggression against any private property location increases with the proximity and the number and resources of potential aggressors. Thus, insurers would be interested in gathering information on actual crimes and known criminals and their locations, and it would be in their mutual interest of minimizing property damage to share this information with each other (just as banks now share information on bad credit risks with each other). Furthermore, insurers would also be particularly interested in gathering information on potential (not yet committed and known) crimes and aggressors, and this would lead to a fundamental overhaul of and improvement in current—statist—crime statistics. In order to predict the future incidence of crime

14. On crime and punishment, past and present, see Terry Anderson and P. J. Hill, "The American Experiment in Anarcho-Capitalism: The Not So Wild, Wild West," *Journal of Libertarian Studies* 3, no. 1 (1979); Bruce L. Benson, "Guns for Protection, and Other Private Sector Responses to the Government's Failure to Control Crime," *Journal of Libertarian Studies* 8, no. 1 (1986); Roger D. McGrath, *Gunfighters, Highwaymen, and Vigilantes: Violence on the Frontier* (Berkeley: University of California Press, 1984); James Q. Wilson and Richard J. Herrnstien, *Crime and Human Nature* (New York: Simon and Schuster, 1985); Edward C. Banfield, *The Unheavenly City Revisited* (Boston: Little, Brown, 1974).

and thus calculate its current price (premium), insurers would correlate the frequency, description, and character of criminals and crimes with the social surroundings in which they occur and operate, and develop and under competitive pressure continually refine an elaborate system of demographic and sociological crime indicators.[15] That is, every neighborhood would be described, and its risk assessed, in terms and in light of a multitude of crime indicators, such as the composition of sexes, age groups, races, nationalities, ethnicities, religions, languages, professions, and incomes.

Consequently, and in distinct contrast to the present situation, all inter-local, regional, racial, national, ethnic, religious, and linguistic income, and wealth redistribution would disappear, and a constant source of social conflict would be removed permanently. Instead, the emerging price (premium) structure would tend to accurately reflect the risk of each location and its particular social surrounding, such that no one would be forced to pay for the insurance risk of anyone but his own and that associated with his particular neighborhood. More importantly, based on its continually updated and refined system of statistics on crime and property values and further motivated by the noted migration tendency from high-risk–low-value (henceforth "bad") to low-risk–high-value (henceforth "good") locations, a system of competitive aggression insurers would promote a tendency toward civilizational progress (rather than de-civilization).

Governments — and democratic governments in particular — erode "good" and promote "bad" neighborhoods through their tax and transfer policy. They do so also, and with possibly an even more damaging effect, through their policy of forced integration. This policy has two aspects. On the one hand, for the owners and residents in "good" locations and neighborhoods who are faced with an immigration problem, forced integration means that they must accept, without discrimination, every domestic immigrant, as transient or tourist on public roads, as customer, client, resident, or neighbor. They are prohibited by their government from excluding anyone, including anyone they consider an undesirable potential risk, from immigration. On the other hand, for those owners and residents

---

15. For an overview of the extent to which official—statist—statistics, in particular on crime, deliberately ignore, misrepresent, or distort the known facts for reason of so-called public policy (political correctness), see J. Philippe Rushton, *Race, Evolution, and Behavior* (New Brunswick, N.J.: Transaction Publishers, 1995); Michael Levin, *Why Race Matters* (Westport, Conn.: Praeger, 1997).

in "bad" locations and neighborhoods, who experience emigration rather than immigration, forced integration means that they are prevented from effective self-protection. Rather than being allowed to rid themselves of crime through the expulsion of known criminals from their neighborhood, they are forced by their government to live in permanent association with their aggressors.[16]

The results of a system of private protection insurers would be in striking contrast to these all too familiar de-civilizing effects and tendencies of statist crime protection. To be sure, insurers would be unable to eliminate the differences between "good" and "bad" neighborhoods. In fact, these differences might even become more pronounced. However, driven by their interest in rising property values and falling protection costs, insurers would promote a tendency to improve by uplifting and cultivating both "good" and "bad" neighborhoods. Thus, in "good" neighborhoods insurers would adopt a policy of selective immigration. Unlike states, they could not and would not want to disregard the discriminating inclinations among the insured toward immigrants. To the contrary, even more so than any one of their clients, insurers would be interested in discrimination: in admitting only those immigrants whose presence adds to a lower crime risk and increased property values and in excluding those whose presence leads to a higher risk and lower property values. That is, rather than eliminating discrimination, insurers would rationalize and perfect its practice. Based on their statistics on crime and property values, and in order to reduce the cost of protection and raise property values, insurers would formulate and continually refine various restrictive (exclusionary) rules and procedures relating to immigration and immigrants and thus give quantitative precision—in the form of prices and price differentials—to the value of discrimination (and the cost of non-discrimination) between potential immigrants (as high- or low-risk and value-productive).

Similarly, in "bad" neighborhoods the interests of the insurers and the insured would coincide. Insurers would not want to suppress the expulsionist inclinations among the insured toward known criminals. They would rationalize such tendencies by offering selective price cuts (contingent on specific cleanup operations). Indeed, in cooperation with one another, insurers would want to expel known criminals not just from their immediate

---

16. See Hans-Hermann Hoppe, "Free Immigration or Forced Integration," *Chronicles* (July 1995).

neighborhood, but from civilization altogether, into the wilderness or open frontier of the Amazon jungle, the Sahara, or the polar regions.

VIII. INSURING AGAINST STATE AGGRESSION

Yet what about defense against a state? How would insurers protect us from state aggression?

First, it is essential to remember that governments *qua* compulsory, tax-funded monopolies are inherently wasteful and inefficient in whatever they do. This is also true for weapons technology and production, military intelligence and strategy, especially in our age of high technology. Accordingly, states would not be able to compete within the same territory against voluntarily financed insurance agencies. Moreover, most important and general among the restrictive rules relating to immigration and designed by insurers to lower protection cost and increase property values would be the one concerning government agents. States are inherently aggressive and pose a permanent danger to every insurer and insured. Thus, insurers in particular would want to exclude or severely restrict—as a potential security risk—the immigration (territorial entry) of all known government agents, and they would induce the insured, either as a condition of insurance or of a lower premium, to exclude or strictly limit any direct contact with any known government agent, be it as visitor, customer, client, resident, or neighbor. That is, wherever insurance companies operated—in all free territories—state agents would be treated as undesirable outcasts, potentially more dangerous than any common criminal. Accordingly, states and their personnel would be able to operate and reside only in territorial separation from, and on the fringes of, free territories. Furthermore, owing to the comparatively lower economic productivity of statist territories, governments would be continually weakened by the emigration of their most value-productive residents.

Now, what if such a government should decide to attack or invade a free territory? This would be easier said than done! Who and what would one attack? There would be no state opponent. Only private property owners and their private insurance agencies would exist. No one, least of all the insurers, would have presumably engaged in aggression or even provocation. If there were any aggression or provocation against the state at all, this would be the action of a particular person, and in this case the interest of the state and insurance agencies would fully coincide. Both would want to see the attacker punished and held accountable for all damages caused. But without any aggressor-enemy, how could the state justify an attack and even more so any indiscriminate attack? And surely it would have to justify it! For the power of every government, even the most despotic one, rests ultimately on opinion and consent, as La Boétie, Hume, Mises and Rothbard have explained.[17] Kings and presidents can issue an order to attack, of course. But there must be scores of others willing to execute their order to put it into effect. There must be generals receiving and following the order, soldiers willing to march, kill, and be killed, and domestic producers willing to continue producing to fund the war. If this consensual willingness were absent because the orders of the state rulers were considered illegitimate, even the seemingly most powerful government would be rendered ineffectual and collapse, as the recent examples of the Shah of Iran and the Soviet Union have illustrated. Hence, from the viewpoint of the leaders of the state an attack on free territories would have to be considered extremely risky. No propaganda effort, however elaborate, would make the public believe that its attack were anything but an aggression against innocent victims. In this situation, the rulers of the state would be happy to maintain monopolistic control over their present territory rather than running the risk of losing legitimacy and all of their power in an attempt at territorial expansion.

However, as unlikely as this may be, what would happen if a state still attacked and/or invaded a neighboring free territory? In this case the aggressor would not encounter an unarmed population. Only in statist territories is the civilian population characteristically unarmed. States everywhere aim to disarm their own citizenry so as to be better able to tax and expropriate it. In contrast, insurers in free territories would not want to disarm the insured. Nor could they. For who would want to be protected by someone who required him as a first step to give up his ultimate means of self-defense? To the contrary, insurance agencies would encourage the ownership of weapons among their insured by means of selective price cuts.

Moreover, apart from the opposition of an armed private citizenry, the aggressor state would run into the resistance of not only one but

---

17. Etienne de La Boétie, *The Politics of Obedience: The Discourse of Voluntary Servitude* (New York: Free Life Editions, 1975); David Hume, "The First Principles of Government," in idem, *Essays: Moral, Political, and Literary* (Oxford: Oxford University Press, 1971); Ludwig von Mises, *Liberalism: In the Classical Tradition* (San Francisco: Cobden Press, 1985); Murray N. Rothbard, *Egalitarianism as a Revolt Against Nature and Other Essays* (Washington, D.C.: Libertarian Review Press, 1974).

in all likelihood several insurance and reinsurance agencies. In the case of a successful attack and invasion, these insurers would be faced with massive indemnification payments. Unlike the aggressing state, however, these insurers would be efficient and competitive firms. Other things being equal, the risk of an attack—and hence the price of defense insurance— would be higher in locations adjacent or in close proximity to state territories than in places far away from any state. To justify this higher price, insurers would have to demonstrate defensive readiness *vis-à-vis* any possible state aggression to their clients, in the form of intelligence services, the ownership of suitable weapons and materials, and military personnel and training. In other words, the insurers would be prepared—effectively equipped and trained—for the contingency of a state attack and ready to respond with a two-fold defense strategy. On the one hand, insofar as their operations in free territories are concerned insurers would be ready to expel, capture, or kill every invader while at the same time trying to avoid or minimize all collateral damage. On the other hand, insofar as their operations on state territory are concerned insurers would be prepared to target the aggressor—the state— for retaliation. That is, insurers would be ready to counterattack and kill, whether with long-range precision weapons or assassination commandos, state agents from the top of the government hierarchy of king, president, or prime minister on downward while at the same time seeking to avoid or minimize all collateral damage to the property of innocent civilians (non-state agents), and they would thereby encourage internal resistance against the aggressor government, promote its de-legitimization, and possibly incite the liberation and transformation of the state territory into a free country.

IX. Regaining Our Right to Self-Defense

I have thus come full circle with my argument. First, I have shown that the idea of a protective state and state protection of private property is based on a fundamental theoretical error, and that this error has had disastrous consequences: the destruction and insecurity of all private property and perpetual war. Second, I have shown that the correct answer to the question of who is to defend private property owners from aggression is the same as for the production of every other good or service: private property owners, cooperation based on the division of labor, and market competition. Third, I have explained how a system of private profit-loss insurers would effectively minimize aggression, whether by private criminals or states, and promote a tendency toward civilization and perpetual peace. The only task outstanding, then, is to implement these insights: to withdraw one's consent and willing cooperation from the state and to promote its de-legitimization in public opinion so as to persuade others to do the same. Without the erroneous public perception and judgment of the state as just and necessary and without the public's voluntary cooperation, even the seemingly most powerful government would implode and its powers evaporate. Thus liberated, we would regain our right to self-defense and be able to turn to freed and unregulated insurance agencies for efficient professional assistance in all matters of protection and conflict resolution.

13

Reflections on State and War

Conventionally, the state is defined as an agency with two unique characteristics. First, it is a compulsory territorial monopolist of ultimate decision-making (jurisdiction). That is, it is the ultimate arbiter in every case of conflict, including conflicts involving itself. Second, the state is a territorial monopolist of taxation. That is, it is an agency that unilaterally fixes the price citizens must pay for its provision of law and order.

Predictably, if one can only appeal to the state for justice, justice will be perverted in favor of the state. Instead of resolving conflict, a monopolist of ultimate decision-making will provoke conflict in order to settle it to his own advantage. Worse, while the quality of justice will fall under monopolistic auspices, its price will rise. Motivated like everyone else by self-interest but equipped with the power to tax, the state agents' goal is always the same: to maximize income and minimize productive effort.

I. STATE, WAR, AND IMPERIALISM

Instead of concentrating on the internal consequences of the institution of a state, however, I will focus on its external consequences, i.e., foreign rather than domestic policy.

For one, as an agency that perverts justice and imposes taxes, every state is threatened with "exit." Especially its most productive citizen may leave to escape taxation and the perversions of law. No state likes this. To the contrary, instead of seeing the range of control and tax base shrink, state agents prefer that they be expanded. Yet this brings them in conflict with other states. Unlike competition between "natural" persons and institutions, however,

---

• A speech delivered in Auburn, Alabama, on the occasion of Professor Hoppe's receiving the Mises Institute's 2006 Gary G. Schlarbaum Liberty Prize.

the competition between states is eliminative. That is, there can be only one monopolist of ultimate decision-making and taxation in any given area. Consequently, the competition between different states promotes a tendency toward political centralization and ultimately one single world state.

Further, as tax-funded monopolists of ultimate decision-making, states are inherently aggressive institutions. Whereas "natural" persons and institutions must bear the cost of aggressive behavior themselves (which may well induce them to abstain from such conduct), states can externalize this cost onto their taxpayers. Hence, state agents are prone to become provocateurs and aggressors and the process of centralization can be expected to proceed by means of violent clashes, i.e., interstate wars.

Moreover, given that states must begin small and assuming as the starting point a world composed of a multitude of independent territorial units, something rather specific about the requirement of success can be stated. Victory or defeat in interstate warfare depend on many factors, of course, but other things such as population size being the same, in the long run the decisive factor is the relative amount of economic resources at a state's disposal. In taxing and regulating, states do not contribute to the creation of economic wealth. Instead, they parasitically draw on existing wealth. However, state governments can influence the amount of existing wealth negatively. Other things being equal, the lower the tax and regulation burden imposed on the domestic economy, the larger the population will tend to grow and the larger the amount of domestically produced wealth on which the state can draw in its conflicts with neighboring competitors. That is, states that tax and regulate their economies comparatively little — liberal states — tend to defeat and expand their territories or their range of hegemonic control at the expense of less liberal ones.

This explains, for instance, why Western Europe came to dominate the rest of the world rather than the other way around. More specifically, it explains why it was first the Dutch, then the British and finally, in the 20th century, the United States, that became the dominant imperial power, and why the United States, internally one of the most liberal states, has conducted the most aggressive foreign policy, while the former Soviet Union, for instance, with its entirely illiberal (repressive) domestic policies has engaged in a comparatively peaceful and cautious foreign policy. The United States knew that it could militarily beat any other state; hence, it has been aggressive. In contrast, the Soviet Union knew that it was bound to lose a military confrontation with any state of substantial size unless it could win within a few days or weeks.

II. From Monarchy and Wars of Armies to Democracy and Total Wars

Historically, most states have been monarchies, headed by absolute or constitutional kings or princes. It is interesting to ask why this is so, but here I have to leave this question aside. Suffice it to say that democratic states (including so-called parliamentary monarchies), headed by presidents or prime ministers, were rare until the French Revolution and have assumed world-historic importance only after World War I.

While all states must be expected to have aggressive inclinations, the incentive structure faced by traditional kings on the one hand and modern presidents on the other is different enough to account for different kinds of war. Whereas kings viewed themselves as the private *owner* of the territory under their control, presidents consider themselves as temporary *caretakers*. The *owner* of a resource is concerned about the current income to be derived from the resource and the capital value embodied in it (as a reflection of expected future income). His interests are long-run, with a concern for the preservation and enhancement of the capital values embodied in "his" country. In contrast, the *caretaker* of a resource (viewed as *public* rather than private property) is concerned primarily about his current income and pays little or no attention to capital values.

The empirical upshot of this different incentive structure is that monarchical wars tended to be "moderate" and "conservative" as compared to democratic warfare.

Monarchical wars typically arose out of inheritance disputes brought on by a complex network of inter-dynastic marriages. They were characterized by tangible territorial objectives. They were not ideologically motivated quarrels. The public considered war the king's private affair, to be financed and executed with his own money and military forces. Moreover, as conflicts between different ruling families, kings felt compelled to recognize a clear distinction between combatants and non-combatants and target their war efforts exclusively against each other and their family estates. Thus military historian Michael Howard noted about 18th-century monarchical warfare:

> On the [European] continent commerce, travel, cultural and learned intercourse went on in wartime almost unhindered. The wars were

the king's wars. The role of the good citizen was to pay his taxes, and sound political economy dictated that he should be left alone to make the money out of which to pay those taxes. He was required to participate neither in the decision out of which wars arose nor to take part in them once they broke out, unless prompted by a spirit of youthful adventure. These matters were *arcane regni*, the concern of the sovereign alone.[1]

Similarly Ludwig von Mises observed about the wars of armies:

> In wars of armies, the army does the fighting while the citizens who are not members of the army pursue their normal lives. The citizens pay the costs of warfare; they pay for the maintenance and equipment of the army, but otherwise they remain outside of the war events. It may happen that the war actions raze their houses, devastate their land, and destroy their other property; but this, too, is part of the war costs which they have to bear. It may also happen that they are looted and incidentally killed by the warriors—even by those of their "own" army. But these are events which are not inherent in warfare as such; they hinder rather than help the operations of the army leaders and are not tolerated if those in command have full control over their troops. The warring state which has formed, equipped, and maintained the army considers looting by the soldiers an offense; they were hired to fight, not to loot on their own. The state wants to keep civil life as usual because it wants to preserve the tax-paying ability of its citizens; conquered territories are regarded as its own domain. The system of the market economy is to be maintained during the war to serve the requirement of warfare.[2]

In contrast to the limited warfare of the *ancien régime*, the era of democratic warfare—which began with the French Revolution and the Napoleonic Wars, continued during the 19th century with the American War of Southern Independence, and reached its apex during the 20th century with World War I and World War II—has been the era of total war.

In blurring the distinction between the rulers and the ruled ("we all rule ourselves"), democracy strengthened the identification of the public with a particular state. Rather than dynastic property disputes which could be resolved through conquest and occupation, democratic wars became

---

1. Michael Howard, *War in European History* (New York: Oxford University Press, 1976), p. 73.

2. Ludwig von Mises, *Nationalökonomie: Theorie des Handelns und Wirtschaftens* (Union Genf, 1940), pp. 725–26.

ideological battles: clashes of civilizations, which could only be resolved through cultural, linguistic, or religious domination, subjugation and, if necessary, extermination. It became increasingly difficult for members of the public to extricate themselves from personal involvement in war. Resistance against higher taxes to fund a war was considered treasonous. Because the democratic state, unlike a monarchy, was "owned" by all, conscription became the rule rather than the exception. And with mass armies of cheap and hence easily disposable conscripts fighting for national goals and ideals, backed by the economic resources of the entire nation, all distinctions between combatants and non-combatants fell by the wayside. Collateral damage was no longer an unintended side-effect but became an integral part of warfare. "Once the state ceased to be regarded as 'property' of dynastic princes," Michael Howard noted, and

> became instead the instrument of powerful forces dedicated to such abstract concepts as Liberty, or Nationality, or Revolution, which enabled large numbers of the population to see in that state the embodiment of some absolute Good for which no price was too high, no sacrifice too great to pay; then the "temperate and indecisive contests" of the rococo age appeared as absurd anachronisms.[3]

Similar observations have been made by the military historian Major General J. F. C. Fuller:

> The influence of the spirit of nationality, that is of democracy, on war was profound, ... [it] emotionalized war and, consequently, brutalized it; ... National armies fight nations, royal armies fight their like, the first obey a mob—always demented, the second a king, generally sane.... All this developed out of the French Revolution, which also gave to the world conscription—herd warfare, and the herd coupling with finance and commerce has begotten new realms of war. For when once the whole nation fights, then is the whole national credit available for the purpose of war.[4]

And William A. Orton thus summarized matters:

> Nineteenth-century wars were kept within bounds by the tradition, well recognized in international law, that civilian property and business were outside the sphere of combat. Civilian assets were not

---

3. Howard, *War in European History*, pp. 75–76.
4. John F. C. Fuller, *War and Western Civilization* (Freeport, N.Y.: Books for Libraries, 1969), pp. 26–27.

exposed to arbitrary distraint or permanent seizure, and apart from such territorial and financial stipulations as one state might impose on another, the economic and cultural life of the belligerents was generally allowed to continue pretty much as it had been. Twentieth-century practice has changed all that. During both World Wars limitless lists of contraband coupled with unilateral declarations of maritime law put every sort of commerce in jeopardy, and made waste paper of all precedents. The close of the first war was marked by a determined and successful effort to impair the economic recovery of the principal losers, and to retain certain civilian properties. The second war has seen the extension of that policy to a point at which international law in war has ceased to exist. For years the Government of Germany, so far as its arms could reach, had based a policy of confiscation on a racial theory that had no standing in civil law, international law, nor Christian ethics; and when the war began, that violation of the comity of nations proved contagious. Anglo-American leadership, in both speech and action, launched a crusade that admitted of neither legal nor territorial limits to the exercise of coercion. The concept of neutrality was denounced in both theory and practice. Not only enemy assets and interests, but the assets and interests of any parties whatsoever, even in neutral countries, were exposed to every constraint the belligerent powers could make effective; and the assets and interests of neutral states and their civilians, lodged in belligerent territories or under belligerent control, were subjected to practically the same sort of coercion as those of enemy nationals. Thus "total war" became a sort of war that no civilian community could hope to escape; and "peace loving nations" will draw the obvious inference.[5]

III. Excursus: The Doctrine of Democratic Peace

I have explained how the institution of a state leads to war; why, seemingly paradoxical, internally liberal states tend to be imperialist powers; and how the spirit of democracy has contributed to the de-civilization in the conduct of war.

More specifically, I have explained the rise of the United States to the rank of the world's foremost imperial power; and, as a consequence of its successive transformation from the early beginnings as an aristocratic

---

5. William A. Orton, *The Liberal Tradition: A Study of the Social and Spiritual Conditions of Freedom* (New Haven, Conn.: Yale University Press, 1945), pp. 251–52.

republic into an unrestricted mass democracy which began with the War of Southern Independence, the role of the United States as an increasingly arrogant, self-righteous and zealous warmonger.

What appears to be standing in the way of peace and civilization, then, is above all the state and democracy, and specifically the world's model democracy: the United States. Ironically if not surprisingly, however, it is precisely the United States which claims that it is the solution to the quest for peace.

The reason for this claim is the doctrine of democratic peace, which goes back to the days of Woodrow Wilson and World War I, has been revived in recent years by George W. Bush and his neo-conservative advisors, and by now has become intellectual folklore even in liberal-libertarian circles. The theory claims:

- *Democracies do not go to war against each other.*
- *Hence, in order to create lasting peace, the entire world must be made democratic.*

And as a—largely unstated—corollary:

- *Today, many states are not democratic and resist internal—democratic— reform.*
- *Hence, war must be waged on those states in order to convert them to democracy and thus create lasting peace.*

I do not have the patience for a full-blown critique of this theory. I shall merely provide a brief critique of the theory's initial premise and its ultimate conclusion.

First: Do democracies not go to war against each other? Since almost no democracies existed before the 20th century the answer supposedly must be found within the last hundred years or so. In fact, the bulk of the evidence offered in favor of the thesis is the observation that the countries of Western Europe have not gone to war against each other in the post–World War II era. Likewise, in the Pacific region, Japan and South Korea have not warred against each other during the same period. Does this evidence prove the case? The democratic-peace theorists think so. As "scientists" they are interested in "statistical" proof, and as they see it there are plenty of "cases" on which to build such proof: Germany did not war against France, Italy, England, etc.; France did not war against Spain, Italy, Belgium, etc. Moreover, there are permutations: Germany did not attack France, nor did France attack Germany, etc. Thus, we have seemingly dozens of confirmations—and that for some 60 years—and not a single counterexample. But do we really have so many confirming cases?

The answer is no: we have actually no more than a single case at hand. With the end of World War II, essentially all of—by now, democratic—Western Europe (and democratic Japan and South Korea in the Pacific region) has become part of the U.S. Empire, as indicated by the presence of U.S. troops in practically all of these countries. What the post–World War II period of peace then "proves" is not that democracies do not go to war against each other but that a hegemonic, imperialist power such as the United States did not let its various colonial parts go to war against each other (and, of course, that the hegemon itself did not see any need to go to war against its satellites—because they obeyed—and they did not see the need or did not dare to disobey their master).

Moreover, if matters are thus perceived—based on an understanding of history rather than the naïve belief that because one entity has a different name than another their behavior must be independent from one another—it becomes clear that the evidence presented has nothing to do with democracy and everything with hegemony. For instance, no war broke out between the end of World War II and the end of the 1980s, i.e., during the hegemonic reign of the Soviet Union, between East Germany, Poland, Czechoslovakia, Romania, Bulgaria, Lithuania, Estonia, Hungary, etc. Was this because these were communist dictatorships and communist dictatorships do not go to war against each other? That would have to be the conclusion of "scientists" of the caliber of democratic-peace theorists! But surely this conclusion is wrong. No war broke out because the Soviet Union did not permit this to happen—just as no war between Western democracies broke out because the United States did not permit this to happen in its dominion. To be sure, the Soviet Union intervened in Hungary and Czechoslovakia, but so did the United States at various occasions in Central America, such as in Guatemala for instance. (Incidentally: How about the wars between Israel and Palestine and Lebanon? Are not all these democracies? Or are Arab countries ruled out by definition as undemocratic?)

Second: What about democracy as a solution to anything, let alone peace? Here the case of democratic-peace theorists appears even worse. Indeed, the lack of historical understanding displayed by them is truly frightening. Here are only some fundamental shortcomings:

First, the theory involves a conceptual conflation of democracy and liberty (freedom) that can only be called scandalous, especially coming from self-proclaimed libertarians. The foundation and cornerstone of liberty is the institution of private property; and private—exclusive—property is logically incompatible with democracy—majority rule. Democracy has nothing to do with freedom. Democracy is a soft variant of communism, and rarely in the history of ideas has it been taken for anything else. Incidentally, before the outbreak of the democratic age, i.e., until the beginning of the 20th century, government (state) tax-expenditures (combining all levels of government) in Western European countries constituted somewhere between 7 and 15% of national product, and in the still young United States even less. Less than a hundred years of full-blown majority rule have increased this percentage to about 50% in Europe and 40% in the United States.

Second, the theory of democratic peace distinguishes essentially only between democracy and non-democracy, summarily labeled dictatorship. Thus not only do all aristocratic-republican regimes disappear from view but, more importantly for my current purposes, so do all traditional monarchies. They are equated with dictatorships à la Lenin, Mussolini, Hitler, Stalin, Mao. In fact, however, traditional monarchies have little in common with dictatorships (while democracy and dictatorship are intimately related).

Monarchies are the semi-organic outgrowth of hierarchically structured natural—stateless—social orders. Kings are the heads of extended families, of clans, tribes, and nations. They command a great deal of natural, voluntarily acknowledged authority, inherited and accumulated over many generations. It is within the framework of such orders (and of aristocratic republics) that liberalism first developed and flourished. In contrast, democracies are egalitarian and redistributionist in outlook; hence, the above-mentioned growth of state power in the 20th century. Characteristically, the transition from the monarchical age to the democratic one, beginning in the second half of the 19th century, has seen a continuous decline in the strength of liberal parties and a corresponding strengthening of socialists of all stripes.

Third, it follows from this that the view democratic-peace theorists have of conflagrations such as World War I must be considered grotesque, at least from the point of view of someone allegedly valuing freedom. For them, this war was essentially a war of democracy against dictatorship; hence, by increasing the number of democracies, it was a progressive, peace-enhancing, and ultimately justified war.

In fact, matters are very different. To be sure, pre-war Germany and Austria may not have qualified as *democratic* as England, France, or the United States at the time. But Germany and Austria were definitely not dictatorships. They were (increasingly emasculated) monarchies and as such arguably as *liberal*—if not more so—than their counterparts. For instance, in the United States, anti-war proponents were jailed, the German language was essentially outlawed, and citizens of German descent were openly harassed and often forced to change their names. Nothing comparable occurred in Austria and Germany.

In any case, however, the *result* of the crusade to make the world safe for democracy was *less liberal* than what had existed before (and the Versailles peace dictate precipitated World War II). Not only did state power grow faster after the war than before. In particular, the treatment of minorities deteriorated in the democratized post-World War I period. In newly founded Czechoslovakia, for instance, the Germans were systematically mistreated (until they were finally expelled by the millions and butchered by the tens of thousands after World War II) by the majority Czechs. Nothing remotely comparable had happened to the Czechs during the previous Habsburg reign. The situation regarding the relations between Germans and southern Slavs in pre-war Austria versus post-war Yugoslavia respectively was similar.

Nor was this a fluke. As under the Habsburg monarchy in Austria, for instance, minorities had also been treated fairly well under the Ottomans. However, when the multicultural Ottoman Empire disintegrated in the course of the 19th century and was replaced by semi-democratic nation-states such as Greece, Bulgaria, etc., the existing Ottoman Muslims were expelled or exterminated. Similarly, after democracy had triumphed in the United States with the military conquest of the Southern Confederacy, the Union government quickly proceeded to exterminate the Plains Indians. As Mises had recognized, democracy does not work in multi-ethnic societies. It does not create peace but promotes conflict and has potentially genocidal tendencies.

Fourth, and intimately related, the democratic-peace theorists claim that democracy represents a stable "equilibrium." This has been expressed most clearly by Francis Fukuyama, who labeled the new democratic world order as the "end of history." However, overwhelming evidence exists that this claim is patently wrong.

On theoretical grounds: How can democracy be a stable equilibrium if it is possible that it be transformed *democratically* into a dictatorship, i.e., a system that is considered *not* stable? Answer: that makes no sense!

Moreover, empirically democracies are anything *but* stable. As indicated, in multicultural societies democracy regularly leads to the discrimination, oppression, or even expulsion and extermination of minorities—hardly a peaceful equilibrium. And in ethnically homogeneous societies, democracy regularly leads to class warfare, which leads to economic crisis, which leads to dictatorship. Think, for example, of post-Czarist Russia, post-World War I Italy, Weimar Germany, Spain, Portugal, and in more recent times Greece, Turkey, Guatemala, Argentina, Chile, and Pakistan.

Not only is this close correlation between democracy and dictatorship troublesome for democratic-peace theorists; worse, they must come to grips with the fact that the dictatorships emerging from crises of democracy are by no means always worse, from a classical liberal or libertarian view, than what would have resulted otherwise. Cases can be easily cited where dictatorships were preferable and an improvement. Think of Italy and Mussolini or Spain and Franco. In addition, how is one to square the starry-eyed advocacy of democracy with the fact that dictators, quite unlike kings who owe their rank to an accident of birth, are often favorites of the masses and in this sense highly democratic? Just think of Lenin or Stalin, who were certainly more democratic than Czar Nicholas II; or think of Hitler, who was definitely more democratic and a "man of the people" than Kaiser Wilhelm II or Kaiser Franz Joseph.

According to democratic-peace theorists, then, it would seem that we are supposed to war against foreign dictators, whether kings or demagogues, in order to install democracies, which then turn into (modern) dictatorships, until finally, one supposes, the United States itself has turned into a dictatorship, owing to the growth of internal state power which results from the endless "emergencies" engendered by foreign wars.

Better, I dare say, to heed the advice of Erik von Kuehnelt-Leddihn and, instead of aiming to make the world safe for democracy, we try making it safe from democracy—everywhere, but most importantly in the United States.

IV. Making the World Safe from Democracy
or: How to Defend Oneself Against the United States

After this excursion into the theory of democratic peace I am back to the proposition that there is no greater threat to lasting peace than the democratic state, and in particular the United States. Thus the question is: how to defend oneself against the U.S.

Incidentally, this is not only a question for foreigners but Americans as well. After all, the territory constituting the U.S. too is occupied territory— conquered by the U.S. government.

Let us assume, then, that a small territory within the borders of the current U.S.—a village, a town, a county—declares its independence and secedes from the U.S. What can and will the U.S. do in response?

It is possible that the U.S. will invade the territory and crush the secessionists. This is what the French Republic did to the Vendée during the French Revolution, what the Union did to the Confederacy, and on a much smaller scale, what the U.S. government did in Waco. But history also provides examples to the contrary: the Czechs and Slovaks separated peacefully, Russia let Lithuania, Estonia and Latvia go; the Slovenes were let go; Singapore was even expelled from a previous union with Malaysia.

Obviously, the relative population size matters in the decision to war or not to war. Likewise it matters what resources are at the secessionists' disposal. Also the geographical location can weigh in favor or against intervention. But this cannot be all. For how is one to explain, for instance, that France has not long ago conquered Monaco, or Germany Luxemburg, or Switzerland Liechtenstein, or Italy Vatican City, or the U.S. Costa Rica? Or how is one to explain that the U.S. does not "finish the job" in Iraq by simply killing all Iraqis. Surely, in terms of population, technology and geography such are manageable tasks.

The reason is not that French, German, Swiss, Italian or U.S. state rulers have scruples against conquest, confiscation, and the imprisonment or killing of innocents—they do these things on a daily basis to their "own" population. Bush, for instance, has no compunction ordering to kill innocent Iraqis. He does so every day. Rather, what constrains the conduct of state rulers is public opinion.

As La Boétie, Hume, Mises and Rothbard have explained, government power ultimately rests on opinion, not brute force. Bush does not himself kill or put a gun to the head of those he orders to kill. Generals and soldiers follow his orders on their own. Nor can Bush "force" anyone to continue providing him with the funds needed for his aggression. The citizenry must do so on its own. On the other hand, if the majority of generals, soldiers and citizens stop believing in the legitimacy of Bush's commands, his commands turn into nothing more than hot air. It is this need for legitimacy that explains why state governments itching to go to war must offer a reason. The public is not typically in favor of killing innocent bystanders for fun or profit. Rather, in order to enlist the public's assistance "evidence" must be manipulated so as to make aggression appear as defense (for what reasonable person could be against defense). We know the catchwords: Fort Sumter, the U.S.S. Maine, the Lusitania, Pearl Harbor, 9–11.

It thus turns out that not even an overwhelming size advantage is decisive in determining the course of action. That David Koresh and his followers in Waco could be brutally killed by the U.S. government was due to the fact that they could be portrayed as a bunch of child molesters. Had they been "normal people" an invasion might have been considered a public relations disaster. Moreover, regardless of whatever disadvantage the secessionists have in terms of size, resources or location, this can be made up by a favorable international public opinion, especially in the internet age when the spread of news is almost instantaneous.

These considerations bring me to the final points. The new secessionist country can be another state or it can be a free, stateless society. I will argue that the likelihood of successful defense against U.S. aggression is higher if the secessionists form a stateless society than if they opt for another state; for whether large or small, states are good at aggression and bad at defense. (Granting, maybe prematurely, that the U.S. had nothing to do with 9–11 directly, the events of that day certainly show that the U.S. was not good at defending its own citizens: first, by provoking the attacks and, secondly, in having its population disarmed and defenseless *vis-à-vis* box-cutter wielding foreign invaders.)

How would the defense of a free society differ from that of a state?

As explained, the likelihood of an attack depends essentially on the ease of manipulating the evidence so as to camouflage aggression as defense—and to "discover" such evidence is much easier in the case of a state. Even the most liberal state has a monopoly of jurisdiction and taxation and thus cannot but create victims who, properly stylized as "victims of human rights violations," may provide the "excuse" for an invasion. Worse, if the new state is a democracy it is unavoidable that one group—the Catholics or the Protestants, the Shiites or the Sunnis, the Whites or the Blacks—will use its power to dominate another—and again there exists an "excuse" for invasion: to "free an oppressed minority." Better still: the oppressed are incited to "cry out" for help. Moreover, in reaction to domestic oppression terrorists may grow up who try to "revenge" the injustice: just think of the Red Brigades, the RAF, the IRA, the ETA—and both: their continued existence as well as the attempt of eradicating them may provide "reason" to intervene (to prevent the spread of terrorism or to come to the rescue of freedom fighters).

In contrast, in a free society only private property owners and firms, including insurers, police, and arbitrators, exist. If there are any aggressions, they are those of criminals—of murderers, rapists, burglars, and plain frauds—and it is difficult to portray the treatment of criminals as criminals as a reason for an invasion.

What if the attack does occur? In that case it might well be best to give up quickly, especially if the secessionist territory is very small. Thus Mogens Glistrup, founder of the Danish Progress Party, once recommended that the Defense Department of tiny Denmark be replaced with an answering machine announcing (to the Russians) that "we surrender." This way, no destruction occurs and yet the reputation of the invading government as a "defender and promoter of liberty" is soiled forever.

This leads to our central question regarding the effectiveness of states versus free societies in matters of defense. As a monopolist of ultimate decision-making, the state decides for everyone bindingly whether to resist or not; if to resist, whether in the form of civil disobedience, armed resistance or some combination thereof; and if armed resistance, of what form. If it decides to put up no resistance, this may be a well-meaning decision or it may be the result of bribes or threats by the invading state—but in any case, it will be contrary to the will of many who would have liked to resist and who are thus put in double jeopardy because as resisters they now disobey their own state as well as the invader. On the other hand, if the state decides to resist, this again may be a well-meaning decision or it may be the result of pride or fear—but in any case, it too will be contrary to the preferences of many who would have liked not to resist or to resist by different means and who are now entangled as accomplices in the state's schemes and subjected to the same collateral fallout and victor's justice as everyone else.

The reaction of a free territory is distinctly different. There is no government which makes one decision. Instead, there are numerous institutions and individuals who choose their own defense strategy, each in accordance with his own risk assessment. Consequently, the aggressor has far more difficulties conquering the territory. It is no longer sufficient to "know" the government, to win one decisive battle or to gain control of government headquarters. Even if one opponent is "known," one battle is won or one defense agency defeated, this has no bearing on others.

Moreover, the multitude of command structures and strategies as well as the contractual character of a free society affect the conduct of both armed and unarmed resistance. As for the former, in state-territories the civilian population is typically unarmed and heavy reliance exists on regular, tax-and-draft-funded armies and conventional warfare. Hence, the defense forces create enemies even among its own citizenry, which the aggressor state can use to its own advantage, and in any case there is little to fear of the aggressor once the regular army is defeated. In contrast, the population of free territories is likely heavily armed and the fighting done by irregular militias led by defense professionals and in the form of guerilla or partisan warfare. All fighters are volunteers and all of their support: food, shelter, logistical help, etc. is voluntary. Hence, guerrillas must be extremely friendly to their own population. But precisely this: their entirely defensive character and near-unanimous support in public opinion can render them nearly invincible, even by numerically far superior invading armies. History provides numerous examples: Napoleon's defeat in Spain, France's defeat in Algeria, the U.S. defeat in Vietnam, Israel's defeat in South Lebanon.

This consideration leads immediately to the other form of defense: civil disobedience. Provided only that the secessionists have the will to be free, the effectiveness of this strategy can hardly be overestimated. Recall that power does not rest alone on brute force but must rely on "opinion." The conquerors cannot put one man next to each secessionist and force him to obey their orders. The secessionists must obey by their own free will. However, if they do not, the conquerors will fail. Most importantly: civil disobedience can occur in many forms and degrees. It can range from ostentatious acts of defiance to entirely unobtrusive ways, thus allowing almost everyone to participate in the defense effort: the courageous and the timid, the young and the old, leaders and followers. One may hide armed fighters or not hinder them. One may publicly refuse to obey certain laws, or evade and ignore them. One may engage in sabotage, obstruction, negligence, or simply display a lack of diligence. One may openly scoff at orders or comply only incompletely. Tax payments may be refused or evaded. There may be demonstrations, sit-ins, boycotts, work-stoppages or plain slacking-off. The conquerors may be maltreated, molested, ridiculed, laughed at or simply ostracized and never assisted in anything. In any case: all of this contributes to the same result: to render the conquerors powerless, make them despair and finally resign and withdraw.

As is often the case, the first step in the anti-imperialist-anti-democratic struggle is the most difficult. Indeed, the difficulties are enormous. Once the first step has been successfully taken, however, things get successively easier. Once the number of secessionist territories has reached a critical mass—and every success in one location will promote imitation by other localities—the difficulties of crushing the secessionists will increase exponentially. In fact, the more time passes the greater will the comparative economic and technological advantage of free territories become, and in light of the ever increasing attractiveness and economic opportunities offered by the free territories the imperialist powers will be increasingly happy if they can hang on to their power rather than risk whatever legitimacy they still have in an attack.

Part Three

Economic Theory

14

On Certainty and Uncertainty

"The honest historicist would have to say: Nothing can be asserted about the future." —Ludwig von Mises[1]

"The future is to all of us unknowable." —Ludwig Lachmann[2]

I.

It is possible to imagine a world characterized by complete certainty. All future events and changes would be known in advance and could be predicted precisely. There would be no errors and no surprises. We would know all of our future actions and their exact outcomes. In such a world, nothing could be learned, and accordingly, nothing would be *worth knowing*. Indeed, the possession of consciousness and knowledge would be useless. For why would anyone want to know anything if all future actions and events were completely predetermined and it would not make any difference for the future course of events whether or not one possessed this or any knowledge? Our actions would be like those of an automaton—and an automaton has no need of any knowledge. Thus, rather than representing a state of perfect knowledge, complete certainty actually eliminates the value of all knowledge.

Obviously, we do not inhabit a world of complete certainty. We cannot predict all of our future actions and their outcome. There are in our world surprises. Our knowledge of future events and outcomes is less than perfect.

• Originally published in *Review of Austrian Economics* 10, no. 1 (1997).

1. Ludwig von Mises, *Theory and History* (Auburn, Ala.: Ludwig von Mises Institute, 1985), p. 203.

2. Ludwig Lachmann, "From Mises to Shackle: An Essay on Austrian Economics and the Kaleidic Society," *Journal of Economic Literature* 14 (1976): pp. 55–59.

We make errors, can distinguish between failure and success, and are capable of learning. Unlike for an automaton, for us knowledge is valuable. To know something or not makes a difference. Knowledge is not of predetermined events and states of affairs, but knowledge of how to *interfere with* and *divert* the natural course of events so as to *improve* our *subjective wellbeing*. Knowledge does not help us predict an unalterable course of events but is a tool of purposefully *changing* and hopefully *bettering* future outcomes and events. Our actions, unlike the operations of an automaton, are not a series of predetermined events, which the knower cannot influence and with respect to whose outcome he is indifferent. Rather, our actions are sequences of decisions (choices) of altering the predetermined course of events to our advantage. We are never neutral or indifferent toward the course of future events. Instead, we always *prefer* one course of events to another, and we use our knowledge to bring about our preferences. For us, knowledge is practical and effective, and while it is imperfect and subject to error, it is the only means of achieving human betterment.

II.

From the recognition of the fact that perfect foresight eliminates the very need of knowing and knowers, and that such a need only arises if, as in our world, foresight is less than perfect, and insofar as knowledge is a means of bringing about preferences, it does not follow that everything is uncertain. Quite to the contrary. In a world where everything is certain, the idea of certainty would not even come into existence. The idea of certain knowledge requires, as its logical counterpart, the idea of uncertainty. Certainty is defined in contrast to uncertainty, and not everything can be certain. Likewise, uncertainty cannot be defined without reference to certainty, and not all knowledge can be uncertain. It is this latter part of one and the same conclusion which critics of the model of perfect foresight, such as Ludwig Lachmann, have failed to recognize. From the correct insight that we do not inhabit a world of perfect knowledge it does not follow that we live in a world of perfect uncertainty; i.e., in a world with no certainty at all, and from the fact that I cannot predict all of my and others' future actions it does not follow that I can say nothing at all about them. In fact, even if I do not know everything about my future actions, for instance, I do know something to be true about each and every one of them: that I will, as long as I act, employ my knowledge to interfere in the natural course of events so as to—hopefully—bring about a more preferable state of affairs.

Later on, more will be said about the importance of this insight. But it is worth emphasizing from the outset that the idea of perfect or radical uncertainty (or ignorance) is either openly contradictory insofar as it is meant to say, "everything about the future is uncertain except that there will be uncertainty—about this we are certain," or it entails an implicit contradiction if it is meant to say, "everything is uncertain and that there is nothing but uncertainty, is uncertain, too." (I do know such and such to be the case, and I do not know whether such and such is the case or not.) Only a middle-of-the-road position between the two extremes of perfect knowledge and perfect ignorance is consistently defensible:[3] There exists uncertainty but this we know for certain. Hence, also certainty exists, and the boundary between certain and uncertain knowledge is certain (based on certain knowledge).

III.

Nothing about the external, physical world is or can be known with certainty—except for those rather abstract but universal and real things that are already implied in the certain knowledge of acting and action: that this must be a world of objects and object-qualities (predicates), of countable units, physical magnitudes, and quantitative determinateness (causality). Without objects and object-qualities there can be no such thing as propositions; without countable units there can be no arithmetic; and without quantitative determinateness the fact that definite quantities of causes only bring about definite (limited) effects—there can be no ends and means (goods), i.e., no active interference in the course of external events with the purpose of bringing about a more highly-valued end (preferred effect). Apart from the laws of propositional logic, arithmetic, and causality, however, all other knowledge about the external world is uncertain (*a posteriori*). We do not and cannot know with certainty (*a priori*) what kinds of objects and object-qualities exist, how many units of what physical

---

3. See Oskar Morgenstern, "Perfect Foresight and Economic Equilibrium," in A. Schotter, ed., *Selected Economic Writings of Oskar Morgenstern* (New York: New York University Press, 1976), esp. p. 175; Roger W. Garrison, "Austrian Economics as Middle Ground," in Israel Kirzner, ed., *Method, Process, and Austrian Economics* (Lexington, Mass.: Lexington Books, 1982); idem, "From Lachmann to Lucas: On Institutions, Expectations, and Equilibrating Tendencies," in *Subjectivism, Intelligibility and Economic Understanding: Essays in Honor of Ludwig M. Lachmann* (New York: New York University Press, 1986).

dimensions there are, and what quantitative cause-and-effect relationships exist (or do not exist) between various magnitudes of various objects. All of this must be learned from experience. Moreover, experience is invariably past experience, that of past events. It cannot reveal whether or not the facts and relationships of the past will also hold in the future. We cannot but assume that this will be the case, by and large. But it cannot be ruled out categorically that we might be mistaken, and that the future will be so different from the past that all of our past knowledge will be entirely useless. It is possible that none of our instruments or machines will work anymore tomorrow, that our houses will collapse on top of us, that the earth will open up, and that all of us will perish. It is in this sense that our knowledge of the external physical world must be ultimately regarded as uncertain.

Notwithstanding this ultimate uncertainty of our knowledge concerning the external world, however, as a result of contingent circumstances, the relative stability and regularity in the concatenation of external objects and events, it has been possible for mankind to accumulate a vast and expanding body of practically certain knowledge. This knowledge does not render the future predictable, but it helps us predict the effects to be produced by definite actions. Even though we do not know *why* things work the way they do, and whether or not they *must* always work in this way, we do know with complete practical certitude *that* and *how* certain things will operate now and tomorrow. One would never know it from the writings of the apostles of radical uncertainty but an innumerable and growing number of events (outcomes) can be produced literally at will and predicted with almost perfect exactitude. My toaster will toast, my key will open the door, my computer, telephone, and fax will work as they are supposed to, my house will protect me from the weather, cars will drive, airplanes will fly, cups will still hold water, hammers will still hammer, and nails will still nail. Much of our future is, practically speaking, perfectly certain. Every product, tool, instrument or machine represents a piece of practical certainty. To claim, instead, that we are faced with radical uncertainty and that the future is to all of us unknowable is not only self-contradictory but also appears to be a position devoid of common sense.

IV.

Our practical certainty concerning future outcomes and events extends even further. There are many future events about whose outcome we are practically certain because we literally know how to *produce* them (the outcome is under our complete practical control). We can also predict with practical certainty a great and growing number of outcomes outside and beyond anyone's control. Sometimes my tools, machines, and products are defective. My toaster does not toast, my telephone is silent, a hurricane or an earthquake has destroyed my house, my airplane crashes, or my cup is broken. I had no knowledge that this would happen to me here and now, and hence I could not have acted differently from the way I did. I am thus taken by surprise. But my surprise and my uncertainty must not be complete. For while I may know absolutely nothing about the single event—this cup will now break, this airplane will now crash, my house will be destroyed in an earthquake 2 years from now—and thus cannot possibly predict and alter any such event, I may know practically everything with respect to the whole class of events (broken cups, crashing airplanes, earthquakes) of which this single event is a member. I may know, based on the observation of long-run frequency distributions, that airplanes of a certain type crash every so often, that 1 in 10,000 cups produced is defective, that machines of such and such a type function on the average for 10 years, and that an earthquake strikes a certain region on the average twice a year and destroys, in the long run, 1 percent of the existing housing stock per year. Then, although the single event still comes as a surprise, I do know with practical certainty that surprises such as these exist and how frequent they are. I am surprised neither by the type of surprise nor its long-run frequency. My surprise is only relative. I am surprised that such and such happens here and now rather than elsewhere or later. But I am not surprised that it happens at all, here, there, now, or later. In thus delineating the range and frequency of possible surprises, my uncertainty concerning the future, while not eliminated, is systematically reduced.

Cases of limited surprises or reduced uncertainty are, of course, what Frank Knight first classified as "risk" (as opposed to "uncertainty"), and what Ludwig von Mises, building on Knight and the work on the foundations of probability theory of his mathematician brother, Richard von Mises, would later define as "class probability" (as opposed to "case probability")[4]: "Class probability means: We know or assume to know, with regard to the

4. See Richard von Mises, *Probability, Statistics, and Truth* (London: George Allen and Unwin, 1957), esp. chaps. 1 and 3; Frank Knight, *Risk, Uncertainty, and Profit* (Chicago: University of Chicago Press, 1971), esp. chap. 7; Ludwig von Mises, *Human Action: A Treatise on Economics* (Chicago: Henry Regnery, 1966), esp. chap. 6.

problem concerned, everything about the behavior of a whole class of events or phenomena; but about the actual singular events or phenomena we know nothing but that they are elements of this class."[5] I know nothing about whether this or that cup will be broken, and I know nothing about whether my house or your house will be destroyed by a tornado within the next year, but I do know from the observation of long-run frequency distributions regarding cups and tornadoes, for instance, that no more than 1 in 10,000 cups is defective and that of a thousand houses in a given territory, no more than one per year on the average will be destroyed. If, based on this knowledge, I adopted a strategy of always predicting that the next cup will not be broken, and that my house will not be destroyed next year, I would commit errors. But in the long run, the strategy would assure more successes than errors: my errors would be 'correct' errors. On the other hand, if I adopted the strategy of predicting always that the next cup will be broken and my house destroyed, I might well be correct. But in the long run this strategy would assuredly fail: I would be erroneously correct. Whenever the conditions of class probability are met and we do not know enough to avoid mistakes altogether but enough to make only correct mistakes, it is possible to take out insurance. As a producer of cups, for instance, I know that on the average I will have to produce 10,001 cups in order to have 10,000. I cannot avoid broken cups, but I can insure myself against the risk of broken cups by including it, as a regularly occurring loss, in my cost-accounting, and by thus associating a correspondingly higher cost with my production of cups. Similarly, I cannot avoid tornadoes, but I can insure myself against them. Because tornado losses are large and infrequent in relation to the size and operations of my household, it would be difficult (although not impossible) to provide insurance internally (within my household). But it is possible to pool my tornado risk with yours and that of other households or firms in a given region. Not one of us knows who will be affected by the risk in question, but based on the knowledge of the objective long-run frequency of tornadoes and tornado damage for the entire region, it is possible to calculate a premium against payment of which each one of us can be insured for this hazard.

It is not only the knowledge incorporated in our tools, instruments, and machines, then, which provides practical certain information about our future: in this case, knowledge of how we will generate various singular

<hr/>

5. R. Mises, *Probability, Statistics, and Truth*, p. 109.

events. Also, the knowledge incorporated in any form of insurance, whether internally practiced or by method of pooling, represents practical certain knowledge: in this case, knowledge of how to be prepared for various classes of events whose individual occurrence is beyond anyone's control. To be sure, while the conditions of class probability and insurability can be stated exactly, with certainty, the question of whether or not there exist insurable events, which ones, and the various expenses of insuring against them, cannot be answered with certainty. On the one hand, the knowledge of objective probability distributions must be acquired through observational experience, and as is the case for all knowledge based on such experience, we can never know whether or not past regularities will also hold in the future. We may have to make revisions. On the other hand, even in order to collect such information, it is necessary that various singular events be classified from the outset as falling into one and the same class (of events). This cup or tornado and that cup or that tornado, are both members of the same class of cup or tornado. Yet any such classification is tainted with uncertainty. The joint classification of a series of singular events is only correct (for the purpose of insurance) if it holds that I do not know more about any of the single class members than that each one of them is a member of the same class. If I learned, however, that one cup was made of clay A and another from clay B, for instance, and that this fact makes a difference for the long-run frequency of defects, my initial classification would become faulty. Similarly, I might learn from experience that tornado damage on the east side of a given valley is systematically higher than on its western side. In this case, too, my original classification would have to be changed, new and revised classes and subclasses of insurable events would have to be formed, and new and different insurance premiums would have to be calculated. These uncertainties notwithstanding, however, it deserves to be pointed out that as a contingent fact of human life, the actual range of insurance, and hence of relatively certain information about future events and outcomes, is vast and growing: We know how many ships will likely sink, how many airplanes crash, how often it will rain or shine, how many people of a given age will die, how many hot-water boilers will explode, how many people will be struck by cancer, that more women than men will be affected by breast cancer, that smokers will die earlier than non-smokers, that Jews suffer more frequently from Tay-Sachs disease than Gentiles, and Blacks more from sickle cell anemia than Whites, that tornadoes, earthquakes, and floods occur here but not there, etc. Our future is most definitely not unknowable.

V.

Little of this ever attracts the attention of theoreticians of radical uncertainty. The existence of a practical working technology and of a vast and flourishing insurance industry constitutes an embarrassment for any theory of radical uncertainty. If pressed sufficiently hard, of course, Lachmann and his followers would probably admit the undeniable and, as if all of this did not matter, quickly move on to another problem. So far, it might be pointed out with some justification, attention has been directed almost exclusively either to the technological rather than the economic aspect of action—to accidents rather than to actions. The phenomenon of radical uncertainty, however, arises in a different arena. While it may be possible to predict the physical outcomes *if* such and such an action is taken, and while it may be possible also to predict the pattern of various physical events entirely outside of human control, matters are completely different when it comes to predicting our own future actions. I can predict that my toaster will toast if I employ it in a certain way, and I can predict that toasters generally do not work longer than 10 years, but presumably I cannot predict whether or not I will actually employ my toaster in the future, nor could I have predicted before it actually happened that I ever wanted—and constructed or bought—a toaster in the first place. It is here, in the arena of human choices and preferences, where supposedly radical uncertainty reigns.

Lachmann and his followers are correct in emphasizing that the problem of predicting my and others' future actions is categorically different from that of predicting the physical outcomes of *given* actions or of *natural* events. In fact, the destructive part of Lachmann's argument is largely correct even though it is hardly new (and entirely insufficient to establish his constructive thesis of radical uncertainty).[6] This is the roof that not only the idea of perfect foresight, underlying general equilibrium theory, is mistaken, but likewise the idea, advanced by rational expectations theorists, that all human uncertainty can be subsumed under the heading of insurable risks: that the uncertainty concerning our future actions in particular is no different from that regarding the future of natural events, such that we can, based on our observation of long-run frequency distributions, predict their general

---

6. See Ludwig Lachmann, *The Market as an Economic Process* (Oxford: Basil Blackwell, 1986), chap. 2, esp. pp. 27–29; also Gerald P. O'Driscoll, Jr., and Mario J. Rizzo, *The Economics of Time and Ignorance* (Oxford: Basil Blackwell, 1985), chap. 2, esp. pp. 24–26.

pattern in the same way as we can predict the pattern of earthquakes, tornadoes, cancer, or car accidents, for example.

As Lachmann points out, and as Frank Knight and Ludwig von Mises explained long before, the new theory of rational expectations suffers from essentially the same deficiency as the old general equilibrium model of perfect foresight: it cannot account for the phenomenon of learning and, hence, of knowledge and consciousness. Rational expectation theorists only replace the model of man as a never-failing automaton with that of a machine subject to random errors and breakdowns of known types and characteristics. Rather than possessing perfect knowledge of all singular (individual) actions, man is assumed to possess merely perfect knowledge of the probability distribution of all future classes of actions. He is assumed to commit forecasting errors, but his errors are always correct errors. False predictions never require a revision of a person's given stock of knowledge. There is no learning from success or failure and, hence, there is no change, or only predictable change, in the future pattern of human actions. Such a model of man, Knight, Mises, and Lachmann agree, is no less faulty than the one it is supposed to replace. It not only stands in manifest contradiction to the facts, but any proponent of this model is also inevitably caught up in logical contradictions.

First off, if our expectations (predictions) concerning our future actions were indeed as rational as rational expectation theorists believe them to be, this would imply that it would be possible to give an exhaustive classification of all possible actions (just as one could list all possible outcomes of a game of roulette or all possible locations of a physical body in space). For without a complete enumeration of all possible types of actions there can be no knowledge of their relative frequencies. Obviously, no such list of all possible human actions exists, however. We know of a great number of types of action performed then or now, but this list is always open and incomplete. Indeed, actions are designed to alter the natural course of events in order to bring about something as yet non-existent. They are the result of creative imagination. New and different actions are constantly added to the list, and old ones dropped. For instance, new or different products and services are constantly added to the pre-existing list of products and services, while others disappear from the list. However, something as yet non-existent— a new product—cannot appear on any list until after it has been imagined and produced by someone. Even the producer of a new product X does not know—and could not have predicted—anything regarding the relative frequency of actions such as the supply of or the demand for X before he had actually had the new idea of X—yet any new product idea and any new product must necessarily upset (alter) the entire pre-existing pattern of the relative frequency of various forms of action (and of relative prices).

Moreover, if we could indeed predict our future actions, either perfectly or subject only to random errors, then it would have to be implicitly assumed as well that every actor must possess the same (identical) knowledge as everyone else. I must know what you know, and you must know what I know. Otherwise, if our knowledge were somehow different, it would be impossible that both our predictions could be equally correct or else equally correctly wrong. Instead, either my predictions would have to be correct and yours would have to be wrong, or vice versa, and either my predictions or yours then would have to be wrongly wrong. The error (mine or yours) would not be random but systematic, for it could have been avoided had I (or you) known what you (or I) knew. This precisely is the case, however: our knowledge is not identical. You and I may know some things in common, but I also know things (about myself, for instance) that you do not know, and vice versa. Our knowledge, and hence our predictions and expectations concerning future actions, are in fact different. Yet if different actors possess different knowledge, the likelihood (frequency) of their predicting correctly or incorrectly will be different as well. Hence, neither the success nor the failure of our predictions can be considered purely random but will have to be ascribed instead, at least partially, to a person's more-and-better or less-and-worse individual knowledge.

Most importantly, however, the rational expectations' model of man as a machine which is endowed with perfect knowledge of the relative frequency distribution of all of its possible future classes of actions (but that knows nothing about any particular action falling into any one of these classes except that it is a member of such and such a class and that this class of action has such and such a relative frequency) is fraught with inescapable internal contradictions. On the one hand, as far as the assumption that all actors possess identical knowledge is concerned, any proponent of this view is caught in a performative contradiction: his words are belied by the very fact of uttering them. For there would be no need to say what he is saying if everyone else already knew what he knows. Indeed, if everyone's knowledge were identical to everyone else's, no one would have to communicate at all. That men *do* communicate demonstrates that they must assume instead, contrary to the stated assumption, that their knowledge is not identical.

Rational expectations theorists, too, by virtue of presenting their ideas to the reading public, must obviously assume that the public does not yet know what *they* already know, and hence, that the public's predictions concerning the future course of actions—in contrast to their own predictions—will be systematically flawed until it has successfully absorbed the lesson of rational expectations.

Similarly, anyone proposing the assumption of a given list of all possible forms of human actions, with its implied denial of all learning, is caught up in contradictions. For one, if his knowledge was indeed given, this would imply assuming that he already knows everything that he will ever know (otherwise, if he could learn something tomorrow that is not already known today, his list of possible classes of actions could no longer be assumed to be complete). Yet if this were the case, then inevitably the question arises how he ever came to know *this*. If he cannot learn, it would appear that he also could not possibly have *learned* to know that there is no human learning. Rather, this knowledge must have always been there, as part of his initial natural endowment, like his hands and fingers. But this idea—that our knowledge is given as our hands and fingers are given—is absurd. Knowledge is always the knowledge *of* something: the knowledge of hands and fingers, for instance, and it cannot possibly be conceived of as anything but sequentially (in time) *acquired* knowledge (as something based upon and learned about some logically and temporarily prior facts). Moreover, the denial of the possibility of learning is again belied by the proponent's action. In proposing his thesis, he cannot but assume that others can understand and possibly learn from him something that they do not yet know. And in waiting for and listening to the response of others to his proposition—by engaging in any form of argumentation—he cannot but also assume that he himself can possibly learn from what others have to say. Otherwise, if he already knew what they would respond and how he would respond to their responses, and so on, there would simply be no purpose to the whole enterprise of communication and argumentation. Indeed, if he knew in advance all of his arguments (propositions) and all possible replies and counter-replies (or at least their relative frequency distribution), it would also be senseless to even engage in any form of internal, intrapersonal argumentation, because his knowledge would already be complete, and he would already possess the answers to all questions. Of course, the rational expectation theorists do engage in argumentation—and no one could argue that he cannot argue without thereby falling into a contradiction—and they do conduct research (which no one would do if he already knew everything there is to know). Hence, they demonstrate through their own actions that their model of man must be considered systematically flawed, and that man must think of himself as capable of learning something as yet unknown (unpredictable).

VI.

What are the consequences as regards the nature of the social sciences that follow from the recognition of man as a learning actor? It is in the answer to this question that Knight and Mises on the one hand, and Lachmann on the other, ultimately part company. They would agree only on one consequence: that there exists a categorical difference between the logic of the natural sciences and that of the social sciences. Indeed, it follows from the recognition of man as a learning actor that the (still) dominating positivist (or falsificationist) philosophy, which assumes that all (empirical) sciences follow the same method—a uniform logic of science— is self-contradictory.[7]

It is one thing to predict the physical outcomes resulting from a given action (technology) or to predict the future pattern of a given class of natural events outside an actor's physical control (insurance). It is an entirely different matter to predict what action an actor will actually perform or against which classes of natural events he will actually want to insure himself. As far as the former problem is concerned, there is no need to dispute what positivism has to say: an actor wants to produce a certain physical result and he has an idea about what type of interference of his is capable of bringing about such a change. His idea is a hypothetical one. The actor never can be ultimately certain that his action will lead to the desired result. He can only try and see what happens. If his action is successful and the anticipated outcome is achieved, his idea is confirmed. However, even then the actor cannot be sure that the same interference will always bring about the same result. All that a confirmation adds to his previous knowledge is the certitude that his hypothesis so far has not yet been shown to be faulty. On the other hand, if his action fails, his idea is falsified and a new, revised or amended hypothesis will have to be formed. Thus, even if certainty is out

---

7. See Hans-Hermann Hoppe, *Kritik der kausalwissenschaftlichen Sozialforschung* (Opladen: Westdeutscher Verlag, 1983); idem, *The Economics and Ethics of Private Property* (Boston: Kluwer Academic Publishers, 1993), chap. 7.

of human reach, it is still possible, through a process of trial and error, that an actor may continuously improve his technological know-how. Likewise, as regards natural events outside one's control, insofar as an actor is not indifferent (unconcerned) about such events but prefers the presence of any such event over its absence, or vice versa, he may form an idea concerning the relative frequency distribution of the entire class of the particular event in question. This idea, based as it is on the joint classification of singular events and the observation of long-run frequencies, is hypothetical, too. In this case, however, the occurrence of a single favorable or unfavorable event does not constitute a confirmation or a falsification of one's hypothesis. Rather, because the hypothesis refers to an entire class of favorable or unfavorable events and does not state anything regarding any singular event except that it is a member of this class, the question whether or not the course of future events confirms or falsifies one's idea can only be decided based on the observation of a large number of cases. This fact, although seemingly less than completely satisfying, does not imply that the experiences of confirmation and falsification, of success and failure, and of scientific progress proceeding through trial and error are any less real, however. In this case, whether or not one's hypothesis is confirmed or falsified can be decided based on the "hard" and objective fact that an insurer—whether a single individual who insures himself over time through personal savings or an agency that insures a class of individuals across time against payment of a premium—either has, or has not, saved or collected premiums sufficient to cover the cost resulting from the occurrence of each and all unfavorable singular events. If he has, his hypothesis is temporarily confirmed, and if he has not, his hypothesis is falsified, and he will either have to change his frequency estimate and increase his savings or premiums, or he will have to revise his classification of singular events and introduce a new, further differentiated system of classes and subclasses. Thus, even if certainty is again unattainable, continuous scientific progress is possible also with respect to man's ability to forecast accidents (natural events outside of his control).

Granted that this is so, however, the question arises if it is also true, as positivists maintain, that man can be thought of as following the same logic—of hypothetical conjecture, confirmation or falsification, and of scientific progress proceeding through a process of trial and error—when it comes to the problem of predicting his own future actions. But this must be categorically denied. For in proceeding in the way he does regarding the world of physical events inside or outside his control, an actor must necessarily conceive of himself as capable of learning (otherwise, why conduct any research at all?). Yet if man can learn and possibly improve his predictive mastery over nature, it must be assumed that he cannot only alter his knowledge, and hence his actions, in the course of time, but also that these possible changes must be regarded by him as in principle unpredictable (such that any progress in his ability to predict these changes must be considered systematically impossible). Or putting things somewhat differently, if man proceeds, as positivists say he does, to interpret a predictive success as a confirmation of his hypothesis such that he would, given the same circumstance, employ the same knowledge in the future, and if he interprets a predictive failure as a falsification such that he would not employ the same but a different hypothesis in the future, he can only do so if he assumes—even if only implicitly—that the behavior of the objects under consideration does not change over the course of time. Otherwise, if their behavior were not assumed to be time-invariant—if the same objects were to behave sometimes this way and at other times in a different way—no conclusion as to what to make of a predictive success or failure would follow. A success would not imply that one's hypothesis had been temporarily confirmed, and hence, that the same knowledge should be employed again in the future. Nor would any predictive failure imply that one should *not* employ the same hypothesis again under the same circumstances. But this assumption—that the objects of one's research do not alter their behavior in the course of time—*cannot* be made with respect to the very subject engaging in research without thereby falling into a self-contradiction. For in interpreting his successful predictions as confirmations and his failed predictions as falsifications, the researcher must necessarily assume *himself* to be a learning subject—someone who can learn about the behavior of objects conceived by him as non-learning objects. Thus, even if everything else may be assumed to have a constant nature, the researcher cannot make the same assumption with respect to himself. *He* must be a different person after each confirmation or falsification than he was before, and it is then *his* nature to be able to change his personality over the course of time.[8]

---

8. Likewise, it would be self-contradictory for me to state about my actions performed over the course of time what would have to be assumed if I wanted to consider them instances of insurable events (class probability): that I know nothing about any one of my actions except that they are *my* actions (in the same way as one may legitimately say, for instance, that I know nothing about any singular outcome of a game of roulette except that

But if the positivist-falsificationist view of a uniform logic of science is rejected and the logic of the social sciences considered categorically different from that applying to the natural sciences, as Knight, Mises, and Lachmann would agree, then what is the method appropriate for the study of human action? It is here that Knight and Mises would fundamentally disagree with Lachmann. Knight and Mises argue—correctly, as will be seen—that it does not follow from the recognition of man as a learning actor that everything concerning the future of human actions must be considered unknowable—indeed, they would consider such a view self-contradictory—but rather only that one must admit the existence of two categorically different branches within the social sciences: of *apodictic* (*aprioristic*) theory (economics) on the one hand and of history and entrepreneurship on the other.[9] Lachmann and his followers conclude precisely this: (1) that there can be no such thing as economic theory capable of prediction at all, that all of the social sciences are nothing but history and "economists must confine their generalizations to the knowable past"[10]; and (2) that all of our predictions concerning human actions, which we must venture day in and day out, are nothing but haphazard guesses, that "man in his true humanity," as Lachmann approvingly cites Shackle, "can neither predict nor be predicted."[11]

VII.

Regarding the first of Lachmann's two contentions on the impossibility of economic theory—it should be noted from the outset that this thesis—contrary to Lachmann's own claim, and in particular the self-congratulatory attitude found among some of his younger disciples—is anything but new and original, but represents instead a return to Lachmann's intellectual beginnings as a student of Werner Sombart and the "historicist" teachings

---

each one is the outcome of the same roulette). In fact, I do know more about each of them. I know that each action is influenced by my knowledge, and that my knowledge will be changed dependent on the outcome of each action, such that each action will be performed by a *different me* and must be considered a *unique* event (forming an entire class by itself).

9. On the methodological views of Frank Knight in particular, see his *The Ethics of Competition and Other Essays* (New York: Harper Bros., 1935); and, idem, *On the History and Method of Economics* (Chicago: University of Chicago Press, 1956).

10. Lachmann, *The Market as an Economic Process*, p. 32.

11. *Id.*, quoted in G. L. S. Shackle, *Time in Economics* (Amsterdam: North Holland, 1958), p. 105.

of the German *Kathedersozialisten* (and thus most definitely has nothing whatsoever to do with Austrian Economics).[12]

Ludwig von Mises, the twentieth century's foremost Austrian economist and life-long critic of historicism, has thus characterized its doctrine:

> The fundamental thesis of historicism is the proposition that ... there is no knowledge but that provided by history....The honest historicist would have to say: Nothing can be asserted about the future. Nobody can know how a definite policy will work in the future. All we believe to know is how similar policies worked in the past. Provided all relevant conditions remain unchanged, we may expect that the future effects will not widely differ from those of the past. But we do not know whether or not these relevant conditions will remain unchanged. Hence we cannot make any prognostication about the—necessarily future—effects of any measure considered. We are dealing with the history of the past, not with the history of the future.[13]

That this is also an accurate description of Lachmann's position is made perfectly clear by Lachmann's following comment on the so-called Austrian theory of the trade cycle:

> Here we have a body of analytical thought designed to meet the requirements set out above: to depict a recurrent pattern of events with booms and depressions following each other in ceaseless succession. But can we really believe that agents witnessing these events will learn nothing from them and act in successive cycles in identical fashion? Is it not more likely that their action in each cycle will be affected by the lessons they have learnt from its predecessors, even though, as always happens, different people learn different lessons from the same events? Once we admit that people learn from experience, the cycle cannot be reproduced time after time. These considerations suggest that it may be better to give up the doubtful quest for a model of *the* business cycle and to regard phenomena such as cyclical fluctuations in output and prices simply as phenomena of history in the explanation of which changes in human knowledge will naturally play a part, with the events of each successive cycle requiring different, although often enough similar, explanations.[14]

---

12. Austrians from Carl Menger onward considered the German historicists as anti-economists and their intellectual foes. The historicists, in particular their leader Gustav Schmoller and his successor Werner Sombart, amply reciprocated this animosity.

13. L. Mises, *Theory and History*, pp. 199, 203–04.

14. Lachmann, *The Market as an Economic Process*, pp. 30–31.

While in and of itself this does not yet prove Lachmann wrong, it is a first step in the direction of a rigorous refutation that the position taken by Lachmann involves nothing less than an all-out social relativism—indeed: nihilism—that cannot but immediately strike one as entirely counter-intuitive. The relativistic consequences of historicism are hinted at clearly in the just quoted passage from Mises, while they may appear somewhat obscured by Lachmann in restricting his remarks to but one theory, the theory of the trade cycle (incidentally without bothering to explain, even if only briefly, what the theory actually states). However, there can be no doubt whatsoever that the trade cycle theory is cited by Lachmann as an *example* and that he actually believes his argument to be equally applicable to all other economic theorems. In the same way and for the same reason that there can be no such thing as *the* theory of the trade cycle, according to Lachmann, there also can be no such thing as *the* theory of exchange, *the* theory of prices, *the* theory of money, *the* theory of interest, *the* theory of wages, *the* theory of socialism, *the* theory of taxation, *the* theory of wage and price controls, or *the* theory of interventionism. What holds for the phenomenon of cyclical fluctuations supposedly also holds for all other phenomena: that they must be regarded as phenomena of history in the explanation of which changes in human knowledge will naturally play a part, with each successive exchange, price, use of money, interest, wage, socialism, tax, wage and price control, and government intervention requiring different, although often enough similar, explanations. But can we really believe *this*? Can we really believe, as Lachmann does, that we cannot say anything "applying equally to future and past" exchanges, prices, monies, or taxes? Can we really believe that, due to the possibility of learning, it may no longer be true in the future that every voluntary exchange will—*ex ante*—be beneficial to both exchangers, and that every coercive exchange such as a tax will benefit one (the taxman) at the expense of the other (the taxed)? Can we really believe that each successive socialist experiment requires a different explanation, and that it is impossible to say anything applicable to *each and every* form of socialism, so that as long as there exists no private ownership of the means of production, and hence no factor prices, economic calculation (cost-accounting) will be impossible and permanent misallocation (waste) will have to result? Can we really believe that, *as long as socialism is not actually abolished*, this proposition may no longer hold true, because agents can learn from experience and may no longer act in an identical fashion? Can we really believe that if a central bank were to double the paper money supply overnight, this would not, now and forever, lead to a drop in the purchasing power of money as well as a systematic income redistribution in favor of the central bank and the early receivers of the newly-created money at the expense of those receiving it later or not at all? Can we really believe that if the minimum wage were fixed today at one million dollars per hour and if this decree were strictly enforced and no increase in the money supply were to take place, this measure might not lead to mass unemployment and a breakdown of the division of labor because people can learn from experience? To be sure, *Lachmann* believes all of this, and it is easy to understand why some other people—taxmen, socialists, central bankers, and minimum wage legislators—would like us to believe as he does. But it is difficult to imagine how anyone but Lachmann—including even those who would personally benefit from us believing that the future effects of various policies can never be known in advance—can actually consider any of this seriously.

As already indicated in section II above, the fundamental logical error involved in Lachmann's reasoning consists in the fact that it does not follow from the proposition that human actors face an uncertain future that everything regarding our future must be considered uncertain.[15] Nor does it follow from the fact that humans can learn, and hence their actions may change in the course of time, that everything concerning the future of human actions may possibly change in the course of time. Quite the contrary. To draw these conclusions, as Lachmann does, is self-contradictory for evidently Lachmann claims to know for certain the unknowability of future knowledge and, by logical extension, of actions. Yet then he does know something about future knowledge and action. He must assume to know something about knowledge and action as such. Likewise, in claiming to know that humans are capable of learning and altering their actions in accordance with what they may learn, Lachmann must admit knowing something about man as such. He must assume to know not only that man may change his future behavior, but also that these changes are the result of a process of *learning*; that is, that they are the result of man being able to distinguish between success and failure, between confirmation and falsification, and draw *conclusions* dependent upon such categorically distinct experiences; and hence, that all possible changes in the behavior of man, unpredictable as their specific content may be, follow a predictable pattern—a uniform and constant logic

---

15. See also Hoppe, *Kritik der kausalwissenschaftlichen Sozialforschung*, chap. 3, esp. p. 47.

of human action and learning. To use a perfect analogy while it is true that I am unable to predict *everything* that I will say or write in the future, this does not imply that I cannot predict *anything* about my future speaking and writing. I can predict, and indeed I can predict with perfect certainty, and regardless of whether I will speak or write in English or German, that, as long as I will speak or write at all, in any language whatsoever, all of my speaking and writing will have a constant and invariable logical (propositional) structure: that I must use identifying expressions, such as proper names, and predicators to assert or deny some specific property of the identified or named object, for instance.[16] In the same way it holds that even though I cannot predict what goals I may pursue in the future, what means I will deem appropriate to reach these goals, and what other conceivable courses of action I will choose to reject in order to do what I will actually do (my opportunity cost), I can still predict that as long as I act at all, there will be goals, means, choices, and costs; that is, I can predict the general, logical structure of each and every one of my actions, whether past, present or future. And this is precisely what economic theory or, as Mises has termed it, *praxeology*, is all about: providing knowledge regarding actions as such and knowledge about the structure which any future knowledge and learning must have by virtue of the fact that it invariably must be the knowledge and learning of actors.

To be sure, the knowledge of the invariant logical structure of acting and learning is acquired knowledge, too, as is all human knowledge. Man is not endowed with it. However, once learned, the knowledge conveyed by praxeology as well as that conveyed by propositional logic can be recognized

---

16. See Paul Lorenzen, *Normative Logic and Ethics* (Mannheim: Bibliographisches Institut, 1969), chap. 1. Lorenzen explains:

> I call a usage a convention if I know of another usage which I could accept instead.... However, I do not know of another behavior which could replace the use of elementary sentences. If I did not accept proper names and predicators, I would not know how to speak at all.... Each proper name is a convention, ... but to use proper names at all is not a convention: it is a unique pattern of linguistic behavior. Therefore, I am going to call it 'logical'. The same is true with predicators. Each predicator is a convention. This is shown by the existence of more than one natural language. But all languages use predicators. (p. 16)

See also Wilhelm Kamlah and Paul Lorenzen, *Logische Propädeutik* (Mannheim: Bibliographisches Institut, 1968), chap. 1.

as necessarily true—*a priori* valid—knowledge, such that no future learning from experience could possibly falsify it. While all of my knowledge regarding the external world is, and forever will be tainted by uncertainty (it is not inconceivable that the law of gravitation may no longer hold in the future or that the sun will not rise tomorrow), my knowledge concerning the structure of my future action and learning is and forever will be non-hypothetically true: it is inconceivable that, as long as I am alive, I will not act and reach or not reach my goal and revise or not revise my knowledge depending on the outcome of my actions. Learning is the learning from success and failure, and there can be no learning of the fact that there is no success or failure. Thus, writes Mises,

> man as he exists on this planet in the present period of cosmic history may one day disappear. But as long as there are beings of the species Homo sapiens there will be human action of the categorical kind praxeology deals with. In this restricted sense praxeology provides exact knowledge of future conditions.... The predictions of praxeology are, within their range of applicability, absolutely certain.[17]

How is it possible, then, especially in light of the fact that Lachmann was familiar with Mises and his writings, that he could have committed an elementary logical blunder such as not to recognize that it does not follow from the fact that we are capable of learning that *everything* about the future of human actions is unknowable? How could he not recognize that only those aspects of our actions which may actually be affected by learning can be considered unpredictable, while those aspects that are a necessary part of any action and learning and thus cannot be altered by future learning—the underlying logical structure of action and learning itself—cannot? The answer to this riddle lies in the fact that although he considered himself a staunch opponent of the positivist philosophy, Lachmann still fell prey to one of its fundamental misconceptions. Like Friedrich A. Hayek, his second teacher, Lachmann, whether wittingly or not, accepted the view of Hayek's friend and protégé Karl R. Popper that all scientific knowledge must be such that, in principle, it is falsifiable by experience, and that all knowledge that is not falsifiable is not genuine knowledge at all but represents merely

17. Ludwig von Mises, *The Ultimate Foundation of Economic Science* (Kansas City: Sheed Andrews and McMeel, 1978), pp. 84–85.

empirically empty tautologies, i.e., arbitrary definitions (formalisms). It is thus that Lachmann can write in response to the challenge posed to his thesis of an unknowable future by Mises and his idea of a logic of action that

> precisely by virtue of the logical necessity inherent in it, it is impotent to engender empirical generalizations. Its truth is purely abstract and formal truth. The means and ends it connects are abstract entities. In the real world the concrete means used and ends sought are ever-changing as knowledge changes and what seemed worthwhile yesterday no longer seems so today. We appeal in vain to the logic of means and ends to provide us with support for empirical generalizations.[18]

But surely, as popular as this view of regarding all non-hypothetically true propositions—such as the laws of propositional logic, for instance—as empirically empty formalisms has become in the wake of the rise of the positivist philosophy, it is completely fallacious.[19] In referring to highly abstract entities such as objects and properties, rather than concrete ones such as my cactus and its red blossoms, I am still speaking about *real* phenomena. The term "tree" is more abstract than the term "pine tree," but the former has no less an empirical content than the latter. In the same vein, in saying something about ends, means, exchange, money, or interest—rather than about my desire to please my wife with flowers, a trade of two oranges against three apples, U.S. dollars, or my exchange of two present socks for four socks three months hence—I am still stating something about real phenomena with an empirical content. Notes Mises,

> if one accepts the terminology of logical positivism and especially also that of Popper, a theory or hypothesis is "unscientific" if *in principle* it cannot be refuted by experience. Consequently, all *a priori* theories, including mathematics and praxeology, are "unscientific." This is merely a verbal quibble. No serious man wastes

---

18. Lachmann, *The Market as an Economic Process*, p. 31; for the similar views of Hayek see his "Economics and Knowledge," in Friedrich A. Hayek, *Individualism and Economic Order* (Chicago: University of Chicago Press, 1948).

19. See Arthur Pap, *Semantics and Necessary Truth* (New Haven, Conn.: Yale University Press, 1958); Brand Blanshard, *Reason and Analysis* (LaSalle, Ill.: Open Court, 1962); Friedrich Kambartel, *Erfahrung und Struktur* (Frankfurt/M.: Suhrkamp, 1968); Hoppe, *The Economics and Ethics of Private Property*, chap. 6.

his time in discussing such a terminological question. Praxeology
and economics will retain their paramount significance for human
life and action however people may classify and describe them.[20]

In light of Lachmann's multiple logical errors, one can now turn back to
our rhetorical questions raised in response to his claim of the impossibility
of any and all economic theory and prediction. The reason it appeared absurd
that one should be unable to predict anything regarding each and every
voluntary exchange, tax, socialism, money supply increase, and minimum
wage law, is that while man may learn many things and alter his behavior in
many ways, he is unable to experience and learn anything that is at variance
with the laws of logic and the nature of man as an actor. I may not be able to
predict that I will engage in voluntary exchanges, when, what it is that will be
exchanged, or the exchange ratio at which the goods or services in question
will be traded, etc., because all of this may indeed be affected by my and
others' knowledge and change as this knowledge changes. But I can predict
with perfect certitude that *if* a voluntary exchange takes place, regardless of
where, when, what, and at what exchange ratio, both exchange partners must
have had opposite preference orderings and must have expected to benefit
from the exchange. No possible learning can ever change *this*. Likewise, I may
not be able to predict that or when a socialist experiment will be undertaken
or discontinued. Nor will I ever be able to predict such an experiment's many
specific features. All of this may be affected by learning. But regardless of
whatever people may learn and how their learning may shape the peculiar
shape of socialism, I can still predict with absolute certainty that as long as
one is in fact dealing with *socialism*, any and all economic calculation will be
impossible and permanent misallocations of production factors must result
because *this* consequence is already logically implied in what socialism *is*.
Similarly, I may not be able to forecast that a money will actually come into
existence, and it is certainly possible that mankind may one day revert back
to barter. Nor can I predict with certainty what specific *kind* of money will be

---

20. L. Mises, *The Ultimate Foundation of Economic Science*, p. 70. Equally incomprehensible as the charge that praxeology is empirically empty because its propositions are
non-falsifiable is the charge brought against Mises and Menger by Gerald P. O'Driscoll, Jr.,
and Mario J. Rizzo that the belief in the existence of "apodictic praxeological theorems"
and "exact economic laws" implies the assumption of some sort of "rigid determinism"!
(*The Economics of Time and Ignorance*, Oxford: Basil Blackwell, 1985, p. 23) And would one
also have to give up the belief in the existence of universal and unchanging laws of logic if
one were to adopt O'Driscoll's and Rizzo's in-deterministic "dynamic subjectivism"?

employed in the future. But I can predict with perfect certitude that if there is any money in use at all, an increase in its supply must lead to a reduction in its purchasing power below what it otherwise would have been. This follows simply from the definition of money as a *medium of exchange*. Lastly, Lachmann also errs regarding the example of the Austrian theory of the trade cycle. He claims that due to the fact that businessmen can learn—they may hear of or read about Mises's theory—they may possibly alter their future behavior in such a way that the effects predicted by the theory will no longer ensue.[21] But such a claim simply involves a misunderstanding of what the theory actually states. True enough, people can learn from Mises, and this may actually prevent business cycles from occurring at all, just as people may learn from Mises never to engage in a socialist experiment in the first place. However, this is entirely beside the point, for the theory states that *if* a bank creates additional paper-money credit, above and beyond the credit made available by the public's voluntary savings, and *if* this additional credit is in fact placed into the hands of borrowers and the interest rate is thus lowered below what it otherwise would have been, i.e., the natural rate of interest, then, and only then, will there be first a boom—over-investment—and consequently a bust—the systematic liquidation of some of the investments as mal-investment. Whatever businessmen may learn after a credit expansion has actually taken place cannot possibly affect this predicted outcome in the slightest, because an inter-temporal dis-coordination is already logically implied in the stated premises. And if the if-clause is not fulfilled, then the theory of the trade cycle is not refuted, of course. It simply does not apply.[22]

VIII.

Having rejected Lachmann's first contention of the impossibility of economic theory applicable to past and future alike, and having argued the case of Knight's and in particular Mises's instead, not only of the possibility of such theory but, even more strongly, of *a priori* theory and *apodictic* (non-hypothetical) prediction, in this final section Lachmann's second

---

21. Ludwig Lachmann, "The Role of Expectations in Economics as a Social Science," in idem, *Capital, Expectations, and the Market Process* (Kansas City: Sheed Andrews and McMeel, 1977).

22. See Ludwig von Mises, "'Elastic Expectations' and the Austrian Theory of the Trade Cycle," *Economica* 10 (1943): pp. 251–52; also George Selgin, "Praxeology and Understanding," *Review of Austrian Economics* 2 (1988): p. 54.

contention—the "kaleidic" nature of the social world and the haphazard character of entrepreneurial prediction—will have to be examined.

Even if the existence of a logic of action—praxeology—is admitted, as it must be, it does not follow that the knowledge provided by it can render our future certain. Praxeology allows us to predict with certainty *some* future events and aspects of the world of human actions, but its range of applicability is strictly limited. There are many events and aspects, and indeed far more of far greater practical significance, about which praxeology has nothing to say. As Mises explains, "there is, but for Robinson Crusoe before he met his man Friday, no action that could be planned or executed without paying full attention to what the actor's fellow men will do. Action implies understanding other men's reactions."[23]

The task with which acting man, that is, everybody, is faced in all relations with his fellows does not refer to the past; it refers to the future. To know the future reactions of other people is the first task of acting man. . . . It is obvious that this knowledge which provides a man with the ability to anticipate to some degree other people's future attitudes is not *a priori* knowledge. The *a priori* discipline of human action, praxeology, does not deal with the actual content of value judgments; it deals only with the fact that men value and then act according to their valuations. What we know about the actual content of judgments of value can be derived only from experience.[24]

Quite apart from whatever praxeology, technology, and insurance can possibly teach us about the future, then, Mises (as well as Knight) would agree with Lachmann that there remains as one of mankind's most pressing problems the need to predict our fellowmen's concrete value judgments, the specific means they will choose to bring their valued ends about, and their evaluations once the results of their actions are in. And as has already been explained, they would also agree with Lachmann that because humans are capable of learning and their learning may affect their values, choices of means, and evaluations of outcomes, the positivist-falsificationist prescriptions of how to deal with this problem are logically inappropriate and impotent. But what else can we do? Or can nothing be done to deal with this aspect of uncertainty?

While it may appear that Lachmann's answer to these questions is similar to Mises's—both refer throughout their writings to the same group

---

23. L. Mises, *The Ultimate Foundation of Economic Science*, p. 49.
24. L. Mises, *Theory and History*, p. 311.

of philosophers of the *Geisteswissenschaften* and the social sciences, most notably Max Weber and Alfred Schuetz, and both mention the method of understanding (*Verstehen*)—this impression is mistaken (although due to Lachmann's generally less-than-clear writing and a considerable amount of hedging on his part, this issue is admittedly somewhat difficult to decide).[25] For whereas Mises's answer to the above questions is an unambiguous yes, there exists a method of dealing with the ineradicable uncertainty of future human choices, and even though this method is not, and never can be, perfect, by not availing ourselves of it we would rob ourselves of the very intellectual tool of successful action and encounter more frequent disappointments than otherwise would be the case. Lachmann seems to hold precisely this: that regardless of what we do, our successes or failures in predicting our fellow men's future actions are purely random.

As for Mises's position, it is essential to recognize that—and why—he rejects the view that the future of human actions may be considered random or haphazard. To entertain such a view can mean one of two things. It can mean that we know literally nothing. But this is clearly false, for we do know something: we know that the future events in question are human actions and will display the structure inherent in each and every action, and hence, that while our knowledge may be deficient, we are still in a position to say more than simply *ignoramus*.[26] Or it can mean that with regard to the problem of future human choices, we know everything about the behavior of the whole class of events, but we do not know anything about any singular choice except that it is an element of the entire class of human choices. The view that human actions may be regarded as instances of "class probability" has already been rejected above. We do not, and never will, know everything about the whole class of human actions. But from this it does not follow that we will have to confess complete ignorance regarding singular human choices (apart from the known fact that they are all choices). In fact, we do know something (more) about each singular event: we know that each singular event is the result of *individual* actors acting based on *individual* knowledge subject to changes by *individual* learning, such that each event as it unfolds in human history past and future, must be conceived of as a *unique and non-repeatable* event (with each event being in a class by itself); and we also know that in order to grasp the past or anticipate the future actions of

---

25. For a similar assessment see Selgin, "Praxeology and Understanding."
26. See L. Mises, *Human Action*, p. 107.

our fellow men, we will have to pay attention and try to understand their individual knowledge, their individual values and personal know-how. It is thus that Mises characterizes the epistemological task faced by man in his dealings with his fellows as one of "case probability." "Case probability (or the specific understanding of the sciences of human action) ... means: We know, with regard to a particular event, some of the factors which determine its outcome; but there are other determining factors about which we know nothing."[27] Categorically different as this situation of case probability is from that of class probability, it is hardly a situation in which the future is random or haphazard. Indeed, in some respect we are in a *better* (not worse) epistemological position in the field of human history, past and future, than we are in the field of natural events, of technology and insurance. For in the latter field we are categorically precluded from the possibility of understanding. Each singular event must be treated as a member of a class of *homogeneous*, except for their class membership *indistinguishable* singular events. In contrast, in the field of past and future human history, we are capable of distinguishing between every singular event (each event can be treated as *heterogeneous*); and to improve our grasp of the past, and our anticipations of the future actions of our fellows, we know and are capable of learning something about the *individual* causes—the *personal* knowledge— uniquely affecting the outcome of each and every *singular* human event (with each event deserving of its own special attention).

While neither random nor haphazard, then, the task of anticipating our fellows' actions based on an understanding of their individuality is not without its inescapable difficulties and imperfections, for every understanding of an individual is always an understanding of his *past* values and knowledge. However, as Mises was quoted above, our first task in life is to know the *future* reactions of other people. "Knowledge of their past value judgments and actions, although indispensable, is only a means to this end."[28] Thus, in

---

27. *Id.*, pp. 107–10. Mises notes, that

> historical events have one common feature: they are human action. History comprehends them as human actions; it conceives their meaning by the instrumentality cognition and understands their meaning in looking at their individual and unique features. What counts for history is always the meaning of the men concerned: the meaning that they attach to the state of affairs they want to alter, the meaning they attach to their actions, and the meaning they attach to the effects produced by the actions. (*Id.*, p. 59)

28. L. Mises, *Theory and History*, p. 311.

all of our attempts of anticipating the future, in addition to an understanding of the past actions of a given individual, we must also necessarily make a judgment regarding the relative stability or instability of the various parts of his system of values and knowledge as displayed in the past; that is, we must form an opinion about his *personality* or *character*. As Mises explains, we must "assume that, by and large, the future conduct of people will, other things being equal, not deviate without special reason from their past conduct, because we assume that what determined their past conduct will also determine their future conduct. However different we may know ourselves to be from other people, we try to guess how they will react to changes in their environment. Out of what we know about a man's past behavior, we construct a scheme about what we call his character. We assume that this character will not change if no special reasons interfere, and, going a step farther, we even try to foretell how definite changes in conditions will affect his reactions."[29] Likewise, if we are concerned about the future behavior of groups of individuals (rather than only a single one), we cannot but classify individuals according to the similarity or dissimilarity of their character or personality; that is, we cannot but form ideas of group characters—ideal types—and sort individuals according to their membership in such types. "If an ideal type refers to people," explains Mises, "it implies that in some respect these men are valuing and acting in a uniform or similar way. When it refers to institutions, it implies that these institutions are products of uniform or similar ways of valuing and acting or that they influence valuing and acting in a uniform or similar way."[30]

Our anticipations, based on an understanding of the past, and the construction of character and ideal types and the classification of individuals and groups into such types, are necessarily hypothetical, or rather, tentative predictions. In ascribing a certain character to an actor, we attempt to reduce the uncertainty surrounding his future behavior. We form a tentative judgment concerning more or less stable parts of his personality and predict that the future changes in his behavior, whatever they may be, will be

---

29. L. Mises, *The Ultimate Foundation of Economic Science*, pp. 49–50; and he continues then to say: "Compared with the seemingly absolute certainty provided by some of the natural sciences, these assumptions and all the conclusions derived form them appear as rather shaky; the positivists may ridicule them as unscientific. Yet they are the only available approach to the problems concerned and indispensable for any action to be accomplished in a social environment."

30. L. Mises, *Theory and History*, p. 316.

changes in line with his character, i.e., changes which follow a general—predictable—pattern. Our prediction may turn out to be successful or not. We may have misclassified the actor(s). Or, contrary to our judgment, the actor(s) may change their very character; and indeed, over the course of time some character types may die out and new ones may emerge, requiring the development of a different and changing system of classification. Or our character constructs may turn out too abstract or too specific; that is, even though they may yield correct predictions, we may find, in retrospect, that what they predict is of lesser importance than anticipated. The prediction may turn out to say too little of much importance, or too much of little importance, requiring further typological revisions. Moreover, whether we evaluate our predictions as successful or not, the meaning of success and failure is necessarily ambiguous. In the natural sciences, success means that so far your hypothesis has not been falsified; apply it again; and failure means that your hypothesis as it stands is wrong; change it. In our dealings with our fellow men, the implications are not, and never can be, as clear-cut. Maybe our prediction was wrong because some people, as can happen sometimes, acted out of character—in this case we would want to use our hypothesis again even though it had been apparently falsified. Or maybe our prediction was successful, but the individual in question has meanwhile undergone a change in his character—in this case we would not want to use our hypothesis again even though it had just been seemingly confirmed. Or maybe the actor in question knew our prediction and deliberately acted so as to confirm or falsify our hypothesis, in which case we might or might not want to change our future prediction. Every success and every failure, then, bears only inconclusive results and necessitates another tentative judgment, a new and updated understanding of the actors concerned and a renewed assessment of their characters in light of their most recent actions, and so on. Thus, in contrast to the situation in the natural sciences, where success and failure have an unambiguous meaning, where we are allowed to conclude that what was false in the past will also be so in the future and what worked once will likely work again, and where we may thus successively acquire a growing stock of knowledge, in dealing with the problem of anticipating our fellow men's actions, we can never rest on our past laurels but must always start again fresh and judge the applicability of our past knowledge anew, we can never possess a stock of knowledge that we may blindly rely upon in the future.

Nothing in this—Mises's—view regarding the nature of human history, past and future, is likely to strike anyone as new or revolutionary. Indeed, if it were not for the fact of the very different positivistic view of the matter, it would appear almost trivial and a self-evident truism. As Mises notes,

> the methods of scientific inquiry [in the social sciences] are categorically not different from the procedures applied by everybody in his daily mundane comportment. They are merely more refined and as far as possible purified of inconsistencies and contradictions. Understanding is not a method of procedure peculiar only to historians. It is practiced by infants as soon as they outgrow the merely vegetative stage of their first days and weeks. There is not conscious response of man to any stimuli that is not direct by understanding.[31]

It is not entirely surprising, then, that Lachmann, too, while his methodological considerations (in distinct contrast to Mises's) are largely unsystematic and marred by an abundance of metaphorical expression and a lack of analytical rigor, should at times appear to be in essential agreement with this commonsensical view as embraced by Mises. Lachmann, too, makes frequent reference to understanding, ideal types, and institutions.[32] Yet despite such apparent similarities, Mises and Lachmann reach completely different conclusions as regards the nature of human—entrepreneurial—uncertainty. Whereas for Mises the result of the method of understanding is moderate uncertainty, for Lachmann it is radical uncertainty. How is this to be explained?

In putting the best possible—because it is the most consistent—face on Lachmann, the disagreement between his and Mises's position may be said to boil down to one regarding a contingent—empirical—fact. There is agreement on the method to be employed; there is disagreement only on how successful this method actually is—remarkably so and most of the time, as Mises would contend, or insignificantly and only occasionally so, as would Lachmann. Instead of disagreeing on principle, on methodology, they only disagree on a matter of fact: whether the social world is, in fact, kaleidic or not. But what of the facts, then? Although the empirical question of whether we inhabit a kaleidic world or not may appear to be of rather minor importance, given the fact that we must deal with it in any case and we have nothing but understanding available to us to do so, and although questions of this nature may easily degenerate into idle semantic quibbles such as whether a glass of water is half empty or half full, empirical questions—disagreements on matters of fact—are accessible to empirical research and can, in principle,

---

31. L. Mises, *The Ultimate Foundation of Economic Science*, p. 48.
32. See Lachmann, *The Market as an Economic Process*, pp. 34–42.

be decided upon based on the observation of the facts. In the bright light of empirical facts, however, Lachmann's theory of radical uncertainty fares no better than in the pale light of logic.

So as to generate a radically uncertain world of kaleidic change, Lachmann must assume, as a matter of empirical fact, that individual actors do not possess any such thing as a character. Understanding, as has been explained, is always understanding of past actions. In order to be able to successfully predict future actions based on an understanding of past actions, it is necessary that one assume that the past and the future are somehow related—not in the sense that the past would determine the future, but rather in the sense that the past values and know-how of an individual (which determined his past actions) shape and constrain his future values and know-how (which determine his future actions). Indeed, if this were not assumed to be the case and an individual's past values and actions were viewed as completely unrelated to his future values and actions, the study of history would be entirely useless. We only study an individual's past because we believe that this knowledge is valuable in helping us anticipate something regarding his future conduct. Without this belief, the study of history must be regarded as a sheer waste of time. In Mises's view, the link connecting an individual's past with his future and the empirical reason for our concern for the study of history is the existence of individual characters and personalities. It is the existence of a person's character, changing though it may be over the course of time, that assures the continuity of change: patterned social change instead of kaleidic flux. Accordingly, only if individual actors were assumed to be completely disjointed personalities, such that my actions tomorrow were always entirely unrelated and unaffected by my actions today or yesterday, could Lachmann's scenario of radical uncertainty ever become reality. While this would indeed be a nightmare if it ever existed, it can safely be said that it has no resemblance whatsoever either to us or to the world we inhabit. Indeed, it is difficult to imagine how a world of disjointed personalities could be reconciled even with human biology. Solely on account of our physical bodily nature—which is a contingent fact, but as long as we are alive a relatively stable contingency—we cannot possibly be quite like Lachmann thinks we are, or else we would quickly die out.

As a matter of fact, actors, from the earliest stages of infancy on, display a personal character, they possess a personal identity and conceive of their past and future as forming a whole: their personal life history. We do not start building a house today and then, tomorrow, without any special reason, do something entirely unrelated. Rather, our past actions influence, circumscribe, and constrain our future actions. We do not always begin from scratch, but most of the time we continue what was already begun and planned as a part of a lengthy sequence of actions. And even if we abandon one such integrated plan, we typically adopt another one. Otherwise, if there were no such continuity in our actions, it would be impossible to explain one of the most striking features of human life—the existence and continued employment of a stock of capital goods. To produce a capital good is to begin something stretching into the future, and to employ an existing capital good is to continue something begun in the past. If the future were indeed unrelated to the past, it should be expected that capital goods, insofar as they come into existence at all, will just as quickly be abandoned in the future as they may have been adopted in the past. However, while there exist some ruins of abandoned capital goods, most of yesterday's capital goods are still employed today and tomorrow—which is empirical proof of the past's continuing influence on the future. As the author of a book on capital, Lachmann of all people should have been able to recognize this, and this alone should have given him reason enough to discard his thesis of kaleidic change and radical uncertainty.

Moreover, equally difficult for Lachmann to explain would be another fundamental feature of human history—the existence of enduring differences among various individuals in their ability to forecast the future; that is, not only the fact that I may be better able to predict the actions of A, B, and C, while you may be better able to predict those of D, E, and F, but also the fact that you and I, confronted with one and the same group of individuals, G, H, and J, may display lastingly different forecasting abilities. From Mises's view these facts pose no problem. Different individuals do not, and cannot possibly know (understand) everyone's past equally well. They know different individuals differently well, and accordingly, their forecasting ability should be expected to be different dependent on whose actions need to be predicted. Likewise, assuming that different individuals are concerned with forecasting the actions of the same individual or group of individuals, it should be expected that there will be systematically—and hence enduringly— different success rates among these forecasters. For in Mises's view, every prediction requires not only an understanding of the past but also a tentative judgment, influenced but not determined by the knowledge of the past, as to the underlying character structure of the individual actors concerned. As an essentially cognitive task involving different and complex intellectual operations, nothing should be less surprising than the fact that different individuals, with strikingly different talents in all other areas of intellectual endeavor, will also perform differently when it comes to predicting their fellow men. However, if an individual's past and future were indeed unrelated, as Lachmann believes is the case, then everyone should be expected to predict everyone else's behavior equally well (or badly). A person with an understanding of an individual's past actions should not be able to predict his future actions any more successfully than someone else not so acquainted with the individual in question. Because the past is unconnected to the future, not knowing it cannot make a difference in our forecasting abilities. And since without our knowledge of past actions there is nothing left to go on to form a character judgment, we are all equally ignorant and without a rudder; hence, there also should be no lasting difference in our rate of success or failure. Successes and failures should be expected to be randomly distributed among actors and personal fortunes to dissipate as quickly as they are found.

It is almost needless to say that none of this fits historical reality. Based on my long understanding of my wife, for instance, I can anticipate her actions and reactions in almost all foreseeable circumstances; and vice versa, she can predict me almost to perfection. There are few if any surprises, and probably no one else could predict us better than we can predict each other. Likewise, I can predict, with great precision and better than almost everybody else, the behavior of my children, while they have (still) considerably more difficulty understanding me and my character. Similarly, I can anticipate better than almost anybody else the actions and reactions of many of my family and friends under a great variety of circumstances, and they, knowing me, can successfully predict many or even most of my reactions. There is nothing radical or kaleidic about the uncertainty involved. As well, I know quite a bit about the history of men and women, Germans, Austrians, Turks, Americans, Italians, Mexicans, Protestants, Catholics, Jews, Blacks, Asians, university professors, politicians, businessmen, private and public employees, and so on, and in many respects I can predict the behavior of the members of these groups very successfully, and certainly more successfully than the average person. Moreover, as far as predictions about the behavior of one and the same (group of) individual(s) by different predictors are concerned, even if all predictors have equal access to the record of past events and can base their prediction on an understanding of this past, they are most definitely not equally successful in their predictions. Most importantly, in the narrower field of capitalist-entrepreneurship, where forecasters must estimate their present and current production costs and form a judgment regarding future consumer demand in order to successfully complete an anticipated exchange of present money against future money, and where there exists a set of objective criteria for success—profit and loss, continued operation and bankruptcy, and growth, stagnation, or decline of capital values—the degree of success among different individuals is strikingly different. While many of those who try, fail, and drop from the rank of a capitalist-entrepreneur to become involved in less risky and intellectually demanding tasks, many others succeed to stay in business year after year, and some have succeeded in accumulating great fortunes during their life, and even to bring up heirs capable of preserving or enhancing their fortune beyond their own lifetime. This empirical fact, too, stands in open contradiction to the idea of kaleidic change and rather confirms the great cognitive value of the method of understanding (even more so in light of the fact that the superior predictive capability of the capitalist-entrepreneurs simultaneously reduces the uncertainty facing all of their employees by providing them with a present income even if they themselves could not have correctly anticipated the future demand for their own line of work).

Certainly all of this—the predictive power of the method of understanding as manifested in the empirical facts of capital formation and maintenance, of successful everyday life entrepreneurship (forecasting of family, friends, colleagues, and acquaintances), and of enduring business successes—in conjunction with the *apodictic* certitude provided by praxeology and the wide-ranging practical certainty afforded by technology and insurance should be more than sufficient to dispel all talk about radical uncertainty and kaleidic social change as either contradictory and meaningless or patently false.

15

The Limits of Numerical Probability

Both Frank H. Knight and Ludwig von Mises are recognized as founders of intellectual traditions: the Chicago School and the neo-Austrian School of economics, respectively. During their lifetime, Knight and Mises were engaged in controversies regarding the nature of socialism and capital.[1] My focus here, however, will be on a systematic yet rarely noted *similarity* in the works of Knight and Mises. In particular, both are representatives of the frequency interpretation of probability and share a similar view concerning the limitations of probability theory in economics and the social sciences generally.[2] In the following I will (1) briefly restate the principles of the frequency interpretation of probability; (2) show why Knight and Mises must be considered frequency theorists; and (3) discuss and evaluate the arguments provided by Knight and Mises against the possibility of applying probability theory in the area of economic forecasting (whether on the micro or the macro level).

• Originally published in *The Quarterly Journal of Austrian Economics* 10, no. 1 (Spring 2007).

1. Frank H. Knight, "Professor Mises and the Theory of Capital," *Economica*, n.s. 8, no. 32 (1941): pp. 409–27; idem, "The Place of Marginalist Economics in a Collectivist System," *American Economic Review: Supplement* 26 (1936): pp. 255–66; idem, "Review of Ludwig von Mises, *Socialism*," *Journal of Political Economy* 46 (1938): pp. 267–68; Ludwig von Mises, *Human Action: A Treatise on Economics* (Chicago: Regnery, 1966 [1949]), pp. 490–93, 848 f.

2. Interestingly, however influential Knight and Mises otherwise have been in shaping their respective schools, neither Knight nor Mises have been entirely successful in convincing their followers of this part of their doctrines. Similarly, while they were skeptical about the use of probability, Knight and Mises were also proponents of "a priori" economic theory, and in this regard, too, neither Knight nor Mises has been entirely successful with his students. See Knight, "Review of T. W. Hutchison, *The Significance and Basic Postulates of Economic Theory*," *Journal of Political Economy* 48, no. 1 (1940); and Mises, *Human Action*, chap. 2.

I.

The principal founder and proponent of the frequency interpretation of probability is Richard von Mises, Ludwig's younger brother.[3] There is no reference in Knight to Richard von Mises, and insofar as Knight's work of primary interest here is concerned—his 1921 *Risk, Uncertainty, and Profit*—nothing else can be expected (though Knight read German).[4] More surprising is the fact that there is also no mention of Richard von Mises and his frequency interpretation in Ludwig von Mises's systematic treatment of probability in his 1949 work *Human Action: A Treatise on Economics.*[5] Nonetheless, I assume Richard von Mises's interpretation as the starting point in the following discussion. It will become apparent that Knight is groping toward the solution provided by Richard von Mises, and that Ludwig von Mises was obviously familiar with his brother's work and in his own work presents what is meant to be a refinement of the frequency interpretation provided by Richard.

According to Richard von Mises, probability must be defined and the range of applicability of probability theory be delineated thus:

1. It is possible to speak about probabilities only in reference to a properly defined collective.[6]

2. A collective [appropriate for the application of the theory of probability must fulfill] ... two conditions: (i) the relative frequencies of particular attributes within the collective tend to fixed limits; (ii) these fixed limits are not affected by any place selection. That is to say, if we calculate the relative frequency of some attribute not in the original

---

3. Richard von Mises (1883–1953) was professor of mathematics at the University of Strassburg (1909–1919). In 1921 he was appointed professor of mathematics and director of the Institute of Applied Mathematics at the University of Berlin. When the National-Socialists dismissed him from this post in 1933, Mises went first to Istanbul, Turkey, and in 1939 he emigrated to the U.S., where he finished his career as Gordon McKay Professor of Aerodynamics and Applied Mathematics at Harvard University. Mises's groundbreaking works on the foundations of probability theory appeared in 1919 in two issues of the *Mathematische Zeitschrift*. His main work in this area, originally published in German in 1928, is *Probability, Statistics and Truth*; see also his *Positivism: A Study in Human Understanding* (Cambridge, Mass.: Harvard University Press, 1951).

4. There are a few references to F. Y. Edgeworth, whose views on probability are rather eclectic.

5. The two Mises brothers were long estranged and reconciled only during their common exile in the U.S.

6. Richard von Mises, *Probability, Statistics and Truth* (New York: Dover Publications, 1957), p. 28.

sequence, but in a partial set, selected according to some fixed rule, then we require that the relative frequency so calculated should tend to the same limit as it does in the original set.[7]

3. The fulfillment of the condition (ii) will be described as the Principle of Randomness or the Principle of the Impossibility of a Gambling System.[8]

For the purpose of this article, only three observations regarding Mises's frequency interpretations are in order. First, there is Mises's emphatic insistence that the application of the term probability to single events, such as the "probability" of Mr. X dying in the course of the next year, for instance, is "utter nonsense."[9] "The theory of probability can never lead to a definite statement concerning a single event."[10] Second, Mises is equally insistent that the probabilities of the probability calculus are objective, empirical

---

7. Richard von Mises, *Probability, Statistics and Truth*, pp. 28–29.

8. Richard von Mises further explains the meaning of condition (ii) (randomness) by means of a contrary example:

> Imagine, for instance, a road along which milestones are placed, large ones for whole miles and smaller ones for tenths of a mile. If we walk long enough along this road, calculating the relative frequencies of large stones, the value found in this way will lie around $1/10$.... The deviations from the value 0.1 will become smaller and smaller as the number of stones passed increases; in other words, the relative frequency tends towards the limiting value 0.1. (*Id.*, p. 23)

That is, condition (i) is fulfilled. However, absent in this case is condition (ii), because

> [t]he sequence of observations of large or small stones differs essentially from the sequence of observations, for instance, of the results of a game of chance, in that the first sequence obeys an easily recognizable law. Exactly every tenth observation leads to the attribute "large," all others to the attribute "small." (*Id.*, p. 23)

The essential difference between the sequence of the results obtained by casting dice and the regular sequence of large and small milestones consists in the possibility of devising a method of *selecting the elements* so as to produce a fundamental change in the relative frequencies.

We begin, for instance, with a large stone, and register only every second stone passed. The relation of the relative frequencies of small and large stones will now converge toward $1/5$ instead of $1/10$.... The impossibility of affecting the chances of a game by a system of selection, this uselessness of all systems of gambling, is the characteristic and decisive property common to all sequences of observations or mass phenomena which form the proper subject of probability calculus.... The limiting values of the relative frequencies in a collective must be independent of all possible place selections. (*Id.*, pp. 24–25)

9. *Id.*, pp. 17–18. 10. *Id.*, p. 32.

properties and magnitudes (rather than subjective beliefs or degrees of confidence). They are based on experience, and further experience may lead to revised measurements or the reclassification of various singular events into various collectives. However, only in referring to objective probabilities can the probability calculus ever be of any practical use.[11] And third and by implication, Mises rejects categorically the notion of *a priori* probability.[12] No such thing as *a priori probability* exists.[13]

"In a problem of probability calculus," according to Richard von Mises, "the data as well as the results are probabilities."[14] "From one or more well-defined collectives, a new collective is derived.... The purpose of the theory of probability is to calculate the distribution in the new collective from the known distribution (or distributions) in the initial ones."[15] As in the case of algebra, "[t]here are four, and only four, ways of deriving a collective and all problems treated by the theory of probability can be reduced to a combination of these four fundamental methods."[16] New collectives are derived from known initial ones by means either of *selection* (unchanged distribution), *mixing* (addition rule), *partition* (division rule), and/or *combination* (multiplication rule).[17]

---

11. Regarding subjectivist interpretations of probability, Mises first remarks that subjectivists such as John Maynard Keynes, for instance, fail to recognize "that if we know nothing about a thing, we cannot say anything about its probability," and he then notes that "[t]he peculiar approach of the subjectivists lies in the fact that they consider 'I *presume* that these cases are equally probable' to be equivalent to 'These cases are equally probable,' since, for them, probability is only a subjective notion." (Mises, *Probability, Statistics and Truth*, pp. 75–76)

12. See also footnote 24 below.

13. It is frequently held, explains Mises in this connection, that

> if one plays with a "perfect" ("correct") coin heads or tails and makes sufficiently large numbers of throws, it is almost certain that the proportion of heads will deviate by less than 1 per mille from one half of all cases. With regard to this we only note: The transition from the arithmetic proposition to this empirical proposition can be made only in declaring a "perfect" coin to be one for which the probability of both outcomes is $1/2$ and thus defining probability precisely in the way suggested by us, i.e., as relative empirical frequency in long sequences. (*Lehrbuch des Positivismus*, p. 267)

"How is it possible to be sure," Mises asks the proponents of *a priori* probability, "that each of the six sides of a die is equally likely to appear.... Our answer is of course that we do not actually know this unless the dice ... have been the subject of sufficiently long series of experiments to demonstrate this fact." (R. Mises, *Probability, Statistics and Truth*, p. 71)

14. *Id.*, p. 33.   15. *Id.*, p. 37.   16. *Id.*, p. 38.   17. *Id.*, p. 57.

II.

As economists, Frank Knight and Ludwig von Mises come upon the subject of probability indirectly, in conjunction with the question concerning the source of entrepreneurial profits and losses. Why, Knight and Mises ask, do profits and losses not *disappear* as the result of entrepreneurial competition? Why does competition not bring about a state of affairs where the sum of the prices paid for all input factors equals exactly the price of the output, such that the product sum can be apportioned perfectly among its contributing factors?[18] Knight and Mises both give the same answer: because of "uncertainty." Uncertainty concerning the future constellation of demand and supply is the ultimate and ineradicable source of entrepreneurial profit and loss.[19] And it is in conjunction with their attempt of explaining the nature of uncertainty, then, that both Knight and Mises introduce the concept of "risk," as a contingency categorically distinct from uncertainty.[20]

Explains Knight:

> If all changes were to take place in accordance with invariable and universally known laws, they could be foreseen for an indefinite period in advance of their occurrence, and would not upset the perfect apportionment of product values among contributing agencies, and profit (or loss) would not arise.[21]

However, perfect foresight need not involve the ability to forecast every singular event and the absence of any kind of contingency (or surprise) for profits and losses to disappear. As Knight explains:

---

18. Knight's and Mises's views concerning backward imputation (apportioning) differ significantly. In equilibrium, according to Knight each production factor is paid in accordance with its marginal value product, whereas according to Mises each production factor is paid in accordance with its *discounted* marginal value product, i.e., its marginal value product discounted by the originary rate of interest. This difference does not affect any of the arguments presented here or below, however.

19. See section III below.

20. Frank H. Knight, *Risk, Uncertainty and Profit* (Chicago: University of Chicago Press, 1971), chaps. 7 and 8; L. Mises, *Human Action*, chap. 6, and pp. 289–94.

21. *Risk, Uncertainty and Profit*, p. 198. Similarly, Mises writes:

> If everybody is correct in anticipating the future state of the market of a certain commodity, its price and the prices of the complementary factors of production concerned would already today be adjusted to this future state. Neither profit nor loss can emerge for those embarking upon this line of business. (L. Mises, *Human Action*, p. 290)

[I]t is unnecessary to perfect, profitless imputation that particular occurrences be foreseeable, if only all the alternative possibilities are known and the probability of the occurrence of each can be accurately ascertained. Even though the business man could not know in advance the results of individual ventures, he could operate and base his competitive offers upon accurate foreknowledge of the future if quantitative knowledge of the probability of every possible outcome can be had. For by figuring on the basis of a large number of ventures (whether of his own business alone or in that of business in general) the losses could be converted into fixed costs.[22]

[Thus, for example,] the bursting of bottles does not introduce an uncertainty or hazard into the business of producing champagne; since in the operations of any producer a practically constant and known proportion of bottles burst, it does not especially matter even whether the proportion is large or small. The loss becomes a fixed cost.... And even if a single producer does not deal with a sufficiently large number of cases of the contingency in question ... to secure constancy in its effects, the same result may easily be realized, through an organization taking in a large number of producers. This, of course, is the principle of insurance, as familiarly illustrated by the chance of fire loss. No one can say whether a particular building will burn, and most building owners do not operate on a sufficient scale to reduce the loss to constancy.... But as is well known, the effect of insurance is to extend this base to cover the operations of a large number of persons and convert the contingency into a fixed cost.[23]

With this definition of "empirical-statistical probability" as "insurable" contingency or "risk," Knight is in complete accordance with Richard von Mises's frequency interpretation. At times, he seems to deviate from Mises's interpretation, as when he assumes also the possibility of a priori probability (in addition to empirical-statistical probability). But not only does Knight ascribe no importance to a priori probability in the conduct of business, his deviation turns out little more than a minor if unfortunate slip.[24] In any case, Knight deserves credit for strictly separating *a priori*

---

22. Knight, *Risk, Uncertainty and Profit*, pp. 198–99.

23. *Id.*, pp. 212–13. Similarly, see L. Mises, *Human Action*, pp. 291–92.

24. According to Knight,

> [t]here are two fundamentally different ways of arriving at the probability judgment of the form that a given numerical proportion of X's are also Y's. The first method is by *a priori* calculation.... As an illustration of the first

probability from *empirical-statistical* probability, which alone is of practical importance (and where *a priori* considerations play no role whatsoever), and in particular for excluding "risk" (insurable contingencies) as a possible source of profit and loss and delineating it strictly from "uncertainty," as two categorically distinct sorts of contingency.

Ludwig von Mises reaches the same conclusion. Yet writing four decades later, his treatment of the subject, contrary to that of Knight, is in full awareness of Richard von Mises's frequency interpretation.

Ludwig von Mises first presents a general (wide) definition of probability:

> A statement is probable if our knowledge concerning its content is deficient. We do not know everything which would be required for a definite decision between true and not true. But on the other hand, we do know something about it; we are in a position to say more than simply non liquet or ignoramus.[25]

Within this general category of probabilistic statements, Mises then distinguishes two categorically distinct subclasses. The first one—probability narrowly understood and permitting the application of the probability calculus—is termed "class probability (or frequency probability)."

> Class probability means: We know or assume to know, with regard to the problem concerned, everything about the behavior of a whole class of events or phenomena; but about the actual singular events or phenomena we know nothing but that they are elements of this class.[26]

---

type of probability we may take throwing a perfect die. If the die is really perfect and known to be so, it would be merely ridiculous to undertake to throw it a few hundred thousand times to ascertain the probability of its resting on one face or another. (Knight, *Risk, Uncertainty and Profit*, pp. 214–15)

Richard von Mises's reply to this definition can be inferred from the quote provided in footnote 13 above: Precisely. But this definition only shows that there is no such thing as *a priori* probability. Because in order to classify a die as perfect, one must *first* show this to be true and that cannot be done other than by means of long-run observations.

25. L. Mises *Human Action*, p. 107.
26. *Id.*, p. 107. "Let us assume," Mises further clarifies,

that ten tickets, each bearing the name of a different man, are put into a box. One ticket will be drawn, and the man whose name it bears will be liable to pay 100 dollars. Then an insurer can promise to the loser full

With this definition of class probability, Ludwig von Mises shows himself in complete agreement with his brother. For him, too, there is no such thing as *a priori* probability. Nor is there such a thing as the probability of a singular event. Probability statements refer to "objective" probabilities of collectives (classes). They are based on empirical observations. And they are corrigible by such observations. Yet at the same time Ludwig von Mises's definition of class probability represents an ingenious simplification and refinement of Richard's frequency interpretation. On the one hand, in requiring that one know (or assume to know) everything regarding the behavior of the whole class, Ludwig von Mises circumvents the difficulties associated with Richard's notion of a *limit* and its application to necessarily *finite* sequences of events. On the other hand, in requiring of every singular event that nothing be known about it except that it is a member of a certain class, Ludwig von Mises eliminates the need for the "randomness" criterion to be added to the definition of a collective suitable to treatment by the probability calculus.[27] Ludwig von Mises's definition of class probability already *entails* a definition of randomness (and "logical homogeneity"): to state that nothing is known about any particular event except its membership in a joint (common) class of events is to say the same as that—as far as one knows—each particular event is logically "homogeneous" (as far as the risk under consideration is concerned) to every other event and/or that one knows of no law (and consequently no

---

indemnification if he is in a position to insure each of the ten for a premium of ten dollars. He will collect 100 dollars and will have to pay the same amount to one of the ten. But if he were to insure only one of them at a rate fixed by the calculus, he would embark not upon an insurance business, but upon gambling.... Insurance, whether conducted according to business principles or according to the principle of mutuality, requires the insurance of a whole class or what can be reasonably considered as such.... The characteristic mark of insurance is that it deals with the whole class of events. As we pretend to know everything about the behavior of the whole class, there seems to be no specific risk involved in the conduct of the business.... Neither is there any specific risk in the business of the keeper of a gambling bank or in the enterprise of a lottery. From the point of view of the lottery enterprise the outcome is predictable, provided that all tickets are sold. If some tickets remain unsold, the enterpriser is in the same position with regard to them as every buyer of a ticket is with regard to the tickets he bought. (*Id.*, pp. 108–10)

27. See section I.

method of place selection) governing the sequence of particular events.[28]

However, as pervasive as "risks" (insurable contingencies) are and as important as class or frequency probability accordingly may be, Ludwig von Mises concurs with Knight that risks are *not* the source of entrepreneurial profit and loss. To account for profit and loss another, different sort of contingency (a different sort of "probability") must be postulated. What, then, is the nature of *this* contingency that both Knight and Mises consider as falling outside the realm of phenomena tractable by the probability calculus and giving rise to entrepreneurial profit and loss?

III.

Knight terms this other sort of contingency "true uncertainty" and characterizes it thus:

> The probability in which the student of business risk is interested is an estimate, ... an estimate or intuitive judgment is somewhat like a probability judgment, but very different from either of the types of probability judgment already described [*a priori* and empirical-statistical].[29]

The theoretical difference between the probability connected with an estimate and that involved in such phenomena as are dealt with by insurance is, however, of the greatest importance.... Take as an illustration any typical business decision. A manufacturer is considering the advisability of making a large commitment in increasing the capacity of his works. He "figures" more or less on the proposition, taking account as well as possible of the various factors more or less susceptible of measurement, but the final result is an "estimate" of the probable outcome of any proposed course of action.

---

28. Ludwig von Mises was clearly aware of the advantage of this definition. Thus, he notes:

> The definition of the essence of class probability as given above is the only logically satisfactory one. It avoids the crude circularity implied in all definitions referring to the equiprobability of possible events. In stating that we know nothing about actual singular events except that they are elements of a class the behavior of which is fully known, this vicious circle is disposed of. Moreover, it is superfluous to add a further condition called the absence of any regularity in the sequence of the singular events. (L. Mises, *Human Action*, p. 109)

29. Knight, *Risk, Uncertainty and Profit*, pp. 223–24.

What is the "probability" of error (strictly, of any assigned degree of error) in the judgment? It is manifestly meaningless to speak of either calculating such a probability *a priori* or of determining it empirically by studying a large number of instances. The essential and outstanding fact is that the "instance" in question is so entirely unique that there are no others or not a sufficient number to make it possible to tabulate enough like it to form a basis for any inference of value about any real probability in the case we are interested in. The same obviously applies to most of conduct and not to business decisions alone.[30]

Business decisions

> deal with situations which are far too unique, generally speaking, for any sort of statistical tabulation to have any value for guidance. The conception of an objectively measurable probability or chance is simply inapplicable.... It is this third type of probability or uncertainty which has been neglected in economic theory, and which we propose to put in its rightful place ... that higher form of uncertainty not susceptible to measurement and hence elimination. It is this *true uncertainty* which by preventing the theoretically perfect outworking of the tendencies of competition gives the characteristic form of "enterprise" to economic organization as a whole and accounts for the peculiar income of the entrepreneur.[31]

Noteworthy about Knight's argument is his emphasis on *unique events*. Indeed, if the probability calculus is applicable only to *classes* or *collectives*, then it follows logically that it can*not* be applied to events which are members of *no* class (or, as Ludwig von Mises would say, events that form a class by themselves) and are thus *unique*. However, Knight is less forthcoming as regards the immediately following question: What is it that makes certain events *unique*, such that they *cannot* be (or cannot be conceived as being) in a class with other events; and how do we identify and distinguish such events from events which *can* be classified?[32]

---

30. Knight, *Risk, Uncertainty and Profit*, p. 226.

31. *Id.*, pp. 231–32.

32. Knight is keenly aware of the unsatisfactory character of his explication of uncertainty-probability (vs. risk-probability). Thus, he notes that "[t]his form of probability is involved in the greatest logical difficulties of all, and no very satisfactory discussion of it can be given, but its distinction from the other types must be emphasized." (*Risk, Uncertainty and Profit*, p. 225) Further, "[t]he ultimate logic, or psychology, of these deliberations is obscure, a part

Ludwig von Mises, writing later and in recognition of his brother's frequency interpretation, provides further clarification in this regard. According to Ludwig von Mises (and there is little doubt that Knight would have agreed with this), two categorically distinct types of empirical events exist: on the one hand, natural events or what might be called *accidents*, and on the other hand, human *actions*. Class (or risk) probability is applicable exclusively to the first type of event, i.e., accidents; and it is impermissible to apply it to human action. Rather, human action is the source of "true," non-quantifiable (Knightian) uncertainty and responsible for the emergence of profit and loss. States Ludwig von Mises,

> [t]here are two entirely different instances of probability; we may call them class probability (or frequency probability) and case probability (or the specific understanding of the sciences of human action).[33] The field for the application of the former is the field of the natural sciences, entirely ruled by causality; the field for the application of the latter is the field of the sciences of human action, entirely ruled by teleology.[34]

Unfortunately, in the relevant chapter VI of his *magnum opus* Ludwig von Mises is less than outspoken in explaining *why* human actions (choices) are intractable by probability theory (in the frequency interpretation). His answer can be inferred, however.

The question is: Is it scientifically legitimate to assign quantitative probabilities to the performance of certain actions (whether by individuals or groups of individuals)? Is there a numerical probability that I will watch basketball on TV tonight, that I will spend $5 on beer and $10 on red wine at Von's grocery store on First Street today, that Hillary Clinton will be elected in 2008, that one million German tourists will spend 3 to 3.5 million Euros on about three million Bratwursts in Mallorca in 2007, that Linda will divorce

---

of the scientifically unfathomable mystery of life and mind." (*Id.*, p. 227) And yet,

> [i]t is indisputable that this procedure is followed in fact to a very large extent and that an astounding number of decisions actually rest upon such a probability judgment, though it cannot be placed in the form of a definite statistical determination. That is, men do form, on the basis of experience, more or less valid opinions as to their own capacity to form correct judgments, and even of the capacities of other men in this regard. (*Id.*, p. 228)

33. On case probability see section IV below.
34. L. Mises, *Human Action*, p. 107.

George, that Ben Bernanke will create 5 billion paper dollars next week, that more people will watch MTV than Fox next Christmas night?

For the frequency theorist, the answer to these questions is a clear no. To be sure, we constantly make predictions concerning action-events such as these, but probability calculations do not—and legitimately cannot—play any role in these predictions.

First of all, the frequency theorist will remind us that the application of the term probability to a single event—and all above-mentioned action-events are single events!—is, in Richard von Mises's words, "utter nonsense." "The theory of probability can never lead to a definite statement concerning a single event." "It is possible to speak about probabilities only in reference to a properly defined collective." "The definition of probability ... is only concerned with 'the probability of encountering a certain attribute in a given collective.'"[35]

What, then, are the corresponding collectives or classes to which the above mentioned single events belong as members? What, for instance, is the class to which the event "I watch basketball on TV tonight" belongs; what is the collective of which "one million German tourists spend 3 to 3.5 million Euros on about three million Bratwursts in Mallorca in 2007" is a member; and what is the appropriate collective for "Linda divorces George?" Without a specified collective and a (assumedly) full count of its individual members and their various attributes no numerical probability statement is possible (or is, if made, arbitrary).

From a formal-logical point of view, no difficulties arise in meeting such request. For every single event one (or more) corresponding class(es) can be defined. For instance, "I watch basketball on TV tonight" can be considered a member of the class "people watching/not watching basketball on TV tonight" or "American males" doing so. Or it can be considered an element of the class "I watch basketball on TV nightly." The one million German Bratwurst eaters on Mallorca can be considered a member of the class "annual per capita Bratwurst expenditure by German tourists on Mallorca." "Linda divorces George" can be an element of "females divorcing/not-divorcing males," or "Lindas divorcing/not-divorcing Georges," etc.

However, to have a well-defined—and actually counted and surveyed— collective is only one of the requirements that must be fulfilled to allow

---

35. R. Mises, *Probability, Statistics and Truth*, pp. 17, 33, 28, 12.

the use of numerical probability statements. The second condition to be fulfilled is that of "randomness." In Richard von Mises's words, "only such sequences of events or observations, which satisfy the requirements of complete lawlessness or 'randomness' [are true] collectives." In order to employ the probability calculus, it must be impossible to devise "a method of *selecting the elements* so as to produce a fundamental change in the relative frequencies."[36] "The limiting values of the relative frequencies in a collective must be independent of all possible place selections."[37] Or as Ludwig von Mises expressed the same requirement: for every element of a class it must hold that nothing is known about its attributes under consideration but that it is an element of this class (and that everything is known about the relative frequency of specified attributes for the class as a whole).

It is in connection with this randomness requirement where Ludwig von Mises (and presumably Knight) see insuperable difficulties in applying probability theory to human actions. True, formal-logically for every single action a corresponding collective can be defined. However, ontologically human actions (whether of individuals or groups) cannot be grouped in "true" collectives but must be conceived as unique events. Why? As Ludwig von Mises would presumably reply, the assumption that one know nothing about any particular event except its membership in a known class is false in the case of human actions; or, as Richard von Mises would put it, in the case of human actions we know a "selection rule" the application of which leads to fundamental changes regarding the relative frequency (likelihood) of the attribute in question (thus ruling out the use of the probability calculus).

IV.

The randomness (or homogeneity) assumption can be made *vis-à-vis* events of the accident variety. For instance, we know nothing about the attribute of any particular bottle (will it break or not?) except the bottle's membership in a class of bottles (of which we know the probability of bottles breaking or not); and we know nothing about the attribute of any particular throw of a die (will it be a 6 or not?) except the throw's membership in a class of dice throws (of which we know the probability of throwing sixes).

In the case of human actions this assumption is incorrect, however. In the case of human actions, "we know," writes Ludwig von Mises, "with regard to

---

36. *Id.*, p. 24.   37. *Id.*, pp. 24–25; see also footnote 8 above.

a particular event, *some* of the factors determin[ing] its outcome."[38] Hence, insofar as we know *more* about a single event than merely its membership in a given class of events of which we know the frequency of certain attributes, we are, with regard to human actions, in a *better* position to make predictions than we are in the case of "accidents," where *nothing* about particular events—one bottle's vs. another's breaking—is known.

Whereas natural events—accidents—are occurrences determined by generally, time- and place-invariantly—"blindly" and "indiscriminately"— effective forces within (and constrained by) a "natural environment," we know action-events to be occurrences determined by *individually, at specific times and places held and effective value judgments, knowledge, and property* (acting as a constraint). That is, we know that human choices and actions result from individual (subjective and momentary) value judgments; that value judgments involve the ranking of valued ends and the presumed correct knowledge of how to reach these ends through some combination of means; and that the valuation of ends and the selection of means are constrained by the quantity and quality of property (possessions) at an individual human actor's disposal.[39]

---

38. L. Mises, *Human Action*, p. 110, emphasis added. In fact, in some cases we know all of the factors determining its outcome. See footnote 44 below.

39. It is true that advocates of the positivist-falsificationist research program deny the categorical distinction drawn here between natural events (accidents) and actions and claim that one and the same methodology applies to both realms of phenomena (monism). According to them, both natural events as well as human actions are to be explained by hypothetically valid (and hence empirically falsifiable) general, time- and place-invariantly effective causes. In both cases, we "explain" by formulating causal hypotheses, which are either confirmed or falsified by actual experiences. However, if actions could indeed be conceived of as governed by time- and place-invariantly operating causes just as natural events are, then it is certainly appropriate to ask: what then about explaining the actions of the explainers, i.e., the causal researchers? They are, after all, the persons who carry on the very process of first formulating causal hypotheses and of then assembling confirming or falsifying experience. In order to assimilate confirming or falsifying experiences—to confirm, revise, or replace his initial hypothesis—the causal researcher must assumedly be able *to learn from experience*. Every positivist-falsificationist is forced to admit this. Otherwise why engage in causal research at all? However, if one can learn from experience in as yet unknown ways, then one admittedly cannot know at any given point in time what one will know at a later point in time and, accordingly, how one will act on the basis of this later knowledge. One can only reconstruct the "causes" of one's actions after the event, as one can explain one's knowledge only after one already possesses it. Indeed, no scientific advance could ever alter the fact that one must regard one's knowledge and

Based on this general knowledge concerning the nature of human actions as opposed to accidents, then, we are in possession of a method which, according to Richard von Mises's frequency theory, we are most definitely *not* allowed to possess if the probability calculus is to be applicable: namely a method of "place selection." We know of *no* rule how to distinguish one bottle from another as far as breakage is concerned (otherwise they would not be "classed" together). However, for any presumed collective of *action*-events (such as "men watch basketball on TV tonight" or "I watch basketball on TV nightly") we *do* know of such a rule. We do know of a method of decomposing and de-homogenizing every conceivable action-collective ultimately down to its individual elements (such as "American men, teenagers, I, you, Peter, Paul watch basketball" and "I watch basketball on Monday, Tuesday, Wednesday"). This method of place selection—the possibility of devising a method of selecting the elements so as to produce a fundamental change in the relative frequencies of the attributes in question—is called *"Verstehen"* (understanding).

Ludwig von Mises characterizes this method thus: *Verstehen*

> deals with the mental activities of men that determine their actions.
> It deals with the mental processes that result in a definite kind
> of behavior, with the reactions of the mind to the conditions of
> the individual's environment. It deals with something invisible and
> intangible that cannot be perceived by the methods of the natural
> sciences. . . . This specific understanding of the sciences of human

---

actions based on this knowledge as unpredictable on the basis of constantly operating causes. One might hold this conception of freedom to be an illusion. And this might well be correct from the point of view of a scientist with cognitive powers substantially superior to any human intelligence, or from the point of view of God. But we are not God, and even if our freedom is illusory from His standpoint and our actions follow a predictable path, for us this is a necessary and unavoidable illusion. We cannot predict in advance, on the basis of our previous state of knowledge our future state of knowledge and our actions manifesting this knowledge. We can only reconstruct them after the event. Thus, the positivist-falsificationist methodology is simply contradictory when applied to the field of knowledge and action—which contains knowledge as its necessary ingredient. The positivist-falsificationist who formulates a causal explanation (assuming time- and place-invariantly operating causes) for some action is simply engaged in nonsense. His activity of engaging in an enterprise—research, whose outcome he must admit he cannot know in advance because he must admittedly be able to learn—proves that what he pretends to do cannot be done. See also Hoppe, *Kritik der kausalwissenschaftlichen Sozialforschung* (Opladen: Westdeutscher, 1987); and idem, *Economic Science and the Austrian Method* (Auburn, Ala.: Ludwig von Mises Institute, 2007 [1995]).

action aims at establishing the facts that men attach a definite meaning to the state of their environment, that they value this state and, motivated by these judgments of value, resort to definite means in order to preserve or to attain a definite state of affairs different from that which would prevail if they abstained from any purposeful reaction. Understanding deals with judgments of value, with the choice of ends and of the means resorted to for the attainment of these ends, and with the valuation of the outcome of actions performed.

The methods of scientific inquiry are categorically not different from the procedures applied by everybody in his daily mundane comportment. They are merely more refined and as far as possible purified of inconsistencies and contradictions. Understanding is not a method of procedure peculiar only to historians. It is practiced by infants as soon as they outgrow the merely vegetative stage of their first days and weeks....

The concept of understanding was first elaborated by philosophers and historians who wanted to refute the positivists' disparagement of the methods of history....But the services understanding renders to man in throwing light on the past are only a preliminary stage in the endeavors to anticipate what may happen in the future. ...Understanding aims at anticipating future conditions as far as they depend on human ideas, valuations, and actions.[40]

Unfortunately, in his characterization of the method of *Verstehen*, Ludwig von Mises fails to expressly identify it *as a method of place selection*, which leaves his analysis of the categorical distinction between case and class probability in a less than satisfactory state. However, this shortcoming can be rectified by adding two closely related observations to his characterization of *Verstehen*.

First, it must be added to Mises's characterization that *Verstehen* is reached, and possibly refined, by means of verbal communication (symbolic interaction), whether actual or virtual,[41] with the entity exhibiting (or

---

40. Ludwig von Mises, *The Ultimate Foundation of Economic Science* (Kansas City: Sheed Andrews and McMeel, 1978), pp. 47–49.

41. Obviously, one can communicate only with *present* entities; hence, the distinction between actual and virtual communication. As far as *past*—and to some extent also *distant*—entities are concerned, only virtual communication is possible. I cannot engage in actual communication with Caesar, for instance, in order to find out why he crossed the Rubicon. But I can study Caesar's writings and those of his precursors and contemporaries in order to gain some understanding of his time, his personality, and the situation he faced when he made the decision in question.

expected to exhibit) a certain behavior or attribute. From this two further elementary insights regarding the distinction between natural (accident) events and action-events follow.

On the one hand, it follows that we have an access to some entities: human actors, that we do *not* have to others such as dice, bottles, stones, or the sun. We can communicate with—and hence understand—the former, but not (with) the latter. Accordingly, we can answer questions concerning human actions that are simply unanswerable in the case of natural events. We do not know, and have no way of finding out, *why* dice, bottles, stones, or the sun behave the way they do. True, we can refer to natural laws in explaining their behavior. But we do not know why these laws are the way they are. They happen to be this way rather than that, and in this sense the behavior of dice, bottles, stones, and the sun is and forever remains unintelligible to us. In contrast, we *do* know, and have a method of finding out, *why* human actors behave in the way they do. Actors have *reasons* for acting the way they do, and we can *understand* these reasons, thus rendering their actions *intelligible events* (rather than mere "happenings").[42]

On the other hand, whereas entities such as dice, bottles, stones, and the sun offer "equal access" to every observer, i.e., every person is in a position of acquiring the *same* knowledge of, and reaching the *same* success in predicting their behavior, such equality is absent in the case of human actions. To be sure, as a matter of empirical fact one person might be more successful than another in predicting the behavior of dice, bottles, stones, and the sun. This may be because one observer possesses cognitive (including mathematical) abilities that another simply does not have or one person has made a new, hitherto unknown discovery. However, *in principle*, no obstacle stands in the way of anyone learning what another knows or has newly discovered about the behavior of such entities. All knowledge and every new discovery regarding them is public, open, and ready to be acquired by everyone.

In distinct contrast, the access to human actors by means of verbal communication is not equal and public but *privileged* and *private*. Each person has a privileged access to himself. That is, in principle each person is better equipped than anyone else in understanding and predicting *his very own actions*, and especially his immediately impending actions. By the same token, because every actor has privileged access to himself, the access

---

42. Peter Winch, *The Idea of a Social Science and Its Relation to Philosophy* (London: Routledge and Kegan Paul, 1970).

to *other* actors—what is called *Fremdverstehen* or the understanding of "strangers"—is private. That is, each "other" or "stranger" may or may not communicate with someone else and reveal more or less about himself. Or put differently, human actors can reveal or keep *secrets*, and their investigators accordingly may know more or less about the behavior of this rather than that person, while entities such as dice, bottles, stones, and the sun have no secrets to hide from anyone.

Second, these insights regarding the cognitive accessibility of human actors versus non-communicative entities immediately lead to the final and decisive conclusion: that *Verstehen* via verbal communication represents a unique method of "individualization." To be sure, in using a system of spatial-temporal coordinates we can always distinguish one die, bottle, or stone from another and likewise one stone-throwing event or one sunrise from another regarding the same stone or sun. But it is precisely our inability of using *any other* method of individualization that makes it possible to form "collectives" or "classes" of different stones and bottles and of different stone throws and sun rises of one and the same stone and sun. That is, only because we are unable to distinguish one die, bottle, or stone from another and one stone throw or sun rise from another, *except through their location in space and time*, are we in a position to say, in accordance with Ludwig von Mises's definition of class probability, that everything is known about the relative frequency of specified attributes for a class as a whole and nothing is known about the behavior of a particular entity but that is a member of this class.

In distinct contrast, in the case of human actors communication offers such *other* method of individualization. By means of verbal communication, we are in a position to precisely distinguish one actor from any other actor and one action of a given actor from any other following action of the same actor. That is, verbal communication represents a method of *synchronic as well as diachronic individualization*.

In synchronic perspective, it is impossible to form any actor "collective" made up of Peter, Paul, John, Jim, etc., because it is manifestly untrue to say that we know nothing about their particular actions but that they are the actions of men, American men or American teenage males, for instance, of which we know the relative frequency of some specified attribute such as buying a six-pack of beer today, for instance. We can communicate with Peter, Paul, John, and Jim, and thus find out about *Peter's* value judgments, knowledge, and property constraints, *Paul's* value judgments, knowledge, and property constraints, *John's*, and *Jim's*. Each of them is faced by *his own* property constraints and has *his own* reasons for acting the way he does.

Likewise, in diachronic perspective it is impossible to form any actor "collective" made up of me and my actions performed over time or of Peter and his actions, because it is also false to claim that I know nothing about my actions or Peter's actions today, tomorrow, in one week, or one month from now but that they are *my* actions or *Peter's* actions and I know everything about the relative frequency of certain attributes within the class of all of my actions or all of Peter's actions. To say so is untrue for a twofold reason.

On the one hand, it is untrue because I know more about *my* actions or *Peter's* actions today, tomorrow, in one week, and so on, than that they are my actions or Peter's actions. I know that my and Peter's actions today are the result of my and Peter's *present* value judgments, knowledge, and property constraints, and that my and Peter's actions tomorrow or in one week are the result of my and Peter's *future*—*tomorrow's* and *next week's*—value judgments, knowledge, and property constraints. I know further that regardless of the outcome—success or failure—of my and Peter's *present* actions, my and Peter's *future* value judgments, knowledge, and property constraints will be *changed* as a result of our present actions, such that my and Peter's future actions will be performed by a *different* me and a *different* Peter under *different* constraints. Moreover, I know that the change effected in me and in Peter and our circumstances as a result of our present actions cannot be predicted by us in advance but only be reconstructed *after* the event, thus requiring continuously renewed efforts of *Verstehen*.[43]

---

43. In contrast to the behavior of non-communicative entities, then, which is time-invariant, human actors vary in time and we must communicate with them again and again in order to predict their actions. If man proceeds, as positivists say he does, to interpret a predictive success as a confirmation of his hypothesis such that he would, given the same circumstance, employ the same knowledge in the future, and if he interprets a predictive failure as a falsification such that he would not employ the same but a different hypothesis in the future, he can only do so if he assumes—even if only implicitly—that the behavior of the objects under consideration does not change over the course of time. Otherwise, if their behavior were not assumed to be time-invariant—if the same objects were to behave sometimes this way and at other times in a different way—no conclusion as to what to make of a predictive success or failure would follow. A success would not imply that one's hypothesis had been temporarily confirmed, and hence, that the same knowledge should be employed in the future. Nor would any predictive failure imply that one should *not* employ the same hypothesis again under the same circumstances. But this assumption—that the objects of one's research do not alter their behavior in the course of time—*cannot* be made

On the other hand and by the same token, we cannot say that we know nothing about the attributes of a particular event but everything about the relative frequency of the same attributes for the entire class of my and Peter's actions, because the possible attributes of our actions constitute an "open" or "unending" class. For entities such as dice and bottles, for instance, we know all possible attributes. A throw of a die has six possible outcomes and a bottle can either break or not break. And it is only because the number of possible outcomes is thus "closed," that the notion of a "sufficiently long" series of observations (Richard von Mises) can assume any operational meaning. Only because the number of possible attributes is definite can we reasonably claim that a series of observations has been "sufficiently long" for all attributes having had a chance of showing up and thus allowing us to calculate the relative frequency of any one of them. However, if man can learn in unforeseeable ways and the potential attributes of his actions are open-ended, then no series of observations can ever be considered "sufficiently long," and hence, it becomes impossible to calculate the relative frequency of any given attribute within a class of events.

---

with respect to the very subject engaging in research without thereby falling into self-contradiction. For in interpreting his successful predictions as confirmations and his failed predictions as falsifications, the researcher must necessarily assume *himself* to be a learning subject—someone who can learn about the behavior of objects conceived by him as non-learning objects. Thus, even if everything else may be assumed to have a constant nature, man as a researcher cannot make the same assumption with respect to *himself*. He must be a different person after each confirmation or falsification than he was before, and it is *his* nature to be able to change over the course of time. See also footnote 39 above.

Consequently, whereas in the case of non-communicative entities the meaning of predictive success and failure is unambiguous: success means "so far your hypothesis has not been falsified, thus apply it again" and failure means "your hypothesis as it stands is wrong, thus change it," in the case of human actors the meaning of predictive success and failure is necessarily ambiguous. Because the value judgments, knowledge, and property constraints of a given actor can change in the course of time, we might repeat a specific prediction even if it had proved wrong before or change it even if it had turned out right. That is, we can never rest on our past laurels but must always start again fresh and judge the applicability of our past knowledge anew; and hence, we can never accumulate a stock of knowledge that we may blindly rely upon in the future. See also Hoppe, "On Certainty and Uncertainty," *Review of Austrian Economics* 10, no. 1 (1997): pp. 60–61, 73; reprinted chapter 14 herein.

V. CONCLUSION

This, then, brings us to our final conclusion. Frank H. Knight and Ludwig von Mises are entirely correct in insisting that the use of numerical probabilities is impossible in our daily endeavors of predicting our own and our fellow men's actions. As Richard von Mises, the originator of the frequency interpretation of probability, has unambiguously stated: the application of the term probability to a single event is "utter nonsense." It is possible to speak about numerical probabilities only in reference to a properly defined collective. But ontologically, no such collective exists as far as human actions are concerned. Each human action must be considered a unique event, constituting a class of its own. The method of *Verstehen* through verbal communication represents a technique of synchronic as well as diachronic individualization. By means of *Verstehen* each actor (and each group of actors) can be de-homogenized from any other actor (or group) and every given actor (or group of actors) *today* can be de-homogenized from the same actor (or the same group) *tomorrow*. Or in the words of Richard von Mises, *Verstehen* provides us with a "selection rule" which prohibits every use of "relative frequency" statements, because, by definition, *relative* (numerical) frequencies require a class made up of more than just *one* element.[44]

---

44. While Ludwig von Mises is exclusively concerned with *probability* statements and the categorical distinction between class probability (risk) and case probability (uncertainty), his analysis can be extended to *deterministic* propositions as well, i.e., to statements regarding which our knowledge concerning their content is *not* deficient such that we *do* know everything which would be required for a definite decision between true and not true. In the same way as there exists a categorical distinction between class vs. case probability, so there also exists a categorical distinction between class *determinism* (event or accident-certainty) vs. case *determinism* (action-certainty).

For instance (in synchronic perspective), I am certain about what will happen if a stone is thrown into the air: that it will fall to the ground. In fact, *every* stone will do so, and insofar my certainty extends to every single stone-throwing event. Likewise (in diachronic perspective), I am certain that I will see the sun rise and set in the same constant pattern every day, and insofar my certainty also extends to particular events: to the sun on Monday, Tuesday, Wednesday, etc. However, despite my certainty regarding the outcome of particular events, it still holds true what Ludwig von Mises defines as the *characteristicum specificum* of class probability: namely, that nothing is known about any particular event except its membership in a given class, while everything is known about the behavior of the whole class of events. The objective probability of the events under consideration, based on long-run frequency observations, is 1; *hence*, my certainty regarding each singular event. I can be certain regarding each actual, singular event, *because* I am certain about the behavior of the class, but I have no means to distinguish between the singular events. They are homogeneous as far as the attributes in question are concerned. Each singular event is the outcome of the same general (deterministic) law.

In distinct contrast are the following examples: I am certain that my left arm will rise in a second. I am certain that I will drink a beer tonight. I am certain that I will get out of my bed tomorrow morning. As far as the certainty of these events is concerned, it is no less than that regarding the behavior of stones or the sun. Indeed, one might say that my certainty regarding the former events is even higher than that concerning the latter. After all, the validity of the deterministic laws on which the latter certainty rests is only a hypothetical one, whereas in the former cases it is what one might call a voluntarist-constructivist certainty: I am making the events in question certain; their occurrence depends solely on my will (plus the fact that I am not paralyzed, that I am in possession of a beer, that I own a bed, etc.).

However, as Ludwig von Mises notes regarding probability statements, just as "case probability has nothing in common with class probability but the incompleteness of our knowledge" (*Human Action*, p. 110), so case determinism (action-certainty) has nothing in common with class determinism (event- or accident-certainty) but the completeness of our knowledge. In every other regard the two are entirely different. For one, whereas I do not know why stones and the sun behave the way they do (I may say that they do so because of the law of gravitation or the Newtonian laws of motion, but there is no further answer, then, as to the question why these laws are the way they are: they are the way they are without anyone understanding why this is so), regarding my own actions (lifting my arm, drinking a beer, getting out of bed) I do know their ultimate cause: they happen, because that is the way I want things to be. Moreover, whereas my certainty regarding the behavior of stones and the sun is based on long-run frequency observations (and the fact that these observations have so far revealed only one and the same result, without any exception), my certainty regarding my arm-lifting, beer-drinking, and getting out of bed is solely based on my present understanding of myself and my present circumstances. However, from my certainty regarding this particular case of arm-lifting, beer-drinking, and getting out of bed nothing follows as regards my future acts of arm-lifting, beer-drinking, and getting out of bed. Rather, any certainty regarding any such future acts of mine must be based on another, future act of understanding myself and my circumstances. In contrast, from my certainty regarding the behavior of one particular stone-throw and the behavior of the sun on Monday it follows that I am just as certain about the result of the next stone-throwing event and the behavior of the sun on Tuesday. (Incidentally, apart from these two types of empirical [*a posteriori*] certainty, there also exists a third type: of logical and praxeological [*a priori*] certainty.)

16

In Defense of Extreme Rationalism

I. THE RELATIVISM OF HERMENEUTICS AND RHETORIC AND THE CLAIMS OF RATIONALISM

For some time, the philosophy establishment has been under attack by the likes of Paul Feyerabend, Richard Rorty, Hans G. Gadamer, and Jacques Derrida. A movement of sorts that has already won over numerous members of the philosophy profession is steadily gaining ground, not only in such soft fields as literary criticism and sociology, but even in the hard natural sciences. With Donald McCloskey's *The Rhetoric of Economics*,[1] this movement is ready to invade economics. Yet, it is not only the orthodox, neoclassical Chicago economist McCloskey who preaches the new dispensation; there is also G. L. S. Shackle, and at the fringes of the Austrian school of economics are Ludwig Lachmann and the George Mason University hermeneuticians who lend support to the new creed.

However, this creed is not entirely new. It is the ancient tune of skepticism and nihilism, of epistemological and ethical relativism that is sung here in ever-changing, modern voices. Richard Rorty, one of the outstanding champions of the creed, has presented it with admirable frankness in his *Philosophy and the Mirror of Nature*.[2] The opponent of the new old

---

• Review of Donald McCloskey, *The Rhetoric of Economics*. Originally published in *Review of Austrian Economics* 3 (1989).

1. Donald McCloskey, *The Rhetoric of Economics* (Madison: University of Wisconsin Press, 1985)

2. Richard Rorty, *Philosophy and the Mirror of Nature* (Princeton, N.J.: Princeton University Press, 1979).

movement is *rationalism* and, in particular, *epistemology* as a product of rationalism. Rationalism, writes Rorty:

> is a desire for constraint—a desire to find "foundations" to which one might cling, frameworks beyond which one must not stray, objects which impose themselves, representations, which cannot be gainsaid.[3]

The dominating notion of epistemology is that to be rational, to be fully human, to do what we ought, we need to be able to find agreement with other

> human beings. To construct an epistemology is to find the maximum amount of common ground with others. The assumption that an epistemology can be constructed is the assumption that such common ground exists.[4]

However, Rorty claims that no such common ground exists: hence the false idol of rationalism must fall and a "relativist" position termed hermeneutics must be adopted.

Hermeneutics sees the relations between various discourses as those of strands in a possible conversation, a conversation which presupposes no disciplinary matrix which unites the speakers, but where the hope of agreement is never lost so long as the conversation lasts. This hope is not a hope for the discovery of antecedently existing common ground, but *simply* hope for agreement, or, at least, exciting and fruitful disagreement. Epistemology sees the hope of agreement as a token of the existence of common ground which, perhaps unbeknown to the speakers, unites them in common rationality. For hermeneutics, to be rational is to be willing to refrain from epistemology—from thinking that there is a special set of terms in which all contributions to the conversation should be put—and to be willing to pick up the jargon of the interlocutor rather than translating it into one's own. For epistemology, to be rational is to find the proper set of terms into which all contributions should be translated if agreement is to become possible. For epistemology, conversation is implicit inquiry. For hermeneutics, inquiry is routine conversation.[5]

What Rorty terms hermeneutics, McCloskey calls rhetoric. In *The Rhetoric of Economics*, he attempts to persuade us that in economics, just

---

3. Rorty, *Philosophy and the Mirror of Nature*, p. 315.
4. *Id.*, p. 326.
5. McCloskey, *The Rhetoric of Economics*, p. 318.

as in any other language game that we might play, rationalist and epistemological claims of providing a common ground that makes agreement-on-something-objectively-true possible are out of place. Economics, too, is merely rhetoric. It is another contribution to the conversation of mankind, another attempt to keep a routine going. It exists not for the sake of inquiring about what is true, but for its own sake; not in order to convince anyone of anything based on objective standards, but in the absence of any such standards, simply in order to be persuasive and persuade for persuasion's sake.

> Rhetoric is the art of speaking. More broadly it is the study of how people persuade.[6]

> Rhetoric ... is the box of tools for persuasion taken together, available to persuaders good and bad.[7]

> [Economics should learn its lesson from literary criticism.] Literary criticism does not merely pass judgments of good or bad; in its more recent forms the question seems hardly to arise. Chiefly it is concerned with making readers see how poets and novelists accomplish their result. An economic criticism ... is not a way of passing judgment on economics. It is a way of showing how it accomplishes its result. It applies the devices of literary criticism to the literature of economics.[8]

> [The categories truth and falsehood play no role in this endeavor. Scholars] pursue other things, but things that have only an incidental relation with truth. They do so not because they are inferior to philosophers in moral fiber but because they are human. Truth-pursuing is a poor theory of human motivation and non-operational as a moral imperative. The human scientists pursue persuasiveness, prettiness, the resolution of puzzlement, the conquest of recalcitrant details, the feeling of a job well done, and the honor and income of office.... The very idea of Truth—with a capital T, something beyond what is merely persuasive to all concerned—is a fifth wheel. ... If we decide that the quantity theory of money or the marginal productivity theory of distribution is persuasive, interesting, useful, reasonable, appealing, acceptable, we do not also need to know that it is True.... [There] are particular arguments, good or bad. After making them, there is no point in asking a last, summarizing question: "Well, is it True?" It's whatever it is—persuasive, interesting, useful, and so forth.... There is no reason to search for a general quality called Truth.[9]

---

6. *Id.*, p. 29. 7. *Id.*, pp. 37–38. 8. *Id.*, p. XIX. 9. *Id.*, pp. 46–47.

> [E]conomics in particular, and science in general are like the arts;[10] the law of demand is persuasive or unpersuasive in exactly the same way as a Keats poem;[11] and in just the same way as there exists no methodological formula for advancing artistic expression there exists none for advancing economics. Rhetoric] believes that science advances by healthy conversation, not adherence to a methodology. ...Life is not so easy that an economist can be made better at what he does merely by reading a book.[12]

Surely, after all this one has to catch one's breath. Yet has not rationalism refuted this doctrine time and again as self-contradictory and, if taken seriously, as fatally dangerous nonsense? Books such as McCloskey's may indeed make life better or easier. But is this not only insofar as one ignores their advice; and would not life in fact be worse if one were actually to follow it?

Consider this: after reading Rorty and McCloskey, would it not seem appropriate to ask "What, then, about their own pronouncements?" If there is nothing like truth based on common, objective ground, then all of the preceding talk can surely not claim to say anything true. In fact, it would be self-defeating to do what they seem to be doing: denying that an objective case can be made for any statement, while at the same time claiming this to be the case for their own views. In so doing, one would falsify the content of one's own statement. One cannot argue that one cannot argue.[13] Thus, in order to understand Rorty and McCloskey correctly, one must first realize that they cannot truly be saying what they seem to be saying. Nor can I here say anything claiming to be objectively so and true. No, their talk as well as mine can merely be understood as contributions to their and my entertainment.

But then, why should they or I listen and be entertained? After all, if there is no such thing as truth and, accordingly, no objective distinction between truth-claiming propositions and any others, then we are evidently faced with a situation of all-pervasive intellectual permissiveness.[14] With

---

10. This is also the thesis of a book by Paul Feyerabend, *Wissenschaft als Kunst* (Frankfurt/M.: Suhrkamp, 1984).

11. See the interview with McCloskey in the Institute for Humane Studies Newsletter, *Institute Scholar* 6, no. 1 (1986): p. 7.

12. McCloskey, *The Rhetoric of Economics*, p. 174.

13. On this "Apriori of Argumentation," see K. O. Apel, *Transformation der Philosophie*, vol. II (Frankfurt/M.: Suhrkamp, 1973).

14. In connection with the hermeneutical movement, the phrase *intellectual permissive-*

every statement just another contribution to the conversation of mankind, anything at all that is said is just as good a potential candidate for my entertainment as anything else. But why bother listening to such permissive, everything-goes talk? McCloskey might reply, "Because your talk or my talk is persuasive." But that will not change much, if anything at all. For according to his doctrine, the categories "persuasive" and "unpersuasive" are not simply other names for "true" and "false." The whole point would be lost if they were. No, he is saying that something is persuasive because it has in fact persuaded; because it has resulted in agreement. To go beyond this and ask, "Well, has one been persuaded of something correct?" would be an entirely inappropriate question. As a matter of fact, regarding any such question, he would have to point out that the very problem of determining whether or not a persuasion was based on correct talk would once more have to be decided on the actual persuasion of having been correctly persuaded; hence, that he is consistent in his rejection of the idea of objective truth; that the idea of breaking out of mere talk and of grounding talk in something that is not again simply talk is fallacious; and that truth then is itself no more than the subjective belief that what one believes is objectively true.[15] But if this is his position, then his talk, persuasive or unpersuasive as it may be, can indeed be no more than mere entertainment. Nor can this statement regarding what it means to talk claim to be objectively true; it, too, can only be meant to entertain.

Hence, it seems the first appropriate question regarding such books as McCloskey's would have to be "Are we being entertained?" Without a doubt, many a reader will reply that he is and McCloskey might then think that he has indeed achieved what he intended. But did he? Or was the reader's feeling

---

ness was coined by Henry Veatch in his essay "Deconstruction in Philosophy: Has Rorty Made It the Denouement of Contemporary Analytical Philosophy?" *Review of Metaphysics* 39 (December 1985).

15. McCloskey asks: "[Do we not] need something ... besides the mere social fact that an argument proved persuasive?" No, he counters, "talk against talk is self-refuting. The person making it [i.e., raising the preceding question] appeals to a social, nonepistemological standard of persuasiveness by the very act of trying to persuade someone that mere persuasion is not enough." (McCloskey, *The Rhetoric of Economics*, pp. 38–39)

Ironically, however, this argument does *not* prove his point. On the contrary, the argument can be said to be persuasive only because a self-contradictory position is considered to be false, and not regarded as false because it has been agreed upon. Otherwise, if I did not agree, would not the argument have to be considered false?

of being well entertained only due to the fact that he misinterpreted what he read and understood it as something claiming to be true, which, in fact, it was never meant to be? And would not the reader, once he had realized this, have to change his opinion? For then McCloskey's talk clearly would not fall into any different category from that of a novelist or poet. But as compared with their prose, and in direct competition with any novel or poem written for our entertainment, I submit that McCloskey's book is merely boring and fails miserably in its objective.

Yet, can his book be even *bad* entertainment without still having to be committed indispensably to the notion of a common ground that serves as the basis of objective truth? Rationalism denies that it can. It claims that the notion of truth, of objective truth, of truth grounded in some reality outside that of language itself, is indispensable for talk of any sort, that language presupposes rationality, and hence that it is impossible to rid oneself of the notion of objective truth as long as one is capable of engaging in any language game whatsoever. For how else could we find out whether someone was in fact entertained by something, or that he was persuaded by it, that he understood or misunderstood what it was that had been said to entertain and persuade, and even further, whether there was something that meant anything at all and so could be understood, rather than merely being meaningless rustling in the wind? Clearly enough, we could not claim to know any of this unless we had a common language with commonly understood concepts such as "being persuaded" or "entertained" as well as any other term used in our talk. In fact, we could not meaningfully claim to deny all this without having to presuppose yet another set of commonly understood concepts. And just as clearly, this common ground that must be presupposed if we want to say anything meaningful at all is not simply one of free-floating sounds in harmony with each other in midair. Instead, it is the common ground of terms being used and applied cooperatively in the course of a practical affair, an interaction. And again, in making this claim, one could not possibly deny that this is so without presupposing that one in fact *could* cooperatively establish some common ground with respect to the practical application of some terms.

Language, then, is not some ethereal medium disconnected from reality, but is itself a form of action. It is an offshoot of practical cooperation and as such, via action, is inseparably connected with an objective world. Talk, whether fact or fiction, is inevitably a form of cooperation and thus presupposes a common ground of objectively defined and applied terms.[16] Not in the sense that one would always have to agree on the content of what was said or that one would even have to understand everything said. But rather, in the sense that as long as one claimed to express anything meaningful at all, one would have to assume the existence of *some* common standards, if only to be able to agree on whether or not and in what respect one was in fact in agreement with others, and whether or not and to what extent one in fact understood what had been said. And these common standards would have to be assumed to be objective in that they would involve the application of terms within reality. To say, then, that no common ground exists is contradictory. The very fact that this statement can claim to convey meaning implies that there is such common ground. It implies that terms can be objectively applied and grounded in a common reality of action as the practical presupposition of language.

Thus, if McCloskey were right and there were indeed no objective truth, he could not even claim to entertain anyone meaningfully with his book. His talk would be meaningless, indistinguishable from the rattling of his typewriter. He would advocate even greater intellectual permissiveness than first thought. Not only would he have to drop the distinction between truth-claiming propositions and propositions that merely claim to be entertaining, but his permissiveness would go so far as to disallow any distinction between meaningful talk and a meaningless assemblage of sounds. For one cannot even claim to entertain with talk that involves no truth-claim beyond that of being meaningful talk, without still having to know what objective truth is and be able to distinguish between truth-claiming propositions and those statements (for example, in fictional talk) that do not imply any such claim.

And there is more. For how can McCloskey or Rorty reconcile their view of science as mere talk with their own advocacy of a talk-ethic, an ethic described by McCloskey as follows:

> Don't lie [but how could we, if there were no such thing as objective truth? H.H.H.]; pay attention; don't sneer; cooperate; don't shout; let other people talk; be open-minded; explain yourself when asked; don't resort to violence and conspiracy in aid of your ideas.[17]

---

16. On the inseparable connection between language and action, see esp. Ludwig Wittgenstein, *Philosophische Untersuchungen*, in *Schriften*, vol. I (Frankfurt/M.: Suhrkamp, 1963).

17. McCloskey, *The Rhetoric of Economics*, p. 24.

Why should we follow his advice of paying attention to talk and not resorting to violence, particularly in view of the fact that what is advocated here is talk of the sort where anything goes and where everything said is just as good a candidate for one's attention as anything else? It certainly is not evident that one should pay much attention to talk if that is what talk is all about! Moreover, it would be downright fatal to follow this ethic. For any viable human ethic must evidently allow people to do things other than talk, if only to have a single human survivor who could possibly have any ethical questions; McCloskey's talk-ethic, however, gives us precisely such deadly advice of never to *stop* talking or stop listening to others talk. In addition, McCloskey himself and his fellow hermeneuticians must admit that they can have no objective ground for proposing their ethic anyway. For if there are no objective standards of truth, then it must also be the case that one's ethical proposals cannot claim to be objectively justifiable either.[18] But what is wrong, then, with not being persuaded by all of this and, rather than listening further, hitting McCloskey on the head straightaway rather than waiting until he perishes from following his own prescription of endless talk? Clearly, if McCloskey were right, nothing could be said to be objectively wrong with this. (In fact, would one not have to conclude that McCloskey could not even say that anything objective had happened?) He might not regard my act of aggression as a contribution to the conversation of mankind (though we know by now that he could not even objectively claim to know this to be the case), but if the talk-ethic cannot itself be grounded in something objective outside of talk, then if I happened to be persuaded of an ethic of aggression instead, and I ended our conversation once and for all with a preemptive strike, McCloskey could not find anything objectively wrong with this either.

Thus, it is not only *intellectual* permissiveness that is preached by hermeneuticians and rhetoricians, it is total *practical* permissiveness as well—epistemological *and*, as the other side of the same coin, ethical relativism.[19] Yet such relativism is impossible to follow and thus wrong in the

---

18. On this, see also H. Veatch, "Deconstruction in Philosophy: Has Rorty Made It the Denouement of Contemporary Analytical Philosophy?" esp. p. 319 f.

19. It is by no means an accident, then, that advocates of every conceivable political ideology can be found among the hermeneuticians. The creed goes with libertarianism and anarchism (McCloskey and Feyerabend), with socialism (Ricœur and Foucault), and with fascism (Heidegger) as well as with, in most cases, middle-of-the-roadism. Gadamer—the

most objective sense of being literally incompatible with our nature as actors. Just as it is impossible to say and mean to say that there is no such thing as objective truth without in so doing actually presupposing objective criteria for the application of terms, so is it impossible to actually advocate ethical relativism. Because in order to advocate any ethical position whatsoever, one must be allowed to communicate rather than be coercively shut up and silenced, and thus, contrary to the relativist message itself, its messenger, in bringing it to us, must in fact presuppose the existence of objectively defined absolute rights. More specifically, he must presuppose those norms of action as valid whose observance makes talk as a special form of cooperation between physically separate talkers possible, while they must also allow everybody to do things other than engage in endless talk; and whose validity must then be regarded as objective and absolute in that no one could possibly ever be alive and talkingly challenge them.[20]

---

special hero of Don Lavoie and the George Mason University hermeneuticians and one of the murkiest "thinkers" of them all, who manages to fill hundreds of pages without saying anything and who rambles endlessly about interpreting without ever actually interpreting any text in an intelligible way (witness his masterpiece, *Wahrheit und Methode*, Tübingen: Mohr, 1960, English transl., 1975)—successfully advanced his career under Nazism, communism, and liberal democracy. On his philosophy and his life as a vivid illustration of the meaning of hermeneutics, see the brilliant essay by Jonathan Barnes, "A Kind of Integrity," *London Review of Books* (November 6, 1986); see also David Gordon, "Hermeneutics vs. Austrian Economics," Occasional Paper (Washington, D.C.: Ludwig von Mises Institute, 1986).

20. On the absolutist, a priori foundations of ethics, see Hans-Hermann Hoppe, "From the Economics of Laissez Faire to the Ethics of Libertarianism," in Llewellyn H. Rockwell and Walter Block, eds., *Man, Economy and Liberty* (Auburn, Ala.: Ludwig von Mises Institute, 1988); Hoppe, *Eigentum, Anarchie und Staat* (Opladen: Westdeutscher Verlag, 1986). Ethical absolutism as much as methodological absolutism is very much in disrepute. T. W. Hutchison goes so far as to smear everyone committed to such a position as a dangerous, potential dictator—revealingly, without ever going to the trouble of explaining what the ethical or methodological principles *are* whose a priori grounding allegedly implies such a threat. (*The Politics and Philosophy of Economics*, New York: New York University Press, 1981, esp. pp. 196–97.) Instead, pluralism—ethical and methodological—is what the enlightened person today professes. Only such pluralism, it is said, permits tolerance and freedom. (See as another typical pluralist Bruce Caldwell, *Beyond Positivism*, London: Allen and Unwin, 1982, chap. 13.) Must it be stressed that this doctrine is entirely fallacious? Without a priori foundation, pluralism is itself just another unfounded ideology and there is no reason to adopt it rather than any other one. Only if a priori valid reasons could be given for adopting pluralism could it claim to safeguard tolerance and freedom. A pluralism that would be merely one of plural

II. Hermeneutics versus Empiricism:
Rationalism Against Both—Round I

McCloskey's and Rorty's general thesis then, the very thesis that brought them their notoriety, is dead wrong. In fact, McCloskey and Rorty can only do and say what they do because *what* they say is false.

There is certainly much left to be said about rationalism, the age-old opponent of relativism. However, the perennial claims of rationalism remain unchallenged by this most modern, relativist attack: the claim that there exists a common ground on the basis of which objectively true propositions can be formulated; the claim that a rational ethic objectively founded in the nature of man as actors and talkers exists; and finally, the claim, only somewhat indirectly established in the previous argument and still to be substantiated, that one can know certain propositions to be objectively true a priori (that is, independent of contingent experiences) as they can be derived deductively from basic, axiomatic propositions whose truth cannot be denied objectively without running into a practical contradiction, that is, without presupposing in the very act of denial what is supposedly denied (so that it would be literally impossible to undo the truth of these propositions).[21]

With this fundamental criticism out of the way, what about McCloskey's pronouncements, if for the sake of argument we are willing to ignore that he cannot really claim to say anything? It is not entirely surprising, as will be seen, that the general flaw of the book—its lack of argumentative rigor—also comes to bear here.

---

values would actually be destructive of both. See on this in particular Henry Veatch, *Rational Man: A Modern Interpretation of Aristotelian Ethics* (Bloomington, Ind.: Indiana University Press, 1962), pp. 37–46. As contrasted to our modern pluralists, Benito Mussolini understood all this quite well. Veatch cites him on p. 41: "From the fact that all ideologies are of equal value ... the modern relativist infers that everybody has the right to create for himself his own ideology and to attempt to enforce it with all the energy of which he is capable."

21. In defense of the idea of synthetic a priori propositions, see A. Pap, *Semantics and Necessary Truth* (New Haven: Yale University Press, 1958); B. Blanshard, *Reason and Analysis* (LaSalle, Ill.: Open Court, 1964); P. Lorenzen, *Methodisches Denken* (Frankfurt/M.: Suhrkamp 1968); idem, *Normative Logic and Ethics* (Mannheim: Bibliographisches Institut, 1969); F. Kambartel, *Erfahrung und Struktur* (Frankfurt/M.: Suhrkamp, 1968); F. Kambartel and J. Mittelstrass, eds., *Zum normativen Fundament der Wissenschaft* (Frankfurt/M.: Athenaeum, 1973); Ludwig von Mises, *Human Action: A Treatise on Economics* (Chicago: Henry Regnery, 1966); Murray N. Rothbard, *Man, Economy, and State* (Los Angeles: Nash, 1971).

The very starting point of McCloskey's argument is marked by a misconception of the problem he faces. For in order to advance the thesis that economists should conceive of their jobs as keeping the conversation between economists going without ever claiming to say anything true (i.e., without ever supposing that anyone might ever have a decisive, conversation-stopping argument at his disposal), McCloskey would have to direct his argument against and refute the most extreme available opposition. He would have to choose as his target the claims of *rationalism* regarding the epistemological foundations and methodology of economics. And while only accounting for a small minority among today's theoreticians of economics, there surely exist some such dogmatic, doctrinaire, extremist, absolutist (or whatever other depreciating label one may choose) rationalists.[22] The foremost representatives of this persuasion are Ludwig von Mises and Murray N. Rothbard, who, within the general framework of a Kantian or, respectively, Aristotelian epistemology, conceive of economics as part of a pure theory of action and choice (praxeology).[23] Lionel Robbins advances only slightly less uncompromising views, in particular in the first edition of his *Nature and Significance of Economic Science*.[24] And from a very different position within the political-ideological spectrum are Martin Hollis and Edward J. Nell, who in their *Rational Economic Man* propound similar arch-rationalist claims regarding the logic of economics.[25] McCloskey would have to attack all of them, since they are the most radical conversation stoppers in that they all, despite some important differences, are completely uncompromising in insisting that economics not only can and *does* produce propositions that are objectively true and can be distinguished from propositions that are not, but, moreover, that

---

22. On the faulty reason for the use of such labels, see footnote 20. Recently their use has also become increasingly popular among Austrians such as Mario Rizzo and Don Lavoie in order to characterize and distance themselves from the Mises-Rothbard school within the tradition of Austrianism.

23. Ludwig von Mises, *Epistemological Problems of Economics* (New York: New York University Press, 1981); idem, *Human Action*; idem, *Theory and History* (Washington, D.C.: Ludwig von Mises Institute, 1985); idem, *The Ultimate Foundation of Economic Science* (Kansas City: Sheed Andrews and McMeel, 1978); Murray N. Rothbard, *Man, Economy, and State*; idem, *Individualism and the Philosophy of the Social Sciences* (San Francisco: Cato Institute, 1979); idem, "Praxeology: The Methodology of Austrian Economics," in Edwin Dolan, ed., *The Foundations of Modern Austrian Economics* (Kansas City: Sheed and Ward, 1976).

24. Lionel Robbins, *Nature and Significance of Economic Science* (London: Macmillan, 1932).

25. Marin Hollis and Edward J. Nell, *Rational Economic Man* (Cambridge, Eng.: Cambridge University Press, 1975).

some propositions of economics are grounded in incontestably true axioms or real (as contrasted with arbitrary, stipulative) definitions, and hence can be given an a priori justification.[26]

However, nowhere in his book does McCloskey attack these various representatives of an arch-rationalist methodology of economics, nor does he attack anyone else who falls into this camp. Nowhere in his book does he attack, much less refute, the very position that is the polar opposite of his. Robbins, Rothbard, Hollis, and Nell are never mentioned in McCloskey's text, nor do they appear in his bibliography. Nor does Mises's name appear in the bibliography, but it is mentioned twice in the text in support of some of McCloskey's own pronouncements.[27] Yet there is no reference to Mises's extremist, rationalist position. Austrian methodology is only cited in passing and described in a way that would strike anyone only faintly familiar with this intellectual tradition as no more than a naive misrepresentation: "Austrian methodology says: The history of all hitherto existing societies is the history of interactions among selfish individuals. Use statistics gingerly if at all, for they are transitory figments. Beware of remarks that do not accord with Austrian Methodological precepts."[28]

---

26. Lionel Robbins, just as the earlier Austrians Carl Menger and Eugen von Böhm-Bawerk, admittedly does not use the term *a priori*, but it should be sufficiently clear from his arguments as well as his frequent, approving references to Mises (who does) that Robbins actually *means* to provide an a priori justification of the basic propositions and theorems of economics.

The aprioristic character of economic propositions is explicitly stressed also by Frank H. Knight in "What Is Truth in Economics," in idem, *On the History and Method of Economics* (Chicago: University of Chicago Press, 1956).

For those familiar with the tradition of rationalist philosophy, it hardly needs to be shown that the claim of having produced an a priori true proposition does *not* imply a claim of being infallible. No one is, and rationalism has never said anything to the contrary. Rationalism merely argues that the process of validating or falsifying a statement claiming to be true a priori is categorically different from that of validating or falsifying what is commonly referred to as an empirical proposition. However, since McCloskey does seem to think that rationalism assumes infallibility and, hence, that the fact (triumphantly cited on pp. 33–34) that even in as pure a science as mathematics some alleged water-tight arguments have turned out to be inconclusive after all, constitutes proof of a fundamental flaw in rationalism—assuming here in McCloskey's favor that something such as fundamental flaws can exist at all in the absence of any truly objective standard—this point needs to be stressed here. Revisions of mathematical arguments are themselves a priori. They show only that an argument thought previously to be a priori true is not.

27. McCloskey, *The Rhetoric of Economics*, pp. 15, 65.

28. *Id.*, p. 25. His description of Marxist economic methodology, on the same page, is not much better.

Rather than doing battle with his direct logical adversary, McCloskey chooses to establish his own relativist position through an attack on empiricism-positivism. But knocking down empiricism-positivism is no more than knocking down a straw man, in that from its downfall, absolutely nothing follows in support of McCloskey's own claims. In fact, all of the previously mentioned arch-rationalists have leveled much harsher criticism against empiricism-positivism and still apparently did not think that in so doing they would commit themselves to relativism. On the contrary, it is their view that any criticism of empiricism-positivism, if it is one that has any intellectual weight at all, would have to vindicate the very claims of rationalism. Thus, and this is the fundamental misconstruction of his entire argument, McCloskey, given his objective, simply fires at the wrong target and, worse, does not seem to notice.

However, as much as empiricism-positivism may deserve to be intellectually destroyed, McCloskey does not even succeed here. He begins with a description of empiricism-positivism or of economic modernism, as he terms the application of this philosophy to the field of economics, and lists its major precepts:[29] prediction is what ultimately counts in science; there is no objective truth without observations; only quantifiable observations are objective data; introspection is subjective and worthless; science is positive and does not deal with normative questions; explaining something positively means bringing it under a general law; and a general law's validity is forever hypothetical, requiring permanent testing against objective observational data.

There is little to quarrel with regarding this characterization of modernism. Quite correctly, McCloskey also cites the most influential modern exponents of this creed: the Vienna Circle, analytical philosophy, and Popperianism in philosophy proper,[30] as well as such representative figures

---

29. McCloskey, *The Rhetoric of Economics*, pp. 7–8.

30. Karl R. Popper, in order to distinguish his falsificationism from the verificationism of the early Vienna Circle, prefers to label his philosophy "critical rationalism." To do so, however, is highly misleading if not deceptive, much like the common U.S. practice of calling socialists or social democrats "liberals." For in fact, Popper is in complete agreement with the fundamental assumptions of empiricism (see the following discussion in the text) and explicitly rejects the traditional claims of rationalism, i.e., of being able to provide us with a priori true empirical knowledge in general and an objectively founded ethic in particular. See, for example, his "Why Are the Calculi of Logic and Arithmetic Applicable to Reality," in Karl R. Popper, *Conjectures and Refutations* (London: Routledge and Kegan

within the economics profession as T. W. Hutchison, Milton Friedman, and Mark Blaug.[31] And McCloskey is certainly correct, too, in identifying this modernist worldview as the current textbook orthodoxy. Nonetheless, from the outset, his understanding of empiricism-positivism is insufficient in that he fails to reconstruct the fundamental assumptions of modernism (i.e., those assumptions that underlie its various precepts). He neglects to assign them a specific place in a general, logically unified conceptual structure. He fails to clarify that the various specific modernist precepts flow essentially from the acceptance of one crucial assumption. The assumption, fundamental to modern empiricism, is that knowledge regarding reality, or empirical knowledge, must be verifiable or at least falsifiable by experience; that whatever is known by experience could have been otherwise, or, put differently, that nothing about reality could be known to be true a priori; that all a priori true statements are simply analytical statements that have no factual content, but are true by convention, representing merely tautological information about the use and the transformation rules of signs; that all cognitively meaningful statements are either empirical or analytical, but never both; and hence that normative statements, because they are neither

---

Paul, 1969), where he advances the traditional empiricist thesis that "only if we are ready to accept refutations do we speak about reality" (p. 212), and "refutes" the idea of the rules of logic and arithmetic being laws of reality by pointing out that "if you put 2 + 2 rabbits in a basket, you *may* soon find seven or eight in it" (p. 211). For a correct placement of Popper's philosophy within the general framework of empiricism, see the sovereign discussion by a leading analytical philosopher, W. Stegmueller, *Hauptströmungen der Gegenwartsphilosophie*, vol. I (Stuttgart: Kroener, 1965), chaps. 9–10.

In fact, it is only fair to say that it is Popper who contributed more than anyone else to persuading the scientific community of the modernistic, empiricist-positivist worldview. In particular, it should be emphasized that it was Popper who is responsible for Hayek's and Robbins' increasing deviations from their originally much more Misesian methodological position. See on this Lionel Robbins, *An Autobiography of an Economist* (London: Macmillan, 1976); Friedrich A. Hayek, "The Theory of Complex Phenomena," in idem, *Studies in Philosophy, Politics and Economics* (Chicago: University of Chicago Press, 1964); Hayek, "The Pretence of Knowledge," in idem, *New Studies in Philosophy, Politics, Economics and the History of Ideas* (Chicago: University of Chicago Press, 1978), esp. p. 31 f. See also Hayek's "Einleitung" to Ludwig von Mises, *Erinnerungen* (Stuttgart: Fischer, 1978), and his "Foreword" to Ludwig von Mises, *Socialism* (Indianapolis, Ind.: Liberty Fund, 1981).

31. Terrence W. Hutchison, *The Significance and Basic Postulates of Economic Theory* (London: MacMillan, 1938); Milton Friedman, "The Methodology of Positive Economics," in idem, *Essays in Positive Economics* (Chicago: University of Chicago Press, 1953); Mark Blaug, *The Methodology of Economics* (Cambridge, Eng.: Cambridge University Press, 1980).

empirical nor analytical, cannot legitimately contain any claim to truth, but must be regarded instead as mere expressions of emotions, saying in effect no more than "wow" or "grr."[32] And in failing to clarify this, McCloskey precipitates his subsequent failure to bring even empiricism-positivism, his chosen opponent, down. His attack is simply unsystematic, and it thereby necessarily misses its goal.

McCloskey's first criticism is well targeted. He shows that contrary to the claims of Popper and his school in particular, following the advice of the empiricist-falsificationist philosophy would ultimately lead one to skepticism. Whenever a hypothetical law is empirically tested and found to be lacking, within the very framework of an empiricist methodology it is always possible to immunize one's theory by denying the recalcitrant observations outright and declaring them illusory, by acknowledging them but ascribing their recalcitrance to measurement errors, or by postulating some unobserved, intervening variable, whose lack of control is to blame for the seemingly falsifying observations. Observes McCloskey:

> Insulation from crucial test is the substance of most scientific dis-
> agreement. Economists and other scientists will complain to their
> fellows, "Your experiment was not properly controlled"; "You have
> not solved the identification problem"; "You have used an equilib-
> rium (competitive, single-equation) model when a disequilibrium
> (monopolistic, 500-equation) model is relevant" ... There is no
> "falsification" going on.[33]

And, he remarks further, have we not known since Thomas Kuhn's *Structure of Scientific Revolutions*[34] that the actual history of natural science does not seem to come anything close to the Popperian illusion of science as a rational enterprise steadily advancing through a never-ending process of successive falsification. "Falsification, near enough, has been falsified."[35]

McCloskey also shows some understanding of the socio-psychology of modernist methodology: a philosophy such as empiricism, that starts with the assumption that nothing about reality can be known with certainty and hence everything is possible, and that has no place for anything such as

---

32. See on this the excellent discussion in Martin Hollis and Edward J. Nell, *Rational Economic Man*, "Introduction."

33. McCloskey, *The Rhetoric of Economics*, p. 14.

34. Thomas Kuhn, *Structure of Scientific Revolutions* (Chicago: University of Chicago Press, 1970).

35. *Id.*, p. 15.

objective a priori considerations; an epistemology, that is to say, that puts us under no constraints whatsoever when it comes to choosing our variables to be measured and determining the relation between such variables (except insofar as the chosen relation must fit the data), can be followed by almost everyone and almost everyone can justly feel that if this is what science is all about, he can be as good a scientist as anyone else. Anyone can measure whatever he feels like measuring, then with the help of a computer fit some curves or equations on his data material, and finally change or not change the curves or equations depending on new, incoming material and/or new hypotheses about measurement error or uncontrolled intervening variables. Empiricism is a methodology suited to the intellectually poor, hence its popularity.[36] Notes McCloskey:

> Graduate students in the social sciences view courses in econometrics, sociometrics, or psychometrics as courses in how to become applied economists, sociologists, or psychologists.... The delusion is nourished by democracy, which partly explains its special prevalence in America. Everyone of normal intelligence can after such a course decipher the output of the Statistical Package for Social Sciences. No elite culture is necessary, no longer subordination to Doktor Herr Professor,[37] no knowledge accumulated through middle age.[38]

Quite naturally, he sees all this as strong talk against modernist epistemology. And indeed, it might be enough to persuade someone to cease giving credence to modernism, and that would certainly be for the better. But even if true, does it constitute proof of a systematic flaw in the empiricist-positivist philosophy? And does it constitute proof in the hands of a hermeneutician?

As regards this latter question, it must be noted that for McCloskey himself to understand his statements about modernism as a *criticism* of this philosophy should strike one as simply odd. For in his discussion of empiricism-positivism, he clearly blames this philosophy for allowing scientists to engage in some all-too-pervasive intellectual permissiveness; for producing a science that advances nowhere but is a mere random walk of ideas through time to be understood only ex post by historical or sociological explanation; and thereby for opening the floodgates to the

---

36. See on this also the trenchant observations of Mises, *Human Action*, p. 872 f., "Economics and the Universities."

37. The correct nomenclature is "Herr Professor Doktor."

38. McCloskey, *The Rhetoric of Economics*, p. 163.

invasion of scholarship by intellectual barbarians. Yet McCloskey wants to replace this permissiveness with an even greater one. He wants us to engage in talk, endless and unconstrained by any intellectual discipline whatsoever. Thus, instead of criticizing empiricism-positivism, should he not embrace it enthusiastically for already coming so very close indeed to his own relativist ideals? If empiricism sounds ridiculous to McCloskey, his reason for this can only be that it is just not ridiculous enough, that empiricism is ridiculous because hermeneutics is even more so, and that pure nonsense must prevail over only partial nonsense.

Yet, apart from McCloskey's own position, his arguments directed against modernism cannot count as amounting to anything. "So what," the empiricist could reply. McCloskey has shown that following the modernist precepts leads to a peculiar form of relativism. Admittedly, some empiricists, most notably Popper and his school, have not and still do not recognize this.[39] McCloskey is right in pointing this out again. But then he must admit that this has also been realized by empiricists without causing them much intellectual pain. Was it not Feyerabend who first and most forcefully drove the relativist message home to Popperianism?[40] And was not he himself a leader of this very school who simply drew the ultimate logical conclusions of Popperianism?[41] Empiricism cannot explain the process of

---

39. See Imre Lakatos and Alan Musgrave, eds., *Criticism and the Growth of Knowledge* (Cambridge, Eng.: Cambridge University Press, 1970). Empiricists such as Blaug argue that Popper actually realized the possibility of "immunizing stratagems" yet "solved" this problem and thus escaped relativism and skepticism. (*The Methodology of Economics*, pp. 17 ff.) Nothing could be further from the truth. It is correct that Popper has always been aware of the possibility of immunizing one's hypotheses from falsification. (See his *Logik der Forschung*, Tübingen: Mohr, 1969, chap. 4, sections 19, 20.) His answer to such a threat to his falsificationism, however, can hardly be accepted as a solution. For he actually admits that he cannot show such "conventionalism" to be wrong. He simply proposes to overcome it by adopting the methodological convention of not behaving as conventionalists do. Yet how can such *methodological conventionalism* (i.e., a methodology without epistemological foundation) claim to establish science as a rational enterprise and to stimulate scientific progress? For such an assessment of Popperianism, see A. Wellmer, *Methodologie als Erkenntnistheorie* (Frankfurt/M.: Suhrkamp, 1967). Thus, the preceding classification of Popperianism as relativism and skepticism.

40. See Paul Feyerabend, *Against Method* (London: New Left Books, 1975); Feyerabend, *Science in a Free Society* (London: NLB, 1978).

41. On the complex relation between Feyerabend and Popper, see H. P. Duerr, ed., *Versuchungen. Aufsätze zur Philosophie Feyerabends*, 2 vols. (Frankfurt/M.: Suhrkamp, 1980).

scientific development as a rational enterprise. True enough. But it cannot account for it because the process is not rational. And what is wrong with this? What is wrong with empiricism once it admits its own relativism?

McCloskey gives no answer to these questions. He does not advance any principled arguments that would prove empiricism to be a self-defeating position. Nor does he challenge empiricism on the much more obvious empirical front. It would seem to be evident that at least empiricism's claim of providing us with a correct epistemology of the natural sciences should, in view of the facts, be regarded as incorrect. For whatever the true state of affairs with respect to economics and the social sciences might be, with respect to the natural sciences it seems difficult to deny that hand in hand with their development went a steady, universally recognized process of technological advancement and improvement, and that this fact of technological progress can hardly be brought in line with the empiricist view of science as a relativistic, non-cumulative enterprise. Empiricism then simply seems to have been *empirically* refuted as an appropriate methodology for the natural sciences.[42]

Yet such a refutation in no way supports McCloskey's own position. For the existence of technological progress would have to stand just as much in the way of hermeneutical relativism as in that of empiricism.[43] Only a rationalist methodology of the natural sciences could account for such progress. Only a methodology that begins with the recognition of the fact, as an undeniably true fact of our human nature as actors and talkers, that language in general and scientific theories in particular are ultimately

---

42. Strictly speaking, such an empirical refutation would not be entirely decisive and other, a priori reasons would be required to bring empiricism down. (On such reasons, see the discussion in the following text.) For empiricists could in turn challenge the validity of one's description of the facts as being indeed those of technological progress. They could, given their own framework, deny that one can know even simple facts, much less complex phenomena such as technological progress, to be so or so, because even the description of something as a fact would ultimately be hypothetical and hence one's alleged empirical refutation could not be considered crucial in any strict sense. See on the hypothetical character of basic propositions Karl Popper, *Logik der Forschung* (Tübingen: Mohr, 1969), chap. V and app. X. Ironically, the hypothetical character of basic propositions invalidates Popper's claim, central to his entire falsificationist philosophy, that an asymmetrical relationship between verification and falsification exists (i.e., that one can never verify a hypothesis, but can falsify it). See on this A. Pap, *Analytische Erkenntnistheorie* (Vienna, 1955).

43. See also Jürgen Habermas, "Der Universalitätsanspruch der Hermeneutik," in K. Apel et al., *Hermeneutik und Ideologiekritik* (Frankfurt/M.: Suhrkamp, 1976), esp. pp. 129–31.

grounded in a common, objective reality of action and cooperation can explain why such progress is possible without thereby having to deny some partial correctness of Kuhn and Feyerabend's relativistic portrayals of the history of the natural sciences.

The relativistic impression is due to the fact that Kuhn and Feyerabend, typical of empiricists since Locke and Hume, ultimately misconceive of scientific theories as mere systems of verbal propositions and systematically ignore the foundation of these, or of any, propositions in a reality of action and interaction.[44] Only if one regards observations and theories as being completely detached from action and cooperation, not only does any single theory become immunizable, but any two rival theories whose respective terms cannot be reduced to and defined in terms of each other must then appear completely incommensurable and no rational choice is possible. If statements are merely and exclusively verbal expressions hanging in midair, what reason could there be for any one statement to ever give way to another? Any one statement can perfectly well stand alongside any other one without ever being challenged—unless we simply decide otherwise for whatever arbitrary reason. It is this that Kuhn and Feyerabend demonstrate. But this does not affect the refutability of any one theory and the commensurability of rival theories on the entirely different level of applying these theories in the reality of action, of using them as instruments of action. On the level of mere words, theories may be irrefutable and incommensurable, but practically they can never be. In fact, one could not even state that any single theory was irrefutable or any two theories were incommensurable and in what respect, unless one were to presuppose a common categorical framework that could serve as a basis for such an assessment or comparison. And it is this *practical* refutability and commensurability of theories of natural science that explains the possibility of technological progress—even though it accounted for technological progress in quite a different manner than Popper's failed attempt.[45]

Popper would have us throw out any theory that is contradicted by any fact, which, if at all possible, would leave us virtually empty-handed, going nowhere. In recognizing the insoluble connection between theoretical knowledge (language) and actions, rationalism would instead deem such

---

44. See Hans-Hermann Hoppe, *Handeln und Erkennen* (Bern: Lang, 1976).

45. See on this W. Stegmueller, *Hauptströmungen der Gegenwartsphilosophie*, vol. II (Stuttgart: Kroener, 1975), chap. 5, esp. pp. 523 ff.

falsificationism, even if possible, as completely irrational. There is no situation conceivable in which it would be reasonable to throw away any theory—conceived of as a cognitive instrument of action—that had been successfully applied in a past situation but proves unsuccessful in a new application—unless one already had a more successful theory at hand. And to thus immunize a theory from experience is perfectly rational from the point of view of an actor. And it is just as rational for an actor to regard any two rivals, in their range of application overlapping theories t_1 and t_2 as incommensurable as long as there exists a single application in which t_1 is more successful than t_2 or vice versa. Only if t_1 can be as successfully applied as t_2 to every single instance to which t_2 is applicable but still has more and different applications than t_2 can it ever be rational to discard t_2. To discard it any earlier, because of unsuccessful applications or because t_1 could in some or even in most situations have been applied more successfully, would from the point of view of a knowing actor not be progress but retrogression. And even if t_2 is rationally discarded, progress is not achieved by falsifying it, as t_2 would actually have had some successful applications that could never possibly be nullified by anything (in the future). Instead, t_1 would outcompete t_2 in such a way that any further clinging to t_2, though of course possible, would be possible only at the price of not being able to successfully do everything that an adherent of t_1 could do who could successfully do as much and more than any proponent of t_2.

Trivial as such an account of the possibility of progress (as well as retrogression) in the natural sciences may seem, it is incompatible with empiricism. In systematically ignoring the fact that observations and theories are those of an actor, made and built in order to act successfully, empiricism has naturally deprived itself of the very criterion against which knowledge is continually tested and commensurated: the criterion of successfully or unsuccessfully reaching a set goal in applying knowledge in a given situation.[46] Without the explicit recognition of the universal operativeness of the criterion of instrumental success, relativism was inescapable. However, such relativism would once more literally be impossible to adopt, because it is incompatible with our nature as acting talkers and knowers. Relativism could not even meaningfully claim to deny the operativeness of this criterion, as this very

---

46. See on this also Jürgen Habermas, *Erkenntnis und Interesse* (Frankfurt/M.: Suhrkamp, 1968), esp. chap. II, sections 5–6; and K. O. Apel, *Die Erkären: Verstehen Kontroverse in Transzendental-pragmatischer Sicht* (Frankfurt/M.: Suhrkamp, 1979), esp. p. 284.

denial would itself have to be an action that presupposed some objective standard of success. Rather, in each of our actions, we confirm rationalism's claim (as regards the natural sciences) that one can objectively identify a range of applications for some knowledge and then test it for its success within this range, and, hence, that competing theories must be considered commensurable as regards such ranges of applications and success.

III. HERMENEUTICS VERSUS EMPIRICISM: RATIONALISM AGAINST BOTH — ROUND II

McCloskey's first round against empiricism then is a complete failure. Nor is his second round of criticism any more successful. There, McCloskey takes issue with the modernists' emphasis on prediction as the cornerstone of science. Though he does not deny the possibility of prediction in the natural sciences, he doubts its overwhelming importance. However, prediction in economics, he claims, is impossible. "Predicting the economic future is, as Ludwig von Mises put it, 'beyond the power of any mortal man.' "[47]

In order to defend this thesis, we would expect him to establish two separate but related claims. First would be the claim that something is wrong with methodological monism—the program of an *Einheitswissenschaft*—and methodological dualism should be adopted. Otherwise it makes no sense to say that predictions are possible in one field of inquiry but impossible in another. The second claim would be that on the basis of such a dualist position, it can be demonstrated why predictions are possible in one field but not in another. McCloskey does nothing of this sort. It entirely escapes his notice that his position *vis-à-vis* modernism requires him to attack empiricism on account of its monism; that its monist stand makes it actually impossible for empiricism to explain how predictions, which allegedly constitute the very heart of the empiricist program, can conceivably be possible—and impossible for precisely the same reason that empiricism could not account for the possibility of progress in natural science; and that a dualist position (which McCloskey would be required to take if he wanted to systematically challenge modernism) would be incompatible with hermeneutics—itself being a monist position, though a different sort than empiricism's—and can again only be reconciled with a rationalist methodology, which alone can account for the possibility of the empiricist dream of predictions.

---

47. McCloskey, *The Rhetoric of Economics*, p. 15.

Empiricism is observational monism, stating that all our empirical knowledge is derived from observations and consists in interrelating these observations; and, further, that observations as well as relations have the permanent status of only being true hypothetically. This is the case in economics as well as in any other field concerned with empirical knowledge, and hence the problem of prediction must be the same everywhere. McCloskey does not answer this systematic challenge. He does not present the conclusive refutation of such monism by pointing out that in claiming what empiricism claims, one in fact falsifies the content of one's statement. For to claim what it claims, empiricism must actually presuppose that in addition to observations, meaningful objects exist—words tied to reality via cooperation—that, along with the relations among them, must be understood rather than observed. Hence the need for methodological dualism.[48]

Nor does McCloskey notice the incompatibility of observational monism with the notion of prediction. The idea of prediction and causality (i.e., that there are constant, time-invariantly operating causes that allow one to project past observations regarding the relationship between variables into the future) is something (as empiricism since Hume has noticed) that has no observational basis and hence cannot be said to be justified (within the empiricist framework). One cannot observe the connecting link between observations, except that they are somehow contingently related in time. And even if one could observe it, this observation would still not prove that such an observed connection was time-invariant. Strictly speaking, within the framework of observational monism, it does not even make sense to place observations in objective time.[49] Rather, the observed relationships are those between data in the temporal order in which an observer happens to observe them (clearly something very different from our notion of being able to distinguish between a real, causally effective order and sequence of observations and the mere temporal order in which observations are made). Hence, strictly speaking, according to empiricism, predictions are epistemologically impossible. It is irrational to want to predict, because the

48. See on this also K. O. Apel, "Die Entfaltung der Sprachanalytischen Philosophie und das Problem der Geisteswissenschaften," in idem, *Transformation der Philosophie*, vol. II (Frankfurt/M.: Suhrkamp, 1973); idem, *Die Erkären: Verstehen Kontroverse in Transzendental-pragmatischer Sicht*.

49. See on this also Hans-Hermann Hoppe, *Handeln und Erkennen*, chap. 3 and esp. pp. 62–65; also Immanuel Kant, *Kritik der reinen Vernunft*, in idem, *Werke*, vol. II, ed. by W. Weischedel (Wiesbaden: Insel, 1956), esp. pp. 226 ff.

very possibility of prediction cannot be rationally established. And this, then, is also the ultimate reason for empiricism's skeptical stand regarding the possibility of scientific progress. For if one cannot rationally defend the very idea of causality, how can one expect anything from science but an array of incommensurable observational statements? Progress, as it is commonly understood, is the advancement of predictive knowledge. But surely no such thing can be possible if prediction itself cannot be established as possible.[50]

McCloskey also does not confront the challenge of explaining how hermeneutics accounts for a dualism and the very possibility of prediction (if only in the natural sciences). Nor could he have succeeded in this. For an argument such as dualism would establish that certain propositions can be said to be objectively true—in fact to be a priori true—and this would contradict the relativist message of hermeneutics. Yet as a monist position, hermeneutics cannot account for causality any more than empiricism can. As an observational monism, empiricism would like to reduce all our empirical knowledge to observations and observations of contingent relations between

---

50. It is worth emphasizing here that these remarks on the skeptical, relativistic conclusions of empiricism regarding the possibility of prediction also fully apply to Popperianism. Popper, with great self-assurance, claims to have solved—through adopting his falsificationist methodology—the Humean problem of induction and thereby to have reestablished science as a rational enterprise. (See in particular Karl R. Popper, *Objective Knowledge*, Oxford, Eng.: Oxford University Press, 1972, pp. 85 ff.) Alas, this is simply an illusion. For how can it be possible to relate two or more observational experiences, even if they concern the relations between things that are perceived to be the same or similar, *as falsifying* (or *confirming*) each other, rather than merely neutrally record them as one experience here and one experience there, one repetitive of another or not, and leaving it at that (i.e., regarding them as logically incommensurable) unless one presupposed the existence of time-invariantly operating causes? Only if the existence of such time-invariantly operating causes could be assumed would there by any logically compelling reason to regard them as commensurable and as falsifying or confirming each other. However, Popper, like all empiricists, denies that any such assumption can be given an a priori defense (there are for him no such things as a priori true propositions about reality such as the causality principle would have to be) and is itself merely hypothetical. Yet clearly, if the possibility of constantly operating causes *as such* is only a hypothetical one, then it can hardly be claimed, as Popper does, that any particular predictive hypothesis could ever be falsified or confirmed. For then the falsification (or confirmation) would have to be considered a hypothetical one: any predictive hypothesis would only undergo tests whose status as tests were themselves hypothetical. And hence one would be right back in the muddy midst of skepticism. Only if the causality principle as such could be unconditionally established as true, could any particular causal hypothesis ever be testable, and the outcome of a test provide rational grounds for deciding whether or not to uphold a given hypothesis.

observations, and it is therefore ultimately forced to abandon the idea of time-invariantly operating causes. Hermeneutics would like to reduce it to a talk-monism; to talk disconnected to anything real outside of talk itself; to sequences of talk hanging in midair with no objective, talk-constraining grounding whatsoever. For this reason, hermeneutics cannot account for causality. For in the absence of any common, objective standard, all talk is simply incommensurable, and no objective connection whatsoever can exist between any talk apart from the mere temporal order of talking.

Both dualism and causality can only be explained by rationalism. Rationalism begins with the insight that empiricism is self-refuting, since it cannot actually state its own position without implicitly admitting that in addition to observations and contingent relations of observations, other meaningful things and relations (i.e., words sustained through action and acquiring meaning in the course of such action) must also exist. Similarly, rationalism rejects hermeneutics as self-refuting, because a talk-monism, too, could not be stated without implicitly admitting it as false in that it would have to presuppose the very existence of actions guided by observations, if only in order to sustain talk—thus falsifying the claim of talk ever being unconstrained by anything objective. And rationalism then concludes that the key to the problem of causality must lie in the recognition of the fact (ignored by both empiricism and hermeneutics) that observations as well as words are constrained by action, and that this can be established neither by observation nor by mere talk, but rather must be understood on account of our knowledge of action as the practical presupposition of any observation or talk as an a priori true fact of human nature.

It is from such a priori understanding of action that the idea of causality can indeed be derived.[51] Causality is not a category of observations. It is a category of action whose knowledge as an a priori feature of reality is rooted in our very understanding of our nature as actors. Only because we are actors and our experiences are those of acting individuals can observations be conceived of as occurring objectively earlier or later and as being related to each other through time-invariantly operating causes.[52] No one who did not know what it meant to act could ever experience events occurring in

---

51. See on this (Kantian) idea F. Kambartel, *Erfahrung und Struktur*, chap. 3, esp. pp. 122 f., 127, 144; Hans-Hermann Hoppe, chap. 4, esp. p. 98.

52. See on this Ludwig von Mises, *Human Action*, chap. 1.5; Carl Menger, *Grundsätze der Volkswirtschaftslehre* (Vienna: Braumüller, 1871), pp. 3, 7 ff.

real time and in invariant causal sequences. And no one's knowledge of the meaning of action and causality could ever be said to be derived from contingent observational evidence, as the very fact of experiencing already presupposes action and causally interpreted observations. Every action is and must be understood as an interference with the observational world, made with the intent of diverting the "natural" course of events in order to produce (i.e., to *cause* to come into being) a different, preferred state of affairs—of making things happen that otherwise would not happen—and thus presupposes the notions of events placed in objective time and of time-invariantly operating causes. An actor can err with respect to his particular assumptions about which earlier interference produced which later result, and thus his interference might not actually turn out to be successful. But successful or not, any action, changed or unchanged in light of its success or failure, presupposes that there are constantly connected events in time, even if no particular cause for any particular event can ever be pre-known to any actor at any time. In fact, attempting to disprove that observational events are governed by time-invariantly operating causes would require one to show that some given event cannot be observed or produced based on some earlier interference. Yet trying to disprove this would again necessarily presuppose that the occurrence or nonoccurrence of the phenomenon under scrutiny could, in fact, be effected by taking appropriate action, and that the phenomenon must thus presumably be embedded in a network of constantly operating causes. Hence, rationalism concludes that the validity of the principle of causality cannot be falsified by taking any action, since any action would have to presuppose it.[53]

---

53. Though quite frequently mentioned as an empirical counterexample, it should be noted that quantum physics, or more precisely the indeterminacy or Heisenberg principle of quantum physics, correctly interpreted, is in accordance with this. What has been previously said does not preclude—and this is precisely the situation in quantum physics—that in order to experimentally produce a result, two or more measurement acts must be performed and that because any two separate actions can only be performed sequentially, the performance of the latter act of measurement might change the results of the former one, so that if this proves to be unavoidable, the results in question can only be predicted statistically and a deterministic explanation proves impossible. But even here each separate measurement act presupposes the validity of the constancy principle—otherwise, neither of them would have been performed; and the sequence of acts, too, presupposes constantly operating causes as it would otherwise be simply impossible to repeat two experiments in the field of quantum physics and state this to be the case. Moreover, the experience of quantum physics is in exact line with the preceding

McCloskey notices none of this. And so it is no surprise that the arguments raised in support of his claim regarding the impossibility of prediction in economics are off the mark, too. Though in themselves correct arguments, they simply do not constitute the impossibility theorem that is needed.

What McCloskey offers as proof, which he incidentally claims to be "more precise" than some earlier, related Austrian thoughts,[54] is the following insight: "If economists could do [predict] better than business people, the economists would be rich. They are not."[55] Hence, we should not trust people who claim to have information about future economic events. For if they really did have such knowledge, why would *they* not strike it rich, instead of telling *us* how to do it?[56] Realistically, we should regard economic forecasters as providing information that, generally speaking, is economically worthless in that it tells us no more about future economic events than what concerned people on the average believe and expect anyway and have already accounted for in their present actions.[57]

Good enough. However, a much more succinct presentation than this can already be found in Mises.

There are no rules according to which the duration of the boom or of the following depression can be computed. And even if such rules were available they would be of no use to businessmen. What the individual businessman needs in order to avoid losses is knowledge about the date of the turning point at a time when other businessmen still believe that the crash is farther away than is really the case.... Entrepreneurial judgment cannot be bought on the market. The entrepreneurial idea that carries on and brings profit is precisely that idea which did not occur to the majority. It is not correct foresight as such that yields profits, but foresight better than that of the rest.[58]

conclusion regarding the characteristic of causality as an action-produced phenomenon and as a necessary (known to be valid a priori) feature of reality. If causes can indeed only be measured and identified sequentially, by means of actions that have repercussions for each other, then they can, in principle, only be causes whose constant operation is of a probabilistic kind—and this, to be sure, can again be known to be true a priori. Quantum physics then only reveals that cases such as this are not merely conceivable, but do in fact exist. See on this F. Kambartel, *Erfahrung und Struktur*, pp. 138 ff.; also P. Mittelstaedt, *Philosophische Probleme der modernen Physik* (Mannheim: Bibliographisches Institut, 1968).

54. McCloskey, *The Rhetoric of Economics*, p. 90.
55. *Id.*, p. 93.   56. *Id.*, p. 16.   57. *Id.*, p. 93 f.
58. *Human Action*, pp. 870–71.

Yet this, as Mises but not McCloskey knows, does not prove the impossibility of causal predictions in economics.[59] All it proves is that differential profits can only emerge from *differences* in knowledge. The question is, however, if such knowledge—regardless of whether it is unequally distributed and thus allows for the possibility of differential profits and losses, or equally distributed and thus tends to only account for a uniform rate of return for the forecasters—is such that it could be expressed in a prediction formula that could legitimately make use of the assumption of time-invariant causes and hence could be conceived of as a systematically testable and improvable formula.

Surely McCloskey does not want to deny the possibility of prediction as such in economics. We constantly make such predictions. Moreover, while economic forecasters may not generally be rich and thus evidently may not know more than the rest of us, some of them are, and certainly there are some businessmen who are rich. Evidently, people not only can forecast, but can forecast correctly and successfully. The impossibility theorem cannot be meant to prove that no (successful) prediction whatsoever can be made in the field of economics, but rather only that a certain type of prediction is impossible here that is possible elsewhere. Yet the argument does not prove this. For we have no difficulties applying the idea of differential predictive knowledge and differential returns from forecasting to the field of the natural sciences, and still conceiving of them as gradually progressing and producing ever-improved prediction formulae. One natural-science forecaster may know more than another and even stay ahead of the competition permanently, but this does not imply that his relative advantage is not one that could not possibly be expressed, at all times, in terms of a formula that uses predictive constants and is capable of systematic improvement by means of successive testings. Why, then, should this be any different in the realm of economic forecasting? Why can the rich businessman not have gained his position in the same way as the relatively more successful natural-science forecaster?

This is what must be answered by the impossibility theorem. On this, however, McCloskey is silent. Nor can an answer be formulated by a hermeneutician. For an impossibility theorem would be precisely the kind of

---

59. Mises correctly emphasizes that the decisive argument against causal predictions in economics must be the absence of "constant relations" in the field of human knowledge and actions. See, for instance, *Human Action*, p. 55 f.

conversation-stopping argument that McCloskey claims to be nonexistent. To prove that economic forecasting is categorically different from natural-science forecasting would only mean confirming the claims of rationalism. Such proof would not have relativistic consequences regarding economic predictions as it may at first seem—such as to say that no systematic mistake whatsoever could be made by an economic forecaster and that any economic forecast's failure or success would thus be due entirely to bad or good luck. Instead, even if it were to show that there were indeed some ineradicable element of luck in economic forecasting, making progress as it exists in technological forecasting impossible in the field of economics, at the same time such proof would establish the existence of a priori true propositions on the subject matter of economics, which would then systematically constrain the range of possible predictions about future economic events and open up the possibility of predictions that were systematically flawed in that they would be at variance with such fundamental, a priori valid knowledge.

And indeed, argues rationalism, economic predictions that would make use of the assumption of time-invariantly operating causes must thus be considered systematically flawed.[60] While every action presupposes causality, no actor can conceive of his actions as ever being predictable on the basis of constantly operating causes. Causality can only be assumed to exist outside of the field of human action, and economic predictions as predictions concerning future actions are impossible. This follows from the very modernism that McCloskey criticizes, incidentally proving this position a self-refuting one once again. Empiricism claims that actions, just as any other phenomenon, can and must be explained by means of causal hypotheses that can be confirmed or falsified by experience. Now, if this were the case, empiricism would be forced to assume—contrary to its own doctrine that there is no a priori knowledge about reality—that time-invariantly operating causes with respect to actions exist. One would not know a priori which particular event might be the cause of a particular action. Experience would have to reveal this. But in order to proceed in the way that empiricism wants us to proceed (i.e., to relate different experiences regarding sequences of events as either confirming or falsifying each other and, if falsifying, then responding with a reformulation of the causal hypothesis), a constancy over

---

60. See on the following Hans-Hermann Hoppe, *Kritik der kausalwissenschaftlichen Sozialforschung* (Opladen: Westdeutscher Verlag, 1983); idem, "Is Research Based on Causal Scientific Principles Possible in the Social Sciences," *Ratio* XXV, no. 1 (1983).

time in the operation of causes *as such* must be presupposed. (Without such an assumption, the different experiences would simply be unrelated, incommensurable observations.[61]) However, if this were true and actions could indeed be conceived of as governed by time-invariantly operating causes, what about explaining the explainers (i.e., the persons who carry on the very process of creating hypotheses) of verification and falsification? Evidently, in order to assimilate confirming or falsifying experiences—to replace old hypotheses with new ones—one must presumably be able to learn. However, if one is able to learn from experience, then one cannot know at any given time what one will know at a later time and how one will act based on this later knowledge. Rather, one can only reconstruct the causes of one's actions after the event, as one can only explain one's knowledge after one already possesses it. Thus, the empiricist methodology applied to the field of knowledge and action, which contains knowledge as its necessary ingredient, is simply contradictory—a logical absurdity.[62]

Moreover, it is plainly contradictory to argue that one could ever predict one's knowledge and actions based on antecedent, constantly operating causes. For to argue so is not only absurd because it implies that one can know now what one will know in the future; it is also self-defeating, because to do so would actually be saying that there was something that was not yet understood, but rather had to be learned about and examined as regards the acceptability of its validity claims, with as yet unknown results with respect to the outcome of this (either for our future knowledge, or for our and others' knowledge about the knowledge of others).

Thus, as McCloskey states, yet does not prove, causal empirical explanations regarding knowledge and actions are indeed impossible. Whoever pretends, as empiricist economists invariably do, to be able to predict future knowledge and actions based on constantly operating antecedent variables is simply speaking nonsense. There are no such constants in the field of human action, as Mises insisted over and over again. Economic forecasting is not

---

61. On this, see footnote 50.

62. Interestingly, this proof has been first formulated by Popper in the preface of his *The Poverty of Historicism* (London: Routledge and Kegan Paul, 1957). However, Popper failed to realize that such proof actually invalidates the idea of a methodological monism and demonstrates the inapplicability of his falsificationist philosophy in the field of human action and knowledge. See on this Hans-Hermann Hoppe, *Kritik der kausalwissenschaftlichen Sozialforschung*, pp. 44–49; K. O. Apel, *Die Erklaeren: Verstehen Kontroverse*, pp. 44–46.

and never can be a science, but will always be a systematically unteachable art. Yet, and I shall return to this shortly, this does not mean that such forecasts would not be constrained by anything. While no particular action can ever be predicted scientifically, each and every prediction of future actions and the consequences of actions is constrained by our a priori knowledge of actions as such.

IV. Rationalism and the Foundations of Economics

In the second round of its criticism of empiricism-positivism, hermeneutics fails just as it failed in the first. And again it is philosophical rationalism— equally critical of hermeneutics and empiricism—that is vindicated. Yet McCloskey makes one more point worth mentioning, as he reminds us that modern hermeneutics is an outgrowth of the discipline of interpreting the Bible.[63] In line with this traditionalist orientation, the case for hermeneutics ultimately boils down to an uncritical appeal to and acceptance of authority. We are asked by McCloskey to embrace the new old creed because some authorities tell us to do so. In his view, empiricism is not wrong as such—as a matter of fact, there was a time when it was quite all right to follow empiricist advice. But that was when philosophical authorities were all sold on empiricism. In the meantime, empiricism is out of favor with the philosopher kings and only the practitioners of science still cling to it—not realizing that fashion has changed. It is high time, then, that we shift and follow the new trend setters. Writes McCloskey: "The argument that Hutchison, Samuelson, Friedman, Machlup, and their followers gave for adopting their metaphysics was an argument from authority, at the time correct, namely that this was what philosophers were saying. The trust in philosophy was a tactical error, for philosophy itself was changing as they spoke."[64] And the same goes for the mathematization of economics. Once it was good; now it is becoming bad. The winds of fashion change and we had better pay attention to this. "Economists before the reception of mathematics fell headlong . . . into confusions that a little mathematics would have cleared up." Imagine, they

> could not keep clear, for instance, the difference between a movement
> of an entire curve and a movement along a curve. . . . But now, so long

---

63. See on this H. Albert, *Traktat über kritische Vernunft* (Tübingen: Mohr, 1969), esp. chap. 5, V, VI.

64. McCloskey, *The Rhetoric of Economics*, p. 12.

after the victory, one might ask whether the faith which supported it still serves a social function. One might ask whether the strident talk of Science in economics, which served well in bringing clarity and rigor to the field, has outlived its usefulness.[65]

Surely, this lives up again to truly relativistic form. Yet as we have seen, there is no reason in the world to accept such relativism. Relativism is a self-contradictory position. And just as it is impossible to defend the hermeneutical relativism as the methodology of today, so is it impossible to defend the empiricism-positivism of yesterday. Empiricism-positivism, too, is a self-defeating doctrine, and not only because of its observational monism, which cannot be stated without implicitly admitting its falsehood and accepting a dualism of observable and meaningful phenomena to be understood on account of our knowledge of action and cooperation. Empiricism's fundamental distinction between analytical, empirical, and normative propositions is equally indefensible. What then is the status of the very proposition introducing this distinction? Assuming that empiricist reasoning is correct, it must be either an analytical or an empirical proposition, or it must be an expression of emotions. If it is understood as analytical, then according to its own doctrine it is merely verbal quibble, saying nothing about anything real but rather only defining one sound or sign by another, and hence one would simply have to reply "so what?" The same response would be appropriate, if, instead, the basic empiricist proposition were taken to be an empirical one. For if this were so, it would not only have to be admitted that the propositions might well be wrong. More decisively, as an empirical proposition, the most it could state would be a historical fact and it would thus be entirely irrelevant in determining whether or not it would be *impossible* to *ever* produce either a priori true propositions that were not analytical or normative propositions that were not emotive. And finally, if the empiricist line of reasoning were assumed to be an emotive argument, then according to its own pronouncements, it is cognitively meaningless and one would not have to pay any more attention to it than to a dog's bark. Thus, one must again conclude that empiricism-positivism is an utter failure. If it were correct, its basic premise could not even be stated as a cognitively meaningful proposition; and if it could be so stated and empiricism were

---

65. McCloskey, *The Rhetoric of Economics*, pp. 3–5.

indeed making the proposition that we all along thought it did, then the analytical-empirical-normative distinction would be proven false by the very proposition introducing it.[66]

How then, could it ever have been right to follow a false doctrine? To conceive of economics, or more precisely of actions, as empiricism does, and accordingly to treat economic phenomena as observable variables, measurable and tractable by mathematical reasoning, must have always been wrong. And the surge of positivism in economics could never have added to clarity, but from the very beginning must have helped instead to introduce ever more falsehoods into the field.

There *is* empirical knowledge that is valid a priori. And such knowledge informs us that it has never been correct to represent relationships between economic phenomena in terms of equations containing the assumption of empirical causal constants, because to conceive of actions as being caused by and predictable on the basis of antecedent variables is contradictory. Moreover, the very same a priori knowledge reveals that it is at all times incorrect to conceive of economic variables as observable magnitudes. Rather, all categories of action must be understood as existing only as subjective interpretations of observable events. The fact that knowledge and talk are

---

66. Mises writes:

> The essence of logical positivism is to deny the cognitive value of a priori knowledge by pointing out that all a priori propositions are merely analytic. They do not provide new information, but are merely verbal and tautological.... Only experience can lead to synthetic propositions. There is an obvious objection against this doctrine, viz., that this proposition is in itself a—as the present writer thinks, false—synthetic a priori proposition, for it can manifestly not be established by experience. (*The Ultimate Foundation of Economic Science*, p. 5)

It is remarkable to notice how utterly helplessly empiricists react to such arguments establishing the case for synthetic a priori propositions. Witness, for instance, Mark Blaug, *The Methodology of Economics*, pp. 91–93, where he engages in an all-out smear attack on Mises ("Mises' ... later writings on the foundations of economic science are so cranky and idiosyncratic that we can only wonder that they have been taken seriously by anyone," p. 93) without presenting a single argument and without noticing how strangely his self-assuredness and the apodicticity with which he presents his anti-apriorist methodological pronouncements contrast with his very own professed falsificationism. The same discrepancy between, on the one hand, a complete lack of argument and, on the other, apodictic arrogance, also marks his "discussion" of Hollis and Nell's *Rational Economic Man* on pp. 123–26.

those of an actor, and constrained by our nature as actors, cannot be observed, but rather must be understood. Nor can causality or objective time ever be simply observed, but our knowledge of it is based on our prior understanding of what it is to act. And so it is regarding the rest of the economic categories, as Mises above all has shown. There are no values to be observed, but things can be understood as valued only because of our prior knowledge of action. As a matter of fact, that there is such a thing as actions also cannot be observed, but must be understood. It cannot be observed that with every action, an actor pursues a goal and that whatever his goal, the fact that it is pursued by an actor reveals that he places a relatively higher value on it than on any other goal of action that he at the very start of his action could think of. Further, it can neither be observed that in order to achieve his most highly valued goal an actor must interfere (or decide not to interfere) at an earlier point in time to produce some later result, nor that such interferences invariably imply the employment of some scarce means (at least those of the actor's body, its standing room, and the time absorbed by the interference). It is unobservable (1) that these means must also have value for an actor—a value derived from that of the goal—because the actor must think their employment necessary in order to effectively achieve the goal and (2) that actions can only be performed sequentially, always involving the making of a choice (i.e., taking up that course of action that at some given point in time promises the most highly valued result to the actor and excluding at the same time the pursuit of other, less highly valued goals). It cannot be observed that as a consequence of having to choose and give preference to one goal over another—of not being able to realize all goals simultaneously—each and every action implies the incurrence of costs (i.e., forsaking the value attached to the most highly valued alternative goal that cannot be realized or whose realization must be deferred because the means necessary to effect it are bound up in the production of another even more highly valued end). And lastly, it is unobservable that at its starting point, every goal of action must be considered (1) worth more to the actor than its costs and (2) capable of yielding a profit (i.e., a result whose value is ranked higher than that of the forgone opportunities, and yet that every action is also invariably open to the possibility of a loss if an actor finds, in retrospect, that the actually achieved result—contrary to previous expectations—in fact has a lower value than the relinquished alternative would have had).

All of these categories (values, ends, means, choice, preference, cost, profit and loss, time, and causality) are implied in the concept of action. That one is able to interpret experiences in such categories requires that one already knows what it means to act. No one who is not an actor could ever understand them, as they are not "given," ready to be experienced, but experience is cast in these terms as it is constructed by an actor. And then to treat such concepts, as empiricism-positivism would, as things extending in space and allowing quantifiable measurements is missing the goal entirely. Whatever one might explain in following empiricist advice, it has nothing whatsoever to do with explaining actions and experiences cast in the categories of action. These categories are ineradicably subjective ones. And yet they represent empirical knowledge in that they are conceptual organizations of real events and occurrences. They are not merely verbal definitions; they are real definitions of real things and real observations.[67] Furthermore, they are not only empirical knowledge; contrary to all relativistic aspirations, they incorporate a priori valid empirical knowledge. For it would clearly be impossible to disprove their empirical validity, as the attempt to do so would itself be an action aimed at a goal, requiring means, excluding other courses of action, incurring costs, and subjecting the actor to the possibility of achieving or not achieving the desired goal and so making a profit or suffering a loss. The very possession of such knowledge can never be disputed, and the validity

---

67. Empiricists, of course, would brand such definitions as tautological. Yet it should be perfectly clear that the preceding definition of action is of a categorically different nature than a definition such as *"bachelor"* meaning "unmarried man." Whereas the latter is indeed a completely arbitrary verbal stipulation, the propositions defining action are most definitely not. In fact, while one can define anything as one pleases, one cannot help but make the conceptual distinctions between goals and means and so on as "defining something by something" would itself be an action. It is thus contradictory to deny, as empiricism-positivism does, the existence of "real definitions." Hollis and Nell, *Rational Economic Man*, observe "Honest definitions are, from an empiricist point of view, of two sorts, lexical and stipulative." (p. 177) But

> When it comes to justifying [this] view, we are presumably being offered a definition of *definition*. Whichever category of definition the definition falls in, we need not accept it as of any epistemological worth. Indeed, it would not be even a possible epistemological thesis, unless it were neither lexical nor stipulative. The view [then] is both inconvenient and self-refuting. A contrary opinion with a long pedigree is that there are "real" definitions, which capture the essence of the thing defined. (p. 178)

See also B. Blanshard, *Reason and Analysis*, p. 268 f.

of these concepts can never be falsified by any contingent experience, since disputing or falsifying anything already presupposes its very existence. As a matter of fact, a situation in which these categories of action would cease to have a real existence could itself never be observed, as making an observation is in itself an action.

Economic reasoning has its foundations in this a priori knowledge of the meaning of action.[68] It concerns phenomena that, though existing objectively, cannot be subjected to physical measurements, but must be *understood* as conceptually distinct events. And it concerns phenomena that cannot be predicted based on constantly operating causes; and our predictive knowledge about such phenomena, accordingly, cannot be said to be constrained by contingent empirical laws (i.e., laws that one would have to discover through a posteriori experiences). Instead, it concerns objects and events that are constrained by the existence of a priori valid, logical, or praxeological laws and constraints (i.e., laws whose validity is completely independent of any kind of a posteriori experience). Economic reasoning consists of (1) an understanding of the categories of action and the meaning of a change in values, preferences, knowledge, means, cost, profit, or loss, and so on, (2) a description of a situation in which these categories assume specific meaning and definite individuals are described as actors, with definite things specified as their goals, means, profits, and costs, and (3) a logical deduction of the consequences which result from the introduction of some specified action in this situation, or of the consequences which result for an actor if this situation is changed in a specified way. Provided there is no flaw in the

---

68. Hollis and Nell contend that not "action" but "reproduction of the economic system" is the primary concept on which economics, conceived of as an a priori science, rests. (*Rational Economic Man*, p. 243) Noticing this disagreement among apriorists has led Caldwell to the curious conclusion that something must be wrong with apriorism and to then advocate a do-not-commit-yourself-to-anything pluralism. (*Beyond Positivism*, pp. 131 ff.; see footnote 20) Yet such reasoning is about as conclusive (or, rather, inconclusive) as inferring from the fact that disagreements among people regarding the validity of certain empirical propositions exist, that no empirical facts exist and hence no empirical science is possible. Indeed, Caldwell's conclusion is even more curious, given the fact that in the dispute at hand, the solution is as clear as daylight: Whatever an economic "system" might be, it can certainly not exist or be able to reproduce itself without acting people. Moreover, to say that "reproduction of the system" is the primary concept for economic analysis is plainly contradictory—unless it were simply synonymous with saying that action is such a concept—because saying so would in fact presuppose an actor saying it.

process of deduction, the conclusions that such reasoning yields are valid a priori because their validity would ultimately go back to the indisputable axiom of action. If the situation and the changes introduced into it are fiction or assumptions, then the conclusions are true a priori only of a possible world. If, on the other and, the situation and situational changes can be identified as real, perceived, and conceptualized as such by real actors, then the conclusions are a priori true propositions about the world as it really is. And such realistic conclusions, which are the economists' main concern, act as logical constraints on our actual predictions of future economic events. They do not guarantee correct predictions—even if the empirical assumptions are indeed correct and the deductions are flawless—because in reality, there can be all sorts of situational changes happening concurrently or following the explicitly introduced change in the action-world data. And though they also affect the shape of things to come (and cancel, increase, decrease, accelerate, or decelerate effects stemming from other sources), such concurrent changes can in principle never be predicted or experimentally held constant, because to conceive of subjective knowledge (whose every change has an impact on action) as predictable on the basis of antecedent variables and as capable of being held constant is an outright absurdity. The experimenter who so wanted to hold it constant would in fact have to presuppose that his knowledge, specifically his knowledge regarding the experiment's outcome, could not be assumed to be constant over time. However, while they cannot render any specific future economic event certain or even predictable on the basis of a formula, such a priori conclusions nonetheless systematically restrict the range of possibly correct predictions. Predictions that are not in line with such knowledge would be systematically flawed and would lead to a systematically increased number of forecasting errors—not in the sense that anyone who based his predictions on correct praxeological reasoning would necessarily have to be a better predictor of future economic events than someone who arrived at his predictions through logically flawed deliberations and chains of reasoning, but in the sense that in the long run, ceteris paribus, the first group of forecasters would average a better record than the second.

Regarding any specific forecast, it is very possible to falter despite one's correct identification of a situational change as described in terms of the a priori categories of action and one's correct analysis of the praxeological consequences of such change, because one might err regarding one's identification of other, accompanying changes. It is equally possible to arrive at a correct forecast in spite of the fact that one's inferences drawn from one's correct description of a situational change were praxeologically wrong, because other concurrent events might be of such a kind as to counteract such a wrong assessment of consequences. However, if it is assumed that, on the average, forecasters with or without a solid grasp of praxeological laws and constants are both equally well equipped to anticipate such other concurrent changes in the action-world and to account for them in their predictions, then the group of forecasters that makes its predictions in recognition of and accordance with such laws will be more successful than that which does not.

As are all economic theorems, the law of demand (which causes empiricists as well as hermeneuticians considerable uneasiness because of its apodictically assumed central position in economics) is an a priori true constraint on actual predictions regarding the consequences of certain actions. Empiricism tells us to conceive of it as an in-principle falsifiable hypothesis about the consequences of price changes. Yet, if we accept this and empirically test the law, we frequently find that a price increase, for instance, goes hand in hand with an increase in the quantity demanded, or that a price decrease is accompanied by a reduced demand. The law holds sometimes and for some goods, but at other times, for the same or other goods, it does not. How then, concludes empiricism, can economists assign to this law the axiomatic position that it occupies in economic theory and build a complex network of thought based on it? To do so must seem to an empiricist to be nothing but bad metaphysics that needs to be expelled from the discipline as soon as possible in order to bring economics back onto the right track.[69]

Hermeneutics is no more successful in justifying the law of demand. McCloskey realizes that the empiricist case for the law is weak at best. Yet he believes it acceptable to stick with it—as, despite their professed empiricism, most economists indeed do—because the law of demand is allegedly persuasive in light of other hermeneutical evidence.[70] Such supportive evidence supposedly comes from "introspection," from "thought experiments," and from illustrative case stories; there is the persuasive fact that "business people" believe in the law, and "many wise economists"; the "symmetry of the law" makes it esthetically appealing; "mere definition" adds power; and "above all, there is analogy. That the Law of Demand is true

69. On the empiricist position regarding the law of demand, see Mark Blaug, *The Methodology of Economics*, chap. 6.
70. McCloskey, *The Rhetoric of Economics*, pp. 58–60.

for ice cream and movies, as no one would want to deny, makes it more persuasive also for gasoline."[71] None of this, however, could make the law of demand any better founded and give it the authority it indeed seems to command. To be sure, introspection is the source of our knowledge of the law of demand. This particular law is no more founded in observations than are the laws of logic and mathematics. Yet introspections as such, or thought experiments, can no more establish the law of demand than can observational evidence. Introspective evidence, too, is nothing other than contingent experience. Here and now somebody arrives at this thought, and there and then someone else reaches the same or a different one. As McCloskey himself states, "if properly socialized in economics," introspection and thought experimentation make the law highly persuasive.[72] But, mutatis mutandis, then, if one is not so socialized, introspection might render the law far less appealing. Then, however, introspection as such can hardly be said to lend any systematic support to it. In fact, to appeal to the economists' introspective evidence would amount to a begging of the question, as it would have to be explained why one should accept this economic socialization or brainwashing in the first place. In the same way, case stories or convictions of certain businessmen or wise economists are not proof of anything. Aesthetic criteria and mere definitions, too, have no epistemological value. And conclusions per analogiam are only conclusive if the analogy itself can be said to be correct— besides the fact that it would certainly not be impossible for someone to say that the law of demand sounds unpersuasive even for ice cream and movies.[73] Hence, hermeneutics offers nothing substantive to vindicate our belief in the law of demand.

And yet the law of demand is objectively true despite the fact that it is not based on contingent external or internal experiences. Rather, its foundation lies in our introspective understanding of action as the practical presupposition of our external as well as our internal experiences and in the recognition of the fact that this understanding must be considered epistemologically prior to any contingent act of understanding in that it could not possibly be falsified by it. The fact that in order to exchange successive units of a good A for successive units of a good B, the exchange

---

71. McCloskey, *The Rhetoric of Economics*, p. 60.   72. *Id.*, p. 59.

73. Moreover, why would the argument not also go the other way? If, empirically, the law of demand does not seem to work for some goods, why would not analogy lead us to question it for those in which it does? (I owe this argument to David Gordon.)

ratio of A to B must fall follows from the law of marginal utility: as the supply of A decreases and the marginal utility of a unit of A increases, the supply of B increases and B's marginal utility decreases, and hence successive units of A will become exchangeable for successive units of B only if counteracting these divergent changes in the valuation of As and Bs that follow each exchange, B becomes successively cheaper in terms of A. And as the foundation of the law of demand, this law of marginal utility then follows directly from the undeniably true proposition that every actor always prefers what satisfies him more over what satisfies him less.[74] For then any increase in the supply of a homogeneous good (i.e., a good whose units are considered to be interchangeable and of equal serviceability) by one additional unit can only be employed as a means for the attainment of a goal that is considered less valuable (or the removal of an uneasiness that is deemed less urgent) than the least valuable goal satisfied by means of a unit of such a good if the supply were one unit less.[75] And, as required of any a priori law and again independent of any contingent experiences, this law also precisely delineates its range of application and explains what possible occurrences cannot be considered exceptions or falsifying events. For one thing, the validity of the law of diminishing marginal utility is not at all affected by the fact that the utility of the marginal unit of some good can increase as well as decrease over time. If, for instance, a hitherto unknown use for a unit of some good is found that is considered more valuable than the least urgent present use

---

74. See on this Mises, *Human Action*, p. 124.

75. Robert Nozick believes Austrians to be inconsistent in (1) claiming that actions invariably show preference (and never indifference) and (2) employing the idea of "homogeneity" and "*equal* serviceability" of goods in their formulation of the law of marginal utility. ("On Austrian Methodology," *Synthese* 36 (1977): pp. 37 ff.) However, such a charge would only be correct if "preference" and "indifference" were both considered categories of the same type. This has been correctly pointed out by Walter Block, who insists that "indifference" is not, unlike "preference," a *praxeological* category. ("On Robert Nozick's 'On Austrian Methodology'" *Inquiry* 23 (1980)), Yet his classification of indifference as a "psychological category" instead is also incorrect. (*Id.*, p. 424) In fact, "sameness" is an *epistemological* category: humans are knowers *and* actors; they only act because they know, and they only know because they act. That something is the same (or different) than something else we know *qua* actors who *know*. (Indeed, "sameness" is a universal epistemological category in that one could not even say anything, for instance about actions, without the notion of something being an instance of some particular *type* of thing.) That something that is known to be the same can never actually be treated with indifference we know *qua* knowers who *act*. The law of diminishing marginal utility then is a law regarding knowers who *act*.

of a unit of this good, the utility derived from the marginal employment would be higher now than previously. Yet despite such an increase in marginal utility, there is no question of such a thing as a law of increasing marginal utility. For not only would the actor whose supply of the good in question was unchanged and who realized such new employment have to give up some previously satisfied desire in order to satisfy another one; he would give up the less urgent one. Moreover, if with this new state of affairs regarding an actor's knowledge about possible employments for units of some given good, its supply increases by an additional unit, its marginal utility would decrease as it would be employed to satisfy precisely that desire that previously had to be excluded from satisfaction because of its relatively lesser urgency.

Nor is it an exception to the law of diminishing marginal utility that an increase in the supply of a good from n to $n+1$ units can lead to an increase in the utility attached to one unit of this good if such a larger supply, considered and evaluated as a whole, can be employed for the satisfaction of a want deemed more valuable than the value attached to all the satisfaction that could be attained if the units of supply were each employed separately for the various goals that could be achieved by means of one individual unit of such good.[76] However, in such a case, the increase in supply would not be one of supply-units regarded as equally serviceable, because the units simply would no longer be evaluated separately. Rather, in increasing the supply from n to $n + 1$, a different, larger-sized-unit good would be created that would be evaluated as such, and the law of diminishing marginal utility would then apply to this good in the same way as it applied to the smaller-sized good in that the first unit of this good of size $n + 1$ would again be employed for the most urgent use to which a good of this size could be put, the second unit of supply of such sized good would be employed for the second most important goal to be satisfied by such sized good, and so on.

The law of demand then, as grounded in this a priori valid theorem, has never made the unqualified prediction that less of a good will be bought if its price rises. Rather, it states that this will be the case only ceteris paribus, i.e., if no increase in the demand for the good in question occurs over time and if the increase in its supply does not effect a different, larger-sized-unit good and, mutatis mutandis, the demand for money does not decrease nor does its

---

76. See Mises, *Human Action*, p. 125; M. N. Rothbard, *Man, Economy, and State*, pp. 268 ff.

smaller supply effect separately evaluated smaller-sized money units.[77] Since it is impossible to have a formula that allows one to predict whether or not such changes occur concurrently with the given rise in price (such changes being dependent on people's future states of knowledge and future knowledge being in principle unpredictable based on constantly operating causes), such a priori knowledge then has a rather limited usefulness for one's business of

---

77. Empiricists will complain that such a formulation of the law will make it tautological and un-falsifiable. Both classifications are false. Clearly, the discovery of a new, more highly valued use for, for instance, a unit of a given good, i.e., the event "increase in demand," and the event "a higher price is paid for it" are two conceptually distinct events, and to logically relate such events then is a categorically different thing than to stipulate that "*bachelor* means 'unmarried man'." (See also footnote 67) That the use of ceteris paribus clauses in economics implies an immunization strategy, on the other hand, would be true only if economic propositions were indeed concerned with contingent empirical causal laws. In the natural sciences, where laws do have this status, such complaint would be appropriate—yet there, interestingly enough, one hardly ever finds ceteris paribus clauses. In the natural sciences, predictive hypotheses of the form "If... then" are in fact treated as applicable whenever the if-condition is given, no matter what else is or is not the case. And it is only because this is done that such hypotheses can be validated at all. (There is only one way of testing hypotheses about contingent empirical causal relations: in and through factual applications.) If, contrary to this, one were to demand that in order to apply a hypothesis or to repeat its application, a *full* description of the world at the moment of application be given, or that *everything* be the same in the second application as in the first (beyond the sameness of the condition explicitly stated in the if-clause), the hypothesis would become inapplicable and thus empty for the practical reason that such a demand would literally involve describing all of the universe, and for the theoretical reason that no one at any point in time could possibly know what all the variables are that make up this universe (as this question remains open to new discoveries).

The situation is entirely different in economics, and it is curious indeed that this should not have been realized—given the facts that the use of ceteris paribus clauses in the empirical sciences would render such sciences futile and that such clauses are nonetheless constantly employed in economics. Why, then, not give serious consideration to the idea that economics might be an altogether different science? Indeed, as we have seen, this is the case. Economic propositions can be validated independently of any factual application as implied (or not implied) in the incontestable axiom of action plus certain situations and situational changes described in terms of the categories of action. Yet then ceteris paribus clauses are completely harmless. In fact, their use simply serves to remind us that the deduced consequences only follow if the situation is indeed as described (and not a logically praxeologically different one), and that it is impossible in all actual applications of economic theorems (i.e., whenever the situation analyzed can be identified as real) to hold the ceteris experimentally constant (as the "holding constant" then can, in principle, only be done logically, by means of thought-experimentation). See on this also Hans-Hermann Hoppe, *Kritik der kausalwissenschaftlichen Sozialforschung*, pp. 78–81.

predicting the economic future. Nevertheless it acts as a logical constraint on predictions in that of all forecasters who equally correctly guess that no such concurrent change will take place, only he who recognizes the law of demand will indeed make a correct prediction, while he whose convictions are at variance with the law will blunder. Such is the logic of economic predictions and the function of praxeological reasoning.

Empiricism recommends the law of demand because it supposedly looks good—yet we can neither see it, nor would it survive empirical testing. Hermeneutics, on the other hand, recommends it because it supposedly sounds good—yet to some it sounds bad. And without some objective, extra-linguistic criterion of distinguishing between good or bad, it is impossible to say more in support of the law of demand than somebody said so.

Austrians, as should be clear by now, have no reason to take either the old empiricist fashion or the new hermeneutical one very seriously. Instead, they should take more seriously than ever the position of extreme rationalism and of praxeology as espoused above all by the "doctrinaire" Mises, as unfashionable as such a stand might now be.

17

Two Notes on Preference and Indifference

I. A Note on Preference and Indifference in Economic Analysis

In his celebrated article "Toward a Reconstruction of Utility and Welfare Economics," Murray Rothbard wrote that

> [i]ndifference can never be demonstrated by action. Quite the contrary. Every action necessarily signifies a *choice*, and every choice signifies a definite preference. Action specifically implies the *contrary* of indifference.... If a person is really indifferent between two alternatives, then he cannot and will not choose between them. Indifference is therefore never relevant for action and cannot be demonstrated in action.[1]

This seems to be undeniable, and any attempt to explain why one chooses to do *x* rather than *y* with reference to indifference rather than preference strikes one as a logical absurdity, a "category mistake." Indeed, it seems to be a truth similar to the truth that no "constant" can ever be used to explain a "variable" and why any attempt to explain a variable outcome with reference to some constant conditions is likewise absurd.

Nonetheless, Rothbard and Mises have been criticized by Nozick[2] and Caplan,[3] for inconsistency in admitting the concept of indifference into economic analysis after all, even if only indirectly. These criticisms have

---

• Originally published in *Quarterly Journal of Austrian Economics* 3, no. 4 (Winter 2005): pp. 87–91.

1. Murray N. Rothbard, "Toward a Reconstruction of Utility and Welfare Economics," in idem, *The Logic of Action*, vol. 1 (Cheltenham, Eng.: Edward Elgar 1997), pp. 225–26.

2. Robert Nozick, "On Austrian Methodology," *Synthese* 36 (1977): pp. 353–92.

3. Bryan Caplan, "The Austrian Search for Realistic Foundations," *Southern Economic Journal* 65, no. 4 (1999): pp. 823–38.

been answered by Block[4] and Hülsmann.[5] However, their answers, although largely correct, seem to bring less than full clarity to the matter. Setting out from Nozick's criticism, I hope to remedy this deficiency here.

As correctly noted by Block,[6] aside from some rather confused and easily disposed of remarks, Nozick has but one challenging criticism of Rothbard's and Mises's verdict on indifference. He argues that their views are incompatible with their own formulation of the law of marginal utility. "Indeed," writes Nozick,

> the Austrian theorists *need* the notion of indifference to explain and mark off the notion of a commodity, and of a *unit* of a commodity. ... Without the notion of indifference, and, hence, of an equivalence class of things, we cannot have the notion of a commodity, or of a unit of a commodity; without the notion of a unit ("an interchangeable unit") of a commodity, we have no way to state the law of (diminishing) marginal utility.[7]

To further substantiate his claim, in an attached footnote Nozick provides quotations from Mises's *Human Action*[8] (1966) and Rothbard's *Man, Economy, and State*[9] (1962). He writes,

> on p. 122 [of *Human Action*] Mises says, "All parts—units—of the available stock are considered as equally useful and valuable if the problem of giving up one of them is raised." Here, then, we *do* have *indifference*. Yet a choice will be made, perhaps at random. One particular object will be given up. Yet the person does not prefer giving up *this one* to giving up another one.... [Similarly, Rothbard in *Man, Economy, and State*, pp. 18–19] writes, "in these examples, the units of the good have been *interchangeable from the point of view of the actor*. Thus, any concrete pound of butter was evaluated in this case perfectly equal with any other pound of butter."[10]

---

4. Walter Block, "On Robert Nozick's 'On Austrian Methodology,'" *Inquiry* 23 (1980): pp. 397–444; and idem, "Austrian Theorizing: Recalling the Foundations," *Quarterly Journal of Austrian Economics* 2, no. 4 (1999): pp. 21–39.

5. Jörg Guido Hülsmann, "Economic Science and Neoclassicism," *Quarterly Journal of Austrian Economics* 2, no. 4 (1999): pp. 3–20.

6. Block, "On Robert Nozick's 'On Austrian Methodology,'" pp. 423–25.

7. Robert Nozick, "On Austrian Methodology," *Synthese* 36 (1977): pp. 353–92.

8. Ludwig von Mises, *Human Action: A Treatise on Economics* (Chicago: Henry Regnery, 1966).

9. Murray N. Rothbard, *Man, Economy, and State* (Los Angeles: Nash, 1962).

10. Nozick, "On Austrian Methodology," p. 390.

Block's answer to this challenge is this:

> I think that this problem can be reconciled as follows. *Before* the question of giving up one of the pounds of butter arose, they were all interchangeable units of one commodity, butter. They were all equally useful and valuable to the actor.—But then he decided to give up one pound. No longer did he hold, or can he be considered to have held, a homogeneous commodity consisting of butter pound units. *Now* there are really *two* commodities. Butter *a*, on the one hand, consisting of 99 one-pound units, each (of the 99) equally valued, each interchangeable from the point of view of the actor with any of the other in the 99-pound set; on the other hand, butter *b*, consisting of one pound of butter (the 72nd unit out of the original 100 butter units, the one, as it happens, that he chose to give up when he desired to sell off one of his pounds of butter). In this case, butter *a* would be preferable to butter *b*, as shown by the fact that when push came to shove, butter *b* was jettisoned and butter *a* retained.—Alternatively, we may say that the person was "indifferent" between all 100 units of butter before and apart from any question of *choice* coming into the picture. But "indifference," in this interpretation, existing only in the *absence* of human action, would not be a praxeological, or *economic* category, but a vague, psychological one.... —We can see, then, that with this interpretation, there will be no difficulty with regard to the law of diminishing marginal utility. For one thing, this is because we can have our homogeneity (apart from human action) as well as deny it (when *choice* takes place). Thus, to the extent that homogeneous units of a commodity are required for the operation and application of this law, there is no problem.[11]

My dissatisfaction with Block's solution to the challenge posed by Nozick is twofold.

First, his interpretation of indifference as a "vague, psychological" category seems off the mark. Instead, in accordance with Mises, it must be regarded as a rather precise *epistemological* category implied in the concept of a *class* of objects and involved in any operation of *classification*. "Quantity and quality," explains Mises,

> are categories of the external world. Only indirectly do they acquire importance and meaning for action. Because every thing can only

---

11. Block, "On Robert Nozick's 'On Austrian Methodology'," pp. 424–25; and similarly Block, "Austrian Theorizing: Recalling the Foundations," pp. 22–24.

produce a limited effect, some things are considered scarce and treated as means. Because the effects which things are able to produce are different, acting man distinguishes various classes of things. Because means of the same quantity and quality are apt always to produce the same quantity of an effect of the same quality, action does not differentiate between concrete definite quantities of homogeneous means.[12]

However, if the formation of classes of objects has a realistic and objective foundation, as Mises emphasizes, then Block's escape route appears implausible and *ad hoc*: *before* the choice the units of butter belonged to one class (they were homogeneous), *now*, at the point of choice, they are suddenly members of different classes (they are heterogeneous). In fact, they remain what they were then and what they are now: units of butter.

Block chooses this route because he believes that otherwise the claim might be doubted that actions must be explained with reference to preferences. However, this fear is unjustified. We can have our homogeneity (classes of objects) and still insist that only preferences can explain and are demonstrated in concrete choices.

In order to explain this, it is useful to recall some elementary insights regarding the nature of action—insights that "Austrians" in particular should be familiar with. Actions, *qua* intentional behavior, have an external-behaviorist *and* an internal-mentalist aspect. To give a full and adequate description, both aspects must be taken into account. A quote from John Searle[13] should make this clear:

> If we think about human action, ... it is tempting to think that types of action or behavior can be identified with types of bodily movements. But that is obviously wrong. For example, one and the same set of human bodily movements might constitute a dance, or signaling, or exercising, or testing one's muscles, or none of the above. Furthermore, just as one and the same set of types of physical movements can constitute completely different kinds of actions, so one type of action can be performed by a vastly different number of types of physical movements.... Furthermore, another odd feature about actions which makes them different from events generally is

---

12. Mises, *Human Action*, p. 119.

13. John Searle, *Minds, Brains and Science* (Cambridge, Mass.: Harvard University Press, 1984), pp. 57–58.

that actions seem to have a preferred description. If I am going for a walk to Hyde Park, there are any number of other things that are happening in the course of my walk, but their descriptions do not describe my intentional actions, because in acting, what I am doing depends in large part on what I think I am doing. So for example, I am also moving in the general direction of Patagonia, shaking the hair on my head up and down, wearing out my shoes, and moving a lot of air molecules. However, none of these other descriptions seem to get at what is essential about this action, as the action it is.[14]

Before the backdrop of Searle's observation regarding an action's *preferred description*, we can now proceed to propose a simple yet elegant solution to Nozick's challenge. Keep in mind that, in the above example, "going for a walk to Hyde park" and "moving in the general direction of Patagonia" are behaviorally identical phenomena, but the latter is not part of the preferred description though it *might* be under different circumstances. In his reply to Nozick, Block fails to provide the preferred description.

If the 100 pounds of butter are indeed homogeneous, and I give away one pound (be it in exchange for money, as a present, or for whatever other reason), then it is simply not a part of my action that it is unit 72 that I give away (even though that may be a behaviorally correct description of what I do), just as in the above case it is not a part of my action that I move in the general direction of Patagonia. Instead, the correct (preferred) description is that I give away *a* unit of butter, thus demonstrating that I prefer this dollar—or more likely *a* dollar—or maybe a "thank you" from my neighbor to *a* unit of butter. On the other hand, if it *is* part of the correct description of my action that it is the 72nd unit of butter that I give away (rather than any other), then and only then are we dealing with heterogeneous pounds of butter (and my action then demonstrates that I prefer a dollar, *that* unit of butter or a "thank you" to *this* unit of butter).

Other alleged puzzles concerning ice cream, sweaters, drowning children, and Buridan's ass can be solved in a likewise manner.

To say that I am indifferent to strawberry and vanilla ice cream is to say, for instance, that a correct description of my action should simply speak of ice cream or something cold and creamy. Getting a *strawberry* ice cream in exchange for a dollar is then simply not a part of the description of my choice.

---

14. See also Hoppe, *Economic Science and the Austrian Method* (Auburn, Ala.: Ludwig von Mises Institute, 1995), pp. 40–44.

Instead, my choice demonstrates that I prefer *an* ice cream or *something* cold and creamy to a dollar. On the other hand, if getting a strawberry ice cream *is* part of the correct description of my action, then it is absurd to say that I am indifferent between strawberry and vanilla ice cream.

Similarly, if I am indifferent to blue and green sweaters, then my choice concerns simply *a* sweater, or *a* dark colored sweater; and getting a green (or blue) one is not part of the correct description of my action. Instead my choice demonstrates my preference of a sweater over *a* (or *this*) shirt or to something else.

Likewise, a mother who sees her equally loved sons Peter and Paul drown and who can only rescue one does not demonstrate that she loves Peter more than Paul if she rescues the former. Instead, she demonstrates that she prefers *a* (one) rescued child to none. On the other hand, if the correct (preferred) description is that she rescued Peter, then she was not indifferent as regards her sons.

Lastly, consider Buridan's ass standing between two identical and equidistant bales of hay. The ass is not indifferent and yet chooses one over the other, as Nozick would have it. Rather, it prefers *a* bale of hay (whether it is the left or the right one is simply not part of the preferred choice description), and thus demonstrates its general preference of hay to death.

II. Further Notes on Preference and Indifference: Rejoinder to Block

In response to Block's foregoing criticism of my previously published note on the subject of preference and indifference in economic analysis, I will first summarize our agreements. Then I will reconstruct our differences in the form of a fictive dialogue between Block (B) and Hoppe (H) to conclude that Block has failed to grasp my argument due to his amazing admission that "I do not give two hoots about whether or not we achieve a correct description of someone's actions."

Assume that Block has several ten dollar notes and I have several sweaters. We agree that it is possible and perfectly legitimate for Block to say that each of his notes is "perfectly substitutable" for any other, that they are

---

• Originally published in the *Quarterly Journal of Austrian Economics* 8, no. 4 (Winter 2005).

"homogeneous" goods, or that one is "indifferent" toward one note *vis-à-vis* any other. Whether or not this statement is true (or false) depends on Block's perception. It is true if Block does indeed view each note as "equally serviceable" (given some defined goal or end) as compared to any other; and it is false if he considers them as not equally serviceable (in which case they are heterogeneous goods). The same holds for Hoppe and his sweaters.

Second, we agree that every action, and more specifically, every inter-personal exchange demonstrates, expresses, reveals or manifests a preference (or rather: opposite preferences).

Further, we agree that the law of marginal utility, i.e., the proposition that as the supply of a homogeneous good increases (decreases) the marginal utility decreases (increases), holds true.

Now to our differences: Assume that Block affirms that he considers each of his dollar notes as equally serviceable (as a supply of homogeneous notes), and Hoppe likewise affirms that he considers each of his sweaters as perfectly substitutable for any other. Then an exchange of one ten-dollar note against one sweater takes place. How is this exchange to be analyzed?

B: First, this exchange demonstrates that I prefer a sweater to a ten-dollar note and you prefer a note to a sweater. Second, it demonstrates that I value one note less (the one that I actually give up) than the others (those that I keep) and that the same holds true for you and your sweaters—after all, it is one *particular* note that is being exchanged for one *particular* sweater and there must be a reason why it is *this* note and *this* sweater rather than *that*.

H: I agree with your first statement, but not with the second. In fact, with your second statement you become entangled in a logical contradiction, because on the one hand you have affirmed that you consider all of your notes as *homogeneous* and on the other hand you now affirm that they are *not* homogeneous (but you value one note less than another).

B: Admitted, this is a contradiction if you put the matter in this way. But I don't put it thus. Rather, I say that I considered the notes as homogeneous *before* the action (exchange), but *later*, at the moment of choice, I considered them as different or heterogeneous. Thereby the contradiction disappears.

H: What, however, if you say that you consider them to be homogeneous notes *while* (at the exact same moment when) the exchange takes place? Aren't you then contradicting yourself? Aren't you *then* saying simultaneously *both*: that your notes are homogeneous *and* that they are not homogeneous? Further: Assume that you affirmed the law of marginal utility while we exchanged a ten dollar note for a sweater and said "I herewith give up one of my equally serviceable notes in exchange for one of your sweaters and consequently the marginal utility of a ten dollar note for me is now higher than otherwise would have been the case." Given what you have argued at the outset: that your exchange of a note for a sweater demonstrates, not only your preference of a sweater to a note, but also your preference of some notes (those you keep) over others (the one that you give up)—aren't you then involved in a logical contradiction? Surely, not *both* statements can be true: your affirmation of the law of marginal utility *and* your particular description of the exchange. Isn't your affirmation then falsified by your description of our exchange or *vice versa*?

B: I must admit that I am running into difficulties here with my argument. But aren't you running into similar difficulties with yours? First: How can you accept only the first part of my analysis but deny the second? After all, it cannot be denied that it *is* one *particular* note and one *particular* sweater that are being exchanged. And second: If you don't accept the second part of my analysis, aren't you then saying in effect that indifference *is* and *can* be demonstrated by action? And how do you reconcile *this* with Murray Rothbard's *dictum* (on which we agree) that "indifference can never be demonstrated by action"?

H: First off, I am of course not saying that the second part of your analysis of our exchange is incorrect *under all circumstances*. If you had one note that you regarded as distinct (heterogeneous) from all of your other notes, and I had a sweater that I regarded as distinct from all of my other sweaters, then it would be entirely correct for you to say that our exchange demonstrated your preference of my sweater to this one particular note (as compared to all of your other notes). But by assumption, this is *not* the situation we are supposed to analyze. Rather, the question is whether or not your analysis is correct if, as *per* assumption, you have affirmed that you consider all of your notes as *non*-distinct, homogeneous, and equally serviceable in the pursuit of some given end.

Now to your question: I reject the second part of your analysis, because it involves a contradiction, as I have just explained again. *If* you consider the notes as homogeneous, *then* the correct description of our exchange is that *a—any one*—note has been exchanged against *a—any one*—sweater (but not: *this* note against *this* sweater); and this logically implies that, in fact, it happens to be one particular note that is being exchanged against one particular sweater. So there *is* no problem regarding your first quarrel.

B: Yet how about the more serious second problem I have with your analysis?

H: That problem is readily solved, too.

Not everything that behaviorally "happens" is the result of a *choice* (my original reference to Searle was intended to make precisely this point). If I choose to walk from point A to B, for instance, this walk must begin (and end) with either my left foot or my right foot; that is, behaviorally, my walk can be described as either left-right-left-right, and so on, or as right-left-right-left, and so on. But while this or that particular sequence of steps *may* be the result of a deliberate choice on my part, it *needs* not be so (and it typically isn't). It may just "happen" to be this sequence rather than that without me *choosing* either one (i.e., demonstrating a preference of one lead leg over the other). How do we determine what is the result of choice and what isn't? Obviously, not by mere "observation." Rather, we must inquire of the actor in order to reach a (correct) description of his action. Did he *choose* to put his left or his right foot down first or did it merely *happen* that it was one foot rather than the other? The answer depends on the correct description of the action in question; and what is or isn't the correct description of the action depends on the perception and conceptualization of the action by its very actor: on his description of *his* goal and *his* means available to satisfy this goal.

This applies also to the case at hand. It is incorrect to infer, as you do, from the mere *fact* that one particular note is being exchanged against one particular sweater that this must be the result of a *choice*. It may well be a *coincidence*, and the choice was actually one of *a—any one*—note against *a—any one*—sweater. What is or isn't the case depends on *you*, on *your* description of *your* action. And what *is* the description that you have given of your action? You have stated that you gave up one note viewed as equally serviceable to several other notes in exchange of a sweater. Yet to state this is to say that you did not *choose* between one note and another (notwithstanding the fact that one particular note must have been factually selected).

B: Yet how can you reconcile this analysis with Rothbard's *dictum*?

H: Quite easily; for this is how Rothbard continues his statement: "*if* a person is really indifferent between two alternatives, then he cannot and will not *choose* between them."[15] Note that Rothbard does not say here that there is no such thing as indifference. To the contrary, his statement clearly implies that he thinks there is—only that if and insofar as there is indifference, then no choice is involved. This is exactly what *I* am saying: if you are indeed indifferent toward your notes, i.e., if you believe each of them to be equally serviceable in the pursuit of some given end, then you do not *choose* between them; and that you do not *choose*, because you regard your supply of means as homogeneous, can even be *verified*. For if you are indeed indifferent, then you would be willing to allow *me* (or any third party) to select the note that you are willing to give up in exchange for a better-liked sweater; and this is to say, quite literally, that *you* did *not* choose between your notes. If a choice was made at all, it was a choice made by *someone else*. Insofar as *you* are concerned, *your* choice is one between *a—any one*—note and a sweater.

B: So what, then, is the role of "indifference" in economic analysis?

H: Whenever we act, we employ means to achieve a valued end. This end is a state of affairs that the actor prefers to the actual (and impending) state of affairs. Both states of affairs, at the beginning of action and at its conclusion, are constellations of means (goods) at an actor's disposal, describing the circumstances or conditions under which he must act. On the one hand, *indifference* is part of the *description of such circumstances and conditions* (the start- and end-points of action). On the other hand, *preferences* (*choices*) explain the *change* in these circumstances that an actor wants to achieve through the disposal of means. Any complete analysis of action must involve both: a description

---

15. My emphases.

of the start- and endpoint of action as well as an explanation of the change occurring from one point to another due to preference-demonstrating action. Both concepts, preference *and* indifference, are therefore necessary and complementary parts of every economic (praxeological) analysis.

To explain: The world we human actors must deal with is a world of means (goods). More particularly, it is a world made up of heterogeneous goods. Not every good is suited to reach the same end. We do not inhabit a world made up of some "wonderdough" or "manna" that is equally well-suited to satisfy every conceivable human end. Instead, some goods can satisfy some ends but not others (or not equally well). On the other hand, we also do not live in a world made up exclusively and entirely of heterogeneous goods, such that each particular good can satisfy one and only one specific end. Rather: Our—the *real*—world is characterized by heterogeneity *and* homogeneity: by heterogeneous goods composed of multiple (enumerable and quantifiable) *homogeneous units*, such that each unit is capable of bringing about the same desired end-effect.

Accordingly, every praxeological analysis must begin and end with "indifference" (homogeneity). Every analysis must begin with a description of the starting-point of action; and this involves a specification of the present supply-constellation of *homogeneous units* of *heterogeneous goods* at an actor's disposal. This is where *indifference* (homogeneity) first comes into play. Second, every analysis must then explain the change in this constellation that an actor wants to effect by disposing of (some of) these goods in exchange for other more highly valued ones. Here *preference* enters the scene. Finally, at the conclusion of every analysis must be a description of the results of action (which are at the same time the initial conditions for the *following* action); and this description again must be about a (new and different) supply-constellation of homogeneous units of heterogeneous goods (resulting in a new and different value-scale of the actor).

18

Property, Causality, and Liability

I.

Wherever there is scarcity of resources in relation to human demand, the possibility of conflict arises. The solution to such conflict is the assignment of private property rights—rights of exclusive control. All scarce resources must be owned privately in order to avoid otherwise inescapable conflicts. However, while the assignment of private property rights makes conflict-free interaction *possible*, it does not assure it. The possibility of property rights violations exists, and if there are violations, then there must be rights of self-defense and punishment as well as liability on the part of a wrongdoer.[1]

All this holds true regardless of how and to whom such rights are assigned and who accordingly is or is not considered aggressor or victim in any given case.

We still remain in the realm of "positive" legal analysis when we consider what might be called a *praxeological* requirement of *any* system of assigning property rights. In order to make conflict-free interaction possible, every such system must take into account the fact that man does and must act. In other words, it must be an "operational" system. To accomplish this, based on the system adopted, human actors must be able to determine *ex ante*, at any moment in time, what they are and are not permitted to do. In order to determine this, there need be some "objective" borders, signs, and indicators

---

• Originally published in the *Quarterly Journal of Austrian Economics* 7, no. 4 (Winter 2004).

1. Hoppe, *A Theory of Socialism and Capitalism* (Boston: Kluwer Academic Publishers, 1987); and idem, *The Economics and Ethics of Private Property* (Boston: Kluwer Academic Publishers, 1993).

of ownership and property as well as of wrongful invasion of said ownership and property. Similarly, when considering a case *ex post*, judges must have "objective" criteria of property and aggression to make a determination for or against a plaintiff.

II.

In light of the technical requirements that every property rights system must meet, I will turn to an analysis of a specific—and explicitly normative— proposal of defining private property and property rights violations: the Lockean-Rothbardian solution.

In this intellectual tradition, property is defined as tangible, physical objects which have been "visibly" lifted out of the state of nature of unowned goods through acts of appropriation and production. Through mixing one's labor with specific resources, objectively ascertainable borders of property are established and specific objects connected to particular individuals. There are indicators of owned (as compared to unowned) objects and of who owns them (and who does not), for everyone to "read." Moreover, the theory fulfills perfectly the requirement of being operational in that it traces all present property back to acts of "original appropriation" (up until which time there had only been "nature" or "unowned" resources). Based on this theory, man could indeed have acted from the beginning of time. (In distinct contrast, any theory that makes the assignment of property rights dependent on a "contract" or agreement or on State-declared law [legislation] does *not* allow man to act from the beginning on, but only *after* the conclusion of said contract or the arrival of the State. Accordingly, any such theory must be regarded as "technically" deficient.)

However, here it is not so much the positive definition of property as the complementary negative definition of punishable offense that is of interest. Based on the fundamental *stricture* that just as all property is private so all crime must be private (committed by specific individuals against specific victims), Rothbard has offered the following "strict liability theory" encompassing both criminal and tort law.[2] In every criminal or tort case,

> [e]vidence must be probative in demonstrating a strict causal chain of
> acts of invasion of person or property. Evidence must be constructed

---

2. Currently in the U.S., in criminal cases proof beyond a reasonable doubt is required. In contrast, in tort cases it is sufficient to prove that something is more probable than not (preponderance of evidence).

to demonstrate that aggressor A in fact initiated an overt physical act invading the person or property of victim B.[3]

What the plaintiff must prove, then, beyond a reasonable doubt is a strict causal connection between the defendant and his aggression against the plaintiff. He must prove, in short, that A actually "caused" an invasion of the person or property of B.... To establish guilt and liability, strict causality of aggression leading to harm must meet the rigid test of proof beyond a reasonable doubt. Hunch, conjecture, plausibility, even mere probability are not enough.... Statistical correlation ... cannot establish causation.[4]

One important aspect of this definition: the necessity of establishing *causation*, based on "individualized evidence" rather than mere *probability* (or preponderance of evidence) based on "statistical" evidence is accepted. This not withstanding, Rothbard's proposal must be criticized as overly "objectivistic," for it ignores important "subjective" conditions which must be *combined* with objective indicators to determine liability. "Overly" because Rothbard's objectivism is not warranted by the nature of things nor is it in accord with his own definition of property and original appropriation which contains an important subjective element as well: appropriation implies *intent*. (Not every berry picking counts as an appropriation of the berry bush rather than merely the berry, and not every detour off the beaten path counts as homesteading, for instance.[5])

In contrast, here it is argued that *not* all physical invasions imply liability and, more importantly, that some actions are liable even if *no* overt physical invasion occurs. In this argument Adolf Reinach's illuminating analysis regarding the concept of causality in (Continental European) criminal law will be valuable.[6]

III.

For Rothbard, it appears guilt or fault is established by proof of causation of harm. Reinach, on the other hand, emphasizes that causation and fault are

---

3. Murray N. Rothbard, "Law, Property Rights, and Air Pollution," in idem, *The Logic of Action*, vol. II (Cheltenham, Eng.: Edward Elgar, 1997), p. 137.

4. *Id.*, pp. 140–41.

5. Rothbard, *The Ethics of Liberty* (New York: New York University Press, 1998).

6. Adolf Reinach, "Über den Ursachenbegriff im geltenden Strafrecht," in idem, *Sämtliche Werke*, vol. I. (Munich: Philosophia, 1989).

independent elements, and *both* must be present in order to impose liability. Thus, he writes:

> In the case of a man's death, it is not sufficient that the death resulted from the action of an accountable (sane) person; as an additional requirement of a punishable offense, intent and deliberation (premeditation) or intent without deliberation (negligence) or, as we can summarily say, fault must be present as well. Causation of success *and* fault are requirements of punishment.—Fault must always be found.[7]

However, faultless causation, which remains free of punishment, exists also.

Consider the following examples of harm-causation which do *not* imply liability due to a lack of fault. A drives on the road. B jumps from behind a tree onto the road and is killed. A has caused B's death. Should A be held liable or should he go free? A invites B into his house. The house is struck by lightning, and B is injured. A (and his property) has caused B's injury, for without A's invitation B would have been elsewhere. Is A (or his insurer) liable to B or must B (or his insurer) bear the costs? A's tree, struck by lightning, falls onto B's property, injuring B. Is A (or his insurer) liable to B or must B (or his insurer) bear the costs? A and B go hunting together on B's (or A's) hunting ground. They approach a group of deer from opposite sides and open fire at the same time. A's stray bullet injures B. Is A liable to B or must B assume this risk and the associated costs?

Rothbard would have likely agreed that A is not liable in these cases, and he would have pointed out that he had covered this under the heading of the "proper assumption of risk." Life involves an inescapable element of risk. It is incumbent on each individual to learn how to live with such risk and to insure himself against it. However, this implies admitting that the narrow causality criterion is inadequate. What needs to be added to Rothbard's criterion would seem to be this: No one is liable for "accidents" involving his

---

7. Reinach, "Über den Ursachenbegriff im geltenden Strafrecht," p. 8:

> Liegt der Tod eines Menschen vor, so genügt es nicht, dass der Erfolg durch die Handlung eines Zurechnungsfähigen herbeigeführt wurde, sondern es muss als weitere Strafvoraussetzung Vorsatz und Überlegung, bzw. Vorsatz ohne Überlegung, bzw. Fahrlässigkeit, oder, wie wir umfassend sagen können, Schuld hinzutreten. Strafvoraussetzung ist stets Verursachung des Erfolges und Schuld. — Schuld ist immer erforderlich.

person and property. Instead, the risk of accidents and the insurance against them must be assumed individually (by each person and property owner for himself). People can be held liable only for their *actions*, whether intentional or negligent (but not for *accidents* involving them). Actions, however, involve *both* "objective" (external) *and* "subjective" (internal) elements. Hence, the exclusive inspection of physical events can *never* be considered sufficient in determining liability (there must be *fault*, too, and one can only speak of fault if an event is caused by an *action*).

IV.

Now consider Reinach's definition of action-causality. An action of legal (penal) importance

> is an event that cannot be cancelled without also canceling the effect, insofar as it is of legal importance.[8] ... "Cause" of an event ... is called among other things that condition which must be added to one element of a conceptual whole, so that in place of its second component the event can be conceived of as having occurred.[9] ... To cause an event means to activate a condition of success; to intentionally cause an event means to activate a condition that brings about the success.... To intentionally cause something thus means to activate a condition of success, willing that this condition—of course in conjunction with others—leads to the success.[10] ... The willing thereby must be conscious that he can contribute to the willed success ... [and] that success resulting from his "contribution" and

---

8. *Id.*, p. 29: Eine strafrechtlich relevante Handlung „muss etwas sein, das nicht hinwegfallen kann, ohne dass auch der Erfolg, soweit er rechtlich in Betracht kommt, hinwegfallen müsste."

9. *Id.*, p. 39: „‚Ursache' eines Erfolges ... nennt man unter anderem diejenige Bedingung, die zu dem einen Gliede eines gedachten Zusammen hinzugedacht werden muss, damit an Stelle des zweiten Gliedes der betreffende Erfolg als eintretend gedacht werden könne."

10. *Id.*, p. 30:

> Einen Erfolg verursachen heisst, durch eine Handlung eine Bedingung des Erfolges setzen; ihn vorsätzlich verursachen, heisst, durch eine Handlung eine Bedingung setzen, damit sie den Erfolg herbeiführe. ... Etwas vorsätzlich verursachen, heisst demnach: durch eine Handlung eine Bedingung des Erfolges setzen, wollend, dass diese Bedingung — natürlich im Vereine mit anderen — den Erfolg herbeiführe.

other factors known to him is possible.[11] ... His responsibility
for negligent behavior is similar. In this case the success is not
desired; but I could and should have avoided it. Insofar as it is still
something whose occurrence depended on me: it, too, in a special
way is "mine."[12]

In light of Reinach's definitions, we return to Rothbard's causality
criterion. While his criterion is, on the one hand, too wide in including
accidental invasions among punishable offenses, on the other hand, it appears
too narrow in determining liability.

A few examples, taken from Reinach and slightly modified, illustrate
the point.

A, B's superior, sends B into the woods, hoping that B will be struck by
lightning. His hopes are fulfilled.

Has A caused B's death or injury? Should A be liable? With regard to
causation, Reinach would answer yes: without A's authorized order to B,
B would not have been killed. However, Reinach would deny that A is liable,
not because there is no causality, but because there is no intent or negligence
on A's part (there is just hope). Rothbard also would hold A not liable,
not because of lack of intent but because of lack of causality (verbal orders
presumably do not count as causes, for they are not "physical" causes).

Now let us change the scenario: A is able to calculate exactly when
a particular tree will be hit by lightning. He sends B to this tree, and B is
indeed hit.

Reinach would find causality here in the same way as in the first case.
What makes the two cases different and leads to liability in the second is
intent understood as "willing with the objectively grounded consciousness
of certitude."[13] In the second case, A is liable because he caused the event
with the objectively justified belief that his action, in cooperation with other
factors, would lead to the desired result. In contrast, according to Rothbard's
criterion no causation exists in the second case just as none existed in the

---

11. *Id.*, p. 31: "Der Wollende muss (dabei) das Bewusstsein haben, dass er zu dem
gewollten Erfolg etwas beitragen kann ... (und) dass der Eintritt des Erfolges aus seinem
‚Beitrag' und den übrigen ihm bekannten Faktoren möglich ist."

12. *Id.*, p. 42: "Ähnlich verhält es sich mit der Verantwortung für fahrlässige Vorgehen.
Hier ist der Erfolg zwar nicht von mir gewollt; aber ich hätte ihn vermeiden können und
sollen. Insofern ist er doch etwas, dessen Dasein von mir abhing: auch er ist in besonderem
Grade ‚mein'. "

13. "Wollen mit dem objektiv geforderten Bewusstsein der Gewissheit."

first (the external-phenomenal sequence of events in both cases is in fact the same). Hence, Rothbard would have to let A go free in the second case just as in the first.

How is this possible? Consider another example. A, B's employer, orders B to come directly to him, knowing that halfway there is a concealed trap. B walks into the trap and is injured. Reinach would find A liable. Rothbard would let him go, because there is no "overt physical invasion" initiated by A. A merely says something (which in itself is clearly a noninvasive act) to B; and then "nature" takes its course with no further interference on A's part. That is, entrapment, as an indirectly and by in itself noninvasive means effected physical harm, would have to remain free of punishment.

This does not just stand in opposition to our moral intuition. More importantly, the exclusion of indirectly caused physical harm from the class of punishable offenses has no analogue in the positive theory of property and original appropriation. We have no trouble, for instance, conceiving of an "indirect" act of appropriation. A, B's boss, orders B to clear a piece of previously unowned land and drill for oil. B finds oil. Thereby A, not B, becomes the owner of the oil (although A is only the indirect cause of the act of appropriation). Accordingly, if A orders B to drill for oil, expecting that instead of finding oil B will fall into a trap at the given location, then A should be held responsible for this event as well. If not, why not?

Consider this sequence of cases: A wants B dead and tries to accomplish this through daily prayer. B indeed dies.

In this case neither Reinach nor Rothbard would find liability and presumably for the same reason. No causality exists (only coincidence) and hence there is no liability on A's part.

Now change the scenario: A prays for B's death. B happens to see and hear this and, being superstitious and of extremely delicate physical disposition, dies of fear.

In this case, too, Reinach and Rothbard reach the same verdict, that A is not liable, but they do so for different reasons. Reinach would find that causality is given in the second case. B dies *because* A has prayed for his death. What is missing and thus exculpates A is intent (or negligence) with regard to the outcome. A wants to kill B by means of *praying*, which is simply and objectively ineffective as far as the outcome is concerned. A undertakes no other means than praying. B's death is the result of a causal process that is incidental (accidental) to A's actions. That is why A must go free. Rothbard, on the other hand, would let A go because causality is absent. A has performed no action that can be construed as being invasive of B's person or property.

Consider a second change in the scenario: A prays for B's death. He knows of B's superstition and weak physical condition, and he informs B of his attempt. B dies out of fear.

Reinach would hold A liable in this case, whereas Rothbard would not. For Reinach in this case causality exists in precisely the same way as in the first. And indeed, phenomenally—as far as the outward appearance of things is concerned—the two cases are essentially the same. The only difference is A's *intentional saying* to B what B had discovered accidentally in the first scenario. Liability, according to Reinach, results from the presence of intent or negligence. In the second case, in telling B, A *acts*, whether intentionally or negligently, to bring about B's death. (Reinach would let A go only if A had *not* known anything about B's medical condition. In that case, telling B might be insensitive or cruel. However, while the causal processes involved are exactly the same as under the previous scenario: whether A knows or does not know about B's condition, B dies, A would nonetheless go free because neither intent nor negligence with regard to the outcome exists.) Rothbard, also consistent, would find that just as in the first so in the second case *no* causation exists. There is no overt physical invasion of B by A. A's praying did not cause the death, and informing B in itself did not involve any physical invasion. Hence, A should go completely free. (Based on his causality criterion Rothbard would make no distinction between A knowing or not knowing about B's condition. A is not liable in any case.)

That A should not be held liable in any way, shape or form is not intuitively convincing. Why? What if A could in fact pray people dead, and B died as a result of his praying? There is no physical-causal invasion, yet A has killed B. Should A still go free? Should he be allowed to pray dead whomsoever he wishes dead? More importantly and as indicated before, the exclusive emphasis on direct physical invasion has no analogue in the theory of appropriation. We do not exclude all "indirect" acts of appropriation as invalid *per se*. One can become the owner of things one never touches, i.e., without anything faintly resembling physical causation. Why should matters be different when it comes to aggressive rather than appropriative actions? Why should every "indirect" (covert) aggression (causation mediated through words) be categorically excluded from possible liability? Surely, if A tells B that he wished C were dead, and B kills C, we would not hold A liable. But would we do the same if A paid B, or if A and B were members of an organized gang of which A were the gang's leader, and B killed C? Similarly, if Clinton or Bush ordered their generals to kill Iraqis, the generals told their officers who told the soldiers, and the soldiers then killed as ordered, should only the soldiers be liable because they have "caused" the deaths, or, as we can hardly imagine Rothbard disagreeing should everyone from the president on down to the soldiers be held jointly and severally liable? But then intent matters.

Finally, an example of failed attempt illustrates Rothbard's criterion as too narrow. A wants to kill his wife, B. He buys deadly poison from the pharmacist, and regularly adds it to B's tea. However, the pharmacist has made a mistake. He did not sell A poison but something entirely harmless. B dies in an unrelated car crash. The pharmacist discovers his error and the entire case unravels. Should A be held liable or go free (B's heirs are suing A)?

Reinach would find A liable. There is intent (and hence fault) and there is (failed) causality. A performs a series of actions that he believes to be and which objectively are suited to bringing about the desired result. It is only because of an incidental (accidental) causal event (the pharmacist's error) that the result does not occur as desired.

Rothbard would have to let A go, because no causality as he defines it exists. In fact, as far as the external world is concerned, A has done no harm to B at all. His attempt to take B's life was an all-around failure. (Rothbard himself clearly feels uncomfortable taking this position and comments: "even if the attempted crime created no invasion of property *per se*, if the attempted battery or murder became *known* to the victim, the resulting creation of fear in the victim would be prosecutable as an assault. So the attempted criminal (or tortfeasor) could not get away unscathed."[14])

Again, the principal reason that this solution seems unsatisfactory is the lack of an analogue in the positive theory of property and appropriation. We do not require that an act of original appropriation (homesteading) be successful in order to find that it has taken place and to determine ownership. For example, A clears the underbrush from a previously unowned piece of woodland in order to create a park. However, in doing so he accidentally burns down all trees. A's action was unsuccessful. This is not the outcome he wanted. Is he nonetheless the owner of the burned forest? It seems so. However, if there are unsuccessful attempts of appropriation, which

---

14. Rothbard, "Law, Property Rights, and Air Pollution," p. 163.

count nonetheless as acts of appropriation, why should there not also be unsuccessful attempts of aggression, which nonetheless count as aggression?

V.

Clearly, while "objective" (external, observable) criteria must play an important role in the determination of ownership and aggression, such criteria are not sufficient. In particular, defining aggression "objectivistically" as "overt physical invasion" appears deficient because it excludes entrapment, incitement and failed attempts, for instance. Both the establishment of property rights and their violation spring from actions: acts of appropriation and expropriation. However, in addition to a physical appearance, actions also have an internal, subjective aspect. This aspect cannot be observed by our sense organs. Instead, it must be ascertained by means of understanding (*Verstehen*). The task of the judge cannot—by the nature of things—be reduced to a simple decision rule based on a quasi-mechanical model of causation. Judges must observe the facts and understand the actors and actions involved in order to determine fault and liability.

Part Four

The Intellectuals

19

M. N. Rothbard:
Economics, Science, and Liberty

Murray N. Rothbard (1926–1995) has come to occupy a position of unique influence within the intellectual tradition Austrian economics for a combination of three central reasons.

First, Rothbard is the latest representative of the mainstream within Austrian Economics.[1] As in other intellectual traditions, various interconnected branches can be identified within the Austrian school of economics. Rothbard is the latest exponent of the main rationalist branch of the Austrian school, starting with the school's founder Carl Menger, and continuing with Eugen von Böhm-Bawerk, and Ludwig von Mises. Like Menger, Böhm-Bawerk, and Mises, Rothbard is an outspoken rationalist and critic of all

---

• Originally published in *15 Great Austrian Economists*, edited by Randall Holcombe (Auburn, Ala.: Ludwig von Mises Institute, 1999), pp. 223–41.

1. Among academia in general, currently Friedrich A. Hayek is by far the most prominent Austrian economist. It is worth emphasizing, then, that Hayek is not a representative of the rationalist mainstream of Austrian economics, nor does Hayek claim otherwise. Hayek stands in the intellectual tradition of British empiricism and skepticism, and he is an explicit opponent of the continental rationalism espoused by Menger, Böhm-Bawerk, Mises, and Rothbard. On this topic see further Joseph Salerno, "Ludwig von Mises as Social Rationalist," *Review of Austrian Economics* 4 (1990): pp. 26–54; Jeffrey M. Herbener, "Introduction," in idem, ed., *The Meaning of Ludwig von Mises* (Boston: Kluwer Academic Publishers, 1993); Hans-Hermann Hoppe, "Einführung: Ludwig von Mises und der Liberalismus," in Ludwig von Mises, *Liberalismus* (St. Augustine: Academia Verlag, 1993); idem, "F. A. Hayek on Government and Social Evolution," *Review of Austrian Economics* 7, no. 1 (1994): pp. 67–93, reprinted chapter 20 herein; idem, "Die österreichische Schule und ihre Bedeutung für die moderne Wirtschaftswissenschaft," in Hoppe, Kurt Leube, Christian Watrin, and Joseph Salerno, ed., *Ludwig von Mises's 'Die Gemeinwirtschaft'* (Düsseldorf: Verlag Wirtschaft und Finanzen, 1996); Murray N. Rothbard, "The Present State of Austrian Economics," in idem, *The Logic of Action*, vol. 1 (Cheltenham, Eng.: Edward Elgar, 1997).

variants of social relativism: historicism, empiricism, positivism, falsification-ism, and skepticism. Like his acknowledged predecessors, Rothbard defends the view that economic laws not only exist, but more specifically that they are "exact" (Menger) or "aprioristic" (Mises) laws. In contrast to the propositions of the (empirical) natural sciences, which must be continually tested against ever new data, and thus can never attain more than hypothetical validity, the propositions of economics concern necessary, non-hypothetical relations and assume apodictic validity. According to the Austrian mainstream, all economic laws can be derived deductively from a few elementary facts of nature and man (Menger), or from a single axiom (Mises), i.e., the proposition "man acts," which one cannot dispute without running into a performative contradiction, and which is, thus, indisputably true, and a few empirical—and empirically testable—assumptions. Like his predecessors, Rothbard considers it neither necessary nor indeed possible to test economic propositions by studying data of experience. Experience can illustrate the validity of an economic theorem, but experience can never refute or falsify it, because ultimately its validity rests solely on the indisputable validity of the axiom of action, and on the validity (and correct exercise) of the rules of deductive reasoning and logi-cal inference. Indeed, trying to "empirically test" an economic law involves a category mistake and is a sign of confusion. Further, like Menger, Böhm-Bawerk, and Mises before him, Rothbard adheres firmly to epistemological and methodological individualism. Only individuals act; consequently, all social phenomena must be explained—logically reconstructed—as the result of purposeful individual actions. Every "holistic" or "organicist" explanation must be categorically rejected as an unscientific pseudo-explanation. Like-wise, every mechanistic explanation of social phenomena must be discarded as unscientific. Humans act under conditions of uncertainty. The idea of a social mechanic and equilibrium is useful only insofar as it enables us to grasp what actions are *not*, and in what respect they are fundamentally different and categorically distinct from the operations of machines and automatons.

Second, Rothbard is the latest and most comprehensive system-builder within Austrian economics. Only among rationalists does a constant desire for system and completeness exist. While they contributed much to its foundation, neither Menger nor Böhm-Bawerk accomplished this ultimate intellectual desideratum. This feat was accomplished only by Mises, with the publication of his monumental *Human Action*.[2] "Here at last," Rothbard

---

2. Ludwig von Mises, *Human Action: A Treatise on Economics*, 3rd rev. ed. (Chicago: Contemporary Books, 1949).

wrote about *Human Action*, "was economics *whole* once more, once again an edifice. Not only that—here was a structure of economics with many of the components newly contributed by Professor Mises himself." Since then, only Rothbard has accomplished a similar achievement with the publication of *Man, Economy, and State* and its companion volume *Power and Market*.[3] As it is modeled after Mises's *magnum opus*, and even more comprehensive and complete, what Rothbard stated about Mises and *Human Action* can be said of himself and *Man, Economy, and State*. In fact, no less of an authority than Mises himself did so in reviewing the book for the *New Individualist Review*. Mises hailed Rothbard's treatise

> as an epochal contribution to the general science of human action, praxeology, and its practically most important and up-to-now best elaborated part, economics. Henceforth all essential studies in these branches of knowledge will have to take full account of the theories and criticisms expounded by Dr. Rothbard.[4]

Today Mises's *Human Action* and Rothbard's *Man, Economy, and State* are the two towering and defining achievements of the Austrian school. No one can be considered seriously today, whether as a student of Austrian economics or as its critic, who has not read and studied *Human Action* and *Man, Economy, and State*.

Third, Rothbard is the latest and most systematically political Austrian economist. Just as rationalism implies the desire for system and completeness, so it implies political activism. To rationalists, human beings are above all *rational* animals. Their actions, and the course of human history, are determined by ideas (rather than by blind evolutionary forces of spontaneous evolution and natural selection). Ideas can be true or false, but only true ideas "work" and result in success and progress, while false ideas lead to failure and decline. As the discoverer of true ideas and eradicator of false ones, the scholar assumes a crucial role in human history. Human progress is the result of the discovery of truth and the proliferation of true *ideas*—enlightenment—and is thus entirely in the scholar's hands. The truth is inherently practical, and in recognizing an idea as true (or false), a scholar cannot but want it to be implemented (or eradicated) immediately. For this reason, in addition to pursuing his scholarly ambitions, Menger served as personal tutor to the

---

3. Murray N. Rothbard, *Man, Economy, and State* (Princeton, N.J.: D. Van Nostrand, 1962); idem, *Power and Market* (Menlo Park, Calif.: Institute for Humane Studies, 1970).

4. Ludwig von Mises, "A New Treatise on Economics," *The New Individualist Review* 2, no. 3 (1962): pp. 39–42.

Austrian Crown Prince Rudolf, and as an appointed life-member of the Austrian House of Lords (*Herrenhaus*). Similarly, Böhm-Bawerk served three times as Austrian minister of finance, and was a lifetime member of the *Herrenhaus*. Likewise, Mises was the nationally prominent chief economist of the Vienna Chamber of Commerce and advisor to many prominent figures during Austria's first Republic, and later, in the U.S., he served as advisor to the National Association of Manufacturers and numerous other organizations. Only Mises went even further. Just as he was the first economic system-builder, so was he the first to give the Austrian activism systematic expression by associating Austrian economics with radical-liberal-libertarian-political reform (as laid out in his *Liberalism* of 1927). Only Rothbard, who likewise served in many advisory functions and as founder and academic director of several educational organizations, accomplished something comparable. Proceeding systematically beyond even Mises, Rothbard accomplished—in his *Ethics of Liberty*[5]—to integrate (via the concept of private property) a value-free Austrian economics and libertarian political philosophy (ethics) as two complementary branches of a grand unified social theory, thereby creating a radical—Austro-libertarian—philosophical movement.

In the area of theoretical economics, Rothbard contributed two major advances beyond the standards set by Mises's *Human Action*. First, Rothbard provided systematic clarification of the theory of marginal utility, and then advanced a new reconstruction of welfare economics and, entirely absent in Mises's system, an economic theory of the state.

Building on the foundations of a strictly ordinalist interpretation of marginal utility laid out by Mises as early as 1912 in his *Theory of Money and Credit*,[6] Rothbard explained that the word "marginal" in marginal utility does not refer to increments of utility (which would imply measurability), but rather to the utility of increments of goods (and thus has nothing to do with measurability). The good to which utility is attached, and the increments in its size, can be described in physical terms. The good and its increments extend in space, and thus can be measured and counted as unitary quantitative additions. In distinct contrast, the utility attached to a physical good and its unitary physical increments is a purely intensive magnitude.

---

5. Murray N. Rothbard, *The Ethics of Liberty* (Atlantic Highlands, N.J.: Humanities Press, 1982).

6. Ludwig von Mises, *The Theory of Money and Credit*, trans. by H. E. Batson (Indianapolis, Ind.: Liberty Fund, 1980 [1912]).

It does not extend in space, and hence is immeasurable and intractable by unitary counting and the rules of arithmetic. All attempts to construct a cardinal measure of utility are in vain. *Qua* intensive magnitude, utility can be treated only ordinally; that is, as a rank order on a one-dimensional individual preference scale (and every economic phenomenon, in particular monetary calculation and "objective" cost accounting, must ultimately be reducible to and explained as the simple outcome of ordinal individual rank order judgments). Apart from their placement on one-dimensional individual preference scales, no quantitative relationship between different goods and different quantities of the same good exists. In particular, no such thing as total utility—conceived of as the addition or integration of marginal utilities—exists. Rather, "total" utility is the marginal utility of a larger-sized quantity of a good, and, Rothbard explained,

> [t]here are, then two laws of utility, both following from the apodictic conditions of human action: first, that *given the size of a unit of a good, the (marginal) utility of each unit decreases as the supply of units increases*; second, that *the (marginal) utility of a larger-sized unit is greater than the (marginal) utility of a smaller-sized unit*. The first is the law of diminishing marginal utility. The second has been called the law of increasing total utility. The relationship between the two laws and between the items considered in both is purely one of rank, i.e., ordinal.[7]

Graphically, Rothbard illustrated, the relationship can be represented thus:[8]

Ranks in Value

3 eggs

2 eggs

1 egg

2nd egg

3rd egg

The higher the ranking on this individual value scale for eggs, the higher the value. By the second law, 3 eggs are valued more highly then 2 eggs and 2 eggs more highly than one. By the first law, the 2nd egg will be ranked

---

7. Rothbard, *Man, Economy, and State*, pp. 270–71; emphasis in the original.

8. Murray N. Rothbard, *The Logic of Action*, vol. 1 (Cheltenham, Eng.: Edward Elgar, 1997), p. 222.

below the first on the value scale, and the 3rd below the 2nd. No mathematical relationship exists between, for instance, the marginal utility of 3 eggs and the marginal utility of the 3rd egg except that the former is greater than the latter.

As Lionel Robbins, influenced by Wicksteed and Mises, had first brought home to mainstream economics, from the ordinal character of utility it follows logically that every interpersonal as well as intrapersonal comparison of utility must be regarded as impossible (unscientific), and hence every social welfare proposal involving any such comparison is arbitrary.[9] While mainstream welfare economics was thrown into disarray upon full realization of this conclusion, Rothbard provided a radically new strictly ordinalist reconstruction of welfare economics based on the twin concepts of individual self-ownership and demonstrated preference.[10]

Self-ownership simply means this: every individual owns (controls) his own physical human body. "Man's nature," explained Rothbard, "is a fusion of 'spirit' and matter."[11] Every living human body is appropriated and controlled by a single independent (autonomous) conscious mind and will—a self or ego. Accordingly, as long as it is alive, we refer to a human body as a *persona* (rather than a *corpus*). (Mainstream welfare economics also accepts the concept of self-ownership, even if only implicitly, by virtue of the fact that it speaks of separate *individual* utility maximizers.) The concept of demonstrated preference is implied in that of self-ownership. It simply means "that actual choice reveals, or demonstrates, a man's preferences; that is,

---

9. See Lionel Robbins, *The Nature and Significance of Economic Science* (London: Macmillan, 1932), chap. 6. The impossibility of inter- and intrapersonal utility comparisons does not imply that two individuals or time periods cannot be compared objectively, of course. In fact, every individual can determine objectively whether his quantitative supply of any particular good has increased, decreased, or remained the same. And if his supply of one good has increased (decreased) while the supply of his other goods has remained the same, surely it can be said objectively that this individual is better (worse) off and has attained a higher (lower) rank on his individual value scale. Likewise, every individual participating in a monetary economy can determine objectively whether the monetary value of his assets has increased, decreased, or remained constant.

10. Rothbard's contributions to welfare economics are strewn throughout his entire body of work. They begin with his 1956 essay "Toward a Reconstruction of Utility and Welfare Economics," and reach their completion in 1982 with his *Ethics of Liberty*. See also Hans-Hermann Hoppe, "Book Review of *Man, Economy, and Liberty*," *Review of Austrian Economics* 4 (1990): pp. 257–58; idem, *The Economics and Ethics of Private Property* (Boston: Kluwer Academic Publishers, 1993), pp. 232–33; Jeffrey Herbener, "The Pareto Rule and Welfare Economics," *Review of Austrian Economics* 10, no. 1 (1997): pp. 70–106.

11. Rothbard, *Ethics of Liberty*, p. 31.

that his preferences are deducible from what he has chosen in action."[12] Every action involves a man's purposeful use of his physical body, and thus demonstrates that he values this body as a *good*. Furthermore, in using it in one way rather than another, he simultaneously demonstrates with every action what he considers the most highly valued use of this good at the time of his acting. In accordance with the ordinal character of utility, actions reveal only the *existential fact* of preference orders and ranks. They do not reveal anything about the "differences" or "distances" of ranks or the "intensity" of preference, nor do they ever demonstrate "indifference." Indeed, both "differences" of rank and "indifference," i.e., value-*equality*, presuppose cardinal utility.

Based on the concepts of self-ownership and demonstrated preference, and in accordance with Pareto's strictures concerning the possibility of meaningful ordinalist welfare statements, Rothbard deduced the following set of propositions: If a man uses his body ("labor") to extend his control over (appropriate) other nature-given things (unowned "land"), as he must if only in order to stand, this action demonstrates that such things are also goods for him. Hence, he must have gained in utility by appropriating them. At the same time, his action does not make anyone else worse off, because in appropriating previously unowned resources nothing is taken away from others. Others could have appropriated these resources, too, if they had considered them valuable. Yet, they demonstrably did not do so. Indeed, their failure to appropriate them demonstrates their preference for *not* appropriating them. Hence, they cannot possibly be said to have lost any utility on account of another's appropriation. Proceeding from the basis of acts of original appropriation, any further act, whether of production or consumption, is equally Pareto-superior on demonstrated preference grounds, provided only that it does not affect the physical integrity of the resources appropriated or produced with appropriated means by others. The producer-consumer is better off, while everyone else is left in control of the same quantity of goods as before. As a result, no one can be said to be worse off. Finally, every voluntary exchange of goods proceeding from this basis is a Pareto-superior change as well, because it can only take place if both exchange parties expect to benefit from it, while the supply of goods controlled in action (owned) by others remains unchanged.

---

12. Rothbard, *Logic of Action*, vol. 1, p. 212.

Based on these propositions, Rothbard proceeded to advance an entirely new Austrian theory of the state. While every act of original appropriation, production-consumption, and exchange (the free market) always and necessarily increases social utility, no act of expropriation (the non-consensual unilateral taking of goods from their original appropriator and producer-consumer) can possibly do so. Obviously, this is true of all acts typically considered criminal, such as physical aggression, invasion, robbery, theft, and fraud. While the criminal controls a larger quantity of goods and is thus better off, his victim controls a correspondingly smaller quantity of goods and is made worse off; hence, no criminal act fulfills the Paretian strictures and can ever be said to increase *social* utility. While criminal acts are typically considered illegal and man is permitted to defend himself against them, the same conclusion about utility is true of all acts of government agents: "no act of government whatever can increase social utility."[13] Yet, they are considered legal and one is not permitted to defend oneself against them.

Rothbard's conclusion concerning the rejection of the institution of government on welfare-economic grounds is based on the standard and non-controversial definition of the state

> as that organization which possesses either or both (in actual fact, almost always both) of the following characteristics: (a) it acquires its revenue by physical coercion (taxation); and (b) it achieves a compulsory monopoly of force and of ultimate decision-making power over a given territorial area.[14]

As for its first pillar, it is clear that government agents benefit from acts of taxation; otherwise, they would abstain from them. Just as clearly, the subjects of taxation—the original appropriators—producers of the goods taxed—cannot be said to benefit from such acts; otherwise, they would pay the same quantity of goods voluntarily and no compulsion would be necessary.

Similarly, it is clear that government agents gain in utility by achieving a territorial monopoly of ultimate decision-making (jurisdiction). Most importantly, in doing so the question of whether taxes are justified or not becomes moot and is decided from the outset in favor of government. However, just as clearly, every subject of government's ultimate decision-making power is thereby made worse off. By virtue of his acts of original

---

13. Rothbard, *Logic of Action*, vol. 1, p. 243.
14. Rothbard, *Ethics of Liberty*, p. 171.

appropriation and production, a man demonstrates his preference of exercising exclusive control (jurisdiction) over the appropriated and produced goods. Unless he abandons, sells, or voluntarily surrenders them to someone else (in which case this person would demonstrate *his* preference of gaining exclusive control over them), he cannot possibly be said to have changed this evaluation. If, contrary to his demonstrated preference of *not* giving up his privately appropriated and produced goods, the state attains a territorial monopoly of ultimate decision-making (jurisdiction), this is only possible as the result of an act of expropriation. If the government is the ultimate decision-maker, then by implication no single man has exclusive control over his own appropriated and produced goods. In effect, the state has assumed ownership of all goods appropriated and produced by "its" residents, and has reduced them to the rank of tenants. Whereas the government's range of control is enlarged, every private owner's range of control regarding his own appropriations and products, and their value, is correspondingly reduced. Most importantly, as a tenant no one can exclude the government from access to his privately appropriated and produced goods; that is, everyone is left without means of physical defense *vis-à-vis* possible government intervention or invasion.

Consequently Rothbard concluded, if all government action rests on expropriation, and no expropriation can be said to increase social utility, then welfare economics must call for the abolition of the state. Scores of political philosophers and economists, from Thomas Hobbes to James Buchanan and the modern public-choice economics, have attempted to escape from this conclusion by portraying the state as the outcome of contracts, and hence, a voluntary and welfare-enhancing institution. In reply to such endeavors, Rothbard agreed with Joseph Schumpeter that "the theory which construes taxes on the analogy of club dues or of purchase of services of, say, a doctor only proves how far removed this part of the social sciences is from scientific habits of mind."[15] From Hobbes to Buchanan, statists had tried to overcome the apparent contradiction in the idea of a "voluntary" state equipped with compulsory judicial monopoly and the power to tax by recourse to the intellectual make-shift of "implicit" or "conceptual" agreements, contracts, or constitutions. Rothbard explained that all of these typically tortuous attempts ultimately only lead to the same inescapable conclusion: "implicit" and "conceptual" contracts are the very opposite of contracts, i.e., no

---

15. Rothbard, *Logic of Action*, vol. i, p. 247.

contracts. Hence, it is impossible to derive a welfare-economic justification for the state. No one can possibly—demonstrably—agree to permanently surrender jurisdiction over his person and private property to someone else unless he had sold or otherwise given all of his current possessions away and subsequently committed suicide; likewise no one who is alive, can possibly—demonstrably—enter a contract that permits someone else—his protector—to determine forever unilaterally, without the continued consent of the protected, the tribute that the protected must pay for his protection.

In particular, Rothbard scorned the idea of a "limited" protective state as self-contradictory and incompatible with the promotion of social utility. Limited government always has the inherent tendency to become unlimited (totalitarian) government. Given the principle of government—judicial monopoly and the power to tax—any notion of restraining government power and safeguarding individual life and property is illusory. Under monopolistic auspices, the price of justice and protection will rise and the quality of justice and protection will fall. A tax-funded protection agency is a contradiction in terms—an expropriating property protector—and will lead to more taxes and less protection. Even if a government limited its activities exclusively to the protection of preexisting property rights, the further question of *how much* security to produce would arise. Motivated (like everyone else) by self-interest and the disutility of labor, but with the unique power to tax, a government agent's answer will invariably be the same: to *maximize expenditures* on protection—and almost all of a nation's wealth can conceivably be consumed by the cost of protection—and at the same time to *minimize* the *production* of protection. Moreover, a judicial monopoly will lead to a deterioration in the quality of justice and protection. If one can only appeal to government for justice, justice and protection will be perverted in favor of government, constitutions and supreme courts notwithstanding. Constitutions and supreme courts are government constitutions and courts, and whatever limitations to government action they might contain or find is determined by agents of the very institution under consideration. Predictably, the definition of property and protection will be altered and the range of jurisdiction expanded to the government's advantage.

Instead, in accordance with the "one ethical judgment" that "even the most rigorously *wertfrei* economists have been willing to allow themselves . . . (of feeling) free to recommend any change or process that increases social utility under the Unanimity Rule,"[16] Rothbard reached the same anarchist

---

16. Rothbard, *The Logic of Action*, vol. 1, p. 244.

conclusion as the French-Belgian economist Gustave de Molinari before him: defense, protection, and judicial services

> would therefore have to be supplied by people or firms who (a) gained their revenue voluntarily rather than by coercion, and (b) did not— as the State does—arrogate to themselves a compulsory monopoly of police or judicial protection.... Defense firms would have to be as freely competitive and as noncoercive against noninvaders as are all other suppliers of goods and services on the free market. Defense services, like all other services, would be marketable and marketable only.[17]

Every private property owner would be able to partake of the advantages of the division of labor, and to seek better protection of his property than that afforded by self-defense, through cooperation with other owners and their property. That is, everyone could buy from, sell to, or otherwise contract with anyone else concerning protective and judicial services, and he could at any time unilaterally discontinue any such cooperation with others and fall back on self-reliant defense or change his protective affiliations.

Rothbard's other major advance was in the theory of monopoly and competition. Here too, Rothbard recalled the French tradition of radical laissez-faire economics of Jean-Baptiste Say and his followers (to which Molinari belonged). Rothbard's positive doctrine of competition and monopoly is plain and simple (as a theory should be). Competition is defined as conduct within the framework of the described rules of Pareto-superior action: of original appropriation, production-consumption, and voluntary exchange and contract. More specifically applied to *entrepreneurial* action, competition means the existence of unrestricted "free entry." Every individual is at liberty to employ his own property in any way he sees fit, and to enter any line of production deemed profitable. As long as this free-entry condition is met, Rothbard concluded, all product prices and production costs tend to be minimum prices and minimum costs. In distinct contrast, monopoly and monopolistic competition are defined by the absence of free entry, i.e., as the presence of exclusive privilege. The state, defined as the compulsory territorial monopolist of jurisdiction and protection, is thus the prototype of a monopoly. Every individual—except the agents of the state—is prohibited from using his property for the production of self-defense and justice, and thus from competing with the state. All other monopolies go back to this originary state monopoly of jurisdiction (legislation and regulation) as their

17. Rothbard, *Power and Market*, p. 2.

ultimate source. Every other monopoly involves "a grant of special privilege by the State, reserving a certain area of production to one particular individual or group."[18] Entry into the area is legally restricted to other actual or potential producers, and this restriction is enforced by state police. As long as free entry is restricted or absent, concluded Rothbard, whether in the production of justice and security or that of any other good or service, product prices and production costs will be higher than otherwise, i.e., too high. (Thus, to Rothbard the notion of government anti-monopoly or anti-trust policy was a *contradictio in adjecto*. Competition required instead the abolition of the state's very own territorial monopoly of jurisdiction.)

Moreover, Rothbard refuted every alternative theory as nonsense, non-operational, or false. It is nonsense, for instance, to define a monopolist as someone who has control over his price (a "price-searcher"). Every business-man has perfect control over his price (and no control at all over the quantity bought at that price by consumers). Hence, under this definition, no one exists who is *not* a monopolist. Likewise, is it nonsense to define a monopolist as "the only seller of any given good," for in an objective sense, every seller of every product is always the only seller of his own unique product (brand). Thus, everyone is a monopolist with a one-hundred-percent market share of one's own product. Yet, this circumstance does not affect in the slightest that each entrepreneur must compete at all times with every other entrepreneur for consumer spending, regardless how unique or different one's goods may be. On the other hand, in a subjective sense, no seller of anything can ever be established definitely as a monopolist. According to this interpretation, the term "given good" means "a good as defined by *consumers*." Thus, the determination of whether or not the seller of something is its only seller, or of how large his market-share is, depends on the consumers' definition of what this good is; that is, on their classification of particular *physical objects* into various groups of *homogeneous goods*. Not only can such classifications continually change, but different consumers can classify the same physical objects differently. Hence, in this sense the term monopolist becomes prac-tically useless and non-operational, and all attempts to measure a product's market share must be considered futile.

Finally, Mises's theory of monopoly price is untenable. Mises had argued that

---

18. Rothbard, *Man, Economy, and State*, p. 591.

monopoly is a prerequisite for the emergence of monopoly prices, but it is not the only prerequisite. There is a further condition required, namely a certain shape of the demand curve. The mere existence of monopoly does not mean anything in this regard.... Not every price at which a monopolist sells a monopolized commodity is a monopoly price. Monopoly prices are only prices at which it is more advantageous for the monopolist to restrict the total amount to be sold than to expand its sales to the limit which a competitive market would allow.[19]

As Rothbard explained, this argument is fallacious. First off, it will have to be noted that every restrictive action must, by definition, have a complementary expansionary aspect. The factors of production, which the monopolist releases from employment in some production line A, do not simply disappear. Rather, they must be used otherwise: either for the production of another exchange good B, or for an expansion in the production of the consumer good of leisure for its owner. Thus, even if monopoly prices existed, this would have no negative welfare social-utility implications. From the monopolist's act of not selling, it follows that he must believe himself to be better off keeping rather than selling his goods, and no one else is made worse off because of his act (because everyone else still controls the same quantity of goods as before). Consequently, Mises's monopoly price and the shape of the demand curve facing a monopolist cannot be operationally or conceptually distinguished from any other price and demand curve facing any other seller.

Production, explained Rothbard, *precedes* the sale of final products, and production costs must be incurred *before* consumers can demonstrate their preference for one's products. Hence, it is nonsense, for instance, to define a monopoly price as a price above marginal cost (or of marginal revenue higher than marginal cost) because the cost curves on the one hand and the demand and revenue curves on the other do not exist simultaneously.

The only curves that exist simultaneously with cost curves are entre-preneurially estimated *future* demand and revenue curves. However, in deciding on the quantity of goods to be produced, every producer will always set his output so as to maximize his expected money earnings, *ceteris paribus*. That is, in the monetary calculations leading to his output-decision, expected

---

19. Mises, *Human Action*, p. 359.

price and marginal revenue are never *equal* to marginal cost. No one will produce anything unless he expects its price to *exceed* its cost; and no one will expand his output, unless he expects marginal revenue to be *higher* than marginal cost. Thus, every entrepreneur assumes in his calculations that in the future he will be facing a downward sloping demand curve, with elastic and inelastic stretches. Likewise, at the subsequent point of sale, when all costs have been incurred by the producer and the only relevant demand is that of consumers for existing stocks of produced products, every entrepreneur will assume a downward sloping demand curve. That is, every entrepreneur will set his price at such a height that any price higher than the actually chosen one will encounter an elastic demand, and thus lead to lower sales revenues.

If the actually chosen sale price coincides with the original estimation, and if the market clears at this price, the entrepreneurial forecast has been correct. On the other hand, the actual demand can differ from the initial projection, and one or another type of entrepreneurial forecasting error may be revealed. At the point of sale, the entrepreneur can come to the conclusion that he mistakenly produced either "too little" or "too much." In the first case, actual demand (prices and revenue) is higher than expected yet profits could have been still greater if production had been further expanded. The entrepreneur originally estimated demand beyond a specific output-point to be inelastic (such that a larger output would lead to lower total revenue), while it is now revealed as being elastic beyond this point. In the second case, the actual demand (prices and revenue) is lower than expected. Losses could have been avoided if less had been produced. The entrepreneur estimated demand beyond a certain output-point to be elastic, such that a larger quantity could be sold for a higher total revenue, while it is now revealed as inelastic.

In any case, whether or not his original forecast was correct, every entrepreneur must subsequently make a new output decision. Under the assumption that they regard their past experience (present demand) as indicative of their future experience (demand), three possible decisions exist. Entrepreneurs whose initial forecasts had been correct will produce the same quantity as before. Entrepreneurs who had initially produced "too little" will now produce a larger quantity, and entrepreneurs who had previously produced "too much" will restrict current sales and future production. How, asked Rothbard, can this latter entrepreneurial response to earlier overproduction be distinguished from Mises's alleged "monopoly price" situation? He answered that in fact it could not.

Is the higher price to be gained from such a cutback necessarily a "monopoly price"? Why could it not just as well be a movement from a *subcompetitive* price to a competitive price? In the real world, a demand curve is not simply "given" to a producer, but must be estimated and discovered. If a producer has produced too much in one period and, in order to earn more income, produces less in the next period, *this is all that can be said about the action.* ...Thus, we cannot use "restriction of production" as the test of monopoly vs. competitive price. A movement from a subcompetitive to a competitive price also involves a "restriction" of production of this good, coupled, of course, with an expansion of production in other lines by the released factors. *There is no way whatever to distinguish such a "restriction" and corollary expansion from the alleged "monopoly price" situation....* But if a concept has no possible grounding in reality, then it is an empty and illusory, and not a meaningful, concept. On the free market, there is no way of distinguishing a "monopoly price" from a "competitive price" or a "subcompetitive price" or of establishing any changes as movements from one to the other. No criteria can be found for making such distinctions. The concept of monopoly price as distinguished from competitive price is therefore untenable. We can only speak of the *free-market price.*[20]

In addition to these major innovations, Rothbard contributed many new theoretical insights. Two examples will have to suffice here. For one, Rothbard utilized the well-known Misesian argument concerning the impossibility of economic calculation (cost-accounting) under socialism in order to demonstrate, even more generally, the impossibility of one big cartel on the free market.[21]

[T]he free market placed definite limits on the size of the firm, i.e., the limits of *calculability* on the market. In order to calculate the profits and losses of each branch, a firm must be able to refer its internal operations to *external markets* for *each* of the various factors and intermediate products. When any of these external markets disappear, because all are absorbed *within* the province of a single firm, calculability disappears, and there is no way for the firm rationally to allocate factors to that specific area. The more these limits are encroached upon, the greater and greater will be the sphere

---

20. Rothbard, *Man, Economy, and State*, pp. 607, 614, emphasis in the original.
21. *Id.*, pp. 544–50.

of irrationality, and the more difficult it will be to avoid losses. One big cartel would not be able rationally to allocate producers' goods at all and hence could not avoid severe losses. Consequently, it could never really be established, and, if tried, would quickly break asunder.[22]

The second example, likewise inspired by Mises, is from the area of monetary theory. Mises, stimulated in turn by Menger's work, had demonstrated that money *qua* medium of exchange must originate as a *commodity* money (such as gold). Rothbard complemented Mises's theory of the origin of money—his famous "regression theorem"—with a theory of the destruction or devolution of money by government, or what might be termed a "progression theorem." He demonstrated, most succinctly in his *What Has Government Done to Our Money?*,[23] the praxeologically necessary sequence of actions taken by government in order to achieve—as its ultimate goal—complete money counterfeiting autonomy. Having of necessity to begin with a market-provided commodity money such as gold, a government will first monopolize the minting; next, it will monopolize the issue of money substitutes (titles to money, ready redeemable bank notes); subsequently, it will engage in fractional reserve banking and issue money substitutes in excess of actual money; and finally, as the inevitable result of the bank crisis (bank run) brought about by fractional reserve banking, it will suspend the redeemability of its notes, cut the tie between paper (title) and money (gold), confiscate all privately owned money, and institute a pure fiat money.

Yet, Rothbard's achievements go far beyond his innovations in economic theory. They go far beyond even his accomplishment of integrating these innovations into a grand, comprehensive and unified system of Austrian economics. Although an economist by profession, Rothbard's work encompasses also political philosophy (ethics) and history. Unlike the utilitarian Mises, who denied the possibility of rational ethics, Rothbard recognized the need for an ethical system to complement value-free economics so as to make the case for the free market truly watertight. Drawing on the theory of natural rights, in particular on the work of John Locke, and on the genuinely American tradition of anarchistic thought of Lysander Spooner and Benjamin Tucker, Rothbard developed a system of ethics based on the principles of

---

22. Rothbard, *Man, Economy, and State*, p. 585.
23. Murray N. Rothbard, *What Has Government Done to Our Money?* (Auburn, Ala.: Ludwig von Mises Institute, 1990).

self-ownership and the original appropriation of un-owned natural resources through homesteading. Any other proposal, he demonstrated, either does not qualify as an ethical system applicable to everyone *qua* human being, or it is not viable, for following it would literally imply death while it requires a surviving proponent, and thus leads to performative contradictions. The former is the case with all proposals which imply granting A ownership over B and resources homesteaded by B, but not giving B the same right with respect to A. The latter is the case with all proposals advocating universal (communal) co-ownership of everyone and everything by all, for then no one would be allowed to do anything with anything before he had everyone else's consent to do whatever he wanted to do. And how could anyone consent to anything if he were not the exclusive (private) owner of his body? In *The Ethics of Liberty*, his second *magnum opus*, Rothbard deduced the entire corpus of liberal-libertarian law—from the law of contracts to the theory of punishment—from these first axiomatic principles; and in his *For A New Liberty*,[24] he applied this ethical system to a diagnosis of the present age and the proposal, and economic analysis, of the political reforms necessary to achieve a free and prosperous commonwealth.

Furthermore, although first and foremost a theoretician, Rothbard was also an accomplished historian, and his writing contains a wealth of empirical information rarely matched by any empiricist or historicist. In fact, it is Rothbard's recognition of economics and political philosophy (ethics) as pure aprioristic theory, and of theoretical reasoning as logically anteceding and constraining every historical investigation, which makes his empirical scholarship superior to that of most orthodox historians, and has established him as one of the outstanding "revisionist" historians. Particularly noteworthy in the area of economic history is his book *America's Great Depression*,[25] which applies the Mises-Hayek business cycle theory to explain the 1929 stock market crash and the ensuing economic depression. In political history, it is his four-volume history of colonial America, *Conceived in Liberty*,[26] and in the field of intellectual history it is his posthumously published monumental if uncompleted two-volume history of economic,

---

24. Murray N. Rothbard, *For A New Liberty* (New York: Macmillan, 1973).

25. Murray N. Rothbard, *America's Great Depression* (New York: Richardson and Snyder, 1983).

26. Murray N. Rothbard, *Conceived in Liberty*, 4 vols. (New Rochelle, N.Y.: Arlington House, 1975).

social, and political thought, *Economic Thought Before Adam Smith* and *Classical Economics*.[27] In these and other books and countless articles, Rothbard provided integrated economic-sociological-political analyses of almost every critical episode in American history: from the panic of 1819, the Jacksonian period, the War for Southern Independence, the Progressive era, World War I and Wilsonianism, Hoover, FDR and World War II, to Reagonomics and Clintonianism. With an eye for the minutest detail of history's byways, time and again Rothbard challenged common wisdom and historical orthodoxy and provided his readers with a vision of the process of history as a permanent struggle of good against evil: between truth and falsehood, and between forces of liberty and power elites exploiting and enriching themselves at the expense of others and covering their tracks through lies and deceptions.

These amazing scholarly achievements notwithstanding, Rothbard's academic career, much like Mises's, was hardly a success by conventional standards. The twentieth century has been the age of socialism and interventionism. Schools and universities are government-funded and government-controlled institutions; hence, the most eminent appointments go either to socialists or interventionists, while "intransigent," "dogmatic," or "extremist" proponents of laissez-faire capitalism are excluded or relegated to the fringes of academia. Rothbard had no illusions in this regard, and never complained or appeared to be bitter about his academic fate. His influence did not rest on institutional powers, but solely on the power of his ideas and the force of logic.

Murray Rothbard was born and raised in New York City as the only child of immigrant parents. His father, a chemist, came from Poland and his mother from Russia. Upon winning a scholarship, Rothbard attended private schools and went on to study economics at Columbia University, where, in 1956, he received his Ph.D. with a dissertation written under the economic historian Joseph Dorfman. For more than a decade beginning in 1949, Rothbard also participated in Mises's private seminar at New York University. After working several years for various foundations, most notably the William Volker Fund, Rothbard taught at the Brooklyn Polytechnic Institute, an engineering school, from 1966 until 1986. From 1986 until his death, he was the S. J. Hall Distinguished Professor of Economics at the University

---

27. Murray N. Rothbard, *An Austrian Perspective on the History of Economic Thought*, 2 vols. (Cheltenham, Eng.: Edward Elgar, 1995).

of Nevada, Las Vegas. As one of two economics professors at Brooklyn Polytechnic, Rothbard was member of a social science department, which fulfilled only a subservient function within the university. In Las Vegas, the department of economics, housed in the university's Business College, did not offer a doctoral program. Thus, throughout his academic career Rothbard was prevented from claiming a single doctoral student as his own.

Rothbard's fringe existence in academia did not prevent him from exerting intellectual influence or attracting students and disciples, however. Through the sheer flood of his publications and the unrivaled clarity of his writing, modeled after that of H. L. Mencken, Rothbard became the creator and one of the principal agents of the contemporary libertarian movement, which in the course of three decades has grown from a handful of proponents into a genuine mass movement (including but extending far beyond a party of this name, the Libertarian Party, to a wide and complex network of groups and associations on into the U.S. Congress and many state legislatures). Naturally, in the course of this development, Rothbard and his theoretical position did not remain unchallenged or undisputed. There were ups and downs in institutional alignments, coalitions, breaks, and realignments in his career. However, in association with the Center for Libertarian Studies, under Burton S. Blumert, and the Ludwig von Mises Institute, under Llewellyn Rockwell, and as founder-editor of their scholarly flagships, the *Journal of Libertarian Studies* (1977) and the *Review of Austrian Economics* (1987),[28] Rothbard has remained beyond his death without doubt the most important and highly respected intellectual authority within the entire libertarian movement, and to this day his rationalist-axiomatic-deductive-Austro-libertarianism provides the intellectual benchmark in reference to which not only everyone and everything *within* libertarianism is defined, but increasingly everyone and everything in American politics.

---

28. In 1998 the journal that Rothbard founded became the *Quarterly Journal of Austrian Economics*, published by Transaction Publishers.

20

Hayek on Government and Social Evolution

"As much market as possible, as much state as necessary."
—Motto of the 1959 Godesberg-program of
Germany's Social-democratic Party

I. THESIS ONE

Friedrich A. Hayek is generally known as a champion of the free market economy and an outspoken anti-socialist; indeed, Hayek's life was a noble, and mostly lonely struggle against a rising tide of statism and statist ideologies. These facts not withstanding, however:

(1) Hayek's view regarding the role of market and state cannot systematically be distinguished from that of a modern social democrat; and

(2) the immediate reason for Hayek's social democratic views is his contradictory, and hence nonsensical, definition of "freedom" and "coercion." (Another, fundamental epistemological reason—Hayek's self-contradictory anti-rationalism—will be addressed in Thesis Two.)[1]

• Originally published in *The Review of Austrian Economics* 7, no. 1 (1994).

1. The following essay does *not* consider Hayek's achievements as an economist. As regards these, Hayek deserves great praise. But Hayek's economics is largely the one he adopted from his teacher and mentor Ludwig von Mises and thus is not original with him. What makes Hayek unique, and what fundamentally distinguishes him from Mises, is his political and social philosophy. It is this part of his work, not his contribution to economic theory, that has made Hayek famous. Unfortunately, as will be demonstrated in the following, this *original* part of Hayek's work is entirely false, however.

II. ON GOVERNMENT

According to Hayek, government is "necessary" to fulfill the following tasks (and may acquire the means necessary to do so through taxation)[2]: Not merely for "law enforcement" and "defense against external enemies," but "in an advanced society government ought to use its power of raising funds by taxation to provide a number of services which for various reasons cannot be provided, or cannot be provided adequately, by the market."[3] (Since at all times an infinite number of goods and services which a market does *not* provide exist, Hayek hands government a blank check.) Among these are "protection against violence, epidemics, or such natural forces as floods and avalanches, but also many of the amenities which make life in modern cities tolerable, most roads ... the provision of standards of measure, and of many kinds of information ranging from land registers, maps and statistics to the certification of the quality of some goods or services offered in the market."[4] Additional government functions are "the assurance of a certain minimum income for everyone"[5]; government should "distribute its expenditure over time in such a manner that it will step in when private investment flags"[6]; it should finance schools and research as well as enforce "building regulations, pure food laws, the certification of certain professions, the restrictions on the sale of certain dangerous goods (such as arms, explosives, poisons and drugs), as well as some safety and health regulations for the processes of production and the provision of such public institutions as theaters, sports grounds, etc. ... "[7]; and it should make use of the power of "eminent domain" to enhance the "public good."[8]

---

2. See on the following in particular *The Constitution of Liberty* (Chicago: University of Chicago Press, 1960), chap. 15 and part 3; *Law, Legislation, and Liberty*, 3 vols. (Chicago: University of Chicago Press, 1973–79), chap. 14.

3. *Law, Legislation, and Liberty*, vol. 3, p. 41. Compare this to John Maynard Keynes's statement: "The most important Agenda of the state relate not to those activities which private individuals are already fulfilling but to those functions which fall outside the sphere of individuals, to those decisions which are made by *no one* if the state does not make them. The important thing for government is not to do things which individuals are doing already and to do them a little better or a little worse: but to do those things which are not done at all." (*The End of Laissez Faire*, vol. 9, *Collected Writings*, London: MacMillan, 1973, p. 291)

4. *Law, Legislation, and Liberty*, vol. 3, p. 44.

5. *Id.*, p. 55.

6. *Id.*, p. 59.

7. *Id.*, p. 62.

8. *Id.*, pp. 62–63.

Moreover, it generally holds that "there is some reason to believe that with the increase in general wealth and of the density of population, the share of all needs that can be satisfied only by collective action will continue to grow."[9]

In the *Constitution of Liberty*, Hayek wanted government to provide further for "monetary stability" (while he later on preferred a bizarre scheme for monetary denationalization)[10]; government should implement an extensive system of compulsory insurance ("coercion intended to forestall greater coercion")[11]; public, subsidized housing was a possible government task[12]; likewise, "city planning" and "zoning" were considered appropriate government functions provided that "the sum of the gains must exceed the sum of the losses"[13]; and lastly "the provision of amenities of or opportunities for recreation, or the preservation of natural beauty or of historical sites or places of scientific interest, ... natural parks, nature-reservations, etc.," were regarded as government tasks.[14]

Moreover, Hayek insists we recognize that it is irrelevant how big government is or if and how fast it grows. What alone is important is that government actions fulfill certain formal requirements. "It is the character rather than the volume of government activity that is important."[15] Taxes as such and the absolute height of taxation are not a problem for Hayek. Taxes—and likewise compulsory military service—lose their character as coercive measures,

> if they are at least predictable and are enforced irrespective of how the individual would otherwise employ his energies; this deprives them largely of the evil nature of coercion. If the known necessity of paying a certain amount in taxes becomes the basis of all my plans, if a period of military service is a foreseeable part of my career, then I can follow a general plan of life of my own making and am as independent of the will of another person as men have learned to be in society.[16]

But please, it must be a *proportional* tax and *general* military service!

---

9. *Id.*, p. 53.

10. F. A. Hayek, *Denationalization of Money: The Argument Refined* (London: Institute of Economics Affairs, 1990).

11. *Constitution of Liberty*, p. 286.

12. *Id.*, p. 346.

13. *Id.*, p. 351. What about Hayek's repeated pronouncements, *qua* economist, that all interpersonal comparisons of utility are scientifically invalid?

14. *Id.*, p. 375.   15. *Id.*, p. 222.   16. *Id.*, p. 143.

In light of this terminological hocus-pocus and the above cited list of legitimate government functions, the difference between Hayek and a modern social democrat boils down to the question whether or not the postal service should be privatized (Hayek says yes).

III. On Freedom and Coercion

The last quote in support of the previous thesis is at the same time confirmation of the thesis that Hayek's social-democratic theory of government finds its explanation in the absurdity of his definition of freedom and coercion.[17]

Hayek defines freedom as the absence of coercion. However, contrary to a long tradition of classical liberal thought, he does *not* define coercion as the initiation or the threat of physical violence against another person or its legitimately—via original appropriation, production or exchange—acquired property. Instead, he offers a definition whose only merit is its fogginess. By coercion "we mean such control of the environment or circumstances of a person by another that, in order to avoid greater evil, he is forced to act not according to a coherent plan of his own but to serve the ends of another,"[18] or "coercion occurs when one man's actions are made to serve another man's will, not for his own but for the other's purpose."[19] Freedom, by contrast, is "a state in which each can use his own *knowledge* [not: his own *property*] for his own purposes."[20]

This definition does not contain anything regarding actions, scarce goods and property. Rather, "coercion" refers to a specific configuration of subjective wills (or plans, thoughts and expectations). Yet then it is useless for the following reason. First, it is useless as a guideline for actions (what am I allowed to do here and now if I do not want to commit a coercive act?), because in general I do not know the will or plans of others and in any case, to know all other wills completely would be impossible. Even if I wanted to, I could never be sure from the outset (*ex ante*) that what I was planning to

---

17. See on the following Ronald Hamowy, "Freedom and the Rule of Law in F. A. Hayek," *Il Politico* (1970–71); idem, "Hayek's Concept of Freedom: A Critique," *New Individualist Review* (April 1961); idem, "Law and the Liberal Society: F. A. Hayek's Constitution of Liberty," *Journal of Libertarian Studies* 2 (Winter 1978); Murray N. Rothbard, "F. A. Hayek and the Concept of Coercion," in idem, *The Ethics of Liberty* (Atlantic Highlands: Humanities Press, 1981).

18. *Constitution of Liberty*, pp. 20–21.

19. *Id.*, p. 133.

20. *Law, Legislation, and Liberty*, vol. 1, pp. 55–56.

do would not coerce anyone. Yet individuals obviously must be permitted to act "correctly" *prior* to knowing anything about the plans of others, and even if they knew literally nothing but their own plans. For this to be possible, however, the criterion employed to distinguish between "freedom" and "coercion" must be an *objective* one. It must refer to an event/non-event that possesses a *physical* description (and over whose outcome an actor must possess physical control). Second, Hayek's definition is also useless as a retrospective (*ex post*) criterion of justice (is the accusation of A against B justified; who is guilty and who isn't?). As long as A and B come to the *same* conclusion concerning innocence and guilt (including such questions as compensation and/or punishment), no problem arises for Hayek's criterion. However, in the case of unanimity *no* criterion can ever fail. Hayek's criterion fails miserably in those cases, though, for which it is intended: whenever plaintiff and defendant do *not* agree, and still a verdict must be reached. Since Hayek's definition does not contain any physical (inter-subjectively ascertainable) criteria, his judgments are arbitrary. As mental predicates, Hayek's categories of freedom and coercion are compatible with every real, physical state of affairs. They possess no power to make *real* distinctions.

Correspondingly confused and contradictory are Hayek's attempts to apply his definitions:

1. In applying his definition, Hayek on the one hand reaches the conclusion that the initiation and threat of physical violence constitutes "coercion." "The threat of force or violence is the most important form of coercion."[21] "True coercion occurs when armed bands of conquerors make the subject people toil for them, when organized gangsters extort a levy for 'protection'."[22] On the other hand (witness the quotations above) he classifies acts of the initiation or threat of physical violence such as compulsory military service or taxes as "non-coercive," provided only that the victims of such aggression could have reliably expected and adjusted to it.

2. On the one hand, Hayek identifies physical violence with "coercion." On the other hand, he does not accept the *absence* of physical violence or damage as a criterion for "non-coercion." "The threat of physical force is not the only way in which coercion can be exercised."[23] Even if A has committed no physical aggression against B or his property, he may nonetheless be guilty of "coercion." According to Hayek, this is the case whenever A is guilty of *omitted help vis-à-vis* B, i.e., whenever he has *not* provided B with

---

21. *Constitution of Liberty*, p. 135.   22. *Id.*, p. 137.   23. *Id.*, p. 135.

goods or services of his (A's), which B had expected from him and regarded as "crucial to my existence or preservation of what I most value."[24] Hayek asserts that only a small number of cases actually fit this criterion: The owner of a mine in a mining town who decides to dis-employ a worker allegedly "coerces"; and likewise it is supposedly "coercive" if the owner of the sole water supply in a desert is unwilling to sell this water, or if he refuses to sell it at a price which others deem "fair." But it requires little imagination to recognize that Hayek's criterion is in fact all-encompassing. Any peaceful action a person may perform can be interpreted by others—and indeed any number of them—as constituting "coercion," for every activity is at the same time always the omission of innumerable other *possible* actions, and every omission becomes "coercion" if a single person claims that the execution of the omission was "crucial to the preservation of what I most value."

Whenever cases of omitted help and physical violence are categorically identified as "coercion," however, inescapable contradictions result. [25] If A's omission constitutes "coercion" toward B, then B must possess the right to "defend" himself against A. B's only "defense" would be that he could employ physical violence *against A* (to make A execute what he otherwise would avoid doing)—but then acts of physical violence could no longer be classified as "coercion"! Physical violence would be "defense." In this case, "coercion" would be the peaceful refusal to engage in an exchange as well as the attempt to defend oneself against all forced (under the threat of violence executed) exchange. On the other hand, if physical violence were defined as "coercion," then B would *not* be allowed to "defend" himself against an omissive A; and if B nonetheless attempted to do so, then the right to defense would rest with A—but in this case, omissions could not constitute "coercion."

3. From these conceptual confusions stems Hayek's absurd thesis of "the unavoidability of coercion" and his corresponding, equally absurd "justification" of government. "Coercion, however, cannot be altogether avoided because the only way to prevent it is by the threat of coercion. Free society has met this problem by conferring the monopoly of coercion on

---

24. *Constitution of Liberty*, p. 136.

25. See also Murray N. Rothbard, *Power and Market* (Kansas City: Sheed Andrews and McMeel, 1977), pp. 228–34; Hans-Hermann Hoppe, "Von der Strafunwürdigkeit unterlassener Hilfeleistung," in idem, *Eigentum, Anarchie und Staat* (Opladen: Westdeutscher Verlag, 1977); idem, "On the Indefensibility of Welfare Rights," *Austrian Economics Newsletter* 3 (1989).

the state and by attempting to limit this power of the state to instances where it is required to prevent coercion by private persons."[26] According to both of Hayek's definitions of "coercion," this thesis is nonsensical. If omitted help represents "coercion," then coercion in the sense of physical violence becomes necessary (not: unavoidable). Otherwise, if the initiation and threat of physical violence is defined as "coercion," it can be avoided; first, because each person possesses control over whether or not he will physically attack another; and second, because every person is entitled to defend himself with all of his means against another's physical attack. It is only unavoidable that so long as physical aggression exists, there will also be a need for physical defense. Yet the unavoidability of defensive violence has nothing to do with the alleged "unavoidability of coercion" (unless one confused the categorical difference between attack and defense and asserted that the threat of defending oneself in the event of an attack is the same kind of thing as the threat of attacking). If physical violence is *forbidden*, then it follows that one is *allowed to defend* oneself against it. It is thus absurd to classify attack and defense under the same rubric of "coercion." Defense is to coercion as day is to night.

Yet from the unavoidability of *defense* no justification for a government monopoly of coercion follows. To the contrary. A government is by no means merely a "monopolist of defense" who helps private individuals avoid otherwise "unavoidable" defense expenditures (as a monopolist: inefficiently). Because it could otherwise provide no defense activities, the government's monopoly of coercion includes in particular the *right* of the state to commit violence against private citizens and their complementary *obligation* not to defend themselves against government attacks. But what kind of justification for a government is this: that if a person surrenders unconditionally to an attacker he may save himself otherwise "unavoidable" defense expenditures?

IV. Thesis Two

The fundamental epistemological reason for Hayek's nonsensical theory of government and coercion is to be found in Hayek's systematic anti-rationalism.

(1) This anti-rationalism expresses itself first in the fact that Hayek rejects the idea of a cognitive ethic. Hayek is an ethical relativist (who, as

---

26. *Constitution of Liberty*, p. 21; also *id*., p. 141 f.

already shown, does not even consider an unambiguous moral distinction between attack and defense to be possible).

(2) Second—in an even more dramatic fashion—Hayek's anti-rationalism is expressed in his "theory of social evolution," where purposeful action and self-interest, trial, error and learning, force and freedom as well as state and market (society) have been systematically eliminated as explanatory factors of social change and replaced with an obscure "spontaneity" and a collectivistic-holistic-organizistic principle of "cultural group selection." (Hayek's citation of Carl Menger as precursor of his own theory is false. Menger would have ridiculed Hayek's theory of evolution as mysticism. Menger's successor is not Hayek, but Ludwig von Mises and his "social rationalism."[27])

V. On Ethics

"Moreover, if civilization has resulted from unwanted gradual changes in morality, then, reluctant as we may be to accept this, no universally valid system of ethics can ever be known to us."[28] Furthermore, "Evolution cannot be just.... Indeed, to insist that all future change to be just would be to demand that evolution come to a halt. Evolution leads us ahead precisely in bringing about much that we could not intend or foresee, let alone prejudge for its moral properties."[29] Or: "To pretend to know the desirable direction of progress seems to me to be the extreme of hubris. Guided progress would not be progress."[30] (So much for the question whether or not Hayek can give any advice to the former communist countries of Eastern Europe: he suggests nothing but banking on "spontaneous evolution.")

It is characteristic of Hayek's anti-rationalism that he does not prove this counterintuitive thesis, as is necessary. Indeed, he does not even attempt to make it plausible.

---

27. The documentation of this parenthetical thesis will be kept to a minimum and relegated to footnotes.

On the fundamental difference between Menger and Mises, on the one hand, and Hayek, on the other, see Joseph T. Salerno, "Ludwig von Mises as Social Rationalist," *Review of Austrian Economics* 4 (1990): pp. 26–54; Jeffrey M. Herbener, "Ludwig von Mises and the Austrian School of Economics," *Review of Austrian Economics* 5, no. 2 (1991): pp. 33–50; Murray N. Rothbard, "The Present State of Austrian Economics," Working Paper (Auburn, Ala.: Ludwig von Mises Institute, 1992).

28. F. A. Hayek, *The Fatal Conceit: The Errors of Socialism*, ed. by W. W. Bartley III (Chicago: University of Chicago Press, 1988), p. 20.

29. *Id.*, p. 74.   30. *Law, Legislation, and Liberty*, vol. 3, p. 169.

It is the same anti-rationalism that leads Hayek to state—often merely a few pages apart—something seemingly completely different (logical consistency is not a necessary requirement for an anti-rationalist). For instance, "Where there is no property there is no justice."[31] And John Locke is quoted approvingly with a passage which could not possibly be more rationalist:

> "Where there is no property there is no justice," is a proposition as certain as any demonstration in Euclid: for the idea of property being a right to anything, and the idea to which the name injustice is given being the invasion or violation of that right; it is evident that these ideas being thus established, and these names annexed to them, I can as certainly know this proposition to be true as that a triangle has three angles equal to two right ones.[32]

Lastly, it is characteristic of Hayek when only one page later, while one is still wondering how to square the Lockean idea of an Euclidean ethic with the thesis of the "impossibility" of an universally valid ethic, Hayek returns, in a sudden dialectic twist to his relativistic point of departure. "The institutions of property, as they exist at present, are hardly perfect; indeed, we can hardly yet say in what such perfection might consist."[33] "Traditional concepts of property rights have in recent times been recognized as a modifiable and very complex bundle whose most effective combinations have not yet been discovered in all areas."[34] In particular the investigations of the Chicago school (Coase, Demsetz, Becker and others) "have opened new possibilities for future improvements in the legal framework of the market order."[35]

Hayek does not think it worth mentioning or he does not recognize, that the property theories of Locke and the Chicago school are incompatible. According to Locke, the principles of self-ownership, original appropriation (homesteading), production and voluntary exchange are universally valid ethical norms. Locke's theory of private property is a theory of justice, and Locke is an ethical absolutist. In contrast, the representatives of the Chicago school deny the possibility of a rational, universally valid ethic. There exists no justice in Chicago. Who owns what and who does not, and likewise who is the attacker and who the victim, is for Coase and colleagues not once and for all fixed and settled and does not depend on who has done what in the past. Instead, property titles are to be distributed among people, and with changing circumstances redistributed, in such a way that future economic

---

31. *Fatal Conceit*, p. 33; see also the *Constitution of Liberty*, p. 140.
32. *Fatal Conceit*, p. 34.   33. *Id.*, p. 35.   34. *Id.*, p. 36.   35. *Id.*

efficiency is maximized. The person who is expected to make the most efficient use of a resource—as "measured" in terms of money—becomes its owner; he who will have to bear the lower monetary costs if he were to avoid the disputed activity is declared the attacker in a property-rights dispute; and whenever in the course of time the roles of the most efficient user or the "least cost avoider" change from one person to another, property titles must be accordingly redistributed.[36]

VI. On Social Evolution

The mystic-collectivistic character of Hayek's theory of spontaneous social evolution comes to light in passages such as these:

1. "In the process of cultural transmission, in which modes of conduct are passed on from generation to generation, a process of selection takes place, in which those modes of conduct prevail which lead to the formation of a more efficient order for the whole group, because such groups will prevail over others."[37]

2. "In so far as such rules have prevailed because the group that adopted them was more successful, nobody need ever have known why that group was successful and why in consequence its rules became generally adopted."[38]

3. "Culture ... is a tradition of learnt rules of conduct which have never been 'invented' and whose function the acting individuals usually do not understand ... , the result of a process of winnowing and sifting, directed by the differential advantages gained by groups from practices adopted for some unknown and perhaps purely accidental reasons."[39] "Man did not adopt new rules of conduct because he was intelligent. He became intelligent by submitting to new rules of conduct."[40] "We have never designed our economic system. We were not intelligent enough for that. We have tumbled into it and it has carried us to unforeseen heights and given rise to ambitions which may yet lead us to destroy it."[41]

---

36. See Ronald Coase, *The Firm, the Market, and the Law* (Chicago: University of Chicago Press, 1988); Harold Demsetz, *Ownership, Control, and the Firm* (Oxford: Blackwell, 1988); for a critique see Walter Block, "Coase and Demsetz on Private Property Rights," *Journal of Libertarian Studies* 1, no. 2 (Spring 1977).

37. F. A. Hayek, *New Studies in Philosophy, Politics, Economics and the History of Ideas* (Chicago: University of Chicago Press, 1978), p. 9.

38. *Law, Legislation, and Liberty*, vol. 2, p. 5.

39. *Law, Legislation, and Liberty*, vol. 3, p. 155.   40. *Id.*, p. 163.   41. *Id.*, p. 164.

4. Civilization "resulted not from human design or intention but spontaneously: it arose from unintentionally conforming to certain traditional and largely moral practices, many of which men tend to dislike, whose significance they usually fail to understand, whose validity they cannot prove, and which have nonetheless fairly rapidly spread by means of an evolutionary selection—the comparative increase of population and wealth—of those groups that happened to follow them."[42] "Moral traditions outstrip the capacities of reason."[43] "Mind is not a guide but a product of cultural evolution, and is based more on imitation than on insight or reason."[44]

Hayek's theory, then, consists of these three propositions:

(1) A person initially performs a spontaneous action without knowing why and for what purpose; and a person retains this practice for no reason—whether or not it has resulted in a success (for without purpose and goal there *can* be no success and no failure). (Cultural mutation.)

(2) The new practice is imitated by other group members—again without any motive or reason. The proliferation of the practice comes to a halt once all group members have adopted it. (Cultural transmission.)

(3) Members of other groups do *not* imitate the practice. Those groups which spontaneously adopt and unconsciously imitate a *better* moral practice will exhibit a comparatively higher population growth, greater wealth, or otherwise somehow "prevail." (Cultural selection.)

Hayek claims that this theory explains the evolution of private property, of the division of labor and of exchange, as well as of money and government. In fact, however, these practices and institutions provide perfect examples for demonstrating the theory's entire absurdity (such that Hayek cannot help but contradict his own theory over and over again).[45]

VII. CULTURAL MUTATION

Hayek's theory of spontaneity may apply to vegetables (although it would even run into difficulties here because of Hayek's explicitly assumed "Lamarckism"[46]), but it is definitely not applicable to human actors. Every

---

42. *Fatal Conceit*, p. 6.   43. *Id.*, p. 10.   44. *Id.*, p. 21.

45. See on the following also David Ramsey Steele, "Hayek's Theory of Cultural Group Selection," *Journal of Libertarian Studies* 8, no. 2 (1987).

46. See *The Fatal Conceit*, p. 25.

action involves the purposeful employment of scarce means, and every actor can always distinguish between a successful and an unsuccessful action. The concept of an unconscious-spontaneous action à la Hayek is a *contradictio in adjecto.* Acting is always conscious and rational. Hence Hayek's theory leads to an inescapable dilemma: If one applies Hayek's theory to itself, then his own activity of writing books is nothing but a purposeless emanation regarding which the questions of true or false and of success or failure simply do not arise. Or Hayek's writing represents a purposeful action. In this case his theory is obviously false, however, because in enlightening himself (and us) regarding the course of social evolution, Hayek no longer acts spontaneously but instead tries to shape social change consciously and rationally.

Regarding in particular the problem of the origin of private property; it is only necessary to insert into proposition (1) practices such as the original appropriation of a previously un-owned good or the production of a capital good to immediately recognize its absurdity. Appropriation and capital goods production are purposeful activities. One engages in original appropriation and produces capital goods because one prefers more goods to less and recognizes the greater physical productivity of appropriated land and capitalist production. Even if the *invention* of a capital good such as, for example, a hammer or an axe, first happened by *accident,* the inventor still recognized for what purpose it was useful, and any *repetition* of the invented practice then occurred purposefully and with reason.

VIII. Cultural Transmission

Equally absurd is Hayek's theory of "spontaneous association" through unconscious imitation. The imitation of the practices of original appropriation and indirect, capitalist production by others is likewise motivated by the desire for greater personal wealth. It is a justified imitation. Neither external force, chance nor spontaneity are necessary to explain it. Nor are they required in order to then explain the emergence of the division of labor and interpersonal exchange. People recognize and have always recognized that division of labor and voluntary exchange lead to greater physical productivity than if one were to remain in self-sufficiency.[47] Likewise, for the origin of a monetary

---

47. See Ludwig von Mises, *Human Action: A Treatise on Economics* (Chicago: Henry Regnery, 1966), chap. 8.

If and as far as labor under the division of labor is more productive than isolated labor, and if and as far as man is able to realize this fact, human action itself tends

economy one must not wait for a spontaneous mutation. Under conditions of uncertainty, in any barter economy sales-stoppages are bound to arise (whenever a double coincidence of wants is absent). In this situation a person can nonetheless still increase his own wealth, if he recognizes that goods may be employed not only for personal use but also as a medium of exchange—for resale purposes—and if he then succeeds in acquiring a more marketable good in exchange for a less marketable one. The demand for a good *qua* medium of exchange further increases this good's marketability. The practice

---

toward cooperation and association; man becomes a social being not in sacrificing his own concerns for the sake of a mythical Moloch, society, but in aiming at an improvement in his own welfare. Experience teaches that this condition—higher productivity achieved under the division of labor—is present because its cause—the inborn inequality of men and the inequality in the geographical distribution of the natural factors of production—is real. Thus we are in a position to comprehend the course of social evolution. (*Id.*, pp. 160–61)

"Liberalism ... regards all social cooperation as an emanation of rationally recognized utility." (Ludwig von Mises, *Socialism*, Indianapolis, Ind.: Liberty Fund, 1981, p. 418)

Hayek *rejects* this explanation. According to him, to regard as Mises does

all social cooperation as an emanation of rationally recognized utility ... is wrong. The extreme rationalism of this passage ... seems to me factually mistaken. It certainly was not rational insight into its general benefits that led to the spreading of the market economy. ("Foreword" to *Socialism*, p. xxiii)

One is wondering how else to explain the phenomenon, but Hayek does not say—except through reference to "spontaneous evolution." Still more wondrous must appear the fact that there existed no human society whatsoever that had no private property and no exchange at all. (Hayek's "primordial bands," *Law, Legislation, and Liberty*, vol. 3, "Epilogue"; *Fatal Conceit*, chap. 1, are a myth, similar to the Morgan-Engels myth of primitive communism, for which not a shred of anthropological evidence exists. And the transition from the face-to-face society to the anonymous, faceless economy was not at all a traumatic event, which required fundamentally different motives and habits. The world market is nothing else but the sum of all interpersonal transactions and as such not much more difficult to grasp than a simple bilateral exchange of goods.)

Instead, Hayek then engages in an outright falsification when, despite all historical records to the contrary, he appoints Mises to the position of a somewhat less than fully evolved predecessor of his own (Hayek's) theory.

It seems to me that the thrust of Mises's teaching is to show that we have not adopted freedom because we understood what benefits it would bring: that we have *not* designed, and certainly were not intelligent enough to design, the order which we now have learned partly to understand long after we had plenty of opportunity to see how it worked.... It is greatly to Mises's credit that he largely emancipated himself from that rationalist-constructivist starting point, but that task is still to be completed. (*Id.*, pp. xxiii–xxiv)

In fact, Mises never said anything even remotely similar to what Hayek insinuates; and if credit must be given where it is due, Mises must be credited not for having himself emancipated from his rationalism but for never having abandoned it.

will be imitated by others to solve their own sales problems, and in the course of a self-reinforcing process of imitation, sooner or later a single universal medium of exchange—a commodity money—will emerge, which is uniquely distinguished from all other goods in being the one with the highest degree of resaleability.[48]

None of this is the result of chance. Everywhere, at the origin of private property, exchange and money, individual purpose, insight and self-interested action are at work.

Indeed, so patently wrong is his theory that Hayek frequently withdraws to a second, more moderate variation. According to this version, division of labor and exchange are "the unintended consequences of human action," "the result of human action but not of human design."[49] The process of human association may not proceed entirely unconsciously, but largely so. An actor may be able to recognize his personal gains from acts of appropriation, production, exchange and money—use—and insofar, the process of evolution may appear rational. However, an actor *cannot* recognize the *indirect* consequences of his actions (and it is allegedly these unconscious, unintended consequences for society as a whole which are decisive for the evolutionary success or failure of individual practices). And since *these* consequences *cannot* be known, the process of social evolution is ultimately irrational,[50] motivated not by true or false ideas and insights, but by a blind, unconsciously effective mechanism of group selection.

However, this variant also is contradictory and absurd.

First, it is self-contradictory to characterize actions by their unconscious indirect consequences and then, in the next breath, name these consequences. If the indirect consequences can be named and described, they also can be intended. Otherwise, if they are indeed unconscious, nothing can be said about them. Something about which one cannot say anything obviously cannot have an identifiable influence on anybody's actions; nor can it be made responsible for the different evolutionary success of different

48. See Carl Menger, *Principles of Economics* (New York: New York University Press, 1976), chap. 8; Ludwig von Mises, *Theory of Money and Credit* (Irvington-on-Hudson, N.Y.: Foundation for Economic Education, 1971), chap. 1.

49. F. A. Hayek, *Studies in Philosophy, Politics, and Economics* (Chicago: University of Chicago Press, 1967), chap. 6.

50. Thus Hayek writes that it is "perverted rationalism ... which interpreted the law of nature as the deductive constructions of 'natural reason.'" Law instead is "the undesigned outcome of growth." (*Id.*, p. 101)

groups. Thus, from the outset it is nonsensical to describe—as Hayek does—the task of a social theorist as that of explaining the "unintended patterns and regularities which we find to exist in human society."[51] The task of the social theorist is to explain the direct as well as the indirect (*not*: the intentional and the unintentional) consequences of human actions and to thus contribute to a progressive rationalization of human action—an expansion of the knowledge of possible (intend-able) goals and the mutual compatibility or incompatibility of various goals.[52]

Secondly, the moderate variation also cannot explain the origin of division of labor, exchange and money. One can grant Hayek initially that it may be possible that a person who carries out an exchange or who acquires a medium of exchange for the very first time will thereby recognize only

---

51. *Id.*, p. 97.

52. At this point, one may want to compare Hayek to his alleged predecessor Carl Menger. For Hayek law is "the undesigned outcome of growth." "Our values and institutions are determined not simply by preceding causes but as part of a process of unconscious self-organization of a structure or pattern." (*Fatal Conceit*, p. 9)

In sharp contrast, Carl Menger considers all references in social science explanations to Hayekian categories such as "natural growth," "spontaneous evolution," "primordial nature" or "unconscious self-organization" as sheer mysticism. To *explain* a social phenomenon through forces such as these is not to explain anything at all—a scientific imposture:

> The origin of a phenomenon is by no means explained by the assertion that it *was present from the very beginning* or that it *developed originally* ... a social phenomenon, at least in its most original form, must clearly have developed from individual factors. The [organicist, Hayekian] view here referred to is merely an analogy between the development of social institutions and that of natural organisms, which is completely worthless for the purpose of solving our problem. It states, to be sure, that institutions are unintended creations of the human mind, but not *how* they came about. These attempts at interpretation are comparable to the procedure of a natural scientist who thinks he is solving the problem of the origin of natural organisms by alluding to their "originality," "natural growth," or their "primeval nature" ... attempts to interpret the *changes* of social phenomena as 'organic processes' are no less inadmissible than ... theories which aim to solve 'organically' the problem of the *origin* of unintentionally created social structures. There is hardly any need to remark that the changes of social phenomena cannot be interpreted in a social-pragmatic way, insofar as they are not the intended result of the agreement of members of society or of positive legislation, but are the unintended product of social development. But it is just as obvious that not even the slightest insight into the nature and the laws of the movement of

his own personal gain (but not the indirect, social consequences). He may not know (and mankind at its beginnings certainly did not know) that as an exchanger and a money user he contributes ultimately to the development of a world market, integrated through a single, universally employed commodity money (historically, gold), to steady population growth, to an ever more expansive division of labor and continuously growing global economic wealth. Moreover, it is impossible in principle to predict today (or at any present time) the diversity, quantities, prices and personal distribution of future goods. But from this Hayek's skeptic—anti-rationalist conclusion—that "guided progress is no progress," that "we cannot prejudge the moral properties of evolutionary outcomes," and that "we have never designed our economic system but have tumbled into it, and it may yet lead us to destruction"— does not follow.

For even if a person does not immediately grasp the indirect social consequences of his own actions, it is difficult to imagine how this ignorance could last for long. Once *repeated* exchanges between specific traders occur, or once one sees one's own practice of acquiring a medium of exchange copied by others, one begins to recognize that one's own actions are not only one-sided but *mutually* beneficial. Even if one were still unable to systematically predict the development of future markets and the shape and composition of future wealth, then, with the nature of a bilateral exchange and a medium of exchange one would at the same time recognize the *principle* of interpersonal justice and of individual and universal economic progress: whatever results emerge from voluntary exchanges are just; and economic progress consists of the expansion of the division of labor based upon the recognition of private property and the universalization of the use of money and monetary calculation. Even if the division of labor, money and economic calculation become *routine* in the course of time, the recognition of the foundations of justice and economic efficiency never again completely disappears. Once for whatever reason it comes to a complete breakdown of the division of labor

---

social phenomena can be gained either by the mere allusion to the 'organic' or the 'primeval' character of the processes under discussion, nor even by mere analogies between these and the transformations to be observed in natural organisms. The worthlessness of the above orientation of research is so clear that we do not care to add anything to what we have already said. (Carl Menger, *Investigations into the Method of the Social Sciences with Special Reference to Economics*, New York: New York University Press, 1985, pp. 149–50)

(war) or the currency (hyperinflation), people will be reminded of it. Then they must not unconsciously await the further course of social evolution, their own extinction. Rather, they are capable of recognizing the breakdown as such and know (and have always known) how to begin systematically anew.

Moreover, as the examples cited by Hayek of Carl Menger and Ludwig von Mises clearly demonstrate, it must not even come to a catastrophe before one regains consciousness. As soon as one has comprehended the thoughts of these men, one can act in full understanding of the social consequences of one's activities. The evolution does not proceed *above* the heads of the acting individuals but instead becomes a process of consciously planned and/or experienced social change. Each progression and each mishap in the process of economic integration can be identified and explained, and the conscious identification of mishaps in particular makes it possible that one may either consciously adjust to a catastrophe *before* it actually occurs or that a mistake will be consciously corrected (insofar as one possesses control over it).

Furthermore, just as people are not condemned to blindly tumble toward self-destruction, they also must not remain passive and powerless *vis-à-vis* a foreseen economic decline. Rather, at all times one can systematically expand the range of controllable—and hence correctable—mistakes. For any *institutionalized* derailment in the process of economic integration and association—such as government expropriations, taxes, currency depreciations or trade restrictions—must have the approval of the majority of the public. Without such support in public opinion, however reluctant it may be, their continued enforcement becomes impossible. Thus, in order to prevent a decline, no more—and no less—than a change in public opinion is necessary; and public opinion can be influenced at all times by ideas and ideologies.[53]

---

53. Since Hayek essentially denies the existence (or the importance) of ideas in the course of social evolution, he also (at least in his later writings) gives no mention to public opinion.

In distinct contrast, David Hume, whom Hayek himself claims as his precursor, attaches fundamental importance to ideas and public opinion.

> Nothing appears more surprising to those who consider human affairs with a philosophical eye, than the easiness with which the many are governed by the few, and the implicit submission, with which men resign their own sentiments and passions to those of their rulers. When we inquire by what means this wonder is effected we shall find, that as Force is always on the side of the governed, the governors have nothing to support them but

Ironically, an unconscious economic decline is only possible if the majority of the public follows Hayek's advice to act "spontaneously"—without really knowing why—and free of "the extreme hubris of knowing the direction of progress." One cannot act entirely without consciousness, of course. Yet in accordance with Hayek's recommendation one pays attention exclusively to the direct and immediate causes and consequences of one's actions and wealth. In contrast, knowledge and ideas regarding any indirect, to the naked eye invisible causes and consequences are considered unimportant, arbitrary or even illusory. One participates routinely in the division of labor because one recognizes its direct advantage; and one recognizes the direct harm of taxes, currency depreciations and trade restrictions. However, one does *not* recognize that by participating in the division of labor, one at the same time indirectly advances the welfare of all other market participants literally to the last corner of the earth, and indeed that the higher the personal profit, the greater one's contribution to the public good. Nor does one recognize that the direct harm done through government intervention to others, whether in the immediate neighborhood or at the other end of the world, always indirectly diminishes one's own standard of living. Yet this ignorance has fatal consequences; for he who does not understand the indirect causes and consequences of his actions acts differently. He will either act as if the economic advantage or disadvantage of one person has nothing to do with that of another—and he will accordingly remain neutral or indifferent toward all government intervention which is directed against others. Or he may even act in the belief that one person's gain can be another's loss; and then he may even welcome government expropriation, taxes, currency devaluations or trade restrictions as means of bringing "restitution" to "unfair" losers (preferably oneself and one's own kind). As long as this intellectual attitude prevails in public opinion, a steady increase in government expropriation, taxes, inflation

opinion. It is, therefore, on opinion only that government is founded, and this maxim extends to the most despotic and most military governments, as well as to the most free and most popular. The soldan of Egypt, or the emperor of Rome, might drive his harmless subjects, like brute beasts, against their sentiments and inclination. But he must, at least, have led his mamalukes or praetorian bands, like men, by their opinion. (David Hume, *Essays: Moral, Political and Literary*, Oxford: University of Oxford Press, 1971, p. 19)

See also E. de La Boétie, *The Politics of Obedience: The Discourse of Voluntary Servitude*, ed. and with an intro. by Murray N. Rothbard (New York: Free Life Editions, 1975).

and trade restrictions, and the subsequent continuous economic decline, is indeed unavoidable.

However, Hayek's advice is false and nonsensical. It is impossible to act unconsciously or knowingly to be ignorant. And even if the indirect social causes and consequences of one's actions are unknown, they are still—with some delay and however mediated—effective. Thus, to know them is always and for everyone advantageous. The only beneficiary of Hayek's recommendation to the contrary is government. Only the representatives of state and government can have a personal interest in spreading a Hayekian consciousness (while they themselves recognize it as a "false consciousness"), because *vis-à-vis* an ignorant public it becomes easier for government to grow. Yet the public at large outside the state apparatus has no interest in entertaining a false consciousness (and thus know less than its government). It is personally advantageous to let one's actions be guided by correct ideas, and accordingly one is always receptive to ideological enlightenment. Knowledge is better than ignorance. And because it is better, it is at the same time infectious. However, as soon as the public is enlightened and a majority of it recognizes that everyone's participation in an exchange economy simultaneously benefits all other market participants, and that every government intervention in the network of bilateral exchange relations, regardless where and against whom, represents an attack on one's own wealth, an economic decline is no longer unavoidable. On the contrary, rather than remaining indifferent or even welcoming government intervention, the public will be unsupportive or even hostile to them. In such a climate of public opinion, instead of economic decline, a process of conscious social rationalization and continuously advancing economic integration will result.

IX. Cultural Selection

According to Hayek, however, progress has nothing to do with enlightenment. As little as one is capable of recognizing the reasons for an economic decline, as little is progress due to insight. Just as one tumbles unconsciously and powerlessly into the abyss, so one stumbles blindly forward. It is not true or false ideas that determine the course of social evolution, but mystic fate. Progress occurs *naturally*, without any insight of the participating individuals, as one group with coincidentally *better* practices somehow "prevails" over another with *worse* practices.

Apart from the fact that this theory is incompatible with Hayek's own repeated observation that cultural evolution proceeds faster than biological evolution,[54] it is false for two reasons. First, the theory contains assumptions, which make it inapplicable to human societies. Second, when it is nonetheless applied to them, the theory turns out empty and Hayek again reveals himself—intentionally or unintentionally—as a state apologist.

To make his theory work, Hayek first must assume the existence of *separated* groups. Hayek introduces this assumption when he alleges that a new "spontaneous" practice will be blindly imitated *within* a group, but not (why not?) outside of it. If the practice were imitated universally and if, accordingly, there existed only one single group, cultural group *selection* would by definition be impossible. Without some sort of competitor there can be no selection. Moreover, without selection, the concept of progress can no longer be employed meaningfully. All that can be stated regarding a "spontaneously" without purpose or reason—generated and spontaneously universalized practice is this: that as long as it is practiced, it has not yet died out.

However, the assumption of separated groups, which Hayek must introduce in order to rescue the concept of cultural progress (within his anti-rationalist theory of action and society), immediately produces a series of insurmountable problems for his theory. First, it follows that Hayek's theory cannot be applied to the present. The present world is characterized by the fact that the practices of original appropriation and property, of capital goods production, exchange and monetary calculation are universally disseminated no group in which these practices are completely unknown and absent exists—and that all of mankind is connected through a network of bilateral exchanges. In this regard, mankind is a single group. Whatever competition between different groups may then exist can have no relevance for these universal practices. Universal practices lie—as a constant—outside of any selection mechanism; and according to Hayek's theory, no more could then be said for the justification of original appropriation, capital goods

---

54. Hayek, *Law, Legislation, and Liberty*, vol. 3, pp. 154, 156.

As David Ramsey Steele correctly notes, "if cultural group selection is to be relied upon, human culture would evolve much more slowly than human biology. For the selection of groups is a slower process than the selection of individuals, and group selection according to culture cannot be expected to proceed any faster than group selection according to genes." ("Hayek's Theory of Cultural Group Selection," p. 179)

production, or division of labor and exchange than that such practices have not yet died out.

Hayek's theory is also inapplicable to pre-modern or primitive societies. At this stage in human history, isolated groups existed. Yet even then, the practices of appropriation, production and exchange were universal. There existed no tribe, however primitive, that did not know and practice them. This fact does not cause any problems for a theory of action and society, which recognizes these practices as the result of rational, utility-maximizing action. For such a theory, the fact is easily explainable: Each group comes to recognize independently the very same, universally valid rules. But for Hayek, this elementary fact constitutes a fundamental theoretical problem. For if appropriation, production, exchange and money are the result of spontaneous mutation, blind imitation, infection or mechanical transmission, as Hayek claims, it becomes inexplicable—except by reference to chance—why each group, in complete isolation from all others, should come up with the exact same patterns of action. Following Hayek's theory one should expect instead that mankind, at least at its beginnings, would have generated a variety of very different action and society mutants. In fact, if Hayek were correct, one would have to assume that in the beginning of mankind people would have adopted the practice of *not* appropriating, *not* producing and *not* exchanging as frequently as they adopted the opposite. Since this is obviously *not* the case Hayek would have to *explain* this anomaly. Once he identified the obvious reason for this fact, however, that the adoption of the former practice leads to immediate death,[55] while the latter is an indispensable means for survival—he would have to acknowledge the existence of human rationality and contradict his own theory.

Secondly, even regarding isolated groups Hayek's theory of cultural group selection cannot explain how unconscious cultural progress could be possible. (His explanation of the concept of "prevailing" is accordingly vague.) Isolated groups—and even more so, groups connected by trade—do not compete against each other. The assumption, familiar from the theory of biological evolution, that different organisms are engaged in a zero-sum competition for naturally limited resources cannot be applied to human societies, and hence any attempt to conclude backward from the survival

---

55. Besides, this form of extinction also does not fit Hayek's explanatory scheme, for a person or group that would forego all appropriation, production, etc., would die out on account of its own stupidity, not in the course of cultural group selection.

of a phenomenon to its *better* adaptation (as it is, within limits, possible in biology) fails here. A group of persons isolated from all others, which follows the practices of appropriation, capital goods production and exchange does not thereby reduce the supply of goods of other groups. It enhances its own wealth without diminishing that of others. If it begins to trade with other groups, it even increases their wealth. Between human groups, it is not competition, but self-reliant independence or mutually advantageous cooperation that exists. A mechanism of cultural *selection* thus cannot become effective here.[56]

---

56. Although Hayek notices some obvious differences between biological and cultural evolution (*Fatal Conceit*, p. 25), he does not recognize the categorical difference between social *cooperation* and biological *competition*. Rather, he writes that biological and cultural evolution

> both rely on the same principle of selection: survival or reproductive advantage. Variation, adaptation and competition are essentially the same kind of process, however different their particular mechanism, particularly those pertaining to propagation. Not only does all evolution rest on competition; continuing competition is necessary even to preserve existing achievements. (*Id.*, p. 26)

In contrast, Ludwig von Mises sharply distinguishes between cooperation and competition. He writes:

> Society is concerted action, cooperation. Society is the outcome of conscious and purposeful behavior. This does not mean that individuals have concluded contracts by virtue of which they have founded human society. The actions which have brought about social cooperation and daily bring it about anew do not aim at anything else than cooperation and coadjuvancy with others for the attainment of definite singular ends. The total complex of the mutual relations created by such concerted actions is called society. It substitutes collaboration for the—at least conceivable—isolated life of individuals. Society is division of labor and combination of labor. In his capacity as an acting animal man becomes a social animal. (*Human Action*, p. 143)

What makes friendly relations between human beings possible is the higher productivity of the division of labor. It removes the natural conflict of interests. For where there is division of labor, there is no longer question of the distribution of a supply not capable of enlargement. Thanks to the higher productivity of labor performed under the division of tasks, the supply of goods multiplies. A pre-eminent common interest, the preservation and further intensification of social cooperation, becomes paramount and obliterates all essential collisions. Catallactic competition is substituted for biological competition. It makes for harmony of the interests of all members of society. The very condition from which the irreconcilable conflicts of biological competition arise—viz., the fact that all people by and large strive after the same things—is transformed into a factor making for

Hayek, in his self-made theoretical difficulties, nonetheless indicates several possibilities. "Prevailing" means either that one group becomes wealthier than another, that it displays a comparatively higher population growth, or that it militarily defeats and assimilates another one. Apart from the fact that these criteria are mutually incompatible—what is the case, for instance, if a more populous group is militarily defeated by a less populous one?—they all fail to explain *progress*. The apparently most plausible criterion—wealth—fails because the existence of groups with different wealth has no relevance for their survival or extinction. Two groups practice appropriation, production and exchange independently of each other. However, the members of both groups are neither biologically identical, nor is external nature (land) for both groups the same. From this it follows that the results of their actions—their wealth—will be different as well. This is the case for groups and individuals. For individuals, too, it holds that through the application of one and the same practice of appropriation, production and exchange, *different* wealth results. But then the inference from "greater wealth" to "better culture" is illegitimate. The richer person does not represent a *better* culture, and the poorer a *worse* one, but on the basis of one and the same culture one person becomes comparatively wealthier than another. Accordingly, no selection takes place. Both rich and poor co-exist—while as a result of their shared culture, the absolute wealth of rich and poor alike increases.

Likewise, population size fails as a criterion for cultural selection. Group size, too, implies nothing concerning "better culture." Everything that holds for individuals applies to groups as well. From the fact that a person has no biological offspring, it does not follow that he followed other *worse* practices while he was alive. Rather, different individuals acting on the basis of the same rules produce different numbers of offspring. Just as poor to rich, the childless does not stand in competition to those with children. They exist independently of one another or they cooperate with one another. And even if a group should become literally extinct or if an individual committed suicide, this still would not imply any cultural selection. For the surviving follow the

---

harmony of interests. Because many people or even all people want bread, clothes, shoes, and cars, large-scale production of these goods becomes feasible and reduces the costs of production to such an extent that they are accessible at low prices. The fact that my fellow man wants to acquire shoes as I do, does not make it harder for me to get shoes, but easier. (*Id.*, p. 673)

very same rules of appropriation, production and exchange which the extinct followed while they were alive.

The third criterion, the military conquest, succeeds in bringing groups out of a state of isolated independence or cooperation into one of zero-sum competition. However, military success no more represents moral progress than a murder indicates the moral superiority of the murderer over his victim. Moreover, the occurrence of a conquest (or of a murder) does not affect the validity of *universal* rules, i.e., those that *neither* the murderer *nor* the murdered can do without: In order to introduce a military conflict between groups, Hayek must first make the assumption that in at least one of these groups a new practice spontaneously springs up. Rather than following the practices of original appropriation, capital goods production and exchange, someone must have come up with the idea that one can also increase one's personal wealth by forcibly expropriating appropriators, producers and exchangers. However, as soon as this practice is then, according to Hayek's theory, blindly imitated by all other group members, a war of each against all would ensue. There would soon be nothing left that could still be expropriated, and all group members would die out—not because of a mechanism of cultural displacement or selection, but because of their own stupidity! Every person can independently appropriate, produce and exchange, but not everyone can expropriate appropriators, producers and exchangers. In order for expropriations to be possible, there must be people who continue to follow the practice of appropriation, production and exchange. The existence of a culture of expropriation requires the continued existence of a culture of appropriation, production and exchange. The former stands in a *parasitic* relationship to the latter. Then, however, military conquest cannot generate cultural progress. The conquerors do not represent a fundamentally different culture. Among themselves the conquerors must follow the same practice of appropriation, production and exchange, which was also followed by the conquered. And *after* the successful conquest, the conquerors must return to these traditional practices—either because all the conquered have died out or all booty has been consumed, or because one wishes to institutionalize one's practice of expropriation and therefore needs an ongoing productive population (of conquered people).

However, as soon as Hayek's theory is applied to this only conceivable case of cultural competition (rather than of independence or cooperation) in which a subgroup (the conquerors) follows a parasitic culture of expropriation while the rest of the group (the conquered) simultaneously appropriates, produces and exchanges, the result is an unabashed apology for government and state.

This manifests itself first in the way in which Hayek's theory explains the origin of a culture of expropriation. Just as the culture of appropriation, production and exchange is allegedly the result of an accidental mutation, so the practice of expropriation represents a "spontaneous" development. Just as appropriators, producers and exchangers do not understand the meaning of their activities, so the conquerors do not grasp the meaning of conquest. As appropriator's, producers and exchangers recognize the immediate personal advantage of their activities, so the conquerors can recognize their personal gain from acts of expropriation. Yet as the participants in a market economy are then not capable of understanding that through their activities the wealth of all other participants is simultaneously increased, so the conquerors cannot know that through expropriations the wealth of the expropriated is reduced. Put bluntly: A group of murderers, robbers or slave hunters does not know that the murdered, robbed or enslaved suffer thereby from a loss. They follow their practices as *innocently* as the murdered, robbed and enslaved follow their different practices of appropriation, production and exchange. Expropriation, taxes or trade restrictions are just as much an expression of human spontaneity as are appropriation, production and trade. Every group of conquerors will thank Hayek for so much (mis-)understanding!

Second, Hayek's theory fails just as lamentably in its attempt to explain the rise and fall of historical civilizations—and thereby once again yields absurd statist implications. Indeed, what more could a group of conquerors want to hear than that its own actions have nothing to do with the rise and decline of civilizations. Yet it is precisely this that Hayek's theory implies: For, according to Hayek, cultural progress is only possible, as long as one culture can somehow "prevail" over another. Regarding the relationship between a basic culture of appropriation and a parasitic subculture of expropriation, however, there can be no "prevailing." The parasitic culture cannot prevail, yet as a subculture it can continue to operate as long as a basic culture of appropriation exists. Progress through group selection is impossible within this relationship; and according to Hayek, then, strictly speaking nothing can be stated at all regarding the further course of social evolution. Because the members of the culture of appropriation supposedly do not comprehend that they promote the social welfare through their actions, and because the members of the expropriation culture are equally ignorant of the fact that their actions reduce the general welfare, spontaneous changes in the relative magnitude of both cultures may occur. Sometimes the culture of appropriation will attract more spontaneous adherents; at other times the culture of expropriation will. However, since there is no reason that such spontaneous changes, if they occur at all, should follow any specific, predictable, pattern, there is also no recognizable relationship between spontaneous cultural changes and the rise and fall of civilizations. Everything is chance. No explanation for the rise and the fall of the Roman civilization exists. Likewise, no comprehensible reason for the rise of Western Europe or the United States exists. Such a rise could just as well have happened elsewhere—in India or Africa. Accordingly, it would be "extreme hubris," for instance, to advise India or Africa from the standpoint of Western Europe; for this would imply—oh, how presumptuous—that one knew the direction of progress.

If this theory is rejected as empty, however, and it is pointed out that from the very description of the initial situation—the coexistence of a basic culture of appropriation and a parasitic subculture of expropriation— a fundamental law of social evolution follows, Hayek's entire anti-rationalist system once again breaks down. A relative expansion of the basic culture leads to higher social wealth and is the reason for the rise of civilizations; and a relative expansion of the parasitic subculture leads to lower wealth and is responsible for the fall of civilizations. Yet if one (anyone) has grasped this plain and elementary relationship, then the origin and the relative changes in the magnitudes of both cultures can no longer be interpreted as a *natural* process. The explanation, familiar from biology, of a natural, self-regulated equilibration process—of spontaneously growing parasites, a weakening of the host, a consequent shrinking number of parasites, and finally the host's recovery, etc.—cannot be applied to a situation where host and/or parasite are consciously aware of their respective roles as well as the relationship between them and are capable of choosing between these roles. A comprehended social evolution is no longer natural, but rational. So long as only the members of the parasitic culture understand the nature of the relationship, instead of a natural up and down of both cultures, a planned, steady growth of parasitism will ensue. The members of the parasitic subculture do not vacillate between first faring absolutely better and then absolutely worse. Rather, because of their insight into the relationship between the culture of appropriation and that of expropriation they can act in such a way—by *not* expanding their practices spontaneously, but instead consciously restraining themselves—that their own absolute wealth will always grow (or at least will never fall). On the other hand, to the extent that the members of the basic culture understand the nature of the relationship between both cultures, not only the absolute wealth of the subculture will be threatened but its sheer existence will be endangered. For the members of a parasitic subculture always represent only a minority of the whole group. One hundred parasites can lead a comfortable life on the products of 1,000 hosts. Yet 1,000 parasites cannot live off of 100 hosts. If, however, the members of the productive culture of appropriation always represent a majority of the population, then in the long run the greater physical strength is on their side as well. They can always physically defeat and destroy the parasites, and the continued existence of a subculture of appropriation is then *not* explained by its greater physical-military power, but rather depends exclusively on the power of *ideas*. Government and state must find ideological support, which reaches far into the exploited population. Without such support from the members of the basic culture, even the most brutal and seemingly invincible government immediately collapses (as most recently illustrated dramatically by the fall the Soviet Union and the communist governments of Eastern Europe).

The changes in the relative magnitude of the basic culture and the parasitic subculture that explain the rise and fall of civilizations are in turn explained by *ideological* changes. They do not occur spontaneously but are the result of conscious ideas and their dissemination. In a society in which a majority of the basic culture comprehends that each act of appropriation, production and exchange enhances the welfare of all other market participants, and that each act of expropriation, taxation or trade restriction instead, regardless against whom it is directed, lowers the welfare of all others, the parasitic culture of government and state will continuously die off and a rise of civilization will ensue. On the other hand, in a society, in which the majority of the basic culture does not understand the nature and relationship between basic and subculture, the parasitic expropriation culture will grow and with this a decline of civilization will ensue.[57]

---

57. Writes Mises:

History is a struggle between two principles, the peaceful principle, which advances the development of trade, and the militarist-imperialist principle, which interprets human society not as a friendly division of labor but as the forcible repression of some of its members by others. The imperialist principle continually regains the upper hand. The liberal principle cannot

Hayek, who wants to ban ideas and rationality from the explanation of history, must deny all this. Yet in proposing his own theory of unconscious cultural group selection, he too affirms the existence and effectiveness of ideas, and he too acknowledges—whether he is aware of this or not—that the course of social evolution is determined by ideas and their adoption. Hayek produces ideas and wants to influence the course of human history through ideas, too. However, Hayek's ideas are false; and their proliferation would lead to the eclipse of Western civilization.

X. CONCLUSION

Friedrich Hayek is today acclaimed as one of the most important theoreticians of the market economy and of classical liberalism. Far more than his earlier work in the field of economic theory, his later writings on political philosophy and social theory have contributed to his fame. It is these later writings that currently support and feed an extended, international Hayek dissertation industry.

The preceding investigations demonstrate that Hayek's excursions into the field of political and social theory must be considered a complete failure. Hayek begins with a self-contradictory proposition and ends in absurdity: He denies the existence of human rationality or at least the possibility of recognizing all indirect causes and consequences of human action. He claims

---

maintain itself against it until the inclination for peaceful labor inherent in the masses shall have struggled through to full recognition of its own importance as a principle of social evolution. (*Socialism*, p. 268)

Liberalism is rationalistic. It maintains that it is possible to convince the immense majority that peaceful cooperation within the framework of society better serves the rightly understood interests than mutual battling and social disintegration. It has full confidence in man's reason. It may be that this optimism is unfounded and that the liberals have erred. But then there is no hope left for mankind's future. (*Human Action*, p. 157)

The body of economic knowledge is an essential element in the structure of human civilization; it is the foundation upon which modern industrialism and all the moral, intellectual, technological, and therapeutical achievements of the last centuries have been built. It rests with men whether they will make proper use of the rich treasure with which this knowledge provides them or whether they will leave it unused. But if they fail to take the best advantage of it and disregard its teachings and warnings, they will not annul economics; they will stamp out society and the human race. (*Id.*, p. 885)

that the course of social evolution and the rise and fall of civilizations is incomprehensible, and that no one knows the direction of progress (only to explain progress then as the result of some unconscious process of cultural group selection). He claims that no universally valid ethical standards exist, and that it is impossible to make an unambiguous moral distinction between an attack and a defense or between a peaceful refusal of exchange and a physically coerced exchange. And lastly, he claims that government— whose causes and consequences allegedly are as incomprehensible as those of the market—should take on (financed by taxes) all those tasks which the market does not provide (which anywhere outside of the Garden of Eden amounts to an infinite number of tasks).

Our investigations support the suspicion that Hayek's fame has little to do with his importance as a social theorist, but rather with the fact that his theory poses no threat whatsoever to the currently dominating statist ideology of social democracy, and that a theory which is marked by contradiction, confusion and vagueness provides an unlimited reservoir for hermeneutical endeavors.

He who searches for a champion of the market economy and of liberalism must look elsewhere. But he must look no farther than to Hayek's teacher and mentor: the great and unsurpassed Ludwig von Mises.

Part Five

Autobiographical

21

Interview with The Daily Bell

I. INTRODUCTION

Dr. Hans-Hermann Hoppe, born in 1949 in Peine, West Germany, studied philosophy, sociology, economics, history and statistics at the University of the Saarland, in Saarbrücken, the Johann Wolfgang Goethe University, in Frankfurt am Main, and at the University of Michigan, in Ann Arbor. He received his doctorate (Philosophy, 1974, under Jürgen Habermas) and his "Habilitation" degree (Foundations of Sociology and Economics, 1981) both from the Goethe University in Frankfurt.

In 1985 Hoppe moved to New York City to work with Murray N. Rothbard (1926–1995), the most prominent American student of the Austrian economist Ludwig von Mises (1881–1973). In 1986 Hoppe followed Rothbard to the University of Nevada, Las Vegas, where he served as Professor of Economics until his retirement in 2008. After Rothbard's death, Hoppe also served for many years as editor of the *Quarterly Journal of Austrian Economics* and of the interdisciplinary *Journal for Libertarian Studies*. Hoppe is a Distinguished Fellow of the Ludwig von Mises Institute, in Auburn, Alabama, and founder and president of the Property and Freedom Society. He currently lives with his wife Dr. Gülcin Imre, a fellow economist, in Istanbul, Turkey.

Hoppe is the author of eight books—the best known of which is *Democracy: The God That Failed*—and more than 150 articles in books, scholarly journals and magazines of opinion. As an internationally prominent Austrian School economist and libertarian philosopher, he has lectured

---

• Originally published in *The Daily Bell*, Sunday, March 27, 2011.

all over the world and his writings have been translated into more than twenty languages.

In 2006 Hoppe was awarded the Gary S. Schlarbaum Prize for Lifetime Achievement in the Cause of Liberty, and in 2009 he received the Franz Cuhel Memorial Prize from the University of Economics in Prague. At the occasion of his 60th birthday, in 2009, a Festschrift was published in his honor: Jörg Guido Hülsmann and Stephan Kinsella (eds.), *Property, Freedom and Society: Essays in Honor of Hans-Hermann Hoppe.* Hoppe's personal website is www.HansHoppe.com. There the bulk of his scholarly and popular writings as well as many public lecture recordings are electronically available.

II. Interview

Daily Bell: Please answer these questions as our readers were not already aware of your fine work and considered opinions. Let's jump right in. Why is democracy "The God that failed"?

Dr. Hans-Hermann Hoppe: The traditional, pre-modern state-form is that of a (absolute) monarchy. The democratic movement was directed against kings and the classes of hereditary nobles. Monarchy was criticized as being incompatible with the basic principle of the "equality before the law." It rested on privilege and was unfair and exploitative. Democracy was supposed to be the way out. In opening participation and entry into state-government to everyone on equal terms, so the advocates of democracy claimed, equality before the law would become reality and true freedom would reign. But this is all a big error.

True, under democracy everyone can become king, so to speak, not only a privileged circle of people. Thus, in a democracy no *personal* privileges exist. However, *functional* privileges and privileged functions exist. Public officials, if they act in an official capacity, are governed and protected by "public law" and thereby occupy a privileged position *vis-à-vis* persons acting under the mere authority of "private law." In particular, public officials are permitted to finance or subsidize their own activities through taxes. That is, they are permitted to engage in, and live off, what in private dealings between private law subjects is prohibited and considered "theft" and "stolen loot." Thus, privilege and legal discrimination—and the distinction between rulers and subjects—will not disappear under democracy.

Even worse: Under monarchy, the distinction between rulers and ruled is clear. I know, for instance, that I will never become king, and because of that I will tend to resist the king's attempts to raise taxes. Under democracy, the distinction between rulers and ruled becomes blurred. The illusion can arise "that we all rule ourselves," and the resistance against increased taxation is accordingly diminished. I might end up on the receiving end: as a tax-*recipient* rather than a tax-*payer*, and thus view taxation more favorably.

And moreover: As a hereditary monopolist, a king regards the territory and the people under his rule as his personal property and engages in the monopolistic exploitation of this "property." Under democracy, monopoly and monopolistic exploitation do not disappear. Rather, what happens is this: instead of a king and a nobility who regard the country as their private property, a temporary and interchangeable caretaker is put in monopolistic charge of the country. The caretaker does not own the country, but as long as he is in office he is permitted to use it to his and his protégés' advantage. He owns its current use—*usufruct*—but not its capital stock. This does not eliminate exploitation. To the contrary, it makes exploitation less calculating and carried out with little or no regard to the capital stock. Exploitation becomes shortsighted and capital consumption will be systematically promoted.

Daily Bell: If democracy has failed what would you put in its place? What is the ideal society? Anarcho-capitalism?

Dr. Hans-Hermann Hoppe: I prefer the term "private law society." In a private law society every individual and institution is subject to one and the same set of laws. No public law granting privileges to specific persons or functions exists in this society. There is only private law (and private property), equally applicable to each and everyone. No one is permitted to acquire property by means other than through original appropriation of previously unowned things, through production, or through voluntary exchange, and no one possesses a privilege to tax and expropriate. Moreover, no one is permitted to prohibit anyone else from using his property in order to enter any line of production he wishes and compete against whomever he pleases.

Daily Bell: How would law and order be provided in this society? How would your ideal justice system work?

Dr. Hans-Hermann Hoppe: In a private law society the production of
law and order—of security—would be undertaken by freely financed
individuals and agencies competing for a voluntarily paying (or not-
paying) clientele—just as the production of all other goods and
services. How this system would work can be best understood in
contrast to the workings of the present, all-too-familiar statist system.
If one wanted to summarize in one word the decisive difference—and
advantage—of a competitive security industry as compared to the
current statist practice, it would be: *contract.*

The state operates in a legal vacuum. There exists no contract
between the state and its citizens. It is not contractually fixed, what
is actually owned by whom, and what, accordingly, is to be protected. It
is not fixed, what service the state is to provide, what is to happen if the
state fails in its duty, nor what the price is that the "customer" of such
"service" must pay. Rather, the state unilaterally fixes the rules of the
game and can change them, per legislation, during the game. Obviously,
such behavior is inconceivable for freely financed security providers.
Just imagine a security provider, whether police, insurer or arbitrator,
whose offer consisted in something like this: I will not contractually
guarantee you anything. I will not tell you what I oblige myself to do
if, according to your opinion, I do not fulfill my service to you—but
in any case, I reserve the right to unilaterally determine the price that
you must pay me for such undefined service. Any such security provider
would immediately disappear from the market due to a complete lack
of customers.

Each private, freely financed security producer must instead offer
its prospective clients a contract. And these contracts must, in order
to appear acceptable to voluntarily paying consumers, contain clear
property descriptions as well as clearly defined mutual services and
obligations. Each party to a contract, for the duration or until the
fulfillment of the contract, would be bound by its terms and conditions;
and every change of terms or conditions would require the unanimous
consent of all parties concerned.

Specifically, in order to appear acceptable to security buyers, these
contracts must contain provisions about what will be done in the case
of a conflict or dispute between the protector or insurer and his own
protected or insured clients as well as in the case of a conflict between
different protectors or insurers and their respective clients. And in

this regard only one mutually agreeable solution exists: in these cases the conflicting parties contractually agree to arbitration by a mutually trusted but independent *third party*. And as for this third party: it, too, is freely financed and stands in competition with other arbitrators or arbitration agencies. Its clients, i.e., the insurers and the insured, expect of it, that it come up with a verdict that is recognized as fair and just by all sides. Only arbitrators capable of forming such judgments will succeed in the arbitration market. Arbitrators incapable of this and viewed as biased or partial will disappear from the market.

Daily Bell: Are you denying, then, that we need the state to defend us?

Dr. Hans-Hermann Hoppe: Indeed. The state does not defend *us*; rather, the state aggresses against us and it uses *our* confiscated property to defend *itself*. The standard definition of the state is this: the state is an agency characterized by two unique, logically connected features. First, the state is an agency that exercises a territorial monopoly of ultimate decision-making. That is, the state is the ultimate arbiter and judge in every case of conflict, including conflicts involving itself and its agents. There is no appeal above and beyond the state. Second, the state is an agency that exercises a territorial monopoly of taxation. That is, it is an agency that can unilaterally fix the price that its subjects must pay for the state's service as ultimate judge. Based on this institutional set-up you can safely predict the consequences. First, instead of preventing and resolving conflict, a monopolist of ultimate decision-making will *cause and provoke* conflict in order to settle it to its own advantage. That is, the state does not recognize and protect existing law, but it perverts law through legislation. Contradiction number one: the state is a law-breaking law protector. Second, instead of defending and protecting anyone or anything, a monopolist of taxation will invariably strive to *maximize his expenditures* on protection and at the same time *minimize the actual production* of protection. The more money the state can spend and the less it must work for this money, the better off it is. Contradiction number two: the state is an expropriating property protector.

Daily Bell: Are there any good laws and regulations?

Dr. Hans-Hermann Hoppe: Yes. There are a few, simple good laws that almost everyone intuitively recognizes and acknowledges and that can also be *demonstrated* to be "true" and "good" laws.

First: If there were no interpersonal conflicts and we all lived in perfect harmony there would be no need for any law or norm. It is the purpose of laws or norms to help *avoid* otherwise unavoidable conflict. Only laws that achieve this can be called good laws. A law that *generates* conflict rather than help avoid it is contrary to the purpose of laws, i.e., bad, dysfunctional or perverted law.

Second: Conflicts are possible only if and insofar as goods are *scarce*. People clash, because they want to use one and the same good in different, incompatible ways. Either I win and get my way or you win and get your way. We cannot both be "winners." In the case of scarce goods, then, we need rules or laws helping us decide between rival, conflicting claims. In contrast, goods that are "free," i.e., goods that exist in superabundance, that are inexhaustible or infinitely re-producible, are not and cannot be a source of conflict. Whenever I use a non-scarce good it does not in the slightest diminish the supply of this good available to you. I can do with it what I want and you can do with it what you want at the same time. There is no loser. We are both winners; and hence, as far as non-scarce goods are concerned, there is never any need for laws.

Third: All conflict concerning scarce goods, then, can be avoided if only every good is *privately owned*, i.e., exclusively controlled by one specified individual(s) rather than another, and it is always clear which thing is owned, and by whom, and which is not. And in order to avoid all possible conflict *from the beginning of mankind on*, it is only necessary to have a rule regulating the first, *original appropriation* of previously un-owned, nature-given goods as private property. In sum then, there are essentially three "good laws" that assure conflict-free interaction or "eternal peace": (a) he who first appropriates something previously on owned is its exclusive owner (as the *first* appropriator he cannot have come into conflict with anyone else as everyone else appeared on the scene only *later*); (b) he who produces something with his body and homesteaded goods is owner of his product, provided he does not thereby damage the physical integrity of others' property; and (c) he who acquires something from a previous or earlier owner by means of voluntary exchange, i.e., an exchange that is deemed *mutually* beneficial, is its owner.

Daily Bell: How, then, does one define freedom? As the absence of state coercion?

Dr. Hans-Hermann Hoppe: A society is free, if every person is recognized as the exclusive owner of his own (scarce) physical body, if everyone is free to appropriate or "homestead" previously un-owned things as private property, if everyone is free to use his body and his homesteaded goods to produce whatever he wants to produce (without thereby damaging the physical integrity of other peoples' property), and if everyone is free to contract with others regarding their respective properties in any way deemed mutually beneficial. Any interference with this constitutes an act of aggression, and a society is un-free to the extent of such aggressions.

Daily Bell: Where do you stand on copyright? Do you believe that intellectual property doesn't exist as Kinsella has proposed?

Dr. Hans-Hermann Hoppe: I agree with my friend Kinsella, that the idea of intellectual property rights is not just wrong and confused but dangerous. And I have already touched upon why this is so. Ideas —recipes, formulas, statements, arguments, algorithms, theorems, melodies, patterns, rhythms, images, etc.—are certainly goods (insofar as they are good, not bad, recipes, etc.), but they are not scarce goods. Once thought and expressed, they are free, inexhaustible goods. I whistle a melody or write down a poem, you hear the melody or read the poem and reproduce or copy it. In doing so you have not taken anything away from me. I can whistle and write as before. In fact, the entire world can copy me and yet nothing is taken from me. (If I didn't want anyone to copy my ideas I only have to keep them to myself and never express them.)

Now imagine I had been granted a property right in my melody or poem such that I could prohibit you from copying it or demanding a royalty from you if you do. First: Doesn't that imply, absurdly, that I, in turn, must pay royalties to the person (or his heirs) who invented whistling and writing, and further on to those, who invented sound-making and language, and so on? Second: In preventing you from or making you pay for whistling my melody or reciting my poem, I am actually made a (partial) owner of *you*: of your physical body, your vocal chords, your paper, your pencil, etc., because you did not use anything but your own property when you copied me. If you can no longer copy me, then, this means that I, the intellectual property owner, have expropriated you and your "real" property. Which shows:

intellectual property rights and real property rights are incompatible, and the promotion of intellectual property must be seen as a most dangerous attack on the idea of "real" property (in scarce goods).

Daily Bell: We have suggested that if people want to enforce generational copyright that they do so on their own, taking on the expense and attempting through various means to confront copyright violators with their own resources. This would put the onus of enforcement on the pocket book of the individual. Is this a viable solution—to let the market itself decide these issues?

Dr. Hans-Hermann Hoppe: That would go a long way in the right direction. Better still: more and more courts in more and more countries, especially countries outside the orbit of the U.S. dominated Western government cartel, would make it clear that they don't hear cases of copyright and patent violations any longer and regard such complaints as a ruse of big Western government-connected firms, such as pharmaceutical companies, for instance, to enrich themselves at the expense of other people.

Daily Bell: What do you think of Ragnar Redbeard's *Might Is Right*?

Dr. Hans-Hermann Hoppe: You can give two very different interpretations to this statement. I see no difficulty with the first one. It is: I know the difference between "might" and "right" and, as a matter of empirical fact, might is in fact frequently right. Most if not all of "public law," for instance, is might masquerading as right. The second interpretation is: I don't know the difference between "might" and "right," because there *is* no difference. Might *is* right and right *is* might. This interpretation is self-contradictory. Because if you wanted to defend this statement as a true statement in an argument with someone else you are in fact recognizing your opponent's property right in his own body. You do not aggress against him in order to bring him to the correct insight. You allow him to come to the correct insight on his own. That is, you admit, at least implicitly, that you *do* know the difference between right and wrong. Otherwise there would be no purpose in arguing. The same, incidentally, is true for Hobbes's famous dictum that one man is another man's wolf. In claiming this statement to be true, you actually prove it to be false.

Daily Bell: It has been suggested that the only way to reorganize society is via a return to the clans and tribes that characterized Homo sapiens communities for tens of thousands of years? Is it possible that as part of this devolution, clan or tribal justice could be re-emphasized?

Dr. Hans-Hermann Hoppe: I don't think that we, in the Western world, can go back to clans and tribes. The modern, democratic state has destroyed clans and tribes and their hierarchical structures, because they stood in the way of the state's drive toward absolute power. With clans and tribes gone, we must try it with the model of a private law society that I have described. But wherever traditional, hierarchical clan and tribe structures still exist, they should be supported and attempts to "modernize" "archaic" justice systems along Western lines should be viewed with utmost suspicion.

Daily Bell: You have also written extensively on money and monetary affairs. Is a gold standard necessary for a free society?

Dr. Hans-Hermann Hoppe: In a free society, the market would produce money, as all other goods and services. There would be no such thing as money in a world that was perfectly certain and predictable. But in a world with unpredictable contingencies people come to value goods also on account of their marketability or salability, i.e., as media of exchange. And since a more easily and widely salable good is preferable to a less easily and widely salable good as a medium of exchange, there is an inevitable tendency in the market for a single commodity to finally emerge that differs from all others in being the most easily and widely salable commodity of all. This commodity is called money. As the most easily salable good of all it provides its owner with the best humanly possible protection against uncertainty in that it can be employed for the instant satisfaction of the widest range of possible needs. Economic theory has nothing to say as to what commodity will acquire the status of money. Historically, it happened to be gold. But if the physical make-up of our world would have been different or is to become different from what it is now, some other commodity would have become or might become money. The market will decide. In any case, there is no need for government to get involved in any of this. The market has provided and will provide *some* money-commodity, and the production of that commodity, whatever it is, is subject to the same forces of supply and demand as the production of everything else.

Daily Bell: How about the free-banking paradigm? Is private fractional banking ever to be tolerated or is it a crime? Who is to put people in jail for private fractional banking?

Dr. Hans-Hermann Hoppe: Assume gold is money. In a free society you have free competition in gold mining, you have free competition in gold minting, and you have freely competing banks. The banks offer various financial services: of money safekeeping, clearing services, and the service of mediating between savers and borrower-investors. Each bank issues its own brand of "notes" or "certificates" documenting the various transactions and resulting contractual relations between bank and client. These banknotes are freely tradable. So far so good. Controversial among free bankers is only the status of fractional reserve deposit banking and bank notes. Let's say A deposits 10 ounces of gold with a bank and receives a note (a money substitute) redeemable at par on demand. Based on A's deposit, then, the bank makes a loan to C of 9 ounces of gold and issues a note to this effect, again redeemable at par on demand.

Should this be permitted? I don't think so. For there are now two people, A and C, who are the exclusive owner of one and the same quantity of money. A logical impossibility. Or put differently, there are only 10 ounces of gold, but A is given title to 10 ounces and C holds title to 9 ounces. That is, there are more property titles than there is property. Obviously this constitutes fraud, and in all areas except money, courts have also considered such a practice fraud and punished the offenders. On the other hand, there is no problem if the bank tells A that it will pay interest on his deposit, invest it, for instance, in a money market mutual fund made up of highly liquid short-term financial papers, and make its best efforts to redeem A's shares in that investment fund on demand in a fixed quantity of money. Such shares may well be very popular and many people may put their money into them instead of into regular deposit accounts. But as shares of investment funds they would never function as money. They would never be the most easily and widely saleable commodity of all.

Daily Bell: Where do you stand on the current central banking paradigm? Is central banking as it is currently constituted the central disaster of our time?

Dr. Hans-Hermann Hoppe: Central banks are certainly one of the greatest mischief-makers of our time. They, and in particular the Fed, have been responsible for destroying the gold standard, which has always been an obstacle to inflationary policies, and replacing it, since 1971, with a pure paper money standard (fiat money). Since then, central banks can create money virtually out of thin air. More paper money cannot make a society richer, of course,—it is just more printed paper. Otherwise, why is it that there are still poor countries and poor people around? But more money makes its monopolistic producer (the central bank) and its earliest recipients (the government and big, government-connected banks and their major clients) richer at the expense of making the money's late and latest receivers poorer.

Thanks to the central bank's unlimited money printing power, governments can run ever higher budget deficits and pile up ever more debt to finance otherwise impossible wars, hot and cold, abroad and at home, and engage in an endless stream of otherwise unthinkable boondoggles and adventures. Thanks to the central bank, most "monetary experts" and "leading macro-economists" can, by putting them on the payroll, be turned into government propagandists "explaining," like alchemists, how stones (paper) can be turned into bread (wealth). Thanks to the central bank, interest rates can be artificially lowered all the way down to zero, channeling credit into less and least credit-worthy projects and hands (and crowding out worthy projects and hands), and causing ever greater investment bubble-booms, followed by ever more spectacular busts. And thanks to the central bank, we are confronted with a dramatically increasing threat of an impending hyperinflation when the chicken finally comes home to roost and the piper must be paid.

Daily Bell: We have often pointed out that the Seven Hills of Rome were initially independent societies just like the Italian city-states during the Renaissance and the 13 colonies of the U.S. Republic. It seems great empires start as individual communities where people can leave one community if they are oppressed and go nearby to start afresh. What is the driving force behind this process of centralization? What are the building blocks of Empire?

Dr. Hans-Hermann Hoppe: All states must begin small. That makes it easy for people to run away. Yet states are by nature aggressive, as I have already explained. They can externalize the cost of aggression onto others, i.e., hapless taxpayers. They don't like to see productive people run away and try to capture them by expanding their territory. The more productive people the state controls, the better off it will be. In this expansionist desire, they run into opposition by other states. There can be only one monopolist of ultimate jurisdiction and taxation in any given territory. That is, the competition between different states is eliminative. Either A wins and controls a territory, or B. Who wins? At least in the long run, that state will win—and take over another's territory or establish hegemony over it and force it to pay tribute—that can parasitically draw on the comparatively more productive economy. That is, other things being the same, internally more "liberal" states (in the classic European sense of "liberal") will tend to win over less "liberal," i.e., illiberal or oppressive states.

Looking only at modern history, we can so explain first the rise of liberal Great Britain to the rank of the foremost world Empire and then, subsequently, that of the liberal U.S. And we can understand a seeming paradox: why it is, that internally liberal imperial powers like the U.S. tend to be more aggressive and belligerent in their foreign policy than internally oppressive powers, such as the former Soviet Union. The liberal U.S. Empire was sure to win with its foreign wars and military adventures, while the oppressive Soviet Union was afraid that it might lose.

But empire-building also bears the seeds of its own destruction. The closer a state comes to the ultimate goal of world domination and one-world government, the less reason is there to maintain its internal liberalism and do instead what all states are inclined to do anyway, i.e., to crack down and increase their exploitation of whatever productive people are still left. Consequently, with no additional tributaries available and domestic productivity stagnating or falling, the Empire's internal policies of bread and circuses can no longer be maintained. Economic crisis hits, and an impending economic meltdown will stimulate decentralizing tendencies, separatist and secessionist movements, and lead to the break-up of Empire. We have seen this happen with Great Britain, and we are seeing it now, with the U.S. and its Empire apparently on its last legs.

There is also an important monetary side to this process. The dominant Empire typically provides the leading international reserve currency, first Britain with the pound sterling and then the U.S. with the dollar. With the dollar used as reserve currency by foreign central banks, the U.S. can run a permanent "deficit without tears." That is, the U.S. must not pay for its steady excesses of imports over exports, as it is normal between "equal" partners, in having to ship increasingly more exports abroad (exports paying for imports). Rather: Instead of using their export earnings to buy American goods for domestic consumption, foreign governments and their central banks, as a sign of their vassal status *vis-à-vis* a dominant U.S., use their paper dollar reserves to buy up U.S. government bonds to help *Americans* to continue consuming beyond their means.

I do not know enough about China to understand why it is using its huge dollar reserves to buy up U.S. government bonds. After all, China is not supposed to be a part of the U.S. Empire. Maybe its rulers have read too many American economics textbooks and now believe in alchemy, too. But if only China would dump its U.S. treasuries and accumulate gold reserves instead, that would be the end of the U.S. Empire and the dollar as we know it.

Daily Bell: Is it possible that a shadow of impossibly wealthy families located in the City of London is partially responsible for all this? Do these families and their enablers seek world government by elites? Is it a conspiracy? Do you see the world in these terms: as a struggle between the centralizing impulses of elites and the more democratic impulses of the rest of society?

Dr. Hans-Hermann Hoppe: I'm not sure if conspiracy is still the right word, because in the meantime, thanks to people such as Carroll Quigley, for instance, much is known about what is going on. In any case, it is certainly true that there are such impossibly rich families, sitting in London, New York City, Tel Aviv and elsewhere, who have recognized the immense potential for personal enrichment in the process of State- and Empire-building. The heads of big banking houses played a key role in the founding of the Fed, because they realized that central banking would allow their own banks to inflate and expand credit on top of money and credit created by the central bank, and that a "lender of last resort" was instrumental in allowing them to reap private profits as long as things would go well and to socialize costs if they wouldn't.

They realized that the classical gold standard stood as a natural impediment to inflation and credit expansion, and so they helped set up first a phony gold standard (the gold exchange standard) and then, after 1971, a pure fiat money regime. They realized that a system of freely fluctuating national fiat currencies was still imperfect as far as inflationist desires are concerned, in that the supremacy of the dollar could be threatened by other, competing currencies such as a strong German Mark, for instance; and in order to reduce and weaken this competition they supported "monetary integration" schemes such as the creation of a European Central Bank (ECB) and the Euro.

And they realized that their ultimate dream of unlimited counterfeiting power would come true, if only they succeeded in creating a U.S. dominated world central bank issuing a world paper currency such as the bancor or the phoenix; and so they helped set up and finance a multitude of organizations such as the Council on Foreign Relations, the Trilateral Commission, the Bilderberg Group, etc., that promote this goal. As well, leading industrialists recognized the tremendous profits to be made from state-granted monopolies, from state subsidies, and from exclusive cost-plus contracts in freeing or shielding them from competition, and so they, too, have allied themselves to and "infiltrated" the state.

There are "accidents" in history, and there are carefully planned actions that bring about consequences which are unintended and unanticipated. But history is not just a sequence of accidents and surprises. Most of it is designed and intended. Not by common folks, of course, but by the power elites in control of the state apparatus. If one wants to prevent history from running its present, foreseeable course to unprecedented economic disaster, then, it is indeed imperative to arouse public indignation by exposing, relentlessly, the evil motives and machinations of these power elites, not just of those working within the state apparatus, but in particular also of those staying outside, behind the scenes and pulling the strings.

Daily Bell: It has been our contention that just as the Gutenberg press blew up existing social structures in its day, so the Internet is doing that today. We believe the Internet may be ushering in a new Renaissance after the Dark Age of the 20th century. Agree? Disagree?

Dr. Hans-Hermann Hoppe: It is certainly true that both inventions revolutionized society and greatly improved our lives. It is difficult to imagine what it would be to go back to the pre-internet age or the pre-Gutenberg era. I am skeptical, however, if technological revolutions in and of themselves also bring about moral progress and an advance toward greater freedom. I am more inclined to think that technology and technological advances are "neutral" in this regard. The Internet can be used to unearth and spread the truth as much as to spread lies and confusion. It has given us unheard of possibilities to evade and undermine our enemy the state, but it has also given the state unheard of possibilities of spying on us and ruining us. We are richer today, with the Internet, than we were, let's say, in 1900, without it (and we are richer not because of the state but in spite of it). But I would emphatically deny that we are freer today than we were in 1900. Quite to the contrary.

Daily Bell: Any final thoughts? Can you tell us what you are working on now? Any books or websites you would like to recommend?

Dr. Hans-Hermann Hoppe: I once deviated from my principle not to speak about my work until it was done. I have regretted this deviation. It was a mistake that I won't repeat. As for books, I recommend above all reading the major works of my two masters, Ludwig von Mises and Murray Rothbard, not just once, but repeatedly from time to time. Their work is still unsurpassed and will remain so for a long time to come. As for websites, I go most regularly to mises.org and to lewrockwell.com. As for other sites: I have been called an extremist, a reactionary, a revisionist, an elitist, a supremacist, a racist, a homophobe, an anti-Semite, a right-winger, a theocrat, a godless cynic, a fascist and, of course, a must for every German, a Nazi. So, it should be expected that I have a foible for politically "incorrect" sites that every "modern," "decent," "civilized," "tolerant," and "enlightened" man is supposed to ignore and avoid.

Daily Bell: Thank you for your time in answering these questions. It has been a special honor to address them to you in the context of your remarkable work.

Dr. Hans-Hermann Hoppe: You're welcome.

III. Conclusion

What a great interview. We say this immodestly because with some exceptions (free-banking and money competition being notable ones), Dr. Hans-Hermann Hoppe, one of the finest libertarian thinkers and educators in the world today, actually seemed to agree with some of what has been proposed in these modest pages for several years. Don't take our word for it. Reread the interview if you wish. To have someone of Dr. Hoppe's caliber of mind endorse and elaborate on fundamental perceptions such as we have advanced on occasion is incredibly affirming and even (we don't mind admitting) intellectually satisfying.

On a less frivolous note, what comes across in the interview is that Dr. Hoppe is one of those peculiar individuals who, having glimpsed truth not available to most people, is unable by temperament to temporize about its validity. One sees this characteristic reflected in the work and narratives of Murray Rothbard and Ludwig von Mises to name two brilliant thinkers that come to mind. The inability to avoid the conclusions (or to shy away from voicing them) developed from one's belief system is a telltale sign of intellectual courage and even, we submit, greatness.

It is indeed rare to have the privilege of conducting a dialogue with a truly clarified intellect, someone in fact with a mercilessly resonant frame of reference. If you read the interview closely, you can actually see (or hear) the disciplined approach with which Dr. Hoppe approaches the issues on which he comments. Each position is developed rationally and each conclusion evolves relentlessly from evidence adumbrated.

We won't write much more because like a great musical composition, this interview in our view is best appreciated on its own. Our clumsy commentary probably only detracts from its muscularity and elegant austerity. Of course, you may not appreciate our efforts, dear reader, but please acknowledge the courtesy, wisdom and intellectual courage of one of the world's profound free-market thinkers, Dr. Hans-Hermann Hoppe.

22

Interview with *Philosophie Magazine*

I. Introduction

A few months ago, a French journalist, Mr. Nicolas Cori, approached me with the request for an interview on the subject of taxation, to be published in the French monthly *Philosophie Magazine*, in the context of current "tax reform" debates in France.

I agreed to the interview, it was conducted by email in English, Mr. Cori produced a French translation, my friend Dr. Nikolay Gertchev checked and corrected his translation, and I then sent the authorized translation to Mr. Cori. Since then, more than a month ago, and despite repeated promptings, I have not heard from Mr. Cori. I can only speculate as for the reasons of his silence. Most likely, he did not get permission from his superiors to publish the interview, and he does not possess the courtesy and courage to tell me.

II. Interview

NC: Are taxes consistent with individual freedom and property rights? Is there a level of taxation where it is no more consistent?

Hoppe: No. Taxes are never, at no level of taxation, consistent with individual freedom and property rights. Taxes are *theft*. The thieves—the state and its agents and allies—try their very best to conceal this fact, of course, but there is simply no way around it. Obviously, taxes are not normal, voluntary payments for goods and services, because you are not allowed to stop such payments if you are not satisfied with the

---

• Originally published on www.hanshoppe.com.

product. You are not punished if you do no longer buy Renault cars or Chanel perfume, but you are thrown into jail if you stop paying for government schools or universities or for Mr. Sarkozy and his pomp. Nor is it possible to construe taxes as normal rent-payments, as they are made by a renter to his landlord. Because the French state is not the landlord of all of France and all Frenchmen. To be the landlord, the French state would have to be able to prove two things: first, that the state, and no one else, owns every inch of France, and second, that it has a rental contract with every single Frenchman concerning the use, and the price for this use, of its property. No state—not the French, not the German, not the U.S.-American or any other state—can prove this. They have no documents to this effect and they cannot present any rental contract. Thus, there is only one conclusion: taxation is theft and robbery by which one segment of the population, the ruling class, enriches itself at the expense of another, the ruled.

NC: Is it wrong not to pay taxes?

Hoppe: No. Given that taxes are theft, i.e., a moral "wrong," it cannot be wrong to refuse to pay thieves or to lie to them regarding one's taxable income or assets. This does not mean that it is prudent or wise to do so and not to pay taxes—after all the state is the "coldest of all monsters," as Nietzsche has put it, and it can ruin your life or even destroy you if you do not obey its commands. But there can be no question that it is *just* not to pay taxes.

NC: How do we know that a tax is fair? Are there any criteria? Is a progressive tax better than a flat tax?

Hoppe: We know that *no* tax is fair, whether progressive or flat and proportional. How can theft and robbery be fair? The "best" tax is always the lowest tax—yet even the lowest tax is still a *tax*. The "best," because lowest tax is a head or poll tax, where every person pays the same absolute amount of taxes. Since even the poorest person must be able to pay this amount, such a tax *must* be low. But even a head tax is still theft, and there is nothing "fair" about it. A head tax does *not* treat everyone equally and installs "equality before the law." For something happens with the tax revenue. The salaries of all state employees and dependents (like pensioners and welfare recipients) are paid out of tax revenue, for instance. Accordingly, state employees and dependents pay no taxes at all. Rather, their entire net-income (after payment of their head tax) comes out of tax-payments and they are thus (on net) tax-*consumers* living off income and wealth stolen from others: the tax-*producers*. What is fair about one group of people living parasitically on, and at the expense of, another group of people?

NC: Do all philosophers agree?

Hoppe: No, they don't. But that is hardly surprising. Almost all professional philosophers nowadays are tax-*consumers*. They do not produce any goods or services that they sell on the market to voluntarily buying or not-buying philosophy-consumers. As a matter of fact, as judged by actual consumer demand, the work of most contemporary philosophers must be considered worthless. Rather: Nearly all philosophers today are paid out of taxes. They live off money stolen or confiscated from others. If your livelihood depends on taxes you will likely not oppose the institution of taxation on principled grounds. Of course this is not *necessarily* the case. Our "consciousness" is not *determined* by our "Sein," à la Marx. However, any such opposition is not very likely. Indeed, as most "intellectuals," philosophers typically suffer from an over-inflated ego. They believe to do work of great importance and resent the fact that "society" does not compensate them accordingly. Hence, if the issue of taxation is not simply ignored by them, philosophers have been at the forefront of coming up with tortured attempts of justifying taxes—of masquerading theft as something "good"—and in particular their own, tax-funded philosopher salaries.

NC: Should philosophers consider the economic efficiency of taxation methods, simultaneously with its ethical values?

Hoppe: In order to speak of an action as "efficient," it is necessary that we first define a *purpose*, i.e., a goal or an end. Something can be judged as efficient or inefficient only in light of a *goal* that is assumed as *given*. It is the task of economists and so-called "positive economics" to determine, which measures are effective (or ineffective) in bringing about a *given end*. For instance, if you want to bring about mass unemployment, then economics tells you that it is efficient to raise minimum wages to, let us say, 100 Euros per hour. On the other hand, if it is your goal to minimize unemployment, then economics informs you that all minimum wage laws should be abolished. But economists *qua* economists have nothing to say about the permissibility or desirability of the goals in question. This is the task of the philosopher: to determine which goals are just and permissible and which goals are not. (The economist then informs the philosopher which means are efficient or inefficient, in order to reach such justifiable goals.)

But as I already indicated: the philosophy profession simply has not done its job. Philosophers give plenty of advice about what to do or not to do, of course, but their advice carries little or no intellectual weight. In almost all cases, it is mere opinion: expression of personal tastes, nothing more. If you implore about the "theory of justice," from which their recommendations supposedly follow, they have no such theory. They can offer only some ad-hoc collection of personal value judgments, which typically does not even fulfill the requirement of internal consistency.

Any theory of justice worth its salt must recognize first the most fundamental fact of human life: the *scarcity of goods*, i.e., the absence of super-abundance. For only because of scarcity is it possible that people can have *conflicts* with each other: I want to do *x* with a given, scarce resource, and you want to do *y* with the very same resource. Without conflicts, there would be no need for rules or *norms*; and the purpose of norms then is conflict-*avoidance*. In the absence of a pre-stabilized harmony of all interests, conflicts can be avoided only if all scarce resources are owned *privately*, i.e., by *one* identifiable owner rather than, and at the exclusion of, another. And in order to avoid conflict from the beginning of mankind on, so to speak, any theory of justice must begin with a norm regulating the first, *original appropriation* of scarce resources as *private property*.

Most of contemporary (political) philosophy seems to be unaware of any of this. Indeed, I often have the impression that not even the fact of scarcity itself is recognized or fully comprehended.

NC: What, then, should be the goal of tax policy? Redistribution? Equality? To diminish poverty?

Hoppe: If taxes are theft, then, from the point of view of justice, there should be *no* taxes and *no* tax policy at all. Every discussion about the goals of tax policy and tax reform is a discussion among thieves or advocates of theft, who do not care about justice. They care about theft. There is debate and dispute among them about who should be taxed and how high and what is to be done with the taxes, i.e., who should get how much of the stolen loot. But all thieves and all beneficiaries of theft tend to agree on one thing: the greater the amount of loot and the lower the cost of collecting it, the better are things for them. In fact, this is what all Western democracies practice today: to choose tax rates and forms of taxation, which maximize tax revenue. All current discussions about tax reform, in France, in Germany, in the U.S. and elsewhere: discussions about whether certain forms of taxes such as wealth and inheritance taxes should be introduced or abolished, whether income should be taxed progressively or proportionally, whether capital gains should be taxed as income or not, whether or not indirect taxes such as the VAT should be substituted for direct taxes, etc., etc., and whether the rates of these taxes then should be raised or cut — they are never discussions about justice. They are not motivated by any principled opposition to taxation, but by the desire to make taxation more efficient, i.e., to maximize tax revenue. Every tax reform that is not, at a minimum, "revenue neutral," is considered a failure. And only reforms that *increase* tax revenue are deemed a "success."

I must ask again: How can anyone consider this "fair?" Of course, from the point of view of tax-*consumers* this is all "good." But from the viewpoint of tax-*producers*, i.e., of those who actually *pay* taxes, it is certainly *not* "good," but "worse than bad."

One last remark on the economic effects of taxation: Every tax *is* a redistribution of wealth and income. Wealth and income is forcibly taken from their owners and producers and transferred to people who did *not* own this wealth and did *not* produce this income. The future accumulation of wealth and the production of income are thus *dis*couraged and the confiscation and consumption of existing wealth and income is *en*couraged. As a result, society will be poorer. And as for the effect of the eternally popular, egalitarian proposal of taxing the "rich" to give to the "poor" in particular: Such a scheme does not reduce or alleviate poverty but, quite to the contrary, it *increases* poverty. It reduces the incentive to stay or become rich and be productive, and it increases the incentive to stay or become poor and be un-productive.

NC: Should rich people be treated differently than poor people?

Hoppe: Every person, rich or poor, should be treated the same before the law. There are rich people, who are rich without having defrauded or

stolen from anyone. They are rich, because they have worked hard, they
have saved diligently, they have been productive, and they have shown
entrepreneurial ingenuity, often for several family-generations. Such
people should not only be left alone, but they should be praised as
heroes. And there are rich people, mostly from the class of political
leaders in control of the state-apparatus and from the state-connected
elites of banking and big business, who are rich, because they have been
directly engaged in, or indirectly benefitted from, confiscation, theft,
trickery and fraud. Such people should *not* be left alone, but instead be
condemned and despised as gangsters. The same applies to poor people.
There are poor people, who are honest people, and therefore should be
left alone. They may not be heroes, but they deserve our respect. And
there are poor people who are crooks, and who should be treated as
crooks, regardless of their "poverty."

23

This Crazy World

We live in the age of the American Empire. This Empire may be crumbling, but for the foreseeable future it will last, not only because of its military might but, more importantly, because of its ideological power. For the American Empire has accomplished something truly remarkable: that its core beliefs are internalized in the minds of most people as intellectual taboos. To be sure, all governments rest on aggressive violence and the U.S. government is no exception. It, too, does not hesitate to crush anyone resisting its legislative whims. However, the U.S. government needs astonishing little actual violence to achieve submission to its commands, because the overwhelming majority of the population and in particular of the opinion-molding intellectuals has adopted the value- and belief-system that underlies the American Empire as its very own.

According to the official, U.S.-approved belief system, we are all intelligent and reasonable people confronted with the same hard reality and committed to the facts and the truth. True enough, even at the center of the American Empire, in the U.S., people do not live in the best of all possible worlds. There are still many defects to be fixed. However, with the American system of democratic government, mankind has definitely found the perfect institutional framework allowing for continuous progress on the way toward an ever more perfect world; and if only the American system of democracy is adopted on a world-wide scale, the path to perfection is everywhere clear and open.

The only truly legitimate form of government is democracy. Any other form of government is inferior. There exist monarchies, dictatorships and

---

• Originally delivered as the introductory speech at the Property and Freedom Society's 2009 annual meeting in Bodrum, Turkey, May 21, 2009.

theocracies, and there exist feudal land-lords and war-lords; and since any government is to be preferred to no government at all, democratic governments must, out of necessity, at times cooperate with other, non-democratic governments. Ultimately, however, all governments must be changed according to the American Ideal, because only democracy allows for peaceful change and continuous progress.

Democratic governments such as the U.S. and its European allies are inherently peaceful and do not wage war against each other. If they must wage war at all, their wars are wars of defense against aggressive non-democratic regimes, i.e., just wars. Thus, all countries and territories currently occupied by American troops or those of its European allies have been guilty of aggression, and their occupation by foreign troops is an act of self-defense and of liberation on the part of the democratic West. The aggressiveness of the Islamic world in particular is proven by the very fact that large parts of it are under American-Western occupation and more areas still are provoking such liberating occupation.

Democratic governments are of the people, by the people and for the people. In democracies no one rules over anyone, but the people rule themselves and are hence free. Taxes are contributions and payments for services rendered by government; and tax-evaders are accordingly thieves, who take without paying. Harboring fugitive thieves is then an act of aggression against the people from whom they try to flee.

Private property, markets and profit-making are good and useful institutions, but democratic government must see to it, through proper legislation, that private property and profits are acquired and used in a socially responsible way and that markets function efficiently. Moreover, markets and profit-motivated business cannot produce public goods and thus satisfy social needs, and they cannot take care of the truly needy. Social needs and the needy can be taken care of only by government. Government alone, through the funding of public goods and support given to the needy, can enhance the public welfare and reduce if not eliminate the neediness and number of the needy.

In particular, government social policy must control the private vice of greed and profiteering. Greed and profiteering were also the root cause of the present economic crisis. Reckless financiers created an irrational exuberance in the public that has finally foundered on reality. The market manifestly failed, and only government stood ready to save the situation; and only government, through proper regulation and supervision of the banking industry and financial markets, can prevent anything like this from ever happening again. Banks and businesses went bankrupt. But governments and their central banks stood tall and protected savers' money and workers' jobs.

Advised by the best and best-paid economists in the world, governments have discovered the cause of the crisis and determined that to get out of the current economic mess people must both consume more and invest more. Every penny hoarded under the mattress is a penny withheld from present consumption and investment and so diminishes future consumption and investment. In a recession, under all circumstances and above all, spending must be increased; and if the people do not spend enough of their money, then government must do it for them with its money. Wisely, governments are equipped to do so, because their central banks can produce all necessary liquidity. If billions of dollars or Euros will not do it, trillions will; and if trillions still fail to do the trick then quadrillions surely will. Only massive government spending can avert an otherwise unavoidable economic meltdown. Unemployment in particular is the result of under-consumption: of people not having enough money to buy consumer goods; and it must be cured by giving them higher money wages or higher unemployment benefits.

Once the current economic crisis has been solved, governments can and must again turn to the truly pressing among the remaining problems confronting mankind: the elimination of all unfair discrimination as the ultimate desideratum of democratic egalitarianism, and the control of the global environment and in particular the world climate.

Essentially, all humans are equal. Differences are only apparent, skin-deep and insignificant: some people are white, some brown, and some black; some are tall, and others are short; some are male and some female; some speak English and others Polish or Chinese; some have cancer or AIDS and others don't. These are accidental human characteristics. Some people happen to have them and others not. However, from such accidental differences only trivial consequences follow, such that the tall can reach higher up, that only women can bear children or that some people will die sooner than others. But accidental differences such as these have no systematic bearing on mental traits, such as motivational energy, time-preference or intellectual prowess, and as such they are without explanatory power concerning economic and social success: in particular income and professional status and position. Mental traits have no physical, biological or ethnic basis and are infinitely malleable. Everyone, except for a few pathological cases, is like everyone else in this regard, and every people, throughout history, have made an equal contribution to civilization. Seemingly apparent differences are solely the result of different external circumstances and training opportunities. If properly situated and trained, everyone is capable of the same achievements. All income and achievement differences between Whites, Asians and Blacks, women and men, Latinos, Anglos and Thais, and Hindus, Protestants and Moslems would vanish. Whites could be brought up to compete on a par with Blacks for the highest prizes in the NBA, in the 100 meter sprint and in long-distance running, and Blacks could compete with Whites and Asians in math, chess and engineering. If it is found instead that the representation and distribution of various accidental groups in various social positions of income, wealth or professional status is unequal, then this shows unjustified discrimination; and such discrimination must be rectified by appropriate affirmative action programs, by which the discriminators must compensate the unjustly discriminated.

There is just one possible exception from this general principle of human equality and the evil of discrimination. For, beyond any reasonable doubt, there was one crime in history, committed by one particular people against one particular other people, that is incomparable to any other crime. It cannot be ruled out that this uniquely criminal disposition on the part of one people has genetic roots; and insofar as this possibility cannot be ruled out, it is only fair that the collectively guilty must continue to compensate the collective victims.

Hand in hand with the efforts to eradicate the evil of discrimination, democratic governments must tackle the fundamental task of overcoming the excessive human particularism—the individualism, the localism, provincialism, regionalism and nationalism—ingrained still in the minds of most people and promote instead the ideal of universalism and of the Universal Man and the interests of humanity as such. The necessity of this policy is demonstrated most dramatically by the dangers of global climate change. As the result of countless selfish acts: the unregulated production and consumption of various non-renewable sources of energy, the whole globe is threatened by unimaginable catastrophes: of tidal waves, sharply and suddenly rising sea levels and the emergence of momentous ecological imbalances and instabilities. Only through world-wide concerted government action, and ultimately the establishment of some supra-national world-government, and through minute, scientifically validated and world-wide administered and enforced behavioral regulations of all production and consumption activities can these life-threatening dangers be averted. *Gemeinwohl* (public welfare) *geht vor* (comes before) *Eigenwohl* (private welfare)—this, above all, is what the problem of climate change demonstrates, and it is up to government to finally put this principle into action.

The PFS—and most certainly I, personally—consider all of this just crazy: as utter nonsense and dangerous nonsense at that. Yet this is essentially what we can hear and read day in and day out in the mainstream media and what is proclaimed by every respectable expert and eminence. Only few people can see through the entire charade and even less have the courage to speak up against it. It is the purpose of the PFS and its meetings to assemble such people, to frontally attack the entire craziness and the ruling class perpetrating it on us—and to have fun doing it, at least while we are still permitted to have fun.

24

My Life on the Right

When I first envisioned the idea of this Society, more than 10 years ago and then still a society without a name, I had direct experience with only two other Societies from which to learn.

My first experience was with the Mont Pelerin Society, which Friedrich Hayek had founded in 1947.

During the 1990s, I was three times invited as a speaker to Mont Pelerin Society meetings in Cannes, Cape Town, and Barcelona. Each time, with papers attacking democracy and egalitarianism, defending monarchies versus democracies, eviscerating the classical-liberal idea of a minimal-state as self-contradictory, and propagating a stateless, anarcho-capitalist natural order, my appearance was considered somewhat scandalous: too irreverent, too confrontational, and too sensational.

Whatever the function of the Mont Pelerin Society may have been in the immediate aftermath of WWII, at the time of my encounter with it, I did not find it particularly to my liking.

To be sure, I met many bright and interesting people. But essentially, Mont Pelerin Society meetings were junkets for "free market" and "limited government" think-tank and foundation staffers, their various professorial affiliates and protégés, and the principal donor-financiers of it all, mostly from the U.S., and more specifically from Washington, D.C. Characteristically, Ed Feulner, long-time President of the Heritage Foundation, the major GOP think-tank and intellectual shill to the welfare–warfare state politics of every Republican government administration, from Reagan to Bush, Jr., is a former Mont Pelerin Society president and, more significantly, has been its long-time treasurer.

• Originally published in the *Libertarian Standard*

There had been skepticism concerning the Mont Pelerin Society from the beginning. Ludwig von Mises, Hayek's teacher and friend, had expressed severe doubt concerning his plan simply in view of Hayek's initial invitees: how could a society filled with certified state-interventionists promote the goal of a free and prosperous commonwealth?

Despite his initial reservations, however, Mises became a founding member of the Mont Pelerin Society. Yet his prediction turned out correct. Famously, at an early Mont Pelerin Society meeting, Mises would walk out denouncing speakers and panelists as a bunch of socialists.

Essentially, this was also my first impression when I came in contact with the Mont Pelerin Society and this impression has been confirmed since. The Mont Pelerin Society is a society in which every right-wing social democrat can feel at home. True, occasionally a few strange birds are invited to speak, but the meetings are dominated and the range of acceptable discourse is delineated by certified state-interventionists: by the heads of government-funded or connected foundations and think-tanks, by central bank payrollees, paper-money enthusiasts, and assorted international educrats and researchocrats in and out of government. No discussion in the hallowed halls of the Mont Pelerin Society of U.S. imperialism or the Bush war crimes, for instance, or of the financial crimes committed by the Federal Reserve Bank—and no discussion of any sensitive race issue, of course.

Not all of this can be blamed on Hayek, needless to say. He had increasingly lost control of the Mont Pelerin Society already long before his death in 1992.

But then: Hayek *did* have much to do with what the Mont Pelerin Society had become. For, as Mises could have known already then, and as would become apparent at last in 1960, with the publication of Hayek's *Constitution of Liberty*, Hayek himself was a proven interventionist. In the third part of this famous book, Hayek had laid out a plan for a "free" society so riddled with interventionist designs that every moderate social-democrat— of the Scandinavian-German variety—could easily subscribe. When, at the occasion of Hayek's 80th birthday in 1979, the Social Democratic then-Chancellor of West Germany, Helmut Schmidt, sent Hayek a congratulatory note proclaiming "we are all Hayekians now," this was not an empty phrase. It was true, and Schmidt meant it.

What I came to realize, then, was this: The deplorable development—as judged from a classic-liberal vantage point—of the Mont Pelerin Society was not an accident. Rather, it was the necessary consequence of a fundamental theoretical flaw committed not only by Hayek but, ultimately, also by Mises, with his idea of a minimal state.

This flaw did not merely afflict the Mont Pelerin Society. It afflicted the entire "limited government" think-tank industry that had sprung up as its offspring since the 1960s throughout the Western, U.S.-dominated world, and for which the Mont Pelerin Society had assumed the function of an "International."

The goal of "limited" — or "constitutional" — government, which Friedrich Hayek, Milton Friedman, James Buchanan and other Mont Pelerin Society grandees had tried to promote and that every "free market" think-tank today proclaims as its goal, is an *impossible* goal, much as it is an impossible goal to try squaring the circle. You cannot first establish a territorial monopoly of law and order and then expect that this monopolist will not make use of this awesome privilege of legislating in its own favor. Likewise: You cannot establish a territorial monopoly of paper money production and expect the monopolist not to use its power of printing up ever more money.

Limiting the power of the state, once it has been granted a territorial monopoly of legislation, is impossible, a self-contradictory goal. To believe that it is possible to limit government power—other than by subjecting it to competition, i.e., by not allowing monopoly privileges of any kind to arise in the first place—is to assume that the nature of Man changes as the result of the establishment of government (very much like the miraculous transformation of Man that socialists believe to happen with the onset of socialism).

That is the whole thing: limited government, is an illusory goal. To believe it to be possible is to believe in miracles.

The strategy of Hayek and of the Mont Pelerin Society, then, *had* to fail. Instead of helping to reform—liberalize—the (Western) State, as they intended (or pretended?) to do, the Mont Pelerin Society and the international "limited government" think-tank industry would become an integral *part* of a continuously expanding welfare–warfare state system.

Indicators for this verdict abound: The typical location of the think tanks is in or near the capital city, most prominently Washington, D.C., because their principal addressee is the central government. They react to measures and announcements of government, and they suggest and make proposals to government. Most contacts of think-tankers outside their own institution are with politicians, government bureaucrats, lobbyists, and assorted staffers and assistants. Along with connected journalists, these are also the regular attendees of their conferences, briefings, receptions and cocktail parties. There is a steady exchange of personnel between think tanks and governments. And the leaders of the limited-government industry are frequently themselves prominent members of the power elite and the ruling class.

Most indicative of all: For decades, the limited government movement has been a growth industry. Its annual expenditures currently run in the hundreds of millions of dollars, and billions of dollars likely have been spent in total. All the while, *government expenditures never and nowhere fell*, not even once, but instead always and uninterruptedly increased to ever more dizzying heights.

And yet, this glaring failure of the industry to deliver the promised good of limited government is not punished but, perversely, rewarded with still more ample funds. The more the think tanks fail, the more money they get.

The State and the free-market think-tank industry thus live in perfect harmony with each other. They grow together, in tandem.

For limited government advocates such as Hayek and the entire free-market think-tank industry, this is an embarrassment. They must try to explain it away somehow, as accidental or coincidental. And they typically do so, simply enough, by arguing that without their continued funding and operations matters would be even worse.

Thus excused, then, the industry continues on as before, undisturbed by any fact or event past or future.

But the embarrassing facts are *not* accidental or coincidental and *could* have been systematically predicted—if only one had better understood the nature of the state, and did not believe in miracles.

As a territorial monopolist of legislation and the money-printing press, the State has a natural tendency to grow: to use its "fiat" laws and "fiat" money to gain increasing control of society and social institutions. With "fiat laws," the State has the unique power of threatening and punishing or incentivizing and rewarding whatever it pleases. And with its "fiat money," it can buy up support, bribe, and corrupt more easily than anyone else.

Certainly, an extraordinary institution such as this will have the means at its disposal, legal and financial, to deal with the challenge posed by a limited government industry. Historically, the State has successfully dealt with far more formidable opponents—like organized religion, for instance!

Unlike the Church or churches, however, the limited government industry is conveniently located and concentrated at or near the center of State power, and the industry's entire *raison d'être* is to talk and have access to the State. That is what its donor-financiers typically expect.

Yet so much the easier, then, was it for the State to target and effectively control this industry. The State only had to set up its own bureaucracy in charge of free-market relations and lure the limited-government NGOs (non-government organizations) with conferences, invitations, sponsorships, grants, money and employment prospects. Without having to resort to threats, these measures alone were sufficient to ensure compliance on the part of the free-market think-tank industry and its associated intellectuals. The market demand for intellectual services is low and fickle and hence intellectuals can be bought up cheaply!

Moreover, through its cooperation with the free market industry, the State could enhance its own legitimacy and intellectual respectability as an "economically enlightened," institution—and thus open up still further room for State growth.

Essentially, as with all so-called NGOs, the State managed to transform the limited-government industry into just another vehicle for its own aggrandizement.

What I learned from my experience with the Mont Pelerin Society, then, was that an entirely different strategy had to be chosen if one wanted to limit the power of the State. For socialists or social-democrats, it is perfectly rational to talk and seek access to the State and to try "marching through its institutions," because the Left wants to increase the power of the State. That is, the Left wants what the State is disposed to do anyway, by virtue of its nature as a territorial monopolist of law and order.

But the same strategy is inefficient or even counterproductive if one wants to roll the power of the State *back*—regardless of whether one wants to roll it back completely and establish a stateless natural order or roll it back only "sharply" or "drastically" to some "glorious" or "golden" *status quo ante.*

In any case, this goal can only be reached if, instead of talking and seeking access to the State, the State is openly ignored, avoided and disavowed; and its agents and propagandists are explicitly excluded from one's proceedings. To talk to the State and include its agents and propagandists is to lend legitimacy and strength to it. To ostentatiously ignore, avoid and disavow it and to exclude its agents and propagandists as undesirable is to withdraw consent from the State and to weaken its legitimacy.

In sharp contrast to the Mont Pelerin Society and its multiple offspring, which wanted to reform and liberalize the welfare–warfare state system from within—pursuing a "system-immanent" strategy of change, as Marxists would say—and which failed precisely for this reason and was instead co-opted by the State as part of the political establishment, my envisioned society, the Property and Freedom Society was to pursue a "system-transcending" strategy. That is, it would try to reform, and ultimately revolutionize, the ever more invasive welfare–warfare State system from the outside, through the creation of an anti-statist *counterculture* that could attract a steadily growing number of defectors—of intellectuals, educated laymen and even the much-cited "man on the street"—away from the dominant State culture and institutions. The Property and Freedom Society was to be the international spearhead, the *avant-garde*, of this intellectual counterculture.

Central to this counterculture was this insight into the perversity of the institution of a State: A territorial monopolist of law and order that can make and change laws in its own favor does not and cannot, without assuming miracles, protect the life and property of its subjects (clients); but is and always will be a permanent danger to them—the sure road to serfdom and tyranny.

Based on this insight, then, the Property and Freedom Society was to have a twofold goal.

On the one hand, positively, it was to explain and elucidate the legal, economic, cognitive and cultural requirements and features of a free, stateless natural order.

On the other hand, negatively, it was to unmask the State and showcase it for what it really is: an institution run by gangs of murderers, plunderers and thieves, surrounded by willing executioners, propagandists, sycophants, crooks, liars, clowns, charlatans, dupes and useful idiots—an institution that dirties and taints everything it touches.

For purposes of full disclosure I must add this: At the urging of my friend Jesús Huerta de Soto, who had been inducted at a very young age into the Mont Pelerin Society by Hayek personally, I reluctantly applied for membership sometime in the mid-1990s. Besides Huerta de Soto, the late Arthur Seldon, who was then Honorary President of the Mont Pelerin

Society, had endorsed my membership. Nonetheless, I was turned down—and, as I must admit, deservedly so, because I simply did not fit into such a society.

From reliable sources I have been told that it was, in particular, Leonard Liggio, a former friend of Murray Rothbard's, who must have realized this and most vigorously opposed my membership; seconded, from the German contingent of Mont Pelerin Society movers and shakers, by Christian Watrin. Both Liggio and Watrin would later become Mont Pelerin Society presidents.

My second experience with intellectual societies was with the John Randolph Club [JRC], which had been founded in 1989 by libertarian Murray Rothbard and conservative Thomas Fleming.

From the outset, this society was far more to my liking. For a while, I played a leading role in the John Randolph Club. But I also played a prominent part in its breakup that occurred shortly after Rothbard's death in 1995, and that essentially resulted in the exit of the Rothbardian wing of the society.

Nonetheless, I look back to those early John Randolph Club years with fond memories. So it is no surprise that quite a few of my old John Randolph Club comrades have also appeared here in Bodrum, at Property And Freedom Society meetings: Peter Brimelow, Tom DiLorenzo, Paul Gottfried, Walter Block, Justin Raimondo, Yuri Maltsev, David Gordon. In addition, I should mention my friend Joe Sobran, who had wanted to appear at our inaugural meeting but couldn't attend because of ill health.

In contrast to the "international" Mont Pelerin Society, the John Randolph Club was an "American" Society. This did not mean that the JRC was more provincial, however. To the contrary. Not only had the JRC numerous "foreign" members, but also, whereas the Mont Pelerin Society was dominated by professional economists, the John Randolph Club represented a much broader, interdisciplinary and trans-disciplinary spectrum of intellectual interests and endeavors.

On the average, foreign language proficiency among John Randolph Club-ers ranked well above that encountered in Mont Pelerin Society circles. In its habits and ways, the Mont Pelerin Society was multi-cultural, egalitarian and non-discriminating, while it was highly restrictive and intolerant regarding the range of permissible subjects and intellectual taboos. In sharp contrast, the JRC was a decidedly bourgeois, anti-egalitarian and discriminating society, but at the same time a society far more open and tolerant intellectually, without any taboo-subjects.

In addition, whereas Mont Pelerin Society meetings were large and impersonal—they could exceed 500 participants—John Randolph Club meetings had rarely more than 150 attendees and were small and intimate.

I liked all of these aspects of the John Randolph Club. (I didn't much care for the venues of its meetings: typically some business hotel in the outskirts of a major city. In this regard, Mont Pelerin Society meetings had clearly more to offer—although for a stiff price.)

But, as I indicated, not all was well with the John Randolph Club, and my encounter with it also taught me a few lessons on what not to imitate.

The breakup of the John Randolph Club shortly after Rothbard's death had partly personal reasons. Tom Fleming, the surviving principal of the Club, is, to put it diplomatically, a difficult man, as everyone who has dealt with him can testify. In addition, there were organizational quarrels. The meetings of the John Randolph Club were organized annually alternating by the Center for Libertarian Studies, which represented Murray Rothbard and his men, and by the Rockford Institute, which represented Thomas Fleming and his. This arrangement had perhaps unavoidably led to various charges of free-loading. Ultimately, however, the breakup had more fundamental reasons.

The John Randolph Club was a coalition of two distinct groups of intellectuals. On the one hand was a group of anarcho-capitalist Austro-libertarians, led by Rothbard, mostly of economists but also philosophers, lawyers, historians and sociologists (mostly of a more analytical-theoretical bend of mind). I was a member of this group. On the other hand was a group of writers associated with the conservative monthly *Chronicles: A Magazine of American Culture* and its editor, Tom Fleming. Paul Gottfried was a member of that group. The conservative group did not have any economist of note and generally displayed a more empirical bend of mind. Apart from historians and sociologists, it included in particular also men of letters: of philologists, literary writers, and cultural critics.

On the libertarian side, the cooperation with conservatives was motivated by the insight that while libertarianism may be logically compatible with many cultures, sociologically it requires a conservative, bourgeois core culture. The decision to form an intellectual alliance with conservatives then involved for the libertarians a double break with "Establishment Libertarianism" as represented, for instance, by the Washington DC "free market" Cato Institute.

This Establishment Libertarianism was not only theoretically in error, with its commitment to the impossible goal of limited government (and centralized government at that): it was also sociologically flawed, with its anti-bourgeois—indeed, adolescent—so-called "cosmopolitan" cultural message: of multiculturalism and egalitarianism, of "respect no authority", of "live and let live", of hedonism and libertinism.

The anti-establishment Austro-libertarians sought to learn more from the conservative side about the cultural requirements of a free and prosperous commonwealth. And by and large they did and learned their lesson. At least, I think that I did.

For the conservative side of the alliance, the cooperation with the Austrian anarcho-capitalists signified a complete break with the so-called neoconservative movement that had come to dominate organized conservatism in the US and which was represented, for instance, by such Washington DC think tanks as the American Enterprise Institute and the Heritage Foundation. The paleo-conservatives, as they came to be known, opposed the neo-conservative goal of a highly and increasingly centralized, "economically efficient" welfare–warfare State as incompatible with the traditional conservative core values of private property, of family and family households, and of local communities and their protection. There were some points of contention between the paleo-cons and the libertarians: on the issues of abortion and immigration and on the definition and necessity of government. But these differences could be accommodated in agreeing that their resolution must not be attempted on the level of the central state or even some supra-national institution such as the UN, but always on the smallest level of social organization: on the level of families and of local communities.

For the paleo-cons, secession from a central State was not a taboo, and for the Austro-libertarians secession had the status of a natural human right (while establishment libertarians typically treat it as a taboo subject); hence, cooperation was possible. Moreover, the cooperation with the Austro-libertarians was to afford the conservatives the opportunity of learning sound (Austrian school) economics, which was an acknowledged gap and weakness in their intellectual armor, especially vis-à-vis their neo-conservative opponents. However, with some notable exceptions the conservative group failed to live up to these expectations.

This, then, was the ultimate reason for the breakup of the libertarian-conservative alliance accomplished with the John Randolph Club: that while the libertarians were willing to learn their cultural lesson the conservatives did not want to learn their economics.

This verdict, and the consequent lesson, was not immediately clear, of course. It was driven home only in the course of the events. In the case of the John Randolph Club, the event had a name. It was Patrick Buchanan, TV personality, commentator, syndicated columnist, best-selling book author, including serious works on revisionist history, a very charismatic man, witty and with great personal charm, but also a man with a deep and lasting involvement in Republican Party politics, first as a Nixon speech-writer and then as White House Director of Communications under Ronald Reagan.

Pat Buchanan did not participate directly in the John Randolph Club, but he had personal ties to several of its leading members (on both sides of the Club but especially to the *Chronicles* group, which included some of his closest advisors) and he was considered a prominent part of the counter-cultural movement represented by the John Randolph Club. In 1992, Buchanan challenged then-sitting president George Bush for the GOP presidential nomination. (He would do so again in 1996, challenging Senator Bob Dole for the Republican nomination, and in 2000 he would run as the presidential candidate for the Reform Party.) Buchanan's challenge was impressive at first, nearly upsetting Bush in the New Hampshire primary, and it initially caused considerable enthusiasm in John Randolph Club circles. However, in the course of Buchanan's campaign and in reaction to it open dissent between the two John Randolph Club camps broke out as regards the "correct" strategy.

Buchanan pursued a populist "America First" campaign. He wanted to talk and appeal to the so-called "Middle Americans," who felt betrayed and dispossessed by the political elites of both parties. After the collapse of communism and the end of the cold war, Buchanan wanted to bring all American troops back home, dissolve NATO, leave the UN, and conduct a non-interventionist foreign policy (which his neo-conservative enemies smeared as "isolationist"). He wanted to cut all but economic ties to Israel in particular, and he openly criticized the "un-American" influence of the organized Jewish-American lobby, something that takes considerable courage in contemporary America.

He wanted to eliminate all "affirmative action," non-discrimination and quota laws that had pervaded all aspects of American life, and which were essentially anti-white and especially anti-white-male laws. In particular, he promised to end the non-discriminatory immigration policy that had resulted in the mass immigration of low-class third-world people and the attendant forced integration or, euphemistically, "multiculturalism." Further, he wanted to end the entire "cultural rot" coming out of Washington DC by closing down the federal Department of Education and a multitude of other federal indoctrination agencies.

But instead of emphasizing these widely popular "rightist" cultural concerns, Buchanan, in the course of his campaign, increasingly intoned other, economic matters and concerns, all the while his knowledge of economics was rather skimpy.

Concentrating on what he was worst at, then, he increasingly advocated a "leftist" economic program of economic and social nationalism. He advocated tariffs to protect "essential" American industries and save American jobs from "unfair" foreign competition, and he proposed to "protect" Middle Americans by safeguarding and even expanding the already existing welfare-State programs of minimum wage laws, unemployment insurance, Social Security, Medicaid and Medicare.

When I explained, in a speech before the club, that Buchanan's rightist-cultural and leftist-economic program was theoretically inconsistent and that his strategy must consequently fail to reach its own goal, that you cannot return America to cultural sanity and strengthen its families and communities and at the same time maintain the institutional pillars that are the central cause for the cultural malaise, that protectionist tariffs cannot make Americans more prosperous, but less, and that a program of economic nationalism must alienate the intellectually and culturally indispensible bourgeoisie while attracting the (for us and our purposes) "useless" proletariat, it almost came to an *éclat*. The conservative group was up in arms about this critique of one of its heroes.

I had hoped that, notwithstanding feelings of friendship or personal loyalty, after some time of reflection reason would prevail, especially after it had become clear by the ensuing events that Buchanan's strategy had also failed numerically, at the polls. I thought that the John Randolph Club conservatives would sooner or later come to realize that my critique of Buchanan was an "immanent" critique; that is, that I had not criticized or distanced myself from the goal of the John Randolph Club, and presumably also Buchanan's, of a conservative cultural counterrevolution, but that, based on elementary economic reasons, I had simply found the means—

the strategy—chosen by Buchanan to accomplish this goal unsuitable and ineffective. But nothing happened. There was no attempt to refute my arguments. Nor was there any sign that one was willing to express some intellectual distance to Buchanan and his program.

From this experience I learned a twofold lesson. First, a lesson that I had already come away with from my encounter with the Mont Pelerin Society was reinforced: Do not put your trust in politicians and do not get distracted by politics. Buchanan, notwithstanding his many appealing personal qualities, was still at heart a politician who believed in government, above all, as a means of effecting social change. Second and more generally, however, I learned that it is impossible to have a lasting intellectual association with people who are either unwilling or incapable of grasping the principles of economics. Economics—the logic of action—is the queen of the social sciences. It is by no means sufficient for an understanding of social reality, but it is necessary and indispensible. Without a solid grasp of economic principles, say on the level of Henry Hazlitt's *Economics in One Lesson*, one is bound to commit serious blunders of historical explanation and interpretation.

Thus, I concluded that the property and freedom society not only had to exclude all politicians and government agents and propagandists as objects of ridicule and contempt, as emperors without clothes and the butt of all jokes rather than objects of admiration and emulation, but it also had to exclude all economic ignoramuses.

When the John Randolph Club broke apart, this did not mean that the ideas that had inspired its formation had died out or did no longer find an audience. In fact, in the U.S., a think tank dedicated to the same ideas and ideals had grown up. The Ludwig von Mises Institute, founded in 1982 by Lew Rockwell, with Murray Rothbard as its academic head, had started out as just another limited government think tank—although Rothbard and all other leading Mises Institute associates were anarcho-capitalist Austrians. Yet by the mid-1990s—and I pride myself in having played an important role in this development—Lew Rockwell had transformed the institute, significantly located far away from Washington DC, in provincial Auburn, Alabama, into the very first and only free market think tank that had openly renounced the goal of limited government as impossible and come out instead as an unabashed advocate of anarcho-capitalism, deviating thereby from a narrow, "literal" interpretation of its name sake and yet staying true to his spirit in pursuing the rigorous, Misesian praxeological method to its ultimate conclusion. This move was financially costly at first, but under Rockwell's brilliant intellectual entrepreneurship it had eventually become an enormous success, easily outcompeting its far richer "limited-government libertarian" rivals such as the Cato Institute in terms of reach and influence. Moreover, in addition to the Mises Institute, which focused more narrowly on economic matters, and in the wake of the disappointing experience with the John Randolph Club and its breakup, Lew Rockwell had set up, in 1999, an anti-state, anti-war, pro-market website—LewRockwell.com—that added an interdisciplinary, cultural dimension to the Austro-libertarian enterprise and proved to be even more popular, laying the intellectual groundwork for the present Ron Paul movement.

The Property And Freedom Society was not supposed to compete with the Mises Institute or LewRockwell.com. It was not supposed to be a think tank or another publication outlet. Rather, it was to complement their and other efforts by adding yet another important component to the development of an anti-statist intellectual counterculture. What had disappeared with the break-up of the original John Randolph Club was an intellectual Society dedicated to the cause. Yet every intellectual movement requires a network of personal acquaintances, of friends and comrades in arms to be successful, and for such a network to be established and grow, a regular meeting place, a society, is needed. The Property And Freedom Society was supposed to be this society.

I wanted to create a place where likeminded people from around the world could gather regularly in mutual encouragement and in the enjoyment of unrivalled and uncensored intellectual radicalism. The society was supposed to be international and interdisciplinary, bourgeois, by invitation only, exclusive and elitist: for the few "elect," who can see through the smokescreen put up by our ruling classes of criminals, crooks, charlatans, and clowns.

After our first meeting, 5 years ago, here at the Karia Princess, my plan became more specific still. Inspired by the charm of the place and its beautiful garden, I decided to adopt the model of a salon for the Property And Freedom Society and its meetings. The dictionary defines a salon as "a gathering of intellectual, social, political, and cultural elites under the roof of an inspiring hostess or host, partly to amuse one another and partly to refine their taste and increase their knowledge through conversation." Take the "political" out of this definition—and there you have it what I have tried to accomplish for the last few years, together with Gülcin, my wife and fellow Misesian, without whose support none of this would be possible: to be hostess and host to a grand and extended annual salon, and to make it, with your help, the most attractive and illustrious salon there is.

I hope—and indeed I am confident—that this, our fifth meeting, will mark another step forward toward this end.

Afterword

by Stephan Kinsella[1]

The book you hold in your hands—or that resides in memory bits on your digital device—provides a perfect illustration of the power of Austro-libertarian ideas. Brainpower and genius alone are not enough to provide sound social analysis. One also needs a coherent understanding of economics, in particular of Misesian-Austrian praxeology-based economics. And one needs a coherent and realistic understanding of politics and the state—which is to say, anti-state libertarianism.

We all encounter and learn from brilliant thinkers, but there is often something missing. This is usually because they are insufficiently aware of the true predatorial nature of the state and the role it has played in the history of human society. Or there are, to put it kindly, gaps in their knowledge of economics. How many times have you read a brilliant thinker only to see them err on a crucial issue because of some mainstream economic or statist assumption? It is a frustrating experience.

So genius is not enough. But it helps. After all, the problems and issues at hand are not easy. Great intellect, combined with a realistic, sober view of politics and economics, and with a passion for truth, can achieve great things: a clarifying vision of the nature of the institutions of society. Hoppe was perfectly placed by the currents of fate to become today's leading libertarian social theorist, which is to say: today's leading social theorist.

Professor Hoppe's genius is evident in the razor-sharp clarity and precision of his words and arguments, and his command of philosophy and economics and related fields such as history, sociology, and the philosophy of science. His formal education originated in his studies at the University of Saarland in Saarbrücken, the Johann Wolfgang Goethe University in

---

1. Stephan Kinsella is the executive editor of *Libertarian Papers* (libertarianpapers.org).

Frankfurt am Main, and at the University of Michigan in Ann Arbor, which included a PhD in philosophy under the famous European philosopher Jürgen Habermas and a prestigious "Habilitation" degree on the Foundations of Sociology and Economics.

But Professor Hoppe's *real* education was autodidactic. First, as a mainstream left-winger, his eyes were opened by the Austrian economist Eugen von Böhm-Bawerk's critique of Marxism. Later, after encountering and then rejecting the logical positivism of Milton Friedman and the Chicago school, he discovered Mises and his unique approach. As he wrote in an interview in the *Austrian Economics Newsletter*:

> Independently, I had concluded that economic laws were *a priori* and discoverable through deduction. Then I stumbled on Mises's *Human Action*. That was the first time I found someone who had the same view; not only that, he had already worked out the entire system. From that point on, I was a Misesian.[2]

And then, naturally, he discovered the work of Murray N. Rothbard (1926–1995), the most prominent American student of Mises and the fountainhead of the modern libertarian movement. In the mid-1980s Hoppe moved to the United States to study under, collaborate, and work with Rothbard. Since these days he has produced a cornucopia of political and economic insights, contained in his books: *Handeln und Erkennen* (1976), *Kritik der kausalwissenschaftlichen Sozialforschung* (1983), *Eigentum, Anarchie, und Staat* (1987), his magnum opus *A Theory of Socialism and Capitalism* (1989), *The Economics and Ethics of Private Property* (1993, enlarged 2nd edition 2006), *Democracy: The God that Failed* (2001), and *The Myth of National Defense* (editor, 2003). His works have been translated into at least 23 languages, not counting English.[3]

But the point here is not to provide an encomium to the contributions of a single man. That has been done already, in the *Festschrift Property, Freedom, and Society: Essays in Honor of Hans-Hermann Hoppe* (Mises Institute, 2009). Rather, it is to recognize the power of the anarcho-Austrian-libertarian intellectual framework, which we see realized in the work of Professor Hoppe.

---

2. "Austrians and the Private-Property Society: An Interview With Hans-Hermann Hoppe," *The Austrian Economics Newsletter* vol. 18, 1 (Spring 1998).

3. See www.hanshoppe.com/translations.

Many scholars influenced by Mises and Austrian economics give praxeology—Mises's *apriori* logic of action—lip service. But more so than any other living thinker, Hoppe actually *applies* praxeology, one of the most powerful modes of scientific analysis yet discovered. It permeates his writing. His reasoning is rooted in it. Hoppe swims in the plasma of praxeology.[4] It informs all aspects of his theoretical edifice: not only economic theory and applications, but political theory, ethics, and epistemology.

The power of the Austro-libertarian framework is that it opens up new vistas of understanding in the social sciences. It permits clarity and understanding where before there was muddy water. Professor Hoppe is the best exemplar to date of this methodological approach; his system improves upon that even of his masters, Mises and Rothbard, if only because he has stood on their shoulders. But still. Read this book, and others, like *A Theory of Socialism and Capitalism* (*TSC*) and *The Economics and Ethics of Private Property* (*EEPP*), and you will see something special about Hoppe's work. It is crystal clear, for one thing; what he means is never in doubt. It is rigorous, and systematic, and integrated. It is based on a coherent, realistic, and rational view of the world and of human interpersonal relations. It is obviously motivated by a passion for truth and justice.

And we see this in *The Great Fiction*, a magnificent collection of essays informed by this same spirit and approach. This book contains some of my favorite Hoppean essays, for example, "The Ethics and Economics of Private Property" (ch. 2), "Of Common, Public, and Private Property and the Rationale for Total Privatization" (ch. 5, first published in my journal *Libertarian Papers*), "On Certainty and Uncertainty" (ch. 14), "The Private Production of Defense" (ch. 12), "In Defense of Extreme Rationalism" (ch. 16, a good counterpart to Rothbard's classic "In Defense of 'Extreme Apriorism'"[5]), and "Property, Causality, and Liability" (ch. 18, which I saw Hoppe present at the symposium on Reinach and Rothbard at the Mises Institute in March 2001).

---

4. Here I am borrowing from a vivid metaphor from Shael Herman, "Detrimental Reliance in Louisiana Law—Past, Present, and Future (?): The Code Drafter's Perspective," *Tulane Law Review* 58:3 (1984), pp. 707–57, at 708–709, which observes that legal principles staked out by articles of a civil code embody a "plasma that bathes and nourishes an entire code and its institutions. The obligations articles are traditionally rich in analogies, making them, in Portalis' famous phrase, 'fertile in effects.'"

5. Published in Murray N. Rothbard, *The Logic of Action One* (Edward Elgar, 1997), pp. 100–108.

Let me highlight a few examples of Professor Hoppe's application of
Austrian praxeology and the libertarian-realist understanding of the state to
various issues, in *The Great Fiction* and in his other writings. We may note
first his careful attention to rigorous, essentialist definitions. For example,
Hoppe recognizes that while socialism typically refers to state or collective
ownership of the means of production, its essence is the "institutionalized
interference with or aggression against private property and private property
claims" (*TSC*, 2). In other words, any public or institutionalized aggression is
inherently socialistic, and gives rise to the problems that accompany standard
central planning. Indeed, as Hoppe elsewhere notes, "Societies are not simply
capitalist or socialist. Indeed, all existing societies are socialist to some extent"
(*TSC*, 10). The state is always socialistic, and socialism always implies a state.

As a counterpart to his essentialist definition of socialism, Hoppe's
definition of the state gets straight to the heart of the matter:

> Let me begin with the definition of a state. What must an agent
> be able to do to qualify as a state? This agent must be able to
> insist that all conflicts among the inhabitants of a given territory
> be brought to him for ultimate decision-making or be subject to
> his final review. In particular, this agent must be able to insist that
> all conflicts involving *him* be adjudicated by him or his agent. And
> implied in the power to exclude all others from acting as ultimate
> judge, as the second defining characteristic of a state, is the agent's
> power to tax: to unilaterally determine the price that justice seekers
> must pay for his services.
>
> Based on this definition of a state, it is easy to understand why
> a desire to control a state might exist. For whoever is a monopolist of
> final arbitration within a given territory can *make* laws. And he who
> can *legislate* can also *tax*. Surely, this is an enviable position. [p. 1]

Once you see the state in these clear terms, its nature becomes clear. As
Hoppe elaborates in *TGF*, the state has to coopt the intellectuals to maintain
the illusion—the fiction—that it is necessary and good.

Among Professor Hoppe's signal contributions to political theory is his
recognition of the crucial importance of *scarcity* in political philosophy.
Without scarcity, there would be no social or economic problem to solve.
"A conflict is only possible if goods are scarce. Only then will there
arise the need to formulate rules that make orderly—conflict-free—social
cooperation possible." (p. 9; see also p. 410 et pass.) This also gives rise to his
crucial insight that property rights are rights to control *physical* resources,

and thus are rights only to the physical integrity of these goods—not to the "value" of these resources. As he writes:

> property ownership means the exclusive control of a particular person over specific *physical* objects and spaces. Conversely, property rights invasion means the uninvited *physical* damage or diminution of things and territories owned by other persons. In contrast, a widely held view holds that the damage or diminution of the *value* (or price) of someone's property also constitutes a punishable offense. [p. 15]

The significance of this insight can hardly be overstated, as the fallacious view of property rights in "value" underpins a host of confused ideas, including intellectual property, which Hoppe also rightly, and explicitly, rejects (p. 397).

Hoppe's notion of scarcity, interpersonal conflict, and the need for property allocation norms builds on Mises's praxeological understanding of human action as employing necessarily scarce means to causally achieve one's chosen ends. The ends one chooses and the means one decides to employ to causally bring about one's ends are guided by one's knowledge; scarce means are employed that are causally believed to help accomplish the desired goal. The means, being scarce, rivalrous, can only be used by one agent and thus, property norms are necessary to permit social cooperation. But the information or ideas that guide the actor's selection of ends and knowledge of causal laws to permit him to determine what means to choose, need not be owned—indeed, cannot be owned—as information is nonscarce.

> The idea of intellectual property rights is not just wrong and confused but dangerous. And I have already touched upon why this is so. Ideas—recipes, formulas, statements, arguments, algorithms, theorems, melodies, patterns, rhythms, images, etc.—are certainly goods (insofar as they are good, not bad, recipes, etc.), but they are not scarce goods. Once thought and expressed, they are free, inexhaustible goods. I whistle a melody or write down a poem, you hear the melody or read the poem and reproduce or copy it. In doing so you have not taken anything away from me. I can whistle and write as before. In fact, the entire world can copy me and yet nothing is taken from me. (If I didn't want anyone to copy my ideas I only have to keep them to myself and never express them.)
>
> Now imagine I had been granted a property right in my melody or poem such that I could prohibit you from copying it or demanding a royalty from you if you do. First: Doesn't that imply, absurdly, that

I, in turn, must pay royalties to the person (or his heirs) who invented
whistling and writing, and further on to those, who invented sound-
making and language, and so on? Second: In preventing you from
or making you pay for whistling my melody or reciting my poem,
I am actually made a (partial) owner of *you*: of your physical body,
your vocal chords, your paper, your pencil, etc., because you did not
use anything but your own property when you copied me. If you
can no longer copy me, then, this means that I, the intellectual
property owner, have expropriated you and your "real" property.
Which shows: intellectual property rights and real property rights
are incompatible, and the promotion of intellectual property must
be seen as a most dangerous attack on the idea of "real" property (in
scarce goods). [p. 397]

This passage provides a sparkling example of the power of a consistent
application of Misesian praxeology and Hoppe's insights into the crucial role
of scarcity in the institution of property in addressing the social problem of
conflict. By an almost pure application of praxeological reasoning, Hoppe
realized as far back as 1988, before the Internet, before so-called "intellectual
property" was on the libertarian radar, that IP was incompatible with the
property rights that were aimed at solving the problem of conflict among
actors in the use of scarce resources.[6] This is a brilliant demonstration of the
power of praxeologically-informed social analysis.

By focusing on human action, Hoppe is able to see that the scarce means
employed in action need to be owned, but that the very nature of this need
implies a Lockean-style property assignment rule is the only one that can be
justified. First, any property norm must always answer the question of who
now may use a given item. The norm cannot depend on some future event,
for otherwise the resource may not be used or there would be no conflict-
avoiding norm for the present. As Hoppe explains:

What is the purpose of norms? The avoidance of conflict regarding
the use of scarce physical things. Conflict-generating norms contradict the very purpose of norms. Yet with regard to the purpose
of conflict avoidance, no alternative to private property and original
appropriation exists. In the absence of prestabilized harmony among

---

6. See my blog post, "Hoppe on Intellectual Property," C4SIF Blog (Dec. 27, 2010),
http://c4sif.org/2010/12/hoppe-on-intellectual-property/.

actors, conflict can only be prevented if all goods are always in the private ownership of specific individuals and it is always clear who owns what and who does not. Also, conflicts can only be avoided from the very beginning of mankind if private property is acquired by acts of original appropriation (instead of by mere declarations or words of latecomers). [p. 15]

The emphasis on *latecomers* seems trivial but it is of immense significance. For if a latecomer has a better or equal claim to a given resource than someone who had it earlier, no property is secure, and we are in a might-makes-right situation, not one in which there are applicable norms designed to permit productive, conflict-free use of scarce means. This leads Hoppe to emphasize the importance of the *prior-later distinction*: that it matters, as between two claimants for a given resource, who had it first: "every property right has a *history* (temporal genesis)" [p. 17]. By an almost Misesian monetary regression-theorem like analysis, Hoppe uses these insights to validate the central insight of Lockean-libertarian homesteading: that the first user of a resource has a better claim than anyone else:

All property must go back, then, directly or indirectly, through a chain of mutually beneficial and hence likewise conflict-free property-title transfers, to original appropriators and acts of original appropriation. [p. 87]

The above provides only a sampling of the profound insights and understanding that are possible with an Austro-libertarian foundation — especially when combined with the searing and honest intellect of a thinker like Professor Hoppe.

Index